Catherine of Aragon

Catherine of Aragon

by Garrett Mattingly

ILLUSTRATED

BOSTON · MCMXXXXI

LITTLE, BROWN AND COMPANY

PRINTED IN THE UNITED STATES OF AMERICA

TO GERTRUDE

Foreword

THIS BIOGRAPHY of Catherine of Aragon is the outgrowth of studies in the early history of diplomacy. Turning over the letters of Spanish ambassadors at the Tudor court, it was borne in upon me that the Queen Catherine they were talking about was a different person, more cultured and thoughtful, more forceful and decisive, than the one I had read about elsewhere, and as I followed the history of the Spanish embassy in England, I began to realize that the key to its activities, and to much of what went on in England for a third of a century, lay in the personality and the decisions of this queen. I have tried to restore her figure to something like what her contemporaries saw. Two things in her story have chiefly fascinated me: the way the decisions of persons by no means gifted with genius but strategically placed may influence the course of history, and the way that the divided loyalties common in thoughtful persons during a time of rapid change may affect their conduct in unexpected ways, and consequently give a twist, sometimes, to remote events. Surely Catherine's decisions influenced English history — and therefore the history of the whole world — as vitally, and as unexpectedly, as the decisions of her husband, Henry VIII.

I have spelled the Queen's name "Catherine" following the usual modern practice, instead of "Katharina" as she would probably have spelled it herself, just as I have spelled her mother's name "Isabella of Castile," instead of "Isabel of Castille" as one would be tempted to do. For other spellings I have tried to follow the *Dictionary of National Biography*, or some other guide to modern practice.

The many librarians, archivists, and scholars who have been helpful to me will forgive me if I do not list their names here. I cannot forgo thanking Dr. Otto Schmid of the Vienna *Haus-hof und Stadt Archiv* for his indefatigable assistance, and Dr. Ernst H. Buschbeck of the Vienna *Kunsthistorisches Museum* for courteous aid with problems connected with the Vienna portrait of Catherine. H. M. Hake, Esq., of the National Portrait Gallery, has given me freely the benefit of his great knowledge of sixteenth-century portraiture; and my friends, Dr. E. C. Mack and Dr. J. C. Thirlwall, both of the English Department of the College of the City of New York, have, between them, saved me from many stylistic blunders. My great indebtedness to the continued interest and guidance of Professor R. B. Merriman of Harvard University, to whom ever since my undergraduate days I have constantly looked for help with vexing problems, and never looked in vain, it would be an embarrassment, were it not a pleasure, to acknowledge. A fellowship from the John Simon Guggenheim Memorial Foundation helped me complete the researches on which this book is based.

Contents

Illustrations

The Tudors and some Plantagenets

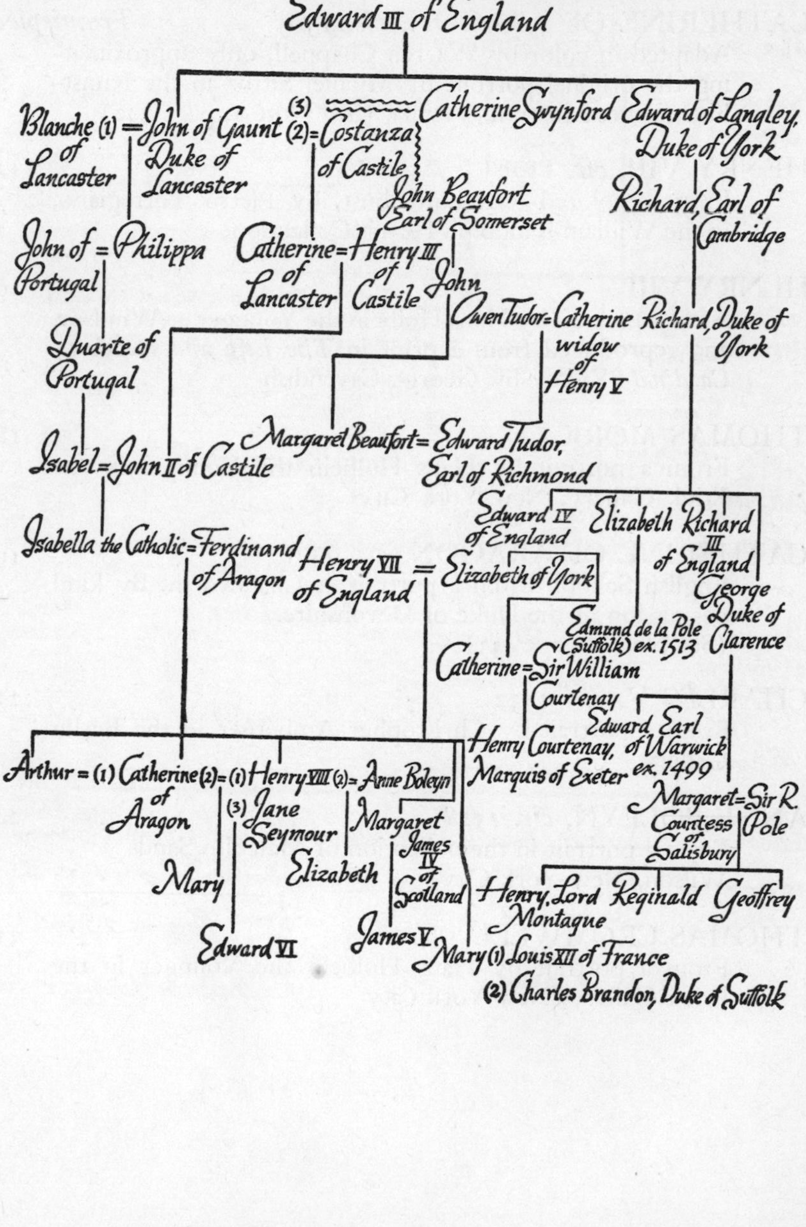
Edward III of England
Blanche (1) of Lancaster
John of Gaunt Duke of Lancaster
(3) Catherine Swynford
(2) Costanza of Castile
Edward of Langley, Duke of York
John Beaufort Earl of Somerset
Richard, Earl of Cambridge
John of Portugal
Philippa
Catherine of Lancaster
Henry III of Castile
John
Owen Tudor
Catherine widow of Henry V
Richard, Duke of York
Duarte of Portugal
Margaret Beaufort
Edward Tudor, Earl of Richmond
Isabel
John II of Castile
Edward IV of England
Elizabeth
Richard III of England
Isabella the Catholic
Ferdinand of Aragon
Henry VII of England
Elizabeth of York
George Duke of Clarence
Edmund de la Pole (Suffolk) ex. 1513
Catherine
Sir William Courtenay
Edward Earl of Warwick ex. 1499
Henry Courtenay, Marquis of Exeter
Arthur
(1) Catherine (2) of Aragon
(1) Henry VIII (2)
Anne Boleyn
(3) Jane Seymour
Margaret
James IV of Scotland
Margaret Countess of Salisbury
Sir R. Pole
Mary
Elizabeth
Henry, Lord Montague
Reginald
Geoffrey
Edward VI
James V
Mary (1) Louis XII of France
(2) Charles Brandon, Duke of Suffolk

Marriage Alliances of the Catholic Kings

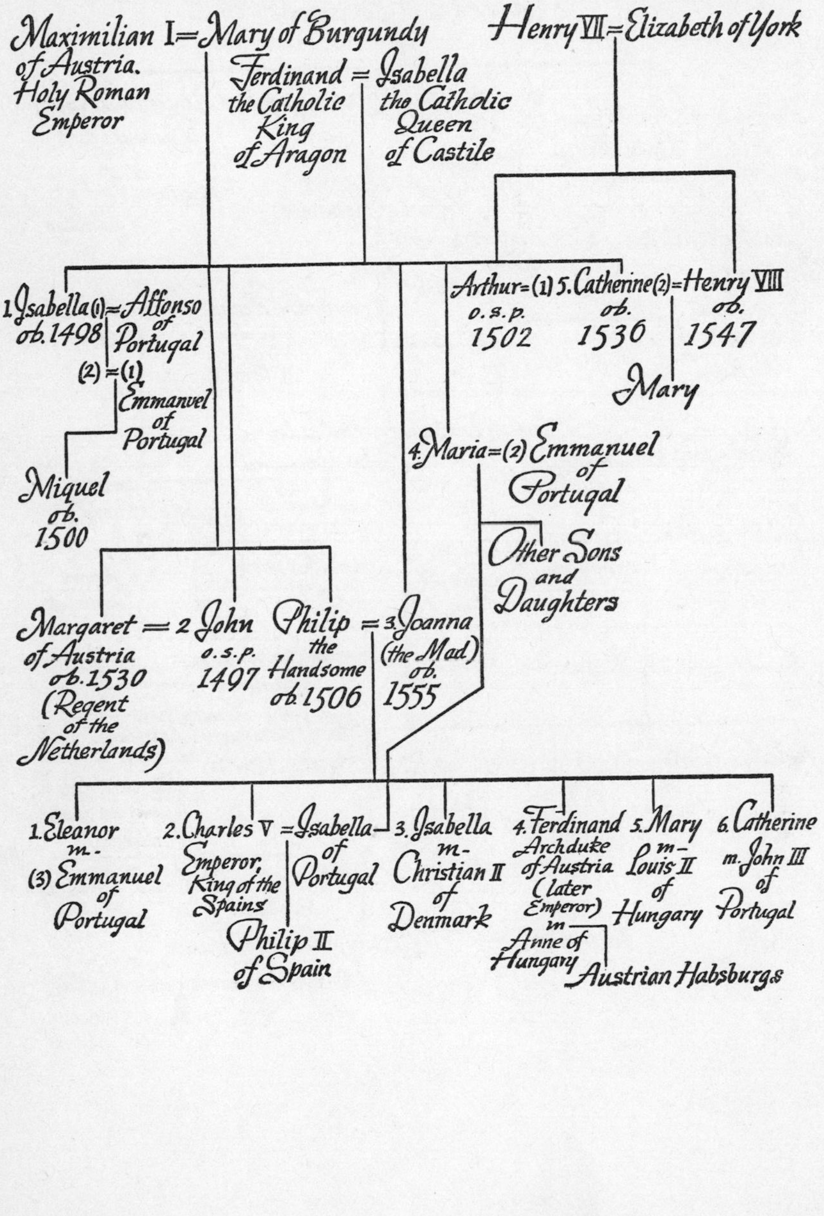

PART I

A SPANISH PRINCESS

(1485–1509)

Chapter One

A SPANISH PRINCESS

SOME CHARACTERS [illegible] tory; some [illegible] torrent of [illegible] which seems to sweep everything before it, and the spectators [illegible] of the river [illegible] for a moment, a rock resists, then the flood sweeps over it, and the spectators note only an individual tragedy, unconscious of the [illegible] that cleaving the current [illegible] less than the fury of [illegible] stream. This is the story of a life which shaped history [illegible] ing with its flow.

Catherine of Aragon was born at a time when [illegible] among some half-dozen families could shape the history of Europe. Under the powerful solvents of [illegible] economy and [illegible] enterprise, of new techniques and new ideas, the old order was breaking up. In the terror and confusion of change [illegible] round the kings. The burghers [illegible] broken the shell of the old society, but who had not yet grown strong enough to master the new, lent the kings money, and became in return for protection [illegible] service new luster for their tarnished prestige and a new authority for their threatened prerogatives. Even the clergy, [illegible] and guardians of the old unity of Christendom, paid royalty a deference increasingly less grudging and reserved. And the power thus thrust into the hands of the kings really could be used [illegible] by the accidents of individual character [illegible] Europe after [illegible]

Chapter One

SOME CHARACTERS appear to triumph with history; some to be overwhelmed by it. The boiling torrent of events throws up one foam-capped wave which seems to sweep everything before it, and the spectators cry "A genius!" and name a whole stretch of the river "the age of so-and-so." Here and there, for a moment, a rock resists, then the flood sweeps over it, and the spectators note only an individual tragedy, unconscious of the solid base cleaving the current below. But the integrity of granite, not less than the fury of rushing water, shapes the final course of the stream. This is the story of a life which shaped history by not moving with its flow.

Catherine of Aragon was born at a time when domestic accidents among some half-dozen families could shape the history of Europe. Under the powerful solvents of a money economy and business enterprise, of new techniques and new ideas, the old order was breaking up. In the terror and confusion of change, society rallied round the kings. The burghers, whose skepticism and daring had broken the shell of the old society, but who had not yet grown strong enough to master the new, lent the kings money and brains in return for protection. The feudal aristocracy found in royal service new luster for their tarnished prestige and a new authority for their threatened prerogatives. Even the clergy, symbols and guardians of the old unity of Christendom, paid royalty a deference increasingly less grudging and reserved. And the power thus thrust into the hands of the kings really could be used by individual wills, by the accidents of individual character and fate, to alter the direction and growth of the new society. For the new organism was still incompletely formed. Though its inner potentialities had already been determined in the womb of the centuries, its bones were still pliable, its features still indefinite. Lacking the elastic resilience of maturity, it would receive and hold the impress of forces much slighter than those which its adult growth would resist with ease. In the events determining one such willful application of royal power, and not the least important, Catherine of Aragon was destined to play a leading part.

The family into which Catherine was born seemed certain to have as large a voice in the fate of Europe as any. Both her parents were kings in their own right, and their marriage, uniting their crowns, made the beginning of a new national state which grew by war and policy and accident throughout Catherine's girlhood to a great dynastic power, enriched by fabulous new-found lands, and struggling for first place in Europe. Her father, Ferdinand, inherited the half-dozen crowns of Aragon, Mediterranean lands mostly, looking towards Italy, tugged at by eddies of Italian rivalries, and being sucked by them into the current of the new times. Into that current Ferdinand steered boldly. Ferdinand, himself, had little Italian culture; his earliest schools had been war and intrigue, and his usual seat from youth the saddle. In his passion for hunting and hawking and fighting, his quasi-illiteracy and conventional piety, he resembled any other feudal nobleman. But no Italian tyrant ever had a more unwavering, single-minded devotion to the realities of power. There was no remnant of medieval idealism about Ferdinand's politics. He did the work of the new times, the consolidation of royal power, with instinctive, tropistic efficiency. Like his Mediterranean kingdoms, Catherine's father belonged to the Renaissance.

What counted most in Spain, however, was Castile; what counted most in the team of the Catholic Kings was the Queen of Castile; what counted most with Catherine was her mother. Castile was not modern; neither was Isabella, though both were willing to take something from the new to reinforce the old. The great central plateau of Spain preserved the psychology of the Middle Ages. Nowhere were the feudal lords prouder and more powerful, nowhere in western Europe were the towns weaker and fewer, nowhere was the Church more firmly lord of the hearts and minds of peasant and hidalgo. And Isabella, though she did the work of the future, belonged, like Castile, to the past. She was more curious than Ferdinand about the new learning, but she sought it not to surrender to its magic but to use it in the work she had to do. Like Ferdinand, and even more than Ferdinand, she had struggled to power, and she had been no more scrupulous than he about the means: fighting, lying, scheming ever since girlhood, leading armies and squirming through conferences, wheedling, meek, fiery, as it served her purpose, but always implacable until she had driven her niece, the rightful heir to the throne, into exile, tamed the grandees, and hammered Castile into one strong kingdom. But unlike Ferdinand, she was restless, not out of simple itch for power, but because God's work is never done and it is laid upon the king to do God's work. Castile was not a prize but a sword.

As soon as she held it firmly, she turned it to the great medieval use of God's sword, the Crusade. Even in Spain the memory of the Crusade was growing faint, and the rest of Europe had almost forgotten it. For two centuries the Moslems held the Holy Land undisturbed. Though the crescent moved westward and Constantinople fell, though the Turk threatened Hungary and raided the Italian coast, no Christian banner stirred. Defense against the Turk had become a phrase in European chanceries, good to embellish a treaty or a declaration of war against one's neighbor. But to Isabella the Crusade was as real as it had been to Saint Bernard; that the conquest of Granada, the last Moslem kingdom in Spain, meant booty and the rounding-out of boundaries, was to her a secondary consideration. Ferdinand might seek power; she sought the glory of God. From different motives husband and wife joined forces, but the main burden lay on Castile, and the driving impulse came from Isabella. Her personal standard was familiar to the Moorish outposts. She rode in armor with her knights along the tracks of the snowy Sierras. She whipped up in her troops something of her own fanatical devotion to the cross. One by one the Moorish fortresses crumbled under the pounding of her modern guns; slowly the Moors gave way before her medieval passion.

When the campaign of 1485 drew to a close, the war against the Moors had lasted four years; it was to last six more. The summer just past had seen some of the hardest fighting so far, and the greatest Spanish success, the capture of the rock-perched city of Ronda. After the taking of Ronda Ferdinand remained in the field, directing operations against the fortified villages which still barred the way to the valley of Granada; Isabella made her headquarters at Cordova, the main army base. As the rains of autumn began Ferdinand rejoined his consort, and the two sovereigns turned northward. It was good policy to spend a part of each year in the older parts of their realms, and prudent not to place too great a strain on the frontier lands, burdened in spring and summer with victualing the army, even though that meant summer in the scorched, airless valleys of the south and winter on the windswept northern plateau. At Alcala de Henares, a cheerless town in winter, northeast of Madrid and not too far from the frontier of Aragon, the Archbishop of Toledo had a castle large enough to accommodate the court. There, on December 16, Isabella gave birth to a daughter, the last of her children. The child was named Catalina after Isabella's grandmother, an English princess, Catherine of Lancaster.[1]

ii

Like her sisters, Catalina grew up amid the bustle of her mother's activities. For nine months the whole royal household was with the

Queen before Granada, hearing the clash of arms as a Moorish sortie was repelled at the edge of the camp, hurried into the night on one occasion when the Queen's tent went up in flames, watching the stones of the beleaguering town of Santa Fé rise day by day. When the last Moorish king rode out of the Alhambra and Their Catholic Majesties entered its gates in triumph, Catalina was six. The court remained in the green valley of Granada, at Granada itself or at Santa Fé, for most of the next year. Then or later Catalina may have acquired a special affection for the most beautifully seated of Spanish cities, but the tradition which makes Granada her usual residence has no authority.[2] She and her sisters followed their parents, and the court was always on the move. Considerations of pleasure – fresh game to be hunted – and of elementary sanitation made most courts of the period itinerant, even when duty was not in question. Ferdinand and Isabella had special reasons to keep moving. Spain was still ill-unified; communications were bad; even after the war with the Moors was over, the sovereigns' presence was necessary, now on one frontier, now on another, now in the north, now in the south. Ferdinand had often to be in his Aragonese realms, and sometimes Isabella went with him. Back and forth along the rocky, dusty roads of Spain labored the straggling procession, horseback, or muleback, or in litters, – the nobles, the *letrados,* the clerics, – all following their sovereigns and carrying most of the machinery of government with them. As part of the royal household, Isabella's children went too.

There were five of them. The Infanta Isabella, born fifteen years before Catherine, was the oldest, and a young lady so preternaturally solemn and unsmiling that the Queen used to refer to her, jestingly, as "my mother-in-law." Next oldest, but eight years younger, came Catherine's dazzling brother Juan, much more nearly a contemporary of the younger girls, though cut off from them by a separate little court and training school, as befitted the heir to all the crowns of Spain. Everyone loved Juan; everyone admired him. The humanists who had begun to flock to the Spanish court strained their vocabularies finding epithets to do justice to his beauty, his gracious bearing, his precocious intelligence, his aptitude for learning and for manly sports. The soberer Spanish chroniclers were almost as extravagant. Behind the cloud of eulogy, from rare letters and infrequent anecdotes, one does seem to discern a singularly winning young man. Great things were predicted for him, and for the Spain over which he was to rule. The three younger girls were Joanna, the beauty of the family, just a year younger than Juan and in some ways very like him; Maria, the docile one; and Catherine, the baby. Their destiny was humbler than their brother's, but only less great and serious. They were to marry kings and bear them children, linking Spain by ties of friendship and blood to the greater crowns of Europe; they were to be queens, and the ambassadresses of Spain to Christendom. For this task Isabella educated them as seriously as she educated Juan.

Isabella herself had had but meager schooling. In her turbulent girlhood she had learned no more than was traditionally considered fitting for a lady of her station: to read and write in Spanish, to dance, to embroider and to draw a little, to sew a fine seam, perhaps to weave and spin. The lessons of her young womanhood were those of a warrior and a statesman: to lead armies, and rule councils, and deal with haughty barons and slippery foreign diplomats. But she was aware of the new stir in the world, of the eagerness with which the humanists were seeking the secrets of the past, of the deference Italians paid to the new learning, and she would not neglect anything which might add to her prestige, or teach her to be a better queen. In the midst of her campaigns she set herself to learn Latin, and though she never acquired any real fluency she learned enough to scan the texts of treaties and charters, and to read with pleasure the Vulgate and Caesar's *Commentaries* – enough to be determined that her children should have what she (and Ferdinand) had missed. Naturally the heir apparent would receive the most elaborate training, but a reigning queen – the only reigning queen in the first century of the Renaissance — could not admit that women's minds were incapable of profiting by classical instruction.

As a matter of course, the princesses were taught the feminine accomplishments appropriate to their station: dancing, drawing, music, sewing and embroidery. Queen Isabella also insisted that they learn the homely, old-fashioned skills of their ancestors: to weave and spin and bake like country wives, and to perform all the services of the great households which later they must direct. They studied heraldry and genealogy and what passed for history (since a great lady must know something of the families she will meet), and (since she must share the interests and amusements of her class) they were drilled in horsemanship and falconry and the voluminous theory and exacting practice of the chase. From Isabella's own inclinations, and from the books in her library, we may judge that her daughters conned the Bible and the Missal, the lives of the saints, and other popular books of devotion. All this, while exceptionally thorough, was usual enough. In addition, however, Isabella engaged for her daughters tutors in the classics from among the leading humanists available, first Antonio Geraldini, and then, after the poet's death, his no less learned brother Alessandro. With them the girls read the Christian poets, Prudentius and Juvencus and their fellows, the Latin fathers Ambrose and Augustine, Gregory and Jerome, the pagan sages, chiefly Seneca, and (because they were to be the wives of rulers and Isabella had a high notion of the duties of a queen) not a little Latin history, and something of the civil and the canon law. They were so well grounded in the classics that later all three of them were able to reply to the speeches of ambassadors in extempore Latin, fluent, classical, and correct, and Catherine appeared to Erasmus and to Luis Vives a miracle of feminine learning. Probably not even in Italy were there three more carefully educated young ladies.[3]

Indeed the phenomenon at the end of the fifteenth century might have seemed more remarkable in Italy than in Spain. Isabella's patronage had stimulated the classical Renaissance in Spain to precocious vigor. Salamanca swarmed with young men eager to study under "that phoenix of scholars," Antonio de Lebrija, or under his chief rival, Arias Barbosa, the Hellenist pupil of Politian. Chairs of Greek and Hebrew were established at Salamanca while the battle of the new learning at Oxford and Paris was still to be begun, and noblemen not only collected manuscripts and scribbled Latin verses as they had begun to do throughout Europe, but competed with the sons of burghers for academic laurels. Before the end of the second decade of Isabella's reign, immigrant Italian humanists on the make were meeting formidable competition from native Spaniards, and the more successful of the Italians, Lucio Marineo, Pietro Martire d'Anghierra, and the Geraldini brothers found more to admire than to patronize in Spanish learning. Since the new studies had developed no stiff tradition, and since the Queen was their patroness, women took more share in them than elsewhere. Italy may have had bluestockings as learned as the Marchioness of Monteagudo and her sister Doña Maria Pacheco, whose attainments astonished their male contemporaries, – may, indeed, have had some as learned as Doña Beatriz de Galinda, Queen Isabella's instructress, called *La Latina*, – but even in Italy women did not lecture regularly on the poets at the great universities as did Doña Lucia de Medrano at Salamanca and Doña Francisca de Lebrija at Alcala.

The fuller participation of women was one of the chief differences of the Spanish Renaissance, the other was the attitude it preserved towards the Church. Into Italy the new studies brought a wave of paganism, so that even the Christian calendar and the Christian deity assumed a classical disguise in the elegant Latin of learned cardinals, and those scholars who did not indulge in dreamy philosophic attempts to melt all religions into one neo-Platonic mist were, for the most part, openly contemptuous of, or blandly indifferent to, the "superstitions" of their gothic forebears. Beyond the Alps, those scholars who escaped Italianate paganism tended to sharpen their humanistic satire, and to aim, more or less consciously, at considerable changes in church discipline and doctrine. But in Spain the Renaissance, while as serious and Christian as in the hands of the most earnest northern reformers, was unquestioningly orthodox. In this difference, as in the matter of feminine participation, something must be attributed to the peculiar temper of Spain, more to the influence of Isabella. Sooner or later most of the leaders of Spanish learning, men and women, natives and foreigners, were drawn into that court circle whose inspiration and chief patroness was also the inspiration and chief patroness of the Spanish Inquisition. Twenty years before Luther began to hatch the eggs Erasmus laid, Isabella was already incubating, in Spain, the Counter Reformation.

iii

Catherine did not learn all her history and statecraft from books. To have seen the fall of Granada was to have seen the triumph of a crusade; after more than seven hundred years Spain was again Christian from the mountains to the straits. Her parents remained in the south until after Catherine's seventh birthday as much to install the Church as to organize the civil government in their new domain. Though all Moslems were not at once expelled, Isabella offered to God another sacrifice in recognition of victory, a sacrifice she had long been preparing. On March 30, 1492, the Spanish Jews were given four months in which to accept baptism or leave the land. More than two hundred thousand of Isabella's subjects, without whose wealth and skill and loyalty Granada might never have fallen, scholars and patrons of the arts like Isaac Abravanel, scientists like Abraham Zacuto, bankers, physicians, lawyers, engineers, the backbone of the middle class in sixty Spanish cities, were cut off from her kingdom with the stroke of a pen, stripped of most of their wealth and driven from the land which had been their home and held the bones of their ancestors for a dozen centuries. Civilized Italy was shocked. In Venice, in the papal states, in the Netherlands, even in Portugal, the exiles found refuge. The Pope made it clear that he exacted of the Most Catholic Kings no such proof of orthodoxy. Even some Spaniards ventured to protest, and Ferdinand, that practical monarch, would have preferred to let the whole matter rest with the levying of blackmail. Only the Sultan was delighted at the folly which thrust into Islam knowledge and skill, energy and potential wealth, more than counterbalancing the loss of Granada. But to Isabella no price was too great to pay for Christian unity, for the preservation of the orthodox Catholic faith. It was an object lesson even a little girl could hardly fail to understand.

Of another event at Granada that year, the departure from court of a needy Italian adventurer, thought by some to be a little mad, but entrusted by Isabella with a letter for the Great Khan and money (to be augmented by the Jews) for some ships, Catherine probably took no notice, though later, much later, her tutor, Alessandro Geraldini, remembered that from the first he alone had supported the daring project of sailing westward, alone had foreseen its tremendous consequences, and alone had brought it to pass. Whether Geraldini drew her attention to his departure or not, Catherine would not forget the Discoverer's return to Barcelona, in April, 1493, when she was seven. Of all the pageants she had seen it was among the most amusing. The Admiral's glittering cavalcade must have seemed a little tawdry, nothing like the style of her cousin, the Admiral of Castile, and the wagonloads of treasure may have bored her; but the queer stuffed birds and beasts, the monkeys perched on the sailors' shoulders, the strange, screaming birds, and the six wild men, if men they were, almost naked except for paint and feathers and golden ornaments, silent in the yelling crowd, and unabashed before the royal throne, were proof even a child could grasp that Europe was confronted with a new world. No child, indeed no adult, could be expected to understand the significance of that confrontation. Orthodox Spain rejoiced at the opportunity to bring so many pagan souls to God. With Isabella, Catherine noted the special favor God paid her family.

Not long after the entry of the Admiral of the Ocean Sea the talk began to be of war with France. The French had always been enemies of Aragon, so that as soon as the Moors were cleared from Granada, and in spite of the fact that the King of France had just signed a treaty with Ferdinand, ceding him two provinces as the price of permanent peace, it was generally agreed that France was next. Before Catherine was ten there were raids back and forth across the Pyrenees and some glorious victories in Naples, all preceded and accompanied by much feverish diplomatic activity. Somehow the whole danger from the French seemed to be mixed up with the Crusade. Christendom could not be safe, Ferdinand insisted, unless the French colossus were encircled by an iron ring of enemies: Milan, Venice, the Habsburgs, and England must join Spain in protecting the Holy Father at Rome against the brutal invaders. It was French aggression in Italy which was stirring up trouble in Europe, and weakening the defense of Christian lands. The King of France, Ferdinand often wrote to his ambassadors, was really worse than the Turk. It would be strange if Catherine did not hear first from her father that phrase which was to become so familiar. Probably she did not know that King Charles VIII of France had announced his occupation of Naples as the first step towards the recovery of the Holy Land; certainly she did not know her father's own ultimate plans about Italy. But she learned thoroughly that in Europe France was the chief enemy of her house, the chief obstacle to its execution of God's will.

To all such lessons her mind held tenaciously. And the lesson about France was the more important because it had to do with her own future. She and her sisters were to seal with their bodies the iron ring designed to hold France in check and overawe the Turk. She could not remember when she had not known this.

Perhaps her earliest recollection was the betrothal of her sister, Isabella, to Alfonso of Portugal. It was uncomfortable and yet exhilarating to stand stiff and silent between Maria and Joanna on the royal dais in the great packed church, to smell the sweet, heavy smell of incense and hear the interminable rumble of the chanting under the shadowy, unfinished vaulting, to catch a glimpse of her sister's white solemn face as she moved forward on her father's hand, and to know that a destiny, immense and awesome and exciting, was beginning to be fulfilled. Or had she an earlier memory still? A bright hot day in the bull ring at Medina del Campo when she was only three? An unusual dress of ceremony, heavy with jewels and stiff brocade, and her mother, in high spirits, holding her up to see the colored darts planted neatly in the flanks of the glossy, charging bulls . . . Dust and sunlight and strange bearded gentlemen, who came to look at her with deference and admiration – the ambassadors of England come to ask her hand for Arthur, Prince of Wales, a baby not yet two . . .[4]

She could not remember being called anything but Princess of Wales, destined for England as her sister Isabella was for Portugal and her sister Joanna for Austria. It may have been a source of juvenile satisfaction to be bespoken before Maria, four years her senior, though, of course, she had not done as well as Isabella and Joanna. Portugal was so near and so like Spain Isabella would hardly find herself a stranger there; Castilian diplomacy always put Portugal first, and now that its king was lord of the African coast and his caravels were pushing farther and farther towards the East, the neighboring kingdom would be more important than ever. Joanna's marriage was impressive too; her fiancé, Philip, was the son of the Emperor Maximilian of Austria, and heir, in his mother's right, to Burgundy and the wealthy Low Countries. One heard tales of the magnificence of the Burgundian court, and Philip had prospects of being not only one of the richest lords in Europe but, in succession to his father, Emperor of the Holy Roman Empire, an office of unique and quasi-divine authority. Portugal and Austria were splendid matches, but there were compensations about England. It was a remote island; a poor, cold place some said; the dynasty there was new and ill-established. But England had a great past. All Europe had heard of Agincourt, and, before that, Spain knew the Black Prince and his brother, John of Gaunt, Catherine's own great-great-grandfather. England was still a land of gallant knights, who, more than other Europeans, did their crusading in Spain, so that even now an occasional English lord wandered in to serve against the Moors. In the old days, England had been a land of enchanted chivalry, Merlin's island of Launcelot and Gawain, Tristram and Galahad. Among the surviving books of Isabella's library, less handsomely bound than the stately tomes of theology and law, or the precious copies of the ancient classics, but more battered with use than any others, are three manuscript volumes in a crabbed Spanish hand that tell the story of King Arthur and the Table Round. It would be odd if those pages had not been thumbed and dog-eared by the fingers of a dreaming child. The dynasty that ruled in England now, however dubious its recent pedigree, claimed descent from the founder of the Round Table, could show an illuminated genealogy to prove it. In memory of that ancient splendor the husband to whom she was promised was named Arthur. A marriage in England might prove the most glorious of all.

Catherine knew, of course, that there were risks in the career marked out for her. Only a few months after the splendid ceremony in Seville, the Princess Isabella returned to her mother's court, pale, unsmiling, clad in black, a widow at twenty. Her husband's sudden death deepened the younger Isabella's seriousness into melancholy asceticism; she denied herself the pleasures of the court, even the society of her family, spent her days shut up in her rooms praying, weeping, fasting, wore the habit of the Little Clares, and begged her parents for permission to take not only the habit but the vows; another marriage, she said, was unspeakably repugnant to her. But the Queen, though she allowed her daughter time to recover from her grief, made it clear that a Spanish princess had no right to follow her own inclinations even if she thought they led her straight towards God. The Infanta Isabella had been unlucky; the Infanta Isabella would have to try again. Spain could not abandon the Portuguese alliance because a woman's heart was broken.

Arrangements to marry the young widow to her late husband's cousin and heir were still in progress when the time came to complete the double wedding with the Habsburgs, the diplomatic masterpiece of the Catholic Kings and the chief disaster of their dynasty. In August, 1496, escorted by a powerful armada, Joanna sailed to be married in Flanders, Joanna whom Catherine loved and was to see only once again, for a few hours, Joanna who was going to her husband without a dowry because her brother would take Philip's sister Margaret so, but who bore with her from the quayside at Laredo, though no one guessed it, the reversion of all the crowns of Spain – gay, moody, beautiful Joanna, whose fate it was to touch all hearts except the one she valued.

Margaret of Austria, whom Catherine welcomed as a sister the next spring, could have told her something of the risks they run whose vocation it is to marry kings. In her infancy Margaret had been betrothed to the greatest catch in Europe, Charles VIII of France. She had been brought up at the French court, addressed as "Madame la Reine," even married to Charles "*per verba de futuro*," the most solemn form of betrothal. When Charles threw her over to marry the heiress of Brittany, Margaret was old enough to feel the injury, old enough never to forget it. After France, a Spanish prince was distinctly second best, and sometimes, as Ferdinand's diplomats bargained, it looked as though Juan, too, might slip away, though he, too, had married her by proxy. When her ship was tossed by a Biscay tempest and seemed ready to founder, the Princess, with wry gaiety, scribbled her own epitaph: –

Ci gist Margot la gentille demoiselle
Mariée deux fois, et si mourut pucelle.

(Here lies Margot, the willing bride,
Twice married – but a virgin when she died.)

But her squadron finally made the harbor of Santander and she found an enthusiastic greeting, and a husband, – not quite so great a catch as the Most Christian King yet heir to more than half a dozen crowns and much better-looking than big-headed, dwarfish Charles. Spanish royalty, not usually given to display, felt that this princess from the most sumptuous court in Europe called for something special, the marriage of the only son of the house for even more. It was a gay and happy summer. From Flanders Philip wrote that Joanna was with child. From England Dr. De Puebla, the Spanish ambassador, reported that the marriage treaty was as good as signed. He lacked only Catherine's power for a marriage by proxy: then she could be sent as soon as her parents liked – the sooner, the better. Another bargain had been driven with Portugal; the Infanta Isabella would marry the new king, Manoel, later to be called the Fortunate, thus not only securing Spain's one vulnerable land frontier, but serving the faith as well, for as a bridal gift, Portugal agreed to expel the Jews. The court moved gaily and confidently across northern Spain.

Then, in September, after Ferdinand and Isabella had left one bride and groom at Valladolid and gone to the border town of Valencia de Alcantara, to deliver a reluctant but obedient daughter to her second husband, the thunderbolts began to fall. While the festivities on the Portuguese frontier were still in progress a courier brought word that Prince Juan lay dangerously ill at Salamanca. The merrymaking broke up, and Ferdinand, stabbed in his most vulnerable spot, his dynastic ambition, for once outrode his wife, to find his only son dying, to send back falsely hearty reports from the bedside, to consider the ruin of his hopes. Some of the council had warned Juan's parents that his adolescent constitution might be endangered by this early marriage, that after the formal consummation it might be better if the young couple were not too much in each other's company, better even if they kept separate establishments. "Whom God hath joined together," Isabella quoted. Nor was it man who put the two asunder. For a while the Catholic Kings hoped still to save their dynasty; Margaret was carrying Juan's child. If it was a boy there would still be one of the house of Trastamara to rule Spain. Then the child was born, prematurely, dead.[5] The crowns of Spain would pass to a foreigner.

For two years Portugal seemed the heir. In July, 1498, young Isabella gave birth to a fine boy, and though the mother did not rally from childbed, the boy seemed strong, and the *cortes* of the realms recognized him as heir apparent. It was bitter to Ferdinand and Isabella to see their kingdoms go to the Portuguese, near neighbors and relatives though they were, but it was some consolation that the whole peninsula would finally be united, that its center of gravity could not fail to be Castile, that their grandson, meanwhile, would be their ward. Then, before he was two, sickness carried off little Dom Miguel. Not long before he died, news came that at Ghent, on February 24, 1500, Joanna had borne a boy to her Habsburg husband. The Flemish baby was heir in his cradle not only to Austria and the wide Burgundian lands, but to all the crowns of Spain. As Charles V he would rule more of Europe than any monarch since Charlemagne.

What history would have been like had Dom Miguel lived is a fascinating question. The Netherlands would have escaped an unnatural domination, and the Habsburgs, undistracted by their southern inheritance, might have welded Germany into a national state in harmony with the tendency of the time. Brought together earlier and under happier auspices, Spain and Portugal might have fused into the single nation for which geography seems to have meant them, and that nation, embracing the whole Iberian peninsula, unburdened by the responsibilities in other parts of Europe under which Spain finally foundered, might have enjoyed centuries of healthy, vigorous growth. Such were the issues which might hang on a single royal baby's life. Ferdinand and Isabella could not see so far, but they could see that their whole position in Europe was altered by the fact that their scepters would ultimately fall to the alien, German, house of Austria.

Whatever the blow to their wider plans, the needs of the moment remained. Maria, their third daughter, would serve to secure Portugal. And now that Spain was bound fatally to the Habsburg lands, the alliance of England, astride the narrow seas, was more necessary than ever. Allied with Spain and Austria, England could threaten the French, Ferdinand hoped, enough to keep them out of the way of his own ambitions in Italy; allied with France, England would make the Austrian alliance merely a liability. So plans for Catherine were unchanged. Her marriage by proxy had been solemnly performed; Dr. De Puebla wrote that the islanders impatiently expected her coming; other diplomats warned against waiting too long [6] – England stood higher in the royal marriage market than it had ten years before. Catherine was to sail as soon after her fifteenth birthday as weather permitted.

iv

She was the last of the children to leave, after all. In October, 1500, Maria departed for Portugal to marry her sister's widower, King Manoel, and the court, once more at Granada and Santa Fé, seemed empty. Its core had been a royal family which, in spite of Isabella's stern devotion to duty and Ferdinand's casual infidelities, had been singularly happy and united, gay and carefree, a family in which the children were petted and indulged at least as much as was good for them, and in which the austere gloom of the eldest sister had once seemed to strike a discordant note. Some of the gaiety had gone with Joanna, the rest when Juan died. The mood of the somber eldest daughter passed like an inheritance to the mother. After the delivery of Margaret's stillborn baby, Isabella gave way to her grief. She withdrew more and more from public appearances. Her health was failing, and she was haunted perhaps by another sense of failure which drove her to long hours of brooding, long fits of weeping, a desperate devotion to prayer and to the offices of the Church. Until her death she wore only black, and, under the black robes, the coarse habit of the third order of St. Francis. Ferdinand, whose restless spirit admitted neither resignation nor sustained regret, immersed himself in business, or in hunting, or in less public pleasures, and spent less and less time in his wife's company. Margaret, in whom Catherine had found a gay companion able to give her lessons in French and endless gossip of the more brilliant northern courts, was glad to escape the Spanish gloom for Brussels and a third try at marriage. In that last winter at Granada, Catherine had only her mother.

The two seemed to have had a special relation. From Catherine's infancy her physical likeness to her mother was striking, and as she grew older observers remarked an increasing resemblance of bearing and mind and character, the same gracious dignity, slightly aloof, the same direct, vigorous intelligence, the same basic gravity and moral earnestness.[7] Something of this, no doubt, was conscious imitation, something the trick of heredity, something a peculiar bond of sympathy. Isabella sensed and returned the child's adoration. Though the excuses she alleged were valid enough, an outbreak of the plague in the northern cities, then a revolt of the Moors at Ronda which made the roads unsafe, one feels in Isabella's letters a reluctance to surrender her youngest daughter. Catherine was still at Granada when she should have been sailing for England.

One may doubt that Catherine shared all her mother's reluctance at parting. She was fifteen, an age at which many queens married, and she had trained for marriage as an athlete trains for a race. From England her husband wrote of his longing for her presence in stilted Latin phrases which sound as if they had been dictated by his schoolmaster. King Henry and Dr. De Puebla wrote more pointedly.[8] The empty Spanish court was like a deserted waiting room in which one last traveler fidgets for the signal to depart. Finally Isabella let her go, the more unwillingly because the Moorish revolt still detained the Queen at Granada and she could not accompany her to the limits of Spain, as she had accompanied her other daughters. On May 21, 1501, Catherine set off towards her high, uncertain destiny, alone.

Alone, that is, for a princess. The Count of Cabra, hero of the Granadan wars, commanded her escort, and, with Alonzo de Fonseca, Archbishop of Santiago, and the Bishop of Majorca, made one of the three high commissioners who were to stand *in loco parentis* at her wedding. Besides the archers and knights who would leave her at the ship, and the nobles and clerics and *letrados* with their servants and retainers whose duty would be done when they saw her safely married, she took a permanent household of some sixty persons, ranging from Doña Elvira Manuel, her duenna, and Doña Elvira's husband, Don Pedro Manrique, her major domo, through Don Alessandro Geraldini (her former tutor and now her confessor and principal chaplain), a chamberlain, a steward, a butler, a marshal, four equerries, and several maids of honor, down to laundresses, page boys, cooks and bakers. The cortege wound along the tracks which passed for roads in Spain, through choking dust and blazing sun, by Toledo, Medina, and Valladolid to the great shrine of Saint James at Compostella, where Catherine passed a night of prayer and made her offering, like a knight going to battle, and thence, a short journey, to Corunna, where a squadron of ships awaited her. On August 17 she sailed.[9]

Her way across Spain, on which she would hurry, so Isabella promised, with the greatest possible speed, took three months. The sea delayed her six weeks more. Even in summer, crossing Biscay was a perilous venture. Isabella had issued elaborate instructions to everyone concerned, and written in her own hand to her daughter's pilots, but the scope for human precautions was small, and the best ships the sixteenth century could build were reasonably safe only in good weather. Four days out of Corunna a storm came boiling from the Atlantic, and the gay squadron was lucky to straggle back into Laredo on the eastern end of the Basque coast with seams started, topmasts and rigging gone overside, and one ship unaccounted for. They were nearly a month refitting, and still unready when Stephen Brett, a famous Devon pilot sent by his king to look for the tardy Spanish princess, poked into Laredo harbor. With Brett showing the way they sailed again on September 27, and this time sighted Ushant in bright weather. Rounding it, however, they were caught in furious squalls breaking never more than three or four hours apart, accompanied by terrific thunder and lightning. Spars carried away and the sea rose so that, as the Licentiate Alcares wrote Isabella, "it was impossible not to be afraid." This time the ships held on their course. Years later, Catherine's friends remembered that she had spoken of the delays and terrors of that voyage as an ill omen; but she showed no fear or indecision at the time. Isabella's daughter had learned to defy augury.

Chapter Two

IN ENGLAND the auguries seemed altogether favorable. Dr. Rodrigo Gonsalez De Puebla, the plebeian lawyer who served as resident ambassador, was delighted with the prospect of a marriage alliance which he regarded as his personal achievement, the crown of thirteen years' arduous negotiation. In 1487 when he had been sent to explore the possibilities of an alliance with the adventurer who had seized the English throne some eighteen months before, his enthusiastic reports had aroused a certain skepticism, and the first treaty of which he had been so proud had been coolly shelved when a turn in Ferdinand's policy made it seem less necessary. In 1495 Ferdinand's plot to oust the French from Italy had involved digging Dr. De Puebla out of relative obscurity and sending him back to England to reweave his broken web. He had been empowered then to renew the treaty of Medina del Campo, signed in 1489, as a bait for the English alliance, and given credentials as resident ambassador – a new sort of post, invented by the Italians, which Spanish diplomacy was just introducing north of the Alps – as an evidence of the importance Spain attached to English friendship. But Henry VII at that time was at war with Scotland and so pestered by pretenders to the throne and on such bad terms with the Emperor Maximilian and with the Netherlands that he seemed in no position to do much harm to France, and Ferdinand and Isabella often wondered whether he was worth bribing with the hand of a daughter. But Dr. De Puebla, who felt his personal credit depended on vindicating the importance of the English match, had an answer to every objection. He minimized the King of England's troubles and magnified his power, even when he had to come dangerously near lying in order to do so. A crafty manipulator of international politics, by worming his way into the confidence of Henry VII, and at the same time getting appointed Ambassador of the Emperor Maximilian in England, he did a shrewd stroke of business for Henry VII and himself by resoldering the old alliance between England and the Burgundian lands Maximilian ruled. In conjunction with a Spanish ambassador whom he persuaded Ferdinand and Isabella to send to Scotland, he jockeyed Perkin Warbeck, the most annoying of the pretenders to Henry's throne, out of Scotland, patched up a peace on the northern border, and helped arrange an Anglo-Scottish royal marriage to make it solid. Dr. De Puebla's path had been anything but rosy. He never had enough money; he was harassed by the suspicions of more aristocratic Spanish envoys; he was accused of base behavior and of being more English than Spanish in his sympathies. At the moment he was involved in a bitter squabble with his colleague, the Spanish Ambassador to Scotland, who, after a taste of life in England, refused to go back where he belonged. But to all his detractors he had one crushing answer: The English king had justified his every expectation. Henry VII had ridden out of the stormy opening of his reign and was now obeyed in every corner of his kingdom as no King of England had ever been before. Since the execution of the Earl of Warwick, his reign was undisputed; there was "no drop of English royal blood" in living veins except what flowed in Henry and his children. The King of England was acknowledged a Solomon for wisdom and for riches; alliance with him would be as honorable and profitable as with any king in Christendom. And it was Dr. De Puebla who, because he had won this king's confidence, was able to confer his alliance upon Spain. The Princess Catherine's marriage would be the triumphant refutation of those who doubted the Doctor's loyalty or his right to the foremost place among the ambassadors of his country.[1]

Henry VII had as much reason to be satisfied with the auguries as had De Puebla. For Henry, the Spanish marriage seemed the seal of public recognition set on his dynasty, the formal admission that he, too, was a member of that little circle of royalty which was beginning to dominate Europe, the guarantee of support from the class into which he had intruded. It would strengthen his hand at home as well as abroad, for the Princess Catherine, descendant of John of Gaunt, and hence of Edward III, had the royal blood of the Plantagenets – and not like the Tudors through a dubious, left-hand marriage, but through an undoubted line of royal kings. Probably Henry admitted to himself that there was too much doubtful blood in his dynasty. The grandson of Owen Tudor, clerk of the Queen's wardrobe and heir to no more than a rocky mountainside and a few goats, could never have come to the English throne had not the Wars of the Roses almost extinguished the Plantagenet stock. Henry's own mother, Margaret Beaufort, Countess of Richmond, gave the King his only drop of royal blood, and though she was descended from John of Gaunt, like the Princess Catherine herself, Margaret Beaufort's grandfather had had the misfortune to be born on the wrong side of the blanket. Like so many of the Italian tyrants, whom they resembled in other ways, the Tudors sprang from bastard stock; and Henry VII knew that, though he had married the daughter of Edward IV to help set things right for his children, his own best claim to the throne was that he had won it by the sword and held it against all comers. The blood of the Spanish princess would strengthen his grandchildren's place among recognized royalty. Meanwhile her dowry would lighten his own task. One had to have money to rule the English. One could not have too much of it.

His passion for money and skill in amassing it are the traits most people remember about Henry VII. They came to him more by necessity than by nature. He was born of no merchant stock, but of wild Welsh adventurers who had mixed their blood with the mad, fickle, talented Valois strain, and the offspring of tough feudal barons. He was reared in no government countinghouse, but in the tiltyards of border castles and on the fringes of the Duke of Brittany's obsolete romantic court. But he had the instinct of survival, and he acquired the traits he needed to survive, intensified, in his case, by the parvenu's haunting sense of insecurity. The years he spent dodging Yorkist assassins affected him less than his years as king. When he first came to the throne, after the bloody scramble of Bosworth, the first things people noticed about him, after his blond good looks, were his generosity and clemency, his fondness for magnificence and for a joke. But the reckless spirit of adventure sank; the caution increased; the humor took a bitter edge. Crowns seemed harder to keep than to win, and the firmer his grasp on his own, the more uneasy he became. The first pretender who came against him he made a turnspit in his kitchen and finally something of a pet; but he hanged the second, and struck off the head of the inoffensive, half-daft Earl of Warwick for good measure, simply because Warwick was the "White Rose." He still loved beautiful things and liked to make a good appearance, but every coin he could lock away in his treasure chests seemed another pledge of security in a tricky world. He was still a fine figure of a man, but the face was beginning to wear a strained look, lines of secrecy and cunning about the mouth, wariness in the eyes.

For Henry had learned what a people he ruled: a people like none in Europe, all Europe agreed, for fickleness and turbulence. Treason and rebellion had been the invariable accompaniment of every English reign for centuries. Since Richard II three kings out of six had died bloodily, two deposed and murdered, the third killed by rebels in battle. The crown had changed hands five times and relatively few persons of royal blood managed to die in bed. In the long wars of the Roses, it is true, the unruly barons had thinned their own ranks by mutual extermination, and many of their great holdings, passing through the hands of the crown, had been broken into smaller fiefs. The country was said to long for peace. But longing for peace is a relative term. Before Henry had been on the throne a year, the North flamed with rebellion. That fire was hardly quenched, when another broke out in Ireland; a boy and a priest, a handful of German mercenaries and wild Irish kerns had shaken the throne and been checked only by a fiercer and more doubtful battle than Bosworth. Then another pretender had arisen, who, with the aid of Burgundy and Scotland, kept Henry uneasy for a decade. It is impossible to tell now, and probably Henry himself did not know, which of his nobles were really faithful to him. Conspiracy was the habit of their class, the profits of revolution their hereditary perquisites. The commons were almost as apt to rebel as the nobles. Twice in a century peasant armies had overrun London itself, and only a few years before an army of Cornishmen had camped on Blackheath and discussed the spoils of the city that lay below them on the Thames. A bad harvest, a crazy prophecy, newer or higher taxes – anything, but particularly taxes – sufficed to set wildfire running across the countryside, a fire of straw for the most part, quickly out, but bright and hot and dangerous while it lasted. Long after Henry's time Europeans still regarded the islanders as probably incapable of orderly government.[2] His granddaughter, Elizabeth, was to complain of the difficulty of ruling "these English wild beasts," and the people themselves had a proverb that the vice of the French was lechery, but the vice of the English was treachery.

Only in times of foreign war, of successful aggressive war, were the English quiet. They could be united and loyal as long as there were Frenchmen or Scotchmen to fight. But though their bellicosity was little diminished since Agincourt, their fighting powers were more suspect. All over Europe the feudal militia were yielding place to professional men-at-arms. In his *compagnies d'ordonnance*, the King of France kept fifteen hundred such; but the King of England could not tax his commons for such luxuries, so England had no professional army, and few of the new weapons, using gunpowder, that were revolutionizing warfare. Henry found it safer to rely on guile – talking a good deal about fighting, but fighting very little, satisfied if he could blackmail the French into an occasional concession. At home, he smote his enemies with a golden dagger, confident that a barony confiscated to the crown in England yielded surer revenues at less cost than a dukedom conquered in France. Meanwhile he fattened his merchants as a farmer fattens his stock, and lent to them at interest from the surplus funds which mounted every year in the royal treasury. To preserve what he had, to be forearmed against every possible danger, to transmit his crown safe and augmented to his children, and his children's children, these were now his constant cares. If not the perfect Machiavellian prince, he was more and more nearly the perfect dynast.

Both as prince and as dynast Henry had reason to be pleased, as he awaited, that summer, the coming of his new daughter from Spain. He was at peace with all the world. The last pretender (so he thought) was dead. The kings of Europe were finally ready to recognize him as one of themselves. One daughter he would give to the King of Scots, one daughter, perhaps, someday to France or Burgundy; meanwhile his eldest son, married to this wealthy Spanish princess, would give him grandchildren, visible pledges of the continuance of the dynasty he had founded. The nobility, what was left of them, would be pleased by Arthur's marriage. If families who were great in England before the Tudors had left their Welsh hillside must yield precedence, they would say, let it at least be to no upstart, but to the blood of a long line of kings. The merchants would be pleased. Spain was a good customer, taking English wool, tin and lead in increasing quantities, corn sometimes, and more and more fish which the men of Bristol caught and salted off Iceland, and paying for them not in such trumpery trash as the Venice galleys brought, but in bow-staves, leather, wax and fine Biscayan iron such as an honest craftsman might rework for gain, or a merchant sell at a profit to the Lubeckers. With a Spanish princess near the throne, trading conditions might be easier in Spain, and business even better.[3] The people would shout for joy, because they were sentimentalists and loved the show of royalty, however unwilling they were to pay for it, and had seen no foreign princesses for many weary years. And because the fact that foreign kings were now willing to marry their daughters in England was a sign the troubled times were over at last, and there would be no more of this politics and fighting and not knowing who, rightly, was king. Nor was this girl one of the false, hateful French, too many of whom had come over as queens, and usually brought bad luck, but a princess from a friendly land, of good Christian parents, who fought infidels and had taken some city or other – possibly Babylon – from them, and best of all she was a descendant (and by a decent marriage) of that ironically popular hero, John of Gaunt. It was best, the people agreed, for princes to marry proper royalty and people to bow to the old blood. Henry and his council could see farther than nobles or merchants or the vulgar, could see that there was no single power in Europe capable of checking the French, unless it was this new power of Spain, none likely to be more influential with the Pope and the Italian states, or more helpful in keeping good relations with the Habsburgs. But for more than these complicated reasons, Henry rejoiced for the same reason his people rejoiced, because Catherine brought the undoubted blood of kings.

ii

Catherine saw the first signs of this popular rejoicing when her battered fleet finally made the Sound and dropped anchor off Plymouth Hoe on a bright Saturday afternoon, the second of October, 1501. For weeks the west country had expected her coming; the topmasts of the foreign ships, the gay flutter of Spanish standards, the familiar cut of Stephen Brett's rigging had packed the quay with gaily dressed citizens among whom were already a sprinkling of squires and their wives, the town barge with the Lord Mayor and a delegation of aldermen floated ready, and, as the first anchors dropped, a welcoming clamor of bells broke out over town and harbor. Catherine may have been a girl not yet sixteen, hardly recovered from seasickness and fright and the wetting which even a princess could not escape in such squalls as her fleet had weathered, but she had been thoroughly trained in what was expected of royalty; when her ship was warped in to the quay she stood in the waist with the Archbishop and the Bishop and the Count of Cabra and her suite of honor ranged ceremoniously behind her, ready to announce to the kneeling Mayor that she would go at once to the church whose steeple rose not far from the quayside to give thanks for her safe arrival in the land of England. In that first procession through the cheering streets of Plymouth, Catherine began to win a hold on English hearts that in all her misfortunes she was never to lose.

Long as the Spanish fleet had been expected, carefully as King Henry's council had drafted and redrafted the plans for its reception, there was no royal officer at Plymouth to bid the Princess welcome; and though hard-riding couriers brought the news of her arrival to Westminster on the Monday, it was a fortnight before the first delegation of Henry's courtiers presented his letter of greeting to her at Exeter. Meanwhile, however, the west country was not wanting in hospitality. Royal instructions had been issued and curiosity was as potent as loyalty. The nobility and gentry of Cornwall and Devon hastened in to form an escort; the commons crowded the roadside to cheer and crane their necks. The welcome at Exeter, bells, banners, bonfires, processions, surpassed that at Plymouth; her suite were lodged as if they had all been grandees; the whole of those first two weeks was a continuous festival. "The Princess could not have been received with greater joy," wrote the elated Licentiate Alcares to Isabella, "had she been the Saviour of the world." [4]

After the stately arrival at Exeter of Lord Willoughby de Broke, high steward of the King's household, supported by Richmond King-at-arms, and Somerset and Rougedragon Heralds, and a goodly array of yeomen and men-at-arms in new green and white liveries, the welcome gained in formality without losing in heartiness. Every stage of the three weeks' journey had been carefully arranged to spare the Princess fatigue, to insure proper lodgings and adequate provisions, to show off the Princess to half a dozen counties, and to delay her arrival at Thameside until the London reception was ready. The high steward in charge of her elaborate itinerary bore, besides the King's own letter of welcome, a sheaf of orders for saddle and draft animals, lodging and entertainment, commands to the local gentry to join the escort in relays, and instructions as to precedence. To act as liaison officer there rode with him Don Pedro de Ayala, papal protonotary and Bishop of the Canaries, ambassador of the Catholic Kings to England and Scotland.

Don Pedro should have been in Scotland, and Dr. De Puebla should have had the honor of welcoming his princess. That the jolly Bishop had succeeded in shouldering his musty colleague out of that pleasant assignment was just another instance of the covert war between the two ambassadors in which the unsuspecting Princess was to play her part. Don Pedro had been sent to Scotland in response to Dr. De Puebla's request for someone to manage that end of his plot to detach James IV from Perkin Warbeck and arrange an Anglo-Scottish peace. Arrived there, Don Pedro began his peace mission by joining a raid across the border into England in the course of which he got most of his staff killed in skirmishes, and endeared himself to his hosts by an unecclesiastical enthusiasm for an all-out, help-yourself fight. James IV liked his ruffling ways so well that he was ready to listen to his advice to get rid of the milksop Perkin, and glad to send the unorthodox Spanish diplomat south with his terms of peace.

Once in London, Don Pedro stayed there. The wine was better

and more copious, the manners more polished, the accommodations more comfortable than in James IV's rude castles, and there was the additional sport of teasing Dr. De Puebla. He had some sort of credentials for England; Henry accepted him, and he was soon as popular at Richmond as he had been at Holyrood. The King could not help liking him. Anyone with half an eye could see that Don Pedro de Ayala was a gentleman and Dr. De Puebla was not, and if Henry preferred to talk business with the Doctor, he preferred to hunt and hawk, drink and dice, with the Bishop – to wink at his brawling, help him out of his scrapes, and from time to time extricate from jail one of the swaggering Scottish sworders with whom Ayala had filled up his war-depleted Spanish suite.

Dr. De Puebla loved his ambassadorial dignity more than anything. To have to share with anyone the glory of making peace with Scotland was bad enough; to have another Spanish resident ambassador – and such a ruffian as Ayala! – dividing his honors in England, meddling in his business and disputing his precedence, was infinitely worse; to be the constant, quivering butt of his colleague's barbed jokes was simply intolerable – more than flesh and blood could bear. The two ambassadors bickered continually. De Puebla, who could keep his temper with everybody else, would explode furiously under Ayala's sly prodding, and the English would chuckle as the imperturbable Don reduced the pompous little doctor to helpless, sputtering rage. The dignity of degrees in the civil and the canon law, of a position as a counselor and ambassador of Their Most Catholic Majesties, turned to shoddy before the effortless poise of authentic blue blood; the mind which could master the most intricate legal problems, find its way unerringly through the most devious maze of diplomatic chicanery, was no match for the nimble repartee of a born courtier. Under Ayala's leadership, baiting Dr. De Puebla became a popular sport. De Puebla wrote to Spain that Don Pedro was an incompetent and impertinent intruder who should be ordered back to Scotland; Don Pedro's letters merely wondered why De Puebla was so anxious to be rid of him unless he wanted to sell out his masters unobserved. De Puebla let it be seen that he considered Don Pedro's ignorance of law and Latin an insult to his profession, and his way of life a disgrace to his cloth. Don Pedro remarked that the Doctor's penny-pinching meanness would be surprising in an ambassador, were it not so obvious that De Puebla was a Jew.

Probably it had not been so obvious in a land where Jews were a rarity, and all Spaniards looked much alike, but after Ayala's remark, De Puebla had to endure cold shoulders and covert sneers from men he had counted his friends, and even coarse jokes from the King himself on the subject of his race. Neither Henry nor Ferdinand and Isabella credited the more serious charges which Ayala's partisans leveled against De Puebla, but Henry, who knew how to value both men, smilingly kept the balance even, and, when the Catholic Kings spoke of recalling Ayala, begged that he be allowed to remain, at least until after the arrival of the Princess, who would find his genial presence a great comfort in her new surroundings. Catherine, no doubt, found Ayala far better company than the stuffy little Doctor, but in the long run it was a grave disservice to her that, falling under the spell of Don Pedro's lazy charm, she learned to share his contempt for the man who later was to be her only champion.[5]

At the time, it was pleasant to amble beside this gay and witty cleric – listening to his fund of stories of the court to which she was going, and of his adventures in the wild land of the Scots; absorbing his friendly, half-paternal advice; storing away in her memory his lively, inaccurate accounts of the history and customs of the land through which they were passing, and of the still stranger land to the north. The land about them was strange enough. Stopping at Honiton and Crokeborne, they rode in easy stages, the more spirited mounts of the gentlemen suiting their pace to the progress of the mules and horse litters and palfreys of the ladies and the priests, while the wains loaded with luggage plodded after, along grassy winding tracks that followed the swelling ridges to the great abbeys of Shirburne and Shaftesbury and Ambresbury. It was a green land, greener now in October than the valley of Granada in May, and over it hung an enchanted mist, softening the outlines of hills that were so much softer already than the uncompromising Spanish ridges, bathing in golden haze the straggling villages and isolated farms which, placidly tucked into folds of the hills or sprawling beside streams, had a confiding, unprotected look after the compact, watchful towns of Spain. The sun which had blazed so fiercely on Spanish rock was veiled until it seemed the sun of another world. Here and there knots of yokels lined the road, staring fixedly, shouting cheerful, incomprehensible greetings; at every stage the local magnates rode in: Paulets, and Lutterels, and Spekes in Dorset, Lyndes and Martins and Newburys in Somerset, Barrowes and Mompessons in Wilts, beefy, red-necked, self-important squires with voices like Andalusian bulls, and weather-beaten, long-toothed wives as assured and nearly as aggressively masculine as their husbands, a boisterous, excitable, demonstrative people, given to loud laughter and bellowing rages and much promiscuous kissing, but, for all their queer manners and appearance, genuinely eager to make a foreign Princess feel at home. Catherine's Spaniards noted that this was a land of soft living and hearty eating, where great fires blazed each evening, where bedding was abundant, and beer and French wine more abundant still, where enough was wasted at every meal to feed another company as large – at least if they were Spaniards; but the Princess had not yet learned to think of the price of provisions. She rode through the flaws of rain that scarcely wetted and the sunshine that barely warmed, listening with half her mind to Don Pedro's droll patter, but wholly wrapped in a golden haze of enchantment.

At Ambresbury Catherine was welcomed by another illustrious company: the Earl of Surrey, Lord Treasurer, and his wife, the titular Duchess of Norfolk, – a proud and influential family, Ayala told her, – also by two bishops, two mitered abbots, two barons and a dozen knights. Here one of the King's servants, William Holybrand, who had been in Spain, and whom Catherine was to know better and like less hereafter, read her a long prepared address in Spanish. After Ambresbury the swollen company moved more slowly, for the November rains were already setting in, by Andover and Basingstoke to the Bishop of Bath's palace at Dogmersfield some fifteen leagues from London Bridge. Still Catherine had not met the King.

Henry's original plans indicate that he meant to receive her when she reached Lambeth on the Surrey side of the Thames; but on November 4, overcome, perhaps, by a fit of his old impatience, he set out with a great company from Richmond, waited at Easthampstead for Arthur, who had been representing the dynasty on the Welsh marches, and then swung down into the plains. Word of the royal cavalcade had preceded them, and it was hardly noon when they were met by the familiar figure of Don Pedro Ayala, cantering briskly on a delicate errand. The Archbishop of Santiago and the Princess's duenna, the formidable Doña Elvira Manuel, had held a hurried council on the news of the English King's approach and had decided to interpret the final instructions of Catherine's parents with Castilian rigidity. Catherine was to observe all the customs of a high-born Spanish bride: until the final benediction had been pronounced at her wedding, not even her future husband was to raise her veil or see her face. Knowing Henry, Ayala delivered the ultimatum with an inner chuckle.

Gnawing his underlip, trying in vain to read the twinkle behind the Bishop's eyes, Henry heard him out, then swung his horse's head towards a field beside the road, barking over his shoulder, "My lords, a council!" Was there, after all, some trickery hidden here? Did the Spaniards expect him to buy a pig in a poke? At Henry's command Ayala put the case again to the wary half-circle of mounted men. With all the formality of Westminster, Henry called for advice. A buzz of whispers ran from saddle to saddle, questioning less the law than the meaning of this contingency; then the King's council gave its unanimous opinion: "The King of England is absolute lord in his own realms; no foreign law or custom can restrain him there. The Princess of Spain, by her marriage to his son, is already one of his subjects; he may dispose of her as he likes."

"Thank you, my lords," said Henry, "we shall meet at Dogmersfield." He shot off at a gallop, the laughing Ayala spurring after him, leaving the bridegroom, the council, and the glittering train to follow at a more dignified pace.

In the great hall at Dogmersfield Henry was met by a solemn deputation: the Archbishop of Toledo, flanked by the Bishop of Malaga and the Count of Cabra. "Tell the King of England," they temporized, "that the Princess is resting. She can see no one."

"Tell the lords of Spain," Henry instructed Ayala, "that the King will see the Princess, even were she in her bed."

But she was not. She was already in the adjoining chamber while her ladies put the last touches to her shawl and her hair, and Doña Elvira frowned disapproval. Henry had his way. Travel-stained as he was, he was led into the chamber where, standing with the light falling on her, her veil lifted, timidly smiling, was his son's bride and the hope of his dynasty. Henry had no Spanish nor enough Latin to serve him at this need; Catherine's scanty French, learned from Margaret of Austria, failed her. For a moment the two eyed each other, then Henry voiced his welcome in English; Catherine, sensing the intention of his words, replied in Spanish; she swept him a deep curtsy, he kissed her hand, and with smiles and nods the two continued to utter courtesies in mutually unintelligible tongues.

Henry needed no words, just the assurance of his eyes, that Spain had sent him no invalid, no cripple, no ugly little monster. He saw a well-grown girl with a beautifully poised head and sturdy supple body, light step and erect carriage, small hands and feet, clear, untroubled gray eyes, a mass of russet-gold hair, half-framing in the Spanish fashion an oval face as freshly pink and white as any English lady's. The English – Henry had set it down in writing – make a great point of beauty; it was almost as important that the bride be beautiful as that she be strong and healthy. Henry was satisfied; his subjects would be too.

Some half-hour behind his father, the bridegroom rode into the courtyard at the head of a column of guards and courtiers, and when father and son had freshened their clothes they were again conducted to the apartments of the Princess, this time for a reception of state. An English bishop turned the formal speeches of the King and the Prince into magniloquent Latin, and a Spanish bishop translated to Catherine and put into Latin her replies. The Princess might have made shift to answer the English bishop herself, but breeding required that she should not show more learning than the King on such an occasion, and there were bishops enough to handle the orations, and to officiate at the formal betrothal which took place on the spot. The two young people had exchanged love letters for years in ardent if formal Latin. Now for the first time their eyes crossed, their hands touched. Catherine saw an elegant youth, blond, with a flush on a skin like snow, a prince from a fairy tale – but young, shorter than she by half a head and slighter, looking less than his almost fifteen years as she looked more than her nearly sixteen. Perhaps her heart went out to him the more because he seemed at once so much younger than herself, and so oddly like, in his slim, blond beauty and his quiet ways, her brother Juan. Perhaps he seemed all she had dreamed of a prince named Arthur, who would restore the ancient glamour of chivalry in the island where it had reached its highest perfection. Or perhaps she only remembered that she was a queen's daughter and that marriage was her destiny. Like most of the two children's sad little idyl, Catherine's thoughts are a matter of conjecture.

Whatever they were, they excited her to unusual self-assertion, unaccustomed gaiety. After supper she invited Henry and his son to her chamber, where minstrels had been summoned, and, after low bows to the King, Catherine and two of her ladies danced one of the stately dances of Spain. Catherine loved dancing, and was proud of her skill in it. Next she and a partner danced a rapid dance, as gay and furious as the other was languorous and slow, and the young prince, encouraged by his father, led out Lady Guildford for an English dance. Candles were lit and the guards were yawning before the company broke up. The terrors of the sea and the hesitations of the diplomats were alike remote, forgotten. England was not only an enchanted land, but a merry one. It would be good to be its queen.

iii

From Dogmersfield, King Henry and his son rode back to Richmond, so that they, with Queen Elizabeth, might row down the Thames in state to Baynard's Castle, the first act in the pageant of the wedding. Catherine and her escort kept on towards Kennington, to be met at Kingston on Thames by another array of peers and ecclesiastics, headed this time by the first nobleman of the realm, Edward Stafford, third Duke of Buckingham. In all the festivities that followed, Buckingham cut the bravest figure, as lineage and wealth and position entitled him to do. The young Duke had been brought up almost as a member of the royal family – his father had been executed by Richard the year before Bosworth – and in Henry's eyes, and in the eyes of many English, no one except Henry's sons stood nearer to the throne. At twenty-three Edward Stafford was, as he was always to be, more a courtier than a soldier or statesman – handsome, charming, extravagant, a little rattle-brained, a little stupid, with an exalted idea of the privileges and security of his position, but a great gentleman, none the less. In him Catherine recognized the proper prop to a throne, an aristocrat as sure of himself and as much to the manner born as any Spanish grandee; in Catherine, Buckingham bowed to an authentic princess. The tie of mutual recognition and respect, the unspoken alliance of persons sure of their respective positions in the world, lasted until Buckingham's death – twenty years, from the field by Kingston to the scaffold on Tower Hill which took the first of Catherine's friends.

Meanwhile another sort of scaffold was being erected in St. Paul's,[6] a great bridge of timber as high as a man's head, running the length of the nave from the west door to the choir, all draped in fine red worsted and ending in an even higher platform large enough to accommodate the King and Queen and their court at one end, and the Lord Mayor and magistrates of London at the other, with room in the middle for the principals of a wedding which Henry was determined should be as sumptuous and as public as possible. This time the King was giving full reign to his taste for magnificence; he knew the value to a ruler of an orderly splendor, and, though he was usually satisfied with a nicely calculated impression of wealth, achieved at a minimum expense, even prudence counseled lavishness on an occasion for which the nobility and the City of London would be obliged to bear much of the cost. So Catherine was conducted from the riverside to the bishop's palace near Paul's to the blare of trumpets and the booming of cannon, through streets hung with draperies and covered with triumphal arches, her progress ornamented and interrupted with all the allegorical pageantry and quaint devices the ingenuity of the Londoners could devise, and thence the next morning to the great bridge of timber in St. Paul's where the Archbishop of Canterbury waited to marry her to a slender, white-clad boy. The boy's brother, a rosy-cheeked strapping youngster with a round cherub's face above a body already bigger and heavier than Arthur's, gave her his right hand down the length of the great church, and stared his wide-eyed, unblinking stare throughout the service. He was Henry, Duke of York, who would be crowned with her, her husband and King, before eight years were out – Henry, now aged ten.

Outside the cathedral, as the kneeling couple rose, a conduit spouted wine and all the bells of the city clanged at once, and the people cheered as if they had not been hoarse already with two days of cheering while the procession formed again to conduct bride and groom to Baynard's castle, a great feast, and a ceremoniously public bridal bed. In court or city few men were sober by the time for that symbolic bedding. London, it was agreed, had never seen a more splendid marriage.

The greatest display, however, was at Westminster.[7] There before Westminster Hall a great tiltyard was set up and platforms richly draped for the King and Queen, the royal family, the Lord Mayor, and the chief notables, while a double tier of wooden benches, solidly constructed, was offered to the common people and by them "were at great cost and price hired." The tournament, the knightly amusement of the middle ages, had degenerated, or been refined, into a sort of circus. It was no longer a pitched field where knights hacked each other in pieces for pleasure and profit and found a rude training ground for their business of war; no longer, even, an open contest of skill where an unknown knight might hope to pick up armor and ransoms and turn an honest penny in the intervals between campaigns. War had become the business of professionals, and the ranks of the nobility were closing to rough soldiers who had only strength and swordsmanship to recommend them, though they were open to wealth, suppleness, and skill in intrigue. The challengers and defenders in such events as this were picked for their social rather than their military qualifications, and the rules were so carefully laid down, the defensive armor was so ponderous, so cunningly jointed and padded, and the marshals so alert to prevent a serious mishap, that the veriest carpet knight might tilt before the King and hope to escape with no more than a few bruises.

As aristocracies become less useful, however, they become more ornamental, and what the tournament lacked in risk and skill it made up, for most spectators, in display. The English, in particular, with their national genius for pageantry, were able to stage a show the like of which Catherine had never seen. Each champion entered in his pavilion, a sort of walking pageant wagon, fantastically ornate. That of Lord William, for instance, was "a red dragon, led by a great giant having a great tree in his hand," a device which would do credit to any Mardi Gras, and the Earl of Essex outdid him with "a mountain of green with many rocks, trees, stones, and marvellous herbs on the side, and on the height a goodly young lady in her hair, pleasantly beseen." Just how the challenger managed to display himself and his horse in the midst of all this painted lath and canvas is not clear, but such shows were admirably adapted to display the contestant's wealth and the quaintness of his taste in allegory, the qualities his society most valued.

On the day after the tournament – which went off admirably, all the contenders breaking their spears skillfully and nobody being hurt – there were festivities in the great hall, where again the English love of allegorical monstrosities formed the main diversion. A castle filled with singing boys was drawn in by four great beasts in chains of gold, two lions, one of gold, the other of silver, a harte and an elk, "in each of them," the chronicler explains scrupulously, "two men, one in the forepart and one in the hinder part, secretly hid and apparelled, nothing of them seen but their legs which were disguised after the proportion and kind of beasts that they were in." A ship followed, bearing Hope and Desire and a figure representing the Princess of Spain, then a hill with eight knights thereon, and a multitude of other devices, dazzling the eyes with gilt and the mind with far-fetched symbolism. For more than a week such entertainments went on – the same four animals, with presumably the same eight men inside them, appearing again and again, to be described each time by the chronicler as if they were quite new, although, as a matter of fact, Henry had used them for several previous spectacles and simply had them repainted for the wedding. More inventive or less canny than their sovereign, the nobles of England required fresh caparisons for each of the three days of harmless jousting, and fresh liveries for their servants. To the gaiety Catherine contributed the antics of her Spanish fool who performed on a high platform grotesquely dexterous feats of tumbling and balancing which kept the onlookers gasping with alternate apprehension and laughter, and she, herself, danced for the company the dances of Spain. Even little Henry, the Prince's brother, danced, performing with such determined energy that to everyone's delight he finally threw off his heavy surcoat and capered in his smallclothes.

Of Arthur, who should have been the chief figure there, the chronicler has little to record. He was too young and fragile for jousting. He danced modestly with Lady Cecil while Catherine led out one of her own ladies, and at dinner he headed a sort of children's table where his sister Margaret and brother Henry also sat, while Catherine sat on the King's right hand with the witty ambassador, Ayala, the Earls of Oxford and Derby, and several of her Spanish ladies. Years later, in the depositions gathered for Henry's divorce, we catch a glimpse of Arthur being publicly and boisterously bedded on his wedding night, and indulging (if one can believe Tudor noblemen deposing in the interests of their sovereign) in certain youthful boasting on the morrow. But in the nuptial pageantry he seems to have played a passive, almost unregarded role, just as he left the arrangements for his household to be settled by his father and his father's ministers in conference with the Spanish ambassador.

The final decision about this was taken at Windsor, whither the

Tudor court, almost as migratory as the Spanish one, though swinging in a much smaller orbit, had arrived by the end of November. So far the bride and groom had had no really separate establishment. The question was whether for the time being they should have one. Arthur, certainly, had to go back to the Welsh marches. Was Catherine not too young and delicate to go with him into the rough border country? Would she not be happier at court with Queen Elizabeth to look after her, and the Princess Margaret, only four years her junior, as companion? Was Arthur robust enough to begin the duties of a husband, and would it not be better if the young couple lived apart for a year or two? The royal council was divided; the King seemed unable to make up his mind. Some of the Spaniards, remembering Juan and Margaret of Austria, thought separate establishments would be wiser. Father Alessandro Geraldini, however, beginning to be a little above himself in his new authority, declared loudly that their Most Catholic Majesties expected Catherine and Arthur to live together at once. Ayala pulled one way, De Puebla the other. Arthur was silent, and Catherine modestly refused to express a preference, leaving the decision entirely to her father-in-law. Though no one guessed all the momentous consequences, there was an awkward moment of pause, while the future hung in the balance. Just what considerations were decisive – politics, the thought of the expense of two separate households, some word from the Prince or his bride, or, least likely of all, the officious tutor-chaplain's opinion about the preference of the King and Queen of Spain, no one can say. When the Prince of Wales started westward, not waiting to keep Christmas at his father's court, Catherine and her Spaniards went with him.

Before they left, and mixed up with the debate over their establishments, there had been another minor wrangle, unimportant to Catherine at the time, but ominous for the future – a wrangle over the plate and jewels she had brought with her from Spain, articles, which, according to the treaty, were to be a part of the final installment on her dowry. We know it only from Ayala, who naturally makes De Puebla the villain of the plot. According to Don Pedro, his colleague advised King Henry to demand immediate possession of Catherine's jewels and plate, although no further payment on the dowry was due for some time, and when the attempt was foiled by the stubborn refusal of Catherine's treasurer to surrender the articles before the date agreed on, an effort was made to trick Catherine into wearing the jewels and using the plate, after which, it was thought, her parents would be ashamed to offer them in payment.[8] Given the hostility between the two ambassadors, the most we can guess from this story is that De Puebla suggested that Henry anticipate the last installment of the dowry and give a receipt for it. The marriage settlement fixed the dowry at two hundred thousand crowns: one hundred thousand to be paid on the wedding day, fifty thousand more within six months, and the final fifty thousand within a year, fifteen thousand in cash, and the jewels and plate Catherine brought with her, valued at thirty-five thousand. The Spanish might anticipate the date of the last two payments if they liked. Had Henry accepted and receipted for the plate in December, 1501, the execution of the treaty would have been simplified, Catherine would have been spared much anxiety, and Ferdinand would have saved, ultimately, about twenty-five thousand crowns. It may be that De Puebla suggested, and Henry tentatively agreed to, such a step. But if either of them believed that by obliging Catherine to use the plate her parents could be shamed into omitting it from the final settlement, they had romantic notions of the ease with which Ferdinand and Isabella could be parted from their money. That De Puebla would have countenanced a scheme which would have complicated outrageously his already complicated task is scarcely credible, and, in fact, nothing came of the imbroglio Ayala reported. If Catherine heard of it from Ayala as she made ready to accompany Arthur towards Wales, she must have thought it a sordid triviality, merely confirming her opinion of the vulgar little Doctor. But the question of her plate and jewels, in another form, was to be the bane of her existence for years.

iv

Wales, towards which the children rode, was a wild land, full of legend and rumor, almost untouched by English influence, almost, one might say, unconquered. In its savage glens the King's writ hardly ran, and its local chieftains settled their differences with scant recourse to the King's justice. During the fifteenth century it had sometimes seemed doubtful whether Wales was ruled from Westminster, or England from the Welsh border – for the marcher lords maintained great retinues of archers and men-at-arms, and could recruit from the solid blocks of their domains and from the lawless mountains beyond hosts of hardy fighting men, greedy for plunder and knowing no loyalty save to their captains, capable, in an age of civil war, of dominating an England grown in its other parts less feudal and less warlike. The ruin, one after another, of the greater of these lords during the civil wars had lessened this danger but also had weakened English influence, and increased the political importance of the Welsh chieftains themselves. Henry, himself, owed his crown in no small measure to his countrymen, who had supplied most of his best troops at Bosworth and who felt that in setting one of Cadwallader's blood on the English throne they had avenged the defeats of centuries. Determined to exploit Welsh loyalty to the full, the King was resolved not to create a new crop of marcher lords to act as the intermediaries of the crown and hold the means of overturning it. Even his chief supporter, the great Rhys ap Thomas, lord of Carewe Castle and of most of South Wales, the King's actual lieutenant in the west, who could call to his standard more fighting men than followed any English earl, was left a simple knight, and as soon as it was possible to do so, Henry sent to supersede him the only kind of representative possible among a people accustomed to ties of personal fidelity, his son Arthur. Arthur had already had one turn of government on the border, where his presence had appealed to the pride and romantic loyalty of the Welsh, and his council, under the guidance of Sir Reginald Bray, had begun the task of rebuilding on the ruins of the civil wars, extending royal influence and authority, and pressing a measure of law and order into the mountain glens. It was essential that Arthur should return to this work as soon as possible.[9]

This time Sir Reginald Bray did not go with him, but Henry gave him an able council, headed by Sir Richard Pole, a dependable wheel horse of Tudor administration, and including, in its array of soldiers, legists, and administrators, several trusty Welshmen like Sir Henry Vernon, Sir David Philips, and Sir William Udall and two bishops, Dr. William Smith and Dr. Charles Booth. Gentlemen, men-at-arms, archers and servants made a little army, and in the train went all of Catherine's permanent household, her chaplain Don Alessandro, her chamberlains, ushers, and pages headed by Don Pedro Manrique, and her maids of honor under the eagle eye of Doña Elvira Manuel. The Archbishop of Santiago and the other Spaniards had been sent, loaded with presents, back to Spain. By Abingdon they rode, and Kenilworth, until, crossing the Severn, they reached Bewdley in Worcestershire, the first of Arthur's own residences in his special domain of the Marches, a charming, comfortable manor house, remodeled during Arthur's first sojourn there in the best modern taste, with glass in many of the windows, handsome hangings and furniture, a neat walled garden, and a sweeping view over green, rolling country. It would have been pleasant to linger at Bewdley more than just long enough for Arthur to show Catherine the little chapel where three years before he had gone through a solemn marriage ceremony with musty, pompous little Dr. De Puebla, standing as her proxy, but duty lay farther on, where, on its rock above the Corve, the grim keep of Ludlow Castle kept its long watch against the mountains of Wales.

We have little record of the short idyl of the two children in their bleak castle. The council debated revisions of the laws and points of administration, and perhaps Arthur sat listening, his boy's brow puckered in concentration, his thin shoulders hunched against the cold. The magnates of Wales rode in to pay their homage. First in power and loyalty Rhys ap Thomas, the simple knight whom Henry VII always called "Father Rhys," bent to kiss Catherine's hand with a courtliness more than Italian, speaking as a prince to princes as he placed himself at the young couple's service and commended his son to their household. After Rhys came others of the Tudor's countrymen, some like fine gentlemen in silk, speaking French or a lisping, lilting English, some shaggy-bearded, in leather and homespun, given to long orations in their native Welsh; some with the manners of grandees, some with the manners of mountain brigands, but all with the dignity and conscious pride of an ancient race, descended from many kings. There must have been feasting in the great hall at Ludlow, lit by the glow of its vast hearths and the smoky glare of cressets, and Catherine's Spanish fool showing his grotesque skill, and wild Welsh harpers chanting their interminable, dirge-like ballads, sweet-voiced, incomprehensible and touching, while young Griffith ap Rhys, her gentleman usher now, lounged behind Catherine's chair and whispered in halting French sketchy translations. One ballad, often sung, he could have told her, was about the son of the red dragon who should spread his wings in Wales, and drive the wild boar of the lowlands, and mate with the silver hind, a union whence should spring another Arthur to renew the glories of the ancient time. Others were of wild loves and wilder hatreds, of lost causes followed to the end, of battles, and defeats and death, and dreams more real than death; and all were so wrapped in the mists of time and allegory that even the Welsh squires hanging on each word hardly knew what they meant, and all were poured out with such fervor and sweetness that even the yawning English, and the bored, impassive Spaniards, were vaguely, uneasily stirred.

Did the children go on with their studies under the learned Alessandro and good Dr. Booth? Did they kill a great stag under Sutterstone Hill and ride home over roads ringing hard with frost to their torch-lit courtyard? Did they stray as far as Wenlocke to see the burning well, and stop the night in the abbey? Did they walk, well wrapped, on the windy battlements, and plan for the time when the rain and blowing mist should clear, and they be free of their dark, damp prison? Whatever they did, it was tragically brief.

We shall never know just how Arthur died. Of a "consumption," it was said later, but a "consumption" in the sixteenth century meant little more than that the patient had wasted away. The plague was abroad in the west that spring, not the terrible black plague, but that curse of the sixteenth-century English, the sweating sickness, perhaps some swift and deadly variety of influenza, which killed strong men within twenty-four hours of its onset, and left survivors weak and spent, susceptible to a relapse, a second or third bout of high fever and profuse sweating which also might be fatal. It came in March to Ludlow, and Catherine seems to have been stricken. Arthur's delicate constitution would have offered little resistance to such an enemy. Whatever the cause, on April 2 he was dead.[10]

At Greenwich, where Sir Richard Pole's courier had arrived at midnight and the anxious council had summoned the King's confessor to break the news, Henry and Elizabeth sought to comfort each other. Elizabeth had borne her husband six children, but the third daughter and the third son had died in infancy; the hope of the Tudor dynasty hung precariously now on the life of a single boy, Henry, who would be the new Prince of Wales. That raised a fear even worse than the grief of Arthur's death, though Elizabeth could remind her husband that they were both young, she thirty-five, he barely ten years older, and they could have more sons; the situation was not so desperate as when he had been born to a widowed mother, the only Tudor of his generation. But three deaths in less than seven years, only three living children after sixteen years of marriage, was not reassuring. The Tudors were not a healthy or prolific stock.

Meanwhile for three weeks, until Saint George's Day, Arthur's body lay in state at Ludlow and the notables of England straggled in along muddy roads to view it, and to hold hushed converse with the Prince's household. By April 23, when the body was removed to the parish church and the requiem sung, the Earl of Surrey had come, representing the King as chief mourner, and the Earls of Shrewsbury and Kent, Lord John Grey of Dorset, Lord Ruthven, Lord Dudley, Lord Powys, and representatives of all the chief families of the west, besides three bishops – Chester, Salisbury, and Lincoln – and other lords and gentlemen of the king's household. From Ludlow to Bewdley the funeral procession wound, Griffith ap Rhys riding just ahead of the black-draped hearse, his own horse draped in black and bearing, reversed, the Prince's banner. Nor was any ceremony omitted, "though the day," says a witness, was "the foulest cold windy and rainy day I have ever seen, and the worst way, so that in some places they were fain to take oxen to draw the charre." From Bewdley the cortege moved on, with eighty flaring torches about it and the black hangings dripping in the wet to Worcester, and there in the choir of the cathedral, with the monks chanting, the coffin was lowered, and "Sir William Udall and Sir Richard Crofts [the prince's chamberlains] broke their staffs and cast them into the grave, and likewise did all the gentleman ushers with their rods. This was a piteous sight to all that beheld it." Catherine did not behold it. She lay ill at Ludlow, and it was many weeks and warm bright weather before she could be brought slowly in a litter to the side of Queen Elizabeth at Richmond.

Chapter Three

IN SPAIN the news of Arthur's death was greeted with consternation. Ferdinand was just reaching the crucial point towards which all his unscrupulous power politics during the past decade had been aimed. He was about to challenge the mighty monarchy of France for the stakes of supremacy in Italy. He was going to need all his allies as he had never needed allies before. Before the coalition which Dr. De Puebla had helped to organize had sent the French scurrying out of Italy faster even than they had entered it, Charles VIII's military promenade had advertised the weakness of the Italian powers, and made it clear that the wealthiest and most civilized part of Europe was destined to be the prey of the strongest of its neighbors. At that time Ferdinand had been content to see the unstable balance of the peninsula restored; he was not ready for conquest on his own account. In 1499 a new king was on the throne of France, Louis XII, a middle-aged intriguer whose itch for adventure had not been discouraged by his unlucky experiences as Duke of Orleans. Having inherited a sort of claim to the duchy of Milan, Louis sent across the Alps, to assert it a new army even more powerful than Charles VIII's, an army which overran Lombardy as easily as Charles VIII's had overrun Naples. Although it was clear that Milan was only a steppingstone to further aggression, that Louis' next objective was Naples where a branch of the House of Aragon ruled weakly, Ferdinand did not stir. He preferred to act the part of accomplice and then collar the swag. By the secret Treaty of Granada he arranged for a joint invasion of his Neapolitan cousin's kingdom, and its partition between the invaders, meaning to let the French bear the brunt of the fighting while a Spanish army established itself in Calabria, and to wait until the vagueness of the Treaty brought the inevitable clash. When the Spaniards fought, it would be not to re-establish Ferdinand's feeble cousin, but to add another crown to Ferdinand's own collection. At Toledo, on May 10, 1502, Ferdinand and Isabella were waiting for news that their troops had met the French, the signal for their effort to drive their partner in crime from his share of the booty.

For years all the policy of the Catholic Kings had envisaged this trial of strength with France. France was the strongest state in Europe, the wealthiest, the most populous, the most warlike and best organized for war; by virtue of his matchless artillery, his iron companies of men-at-arms, above all, by virtue of his almost absolute power to tax his fat provinces at pleasure, Louis XII was the most formidable of possible opponents. Against him Ferdinand felt that Spain – a poor, barren land with only light horsemen and light armed infantry for its soldiers, a land cut up into a dozen separate kingdoms, most of them with disputatious parliaments who grudged every *maravedi* they granted to the crown, a land still burdened with the debts of the Moorish wars – could not be successful without allies. Therefore, he and Isabella had married one daughter to a Habsburg and another to a Tudor to insure help from the north in the coming struggle. But the head of the House of Habsburg, the Emperor Maximilian, always as slippery as an eel, as darting and fickle as a hummingbird, was proving less reliable than ever, now that his grandson Charles of Ghent was heir to all the Spains. Already he looked on Spain as a Habsburg dependency, and felt that Ferdinand should follow his lead, not he Ferdinand's. His all too probable defection would leave only England. And now, as they waited at Toledo, the Catholic Kings heard that in England death again had broken the web of their alliances. Their daughter Catalina was a widow.

Ferdinand and Isabella never flinched in the face of catastrophe. In the early days, when they were fighting for the crown of Castile, more than once defeat seemed certain. In the Moorish wars they had seen their troops ambushed, their camp burned, their best strength hurled in vain against some apparently impregnable town, but always they had collected fresh troops, new guns, and gone on. Twice death had broken their alliance with Portugal; each time a new marriage had rewoven the bond. The King of England had another son, not yet promised. On the same day that news came of Arthur's death, the Catholic Kings in council prepared three hastily drafted documents to be taken by a new special envoy to England, and selected for the mission their councilor and chamberlain, Hernan Duque de Estrada,[1] a gentleman of an old Asturian family, whose knowledge of their views spared much explanation, and who could be trusted to ride with speed. The first document given Hernan Duque was a note to Dr. De Puebla, ordering the resident to follow the special envoy's lead implicitly; the second was a formal power to demand the restitution of the one hundred thousand crowns already paid over on Catherine's dowry, to press her claims to her dower rights of a third of the revenues of Wales, Chester and Cornwall, and to bring her back to Spain. These two were to be shown at once. The third document Duque was to keep in reserve and use at his discretion; it authorized him to arrange the marriage of Catherine to the King's surviving son, Henry, Duke of York, soon to be proclaimed Prince of Wales. Ferdinand and Isabella must have hoped, a little wryly, that the dilemma would force Henry to renew the broken link.[2]

As the council debated at Toledo, Catherine was journeying towards Richmond with all the barbarous funereal pomp due a widowed Princess of Wales, and as Hernan Duque was nearing London, Catherine was being installed in the vacant palace of the Bishop of Durham on the Strand, there to pass the seclusion of her widowhood.

Once behind the walls of Durham House, the Princess might almost have been back in Spain. There were a few English horse-boys in the stables, a few English gardeners in the long pleasant gardens that stretched behind high walls down to the Thames, but, except for these, the great rambling pile of Durham House held only Spaniards, a miniature court in exile, reproducing on a tiny scale all the ordered ceremony, all the gradations of precedence, all the intrigue and backbiting of Toledo or Granada. The offices that English and Welsh had held at Ludlow reverted to their original holders: Don Pedro Manrique was again first chamberlain; Don Alonzo de Esquivel, master of the hall; Don Juan de Cuero, master of the state rooms, second chamberlain and treasurer; Don Alessandro Geraldini, the Princess's confessor, again principal chaplain, each of them prepared to struggle for his share of dignity and influence as bitterly as if a kingdom were at stake, but all of them soon to acknowledge the sway of Doña Elvira Manuel, the duenna.

The brief dreamlike months of independence over, Catherine sank back into the quiescence and tutelage of childhood. She showed no interest in the struggles of her suite; none of which we have record in the political drama. Did she, in the first weeks of loss and homesickness, write to her mother that she had no wish to marry again in England, that she wanted to come home to Spain? If she did, the momentary weakness was unlike her, and the letter has been lost; more likely the letter existed only in a pious seventeenth-century chronicler's fancy, for Isabella's children knew they could not marry where or whom they would. Like a soldier Catherine waited silently for orders, passive, like a good soldier or a good child momentarily forgotten by its parent. Her mother had entrusted her to Doña Elvira; in duty and affection Doña Elvira was her mother's surrogate in England; into Doña Elvira's grasping, competent hands fell the management of Catherine's court.

Dr. De Puebla was the first person to feel the weight of Doña Elvira's authority. He blundered against it in his quest for the solution of what, as a practitioner of the canon law, he saw as the chief difficulty created by Arthur's death. Catherine had certainly been married to the Prince according to the ceremonies of the Church, but had they been married in the sight of God? If the marriage had been consummated, certain aspects of the case were simplified. Perhaps the rest of the dowry would have to be paid over, or compounded for, but there would be no doubt about Catherine's legal status and her dower rights. And should Catherine be carrying Arthur's child, and the child be a boy, the political situation would be excellent. On the other hand, should the marriage have been consummated, but prove to be without issue, things would be more complicated. De Puebla knew enough to anticipate that in this case Ferdinand and Isabella would want their daughter to marry again in England, but there was a hard text in Leviticus forbidding a man to marry his brother's widow, and if Catherine had actually been Arthur's wife, and thus related to Prince Henry in the first degree of affinity, there would be work to do in Rome. Of course a papal dispensation would be necessary in any event, since a mere marriage contract created a canonical obstacle, though a less formidable one, and, of course, whatever the obstacle, light or grave, it could be removed by the Pope. The King of Portugal had had a dispensation to marry his deceased wife's sister, and in the matter of brothers there was a very useful text in Deuteronomy. Dr. De Puebla's lawyer's instinct, rejoicing in the pretty legal problem, favored the more sweeping dispensation as safer in the long run, but he wanted to be sure of the facts. Therefore, he consulted the principal chaplain, and Don Alessandro, swelling with importance, told more than he knew. Assuredly, Don Alessandro said, the marriage had been consummated; very likely there would be issue. Dr. De Puebla dispatched a warning note to Spain, and dropped a hint or so to members of the English council.

Before his letter could reach Spain, Doña Elvira was on him like a thunderbolt. How dare he write lies to Spain and whisper lies among the English? The Princess had never been Prince Arthur's wife in anything but name. She, Doña Elvira, and all the matrons of her lady's household would swear, of their personal knowledge, that the Princess Catherine was *virgo intacta,* a virgin as unspotted as the day she came from her mother's womb, and examination by qualified persons would prove as much. Neither party to this colloquy could guess that the question of Doña Elvira's veracity would be vigorously argued for four hundred years, the disputants being divided less by variations in their common sense and credulity than by their religious antecedents, but both knew that Doña Elvira's assertion was a serious one, and both knew – what some modern historians seem to have forgotten – that, in the canon law, and in sixteenth-century usage, virginity was a term of definite, fixed content, not susceptible of degrees or qualifications, and verifiable in fact. The truth of what Doña Elvira said could be tested and if it proved she was lying, she would never dare face Queen Isabella again. It is hard to see what motive could justify so risky a lie. Dr. De Puebla, at least, was convinced Doña Elvira spoke the truth. He stammered his apologies and his promises to be more careful in the future, and dashed off post-haste the new, authentic version of Catherine's state to Spain.

Doña Elvira also wrote her mistress. She had accepted the Doctor's profuse apologies somewhat grimly, and she added a tart reference to him in her next letter to Isabella which caused the Queen to warn him that hereafter he was to defer to Doña Elvira on every question affecting the Princess, but she did not try to force his recall. Doña Elvira seems to have shared the contempt of other Spanish aristocrats for the little *marrano* – as non-Aryan Christians were slightingly called in Spain – and, having clashed with him once, felt confident of bringing him to heel when she liked. Catherine, she noted with satisfaction, already disliked him. But she took full advantage of Father Alessandro's blunder. By his position as her confessor, by his years as her tutor, by his place in her household and her past, Geraldini had an influence over Catherine second only to Doña Elvira's own, and the duenna had no intention of sharing power with the Italian. What she wrote Isabella about him, plus a blundering letter of Geraldini's own, brought curt directions to Hernan Duque that such a man was obviously unfit to be in the Princess's household and should be shipped back to Spain at once; what Doña Elvira told Catherine left so bitter a memory that Geraldini was unforgiven fifteen years later.[3]

Whether Don Pedro de Ayala also clashed with Doña Elvira is less certain. There was no love lost between Ayala's family and the Manuels, and Ayala was not the man to take a tongue-lashing as meekly as De Puebla. Nor would Doña Elvira wish to share her influence with a witty, graceful worldling who had already connived at one breach of her discipline, and who might lead her charge into ways as shocking for a princess as his own were for a bishop. Since Catherine's marriage Ayala only lingered in England on sufferance; De Puebla had been trying for years to get him recalled, but the *coup de grâce* seems to have been administered by Doña Elvira. Through Hernan Duque, Ayala got orders in September to return to Spain, and Isabella wrote ironically to De Puebla that now his colleague was leaving she hoped to see the wonders he had so often promised once free of that paralyzing presence.[4]

ii

Wonders, in fact, were demanded of De Puebla. Hernan Duque knew his sovereign's wishes in the matter of their daughter's future and the secret springs of their policy, but not how to carry out that policy in England; he was energetic and incorruptible and could be relied on for tedious assignments, but he had no language except Spanish, no previous experience of foreign countries, and none of the arts of diplomacy. He was a gentleman of ancient and unspotted lineage, and his post in the household of the Catholic Kings gave him a certain self-confidence and prestige, but Catherine, whose wits were sharpened in the trying years of her widowhood, remembered him as a fool. Perhaps his sovereigns suspected that he would be unequal to the task his instructions set. They told him precisely what he was to try to do, and advised him to rely in every difficulty on the experience and legal training of their resident ambassador. Dr. De Puebla was to have charge of the actual drafting of the treaty; Dr. De Puebla was to conduct the day-to-day discussions with the English council; in all unforeseen contingencies Hernan Duque was to have recourse to the advice of Dr. De Puebla. Once in England, the special envoy was only too glad to shift most of his burden to the shoulders of his indefatigable colleague.

The difficulties were considerable. One hundred thousand crowns of Catherine's dowry had been paid to Henry, and he had no intention of relinquishing that sum, whomever Catherine married. He had the right to claim payment of the other hundred thousand before putting Catherine in possession of her dower revenues. The complications could be spun out endlessly, while Henry VII watched which way the cat jumped in Italy, and balanced the advantages of the Spanish alliance against the alternatives which his increased prestige was beginning to open to him. Henry had no mind to burn his fingers retrieving Ferdinand's Italian chestnuts, and he had a very clear recollection that Ferdinand had made him wait and sue for the first marriage as if he were a parvenu seeking alliance with an established family. This time, he was determined, Ferdinand should be the suitor.

Spring turned to summer, and summer browned the lawns and gardens of Durham House, while at Westminster the council wrangled over Latin subjunctives and paragraphs of canon law and the winds of Biscay brought bad news from the Spanish border. Autumn came in rawly, the Channel gales delayed Hernan Duque's couriers for weeks, and the King, in mud-spattered hunting boots, told De Puebla that these were grave matters, and there was much division about them in his council, and anyway there was no hurry until word came from Rome. Catherine, in more than Moorish seclusion, stitched, under the vigilant eye of Doña Elvira, new hems on the dresses she had brought from Spain. She was not consulted when Isabella wrote Hernan Duque he might pawn her jewels and plate (the jewels and plate Juan de Cuero had strict orders not to let her touch, the jewels and plate to pay her dowry) if troops could be raised in England for the money. When Hernan Duque, awkwardly playing out the comedy written for him in Spain, ordered a ship to be ready in the Thames and the Princess's household goods to be packed, she may really have thought for a few days that she was going home. Christmas came and went, but her widowhood cut her off from the merrymaking at Richmond, as the silence of her parents and their agents in England cut her off from all but the stark fact that the wrangling over her remarriage was no nearer an end than ever.

Nor was it likely to near an end, while matters were going so badly in Italy. At Terranova, D'Aubigny's iron horsemen rode through and over the fine new army which Ferdinand and Isabella had emptied their treasuries to equip, and the Great Captain huddled his beaten infantry behind fortified lines at Barletta, and watched the French overrun the kingdom he was ordered to conquer. The Catholic Kings wrote that an English invasion of France was imperative, and De Puebla, who knew that Henry VII was not to be hustled, cautiously prepared to lower his terms another notch. It was annoying that money was so short at Durham House. Henry, willing to admit that Catherine's marriage had not been consummated, was not slow to point out that he had no obligation to provide for a Spanish princess whose representatives asserted that she was not legally Princess of Wales; and Ferdinand and Isabella, who needed every *maravedi* for the war, had sent nothing towards their daughter's expenses, nothing for a long time, for that matter, towards their ambassador's salary either. De Puebla saw that it would be a waiting game, and settled down on short rations, like Gonsalvo de Cordova in his trenches, to let events determine the next move. At Durham House, too, rations were short.

The next move was unexpected. The court had come to the City after Christmas, and it was at the Tower of London, on Candlemas, that Elizabeth of York was brought to bed of her seventh child. When news had come, just ten months before, of Arthur's death, Elizabeth had reminded her husband that she was not too old for a queen's first duty, the bearing of children. But this time the bad luck of the Tudors struck a double blow. Elizabeth lived little more than a week after the child's birth. The child, named Catherine after Elizabeth's unhappy sister, wife of the imprisoned Sir William Courtenay – but was the name meant also as a whisper of encouragement to the foreign princess who was under Elizabeth's protection? – "tarried but a small season after her mother."

Historians have noted that the character of Henry VII's reign changes after the death of Elizabeth of York, that the leading roles seem to fall to smaller men and the protagonist himself grows smaller, meaner. That may be one of the illusions of history, but it is certain that, besides whatever private grief the King may have felt at Elizabeth's death, he had a new anxiety. Four of her seven children were dead, and two of the other three were girls. The fate of the Tudor dynasty hung on the life of one twelve-year-old boy. The margin of security was too slight; for the next six years Henry was always thinking of remarriage. After all, he was not yet forty-six, and though a little worn by eighteen years of troubled rule, he had always lived a frugal and active life and was still, ambassadors noted, a fine figure of a man. There was nothing shocking or unreasonable in his proposing to beget more sons to insure the continuance of his dynasty and the tranquillity of his kingdom.

Nor, though some of his biographers have professed to be shocked, was there anything shocking in Henry's first choice – his son's widow. Catherine was past seventeen, a woman mature by sixteenth-century reckoning; she was at hand and a long diplomatic courtship could be spared; one hundred thousand crowns of her dowry had been paid and the rest contracted for; she was distinctly personable and looked quite fit to bear strong sons. From her point of view, Henry may have thought, to exchange an heir apparent for a crowned king, and a boy for a man, would be no such bad bargain. The morals of the century did not forbid, and though Isabella rejected the proposal with instant alarm and wrote that, if the wind lay in that quarter, it would be better to bring Catherine back to Spain at once, her refusal was not occasioned by moral repugnance. It was simply that, from the Spanish point of view, the bargain was not good enough. It could scarcely be hoped that a girl like Catherine could exercise a decisive influence on the foreign policy of a king like Henry VII. And, in the natural course of events, marriage to the middle-aged Henry would doom her to spend most of her life as queen dowager – and a queen dowager who was not even the mother of the new king, a person quite without influence or diplomatic significance, with no power at all to bind England to Spain. Of course Isabella promptly and indignantly refused.[5]

Henry did not insist. The suggestion to De Puebla had been roundabout and tentative, and the King of England was no ogre to take advantage of Catherine's almost helpless position in his realm, as apparently Isabella feared he might do. Instead he cheerfully entertained Isabella's alternative proposal that he marry the widowed Queen of Naples, and sent off an embassy to Spain to ascertain of the proffered lady, among other things, whether her teeth were good, whether her figure was scrawny or acceptably plump, whether her voice and face were pleasing, and (if the ambassadors could get near enough to her to find out) whether her breath was sweet.[6]

Henry did not even drive too hard a bargain in the end over Catherine's betrothal to the new Prince of Wales. A Spanish alliance, as De Puebla had again and again reassured his sovereigns, was Henry's logical, almost his inevitable, choice. To break with Spain, particularly to send Catherine back without her hundred thousand crowns, would be to make a mortal enemy in a Europe where England had no certain friends. A French alliance was unthinkable, and the flighty Emperor Max had recently demonstrated his undependability by taking under his wing yet another pretender to the English throne, Edmund de la Pole, cousin to that Earl of Warwick whom Henry had sent from the Tower to the block as a prelude to Catherine's arrival in England, and, after Warwick's execution, the authentic White Rose. Until Henry could be sure of the Emperor, and of his son Philip, lord of the Netherlands, it would be folly to sacrifice Spanish friendship. So, when Hernan Duque had played his comedy to the end, and when Gonsalvo de Cordova had sprung from his trenches on a French army demoralized by conquest, soundly beaten it in two pitched battles, and entered Naples in triumph, Henry gracefully yielded to De Puebla's cajolery and the new marriage treaty was signed.

That was on June 23, 1503, more than fourteen months after Arthur's death. The treaty was, naturally, favorable to England, but under the circumstances, only moderately so. The chief clauses may be summarized as follows: [7]

Because Catherine had previously contracted a good and valid marriage with Arthur (De Puebla had his way after all, about the dispensation), and thus become related to Henry, his brother, in the first degree of affinity, a canonical impediment to marriage which only a papal dispensation could remove, the contracting parties bound themselves to use all their influence at Rome to obtain the necessary bulls.

The King of England acknowledged that he had received one half of Catherine's dowry, which was fixed, as before, at two hundred thousand crowns.

The marriage (the necessary dispensation having been procured) was to be solemnized as soon as Henry, Prince of Wales completed his fifteenth year, provided that Catherine's representatives could show that the remainder of her dowry was in London, ready to be paid over on demand. This second installment was to consist of 65,000 crowns in gold coin, 15,000 in plate (Catherine's plate) according to the valuation of London goldsmiths, and 20,000 in the jewels and ornaments of the Princess, according to their price in London.

Catherine renounced her claim for the restitution of the first installment of her dowry, and also all claims to her widow's jointure of one third of the revenues of Wales, Cornwall and Chester, in consideration of the promise of an equal jointure upon her new marriage.

By this treaty Catherine was the principal sufferer. She could not remarry for at least two years, and not then unless her dowry was ready; meanwhile, having renounced her dower right, she was obliged to live in England on the bounty of the English King. But Catherine did not protest against these provisions, though she certainly understood them, and her parents did not condole with her on them. Among the great families who were coming to control the destinies of Europe, daughters were necessary pawns, securing friends and tying land to land, just as they were in the feudal families next beneath in the social scale, and in the country gentry families next beneath them, whose quarrels and marriages and schemes to lay field to field reproduced faithfully in miniature the pattern set by the dynasts. Nobody expected that the comfort of the daughters thus used would be consulted.

iii

The marriage treaty was full of loopholes through which the English might slip, but events seemed to be working in Catherine's favor. The success of Spanish arms made the papacy eager to oblige the Catholic Kings, and though Catherine's dispensation was delayed by the deaths of two popes and by the habitual deliberateness of the Roman curia, no one doubted that ultimately it would be granted. Meanwhile, as Henry saw how the war in Italy was going, he became more and more openly a partisan of Spain. First Louis XII, who thought the pension he was paying Henry ample to secure English neutrality, was startled to receive an intimation that England was gravely concerned by the broken peace of Europe, and would gladly act as an impartial mediator; before long, familiar sequel to such offers, the French court was hearing that England in alliance with the Emperor was only waiting for spring to launch a joint attack on the French. Dr. De Puebla had the delightful task of drafting a commercial treaty, granting exceptional privileges to Spanish merchants in England and to English in Spain, and no sooner was this proclaimed than Henry accepted his suggestion for a new, close military alliance, and the doctor's quill raced over fresh parchment, dripping, so he thought, with history.

Catherine's private affairs benefited by the turn of events. In 1502 her parents had told her bluntly that she must accept whatever allowance Henry chose to make her; they sent no money to make that compliance easier, and they curtly negatived the suggestion that she be allowed to pawn a part of her plate to satisfy her creditors and pay the wages of her suite, by then more than a year in arrears. But the King of England, as soon as the treaty was safely signed and the hard bargain sealed, was ready to relieve her necessities. The hundred pounds a month which Henry again allocated for Catherine and her household, the same amount allowed her in the first months of her widowhood, was, it is true, less than half the income she had renounced, and it is true, too, that Henry kept a finger on the spending of it, directing his own councilor, William Holybrand, to see that none was wasted and to keep strict accounts. But a hundred pounds a month was an impressive figure in those days, the revenue of a considerable nobleman. Henry generously told Holybrand that if there was anything left over, after the bills of her household were paid, the Princess might have it to spend as she liked. Fifty hungry Spaniards saw to it that there was nothing left over.

A transient gaiety flitted through Durham House. Until the papal dispensation came, until Prince Henry reached fifteen, until the final installment of the dowry should be ready in London, Catherine was in the embarrassing position of a fiancée who is the permanent, uninvited guest of her intended's father, but for the moment her host was all smiles, and though his prudent bounty did little more than feed the Princess's household, it seemed to be extended with good will. Catherine and her ladies danced at court, she saw again faces she had known at Ludlow, and even had interviews with her fiancé, who celebrated his formal betrothal to her just four days before his twelfth birthday. She visited Richmond and Greenwich, and returned in stately procession to her own palace on the Strand, very much the lady, even though her maids had turned their dresses, and her gentlemen were a little out at elbows. Her health improved, thanks perhaps in part to Henry's solicitude and the services of his physician, thanks also, perhaps, to the improvement in Anglo-Spanish relations, and the promise of the end of her difficulties. She even began to show, hesitantly at first, a disposition to manage her own affairs. During the year after the signing of the marriage treaty at least two obscure intrigues smoldered in her little court. One had to do with whether Juan de Cuero should authorize the use of Catherine's jewels and plate without permission from Doña Elvira, the other with the authority over her pages of Don Iñigo Manrique, Doña Elvira's son. When Hernan Duque involved himself in these squabbles, and incurred the wrath of Doña Elvira, Catherine did not intervene. But after Duque's return in August, 1504, to Spain, where he received tepid compliments on the marriage treaty, and a private scolding from Isabella for interfering with Doña Elvira's arrangements, Catherine herself began to be a little restive. "Some of her household," De Puebla told Ferdinand with discreet indirectness, "think the Princess should enjoy greater freedom." Catherine managed to make some presents to her maids from Juan de Cuero's hoard, and to pawn a few pieces. She appealed to the King of England to settle the dispute about the ushers, apparently with the thought that his authority, at least, would overbear Doña Elvira's, and release her from the duenna's most irksome restrictions. It was a vain hope. Even Henry shrank from a quarrel with Doña Elvira, and whenever Catherine crossed the duenna's plans, she was defeated.

There was, for instance, the matter of Maria de Rojas' dowry. Had Arthur lived, the ladies of Catherine's suite would either have been well married in England before long, or gone back to Spain to find husbands there. But as a Spanish princess living on the bounty of an English king, Catherine had no money to give them dowries, no money indeed to pay their customary wages, and they would soon be past the age at which Spanish ladies expected to marry. For one of them, Maria de Rojas, a grandson of the Earl of Derby had spoken; Maria was willing; the King of England, and the Stanleys, whose real head was the King's mother, the Countess of Richmond, had given their consent. There remained only to arrange the dowry, a part of which Catherine would normally have assumed, and the rest of which would have to come through Isabella, whose ward Maria was. But though Catherine wrote and wrote again to Spain, no word came back. Catherine did not know until later that Doña Elvira had decided that her son, young Iñigo Manrique, master of Catherine's pages, was to marry Maria. On November 26, 1504, Catherine wrote to ask her mother what was delaying Maria's marriage. A filial note to Ferdinand on the same date reminded him that she had had no news of either of her parents for some time; no letter from him for over a year.

That same evening, in her castle looking over Medina del Campo,

Isabella the Catholic lay dying. Only a few days before she had seen Julius II's brief describing the dispensation for her daughter's marriage to Henry, Prince of Wales. A copy was on its way to Dr. De Puebla. The main point in Catherine's future was assured. The rest would have to be left to Doña Elvira.

iv

Catherine always believed that had her mother lived, England and Spain would have remained allies, and she herself would have been spared the worst trials of the next four years. Probably she was right. Not because Isabella was fonder of her daughter than Ferdinand was, or more apt to be moved by mere sentiment, or more skillful in diplomacy, or more anxious to retain English friendship, but because, with her death, the Iberian realms of the Catholic Kings broke in two, and Ferdinand was threatened with the loss of all authority over the larger and more powerful part. In Castile the King of Aragon was merely the Queen's consort, on Isabella's death Castile passed of right, not to Ferdinand, but to Catherine's elder sister, Joanna, the wife of Philip the Handsome. Philip, lord in his mother's right from Friesland to Franche Comté, was now a man grown, a vain, petulant autocrat with more than his father Maximilian's instability and dreamy ambition, but a good deal less than Maximilian's brains. Philip was developing a foreign policy of his own, centered about the Netherlands, the views of whose nobility he shared; his brief, irritating visit to Spain in 1502–1503 had demonstrated his complete incompatibility with Ferdinand. Henry VII fully realized that should Philip succeed in ousting Ferdinand from Castile, Aragon would sink to a second-rate power.

The first sign that Isabella's death meant a change in Anglo-Spanish relations came, however, from another quarter. The long-sought commercial treaty which De Puebla had drafted with so much care and pleasure gave English merchants the same privileges in Spain as native subjects of the Spanish crowns. They could import and export articles on restricted lists, load their ships without waiting for all Spanish ships to be laden, and claim exemption from all the irritating taxes and restrictions devised to annoy foreigners. Spanish merchants were given equivalent privileges in England, and though Spanish commerce was the smaller, it, too, was active and growing. It was an enlightened treaty, too enlightened for the parochial conservatives of Castile, who were sure that if foreigners made money by trading with Spain, Spain must thereby be the poorer. When their resistance delayed ratification of the treaty, Isabella, by special proclamation, relieved English merchants of the restrictions of the Castilian navigation acts, while Henry did as much for Spaniards in England. On Isabella's death, the council of Castile, ignoring Ferdinand, declared that the proclamation had lapsed until renewed by Castile's lawful sovereigns, and in August, 1505, eight hundred English merchants and sailors who had gone to Seville returned to London "all lost and ruined" by the unexpected and rigorous enforcement of the old acts. Henry sent for De Puebla in a towering rage "and the words that came from his mouth were vipers." De Puebla wrote an agonized plea to Ferdinand, but Ferdinand could not risk his small authority in such a contest; commercial relations between England and Spain sank back into chaos. English merchants cried out bitterly against Spanish treachery; and Henry, himself, felt that he had been cheated.

Meanwhile, the embassy which Henry had sent to Spain to investigate Isabella's proffer of the hand of the widowed Queen of Naples returned and reported. Henry was less interested in their assurances that the Queen had a plump neck, white hands, and lively eyes, than in their revelation of the fact, hitherto concealed from him, that she had no reversion whatever in the Kingdom of Naples, lived on the bounty of the King of Aragon, and would bring her husband no money. Henry felt cheated again.

One means of retaliation was near at hand. Catherine and her suite were still living at Durham House, using every penny of Holybrand's hundred pounds a month. Henry did not expel his guest; he merely stopped her allowance. He had already taken a more sinister precaution. There was no sign of the second installment of Catherine's dowry coming from Spain. Now Isabella was dead there was no certainty it would ever come, and there might be better brides in Europe for a Tudor than a castaway Spanish princess. On June 27, 1505, the eve of his fourteenth birthday, Henry, Prince of Wales, appearing before Richard, Bishop of Winchester, and a committee of the privy council, solemnly protested against his betrothal to Catherine, contracted during his minority, declared he would not ratify it, and denounced it as null and void. Not until much later did any Spaniard learn of this act of treachery. We have no clue to the feelings of the young Prince as he repeated the speech he had learned, but we can know what King Henry thought. "My son and I are free [8] – while Ferdinand and his daughter are bound if we choose to have them so." An altogether satisfactory arrangement.

Soon after, events in Europe gave Henry the chance for a more elaborate revenge. Ferdinand of Aragon would not surrender Castile without a struggle. If Maximilian and Philip expected to take two thirds of Spain away from him, they would have to come with an army, and Ferdinand was willing to go to any lengths to prevent their doing so. In March, 1504, he had patched up a truce with France. In the very month of Isabella's death the truce was strengthened and extended, and throughout the summer of 1505 Habsburg and Aragonese diplomats bid against each other for the friendship of a surprised and gratified Louis XII, until, in October, the Treaty of Blois announced the triumph of Aragon. Ferdinand had paid dear for safety, but Louis XII was now his ally and the road by land from the Netherlands to Spain was closed to Philip and his father.

The road by land was closed, but the King of England could open the road by sea. Hostility to this slippery King of Aragon, Henry reflected, might win him overnight the Habsburg alliance, after twenty years of angling with Spanish help had failed. In the end he might not lose Spain either, for his ambassadors reported that all Castile was ripe to welcome Maximilian's son Philip of Burgundy and his wife Joanna of Castile, and their son would someday inherit Ferdinand's crowns as well. Meanwhile, it was worth risking Spain to win Burgundy, the ancient, traditional ally of the English crown, Burgundy, whose iron cavalry joined to English archers made an army the French had never been able to resist, whose wealthy Netherlands took the bulk of English wool and supplied the English with most of their more sophisticated wants, so that the two countries really made one economic unit.

Existing treaties were really more favorable to the Netherlands than to England in matters of trade, yet the burghers of Bruges and Ghent were restive under them, and it was hard to enforce English privileges. Henry could see himself getting a new commercial treaty, stronger and more advantageous. Every pretender to the English throne, every White Rose, true or false, for twenty years had found refuge and aid at the court of Burgundy; at the moment, Max and his son were using the current pretender, Edmund de la Pole, self-styled Duke of Suffolk, to extort loans and commercial concessions; alliance with Philip would mean the end of Suffolk and assurance for the future. Moreover, the Habsburgs, now clearly destined to be the greatest family in Europe, could dispose of marriage alliances beyond the gift of Spain. Philip's sister Margaret, the widow of the Infante Juan, and now widowed again of the Duke of Savoy, was the richest match in Christendom, altogether suitable for a widower king. Philip's daughter Eleanor was just the right age for the Prince of Wales. And to her little brother, Charles, would one day come all the lands of his four grandparents, an unparalleled inheritance of power. Who could be more fitting for

Henry's youngest daughter, Mary? All these marriages were within reach, once he could persuade Philip that England alone could open or close the road by sea. That summer the shrewd Portuguese ambassador in London wrote that all three of these marriages were familiarly discussed at the English court, and the one between the Prince of Wales and Eleanor was almost certain to take place.[9]

Ferdinand of Aragon was conscious of the danger, as he was conscious, though less acutely, of his daughter's distress; but Isabella's death had diminished alike his revenues and his prestige, and he could not afford sentimental gestures or spirited retaliation. To Catherine he wrote counseling patience and submission to the will of heaven, to Henry a long screed warning him against the malice and treachery of the Habsburgs and offering military aid if Henry wished to recover the rebel Suffolk by war. But pious reflections would not pay the expenses of Durham House, and Henry knew cheaper ways to capture Suffolk.

Had Philip of Burgundy known his own mind as clearly as Henry knew his, the diplomatic rapprochement would not have been delayed. But Philip was indolent and vacillating, and the real control of his policy towards Spain – and consequently towards England – swayed between two factions of the Spaniards at his court: the Aragonese, headed by Don Gutierre Gomez de Fuensalida, Ferdinand's ambassador, and the Castilians headed by the able Don Juan Manuel.[10] The Aragonese urged Philip to put all his trust in his father-in-law and to confide the government of his wife's kingdom of Castile to Ferdinand's hands; or, if he wished to go to Spain in person, to go there quietly with a small train, assured of a peaceable and loving welcome. The Castilians, bitter separatists and in close touch with the malcontents at home, counseled a military alliance with England, and an entry into Castile in force, prepared to expel the Aragonese if they resisted.

In the early autumn of 1505 two embassies crossed each other. Herman Rimbre, coming from Philip and his father, appeared at

Henry's court to invite collaboration with the Habsburgs; and Dr. Savage went from England to Brussels to offer that collaboration if the Habsburgs would bid high enough. For once Tudor diplomacy stumbled. Henry was used to dealing with the difficult Habsburg court through Spanish intermediaries. He had no resident ambassador there, and was only dimly aware of the treacherous cross-currents of intrigue, the parties of Castile and of Aragon, the party of the King, the party of the Queen, the factions of the Flemings, the perpetual meddling of the Emperor, which made a straight course so hard to steer. For some time Henry's old friend, Don Pedro de Ayala, had been living at Philip's court; Henry knew of no shrewder courtier, and of no reason not to trust his old friend. Therefore he instructed Savage to go straight to Don Pedro, explain matters and act on his advice. But Don Pedro, though a Castilian, was no friend to the Manuels; he had sworn allegiance to Ferdinand, and expected that wily old hand to triumph in the end over his thick-witted son-in-law. Savage never understood why, under the guidance of so able a man as Don Pedro, he only succeeded in getting more and more snarled in the tangles of court intrigue.

Ayala's stratagem dashed, for a time, the hopes of the Castilian separatists, but their leader was at least as acute an intriguer as Ayala. For twenty years European diplomats unanimously held that the most skillful of their calling and the most dangerous opponent in any negotiation was Don Juan Manuel. As long as Isabella lived, Manuel had served the Catholic Kings with scrupulous loyalty, and with a success which had made him feared and detested in France; on her death, moved by ambition and by hatred of Ferdinand, he became the brains and inspiration of the group of nobles determined to end Ferdinand's rule in Castile. At the moment, Manuel was bent on a strong military alliance between Philip and Henry, to insure the expulsion of the Aragonese and to stiffen Philip's uncertain resolution. Word from England hinted that Henry was ready to talk business, but after Savage's mission, Don Juan despaired of steering so delicate a negotiation through the cross-currents of intrigue at Brussels, and fixed his hopes on a direct interview between the two sovereigns. He could rely on one devoted agent in London – his sister, the Princess's duenna.

Doña Elvira's influence had survived undiminished both Catherine's first timid bid for independence, and the death of Isabella. Henry had refused to interfere with her iron rule of Catherine's household, and in consequence the Princess lived at Richmond and Greenwich and Westminster with "the same good order" that was kept at Durham House. After Isabella's death Catherine seems to have been less inclined to question the duenna's authority. The only drafts on Juan de Cuero's treasury were for presents to Doña Elvira's family. The other Spaniards began to knuckle under to the strong-willed matron, and finally – who knows after what tearful scenes? – it was agreed that Maria de Rojas should be formally betrothed to Don Iñigo Manrique. Doña Elvira carried things with a high hand. She knew that Dr. De Puebla suspected that she was in communication with her malcontent brother in Flanders, but she despised the little Doctor and felt safe in browbeating him as ruthlessly as she browbeat the rest of Catherine's suite, confident that Catherine's dislike of him would prevent his ever shaking her influence. Contemptuously, under the Doctor's very nose, she began to second her brother's scheme for an interview between the kings.

Catherine was not yet twenty, had never been consulted much about her own affairs, was feeling lonely, deserted, bewildered. Ferdinand almost never wrote to her, and his infrequent notes told her nothing. Her English was not good, and anyway, now that she was no longer asked to court, she saw no Englishmen to talk to except gardeners and horseboys. Nor was there any Englishman she knew well enough to consult about this change in her fortunes. Dr. De Puebla could have explained but, thanks to Don Pedro de Ayala, she more than shared Doña Elvira's contempt for the doctor and spoke to him as little and as coldly as possible. Cooped up in

Durham House with her half-dozen fretful ladies in waiting, her elderly, sullen, homesick suite, she had no one to turn to except Doña Elvira, the one person no emergency could shake and no danger discountenance, the guardian to whom her mother had always, up to the very last, commended her. Why, she asked, was she no longer invited to court, no longer allowed even to see her fiancé, treated coldly by the few English she met? Why did this air of defeat and discouragement hang over Durham House, these worn dresses and tattered hangings, these stinking rushes, this stale and meager food? Why, if no money came, not use what wealth she had brought? Why cover rents in court dresses with jewels, and eat bad salt herrings from silver plate? Why was a king's daughter and the betrothed of a king's son left thus neglected?

Doña Elvira had a competent explanation. Of course, her father knew nothing of her plight. Far off in Spain, absorbed by cares of state, he would rely on his ambassador for news of England, and Dr. De Puebla wrote him nothing but sugared lies, to save himself trouble and to please King Henry, who was bribing him. Who knew how much of the King of England's coldness also might be due to De Puebla's lies? The surest recourse, Doña Elvira suggested, was to appeal to Joanna, now Queen of Castile, and bound to fill Isabella's place. Once Joanna learned how her sister was living, she and her husband would set everything right, and Catherine could enjoy once more the comfort and dignity befitting her rank. Having planted this seed, Doña Elvira led Herman Rimbre, King Philip's envoy, to speak of Queen Joanna's eagerness to see her sister Catherine, and when Catherine said wistfully that Joanna could not long to see her as much as she longed to see Joanna, the duenna and the envoy both advised her to write a letter suggesting some sort of meeting. Rimbre had a courier ready to ride with Catherine's timid note, and the answer came back from Flanders with suspicious speed. Joanna would be delighted, and nothing could be easier. If King Henry would only cross to Calais, the Queen–Archduchess and her husband would promise to be at Saint-Omer, eight leagues away. Naturally Catherine would travel with the King. There would be royal festivities, an affectionate reunion; Catherine's little difficulties could be solved out of hand. The prospect made Catherine giddy. Travel, a change of scene, music again and dancing and gallant company, a chance to see Joanna's handsome husband and the splendid Burgundian court, above all a chance to see, after eight years, her pretty, laughing, mercurial sister, and to pour into her ears all the troubles of life in England! Catherine sat down at once to write Henry, forwarding her sister's letter, and urging in the warmest terms that the invitation be accepted.

On that day De Puebla was prowling uneasily about Durham House, warned by an obscure feeling of something in the air. Recently Henry had been unusually affable; he was encouraging the ambassador to go on drafting the new treaty for a military alliance, and had just discussed some clauses with him, and though he did intimate that it was time Ferdinand contributed to his daughter's support, and was, no doubt, vexed by the grievances of the merchants, his tone seemed to imply that he and De Puebla were both sensible men, and with tact and patience little differences could be straightened out. There could be nothing in this new embassy from Flanders, De Puebla reasoned. He had been present at the ambassador's first interview, had, himself, acted as interpreter. It was nothing but Henry's flirting with a new marriage, a matter of the exchange of portraits, and of empty compliments. The Doctor had described to Ferdinand with glee how he had turned the thick-witted Dutch envoy inside out. And yet – had there been other interviews? Did all this coming and going of couriers mean there was something he did not know?

In the corridor he met the Princess, an unsealed letter in her hand. "Ambassador," she cried gaily, her joy for once overcoming her aversion for the little vulgarian, "I hope to see my sister soon. She has written me about it, and I am writing to the King, begging him to grant our request." And she handed De Puebla the letters.

The ambassador felt as if an abyss had opened at his feet. Here, under his very nose, was forming the alliance which Spanish diplomacy throughout Europe was on the alert to scotch, and only an accident had warned him. With an effort he controlled himself. His first thought was to keep these dangerous documents harmless in his own hands. It would be more regular, he suggested, if so momentous a proposal came to Henry through him, as ambassador. But Catherine had a sudden return of her old suspicion and hostility. Something in the queerness of the ambassador's tone, perhaps, had startled her. She took back the letters. There was no reason, she said, why she should not write to the King of England herself. She swept past him. Below in the courtyard a horse was being saddled, and Don Alonzo de Esquivel, the principal chamberlain, stood by, already booted and spurred. Such a messenger could be going only to the King, at Richmond. Dr. De Puebla took his courage in both hands and went to confront Doña Elvira.

For once he dared to speak almost plainly. He reminded Doña Elvira that he had always supported her authority, that his dispatches had always been at her service, that through him she had got from Henry such gifts as were usually reserved for persons of royal blood. Now, he pleaded, his honor was at stake, and the safety of Spain, as well. He accused Don Juan Manuel (he did not quite dare accuse Doña Elvira) of treachery. Perhaps, he said, Doña Elvira did not realize what this interview between Henry and Philip might mean, what grave issues were involved. But he could assure her that nothing could be more harmful to Spain and to the Princess. Ferdinand would never forgive anyone who had helped to bring it about; if it took place it would mean the ruin of every Spaniard in England. Coldly Doña Elvira agreed that perhaps Catherine's letter was a mistake. She, herself, she promised, would prevent its being sent, and would explain matters to Catherine. De Puebla could trust her, leave everything in her hands.

Don Alonzo's horse was led back into the stable and the gouty old ambassador limped off to his modest lodgings in the Strand, his fears partially allayed. But he left a lackey to lounge inconspicuously outside the gates of Durham House. Hardly had the Doctor sat down to his meager dinner when the lackey burst in upon him. Don Alonzo de Esquivel had ridden out of Durham House and taken the road to Richmond.

De Puebla moved faster than he had done for years. No time now for soft words and double meanings and the patient intricate secret game at which he was adept. Only one person could help him now, or Ferdinand, or Spain. He burst into the Princess's chamber, his face livid, drawn with pain and fear, beaded with sweat and streaked with tears. In a voice choking with emotion, he begged the Princess to be calm. He told her the whole story, all the net of war and politics, treachery and intrigue tightened by her simple act. Now, he finished, she alone could frustrate the conspiracy. By persuading Henry against the interview, while still appearing to others to desire it, she could do her father more service than two thousand men-at-arms.

Catherine might have resisted cajolery, intrigue and persuasion; she was an inexperienced girl, but she was no fool and she was uncommonly stubborn. Had he not been desperate, De Puebla might never have hit upon the one means to touch her: a plain straightforward appeal to her sense of duty. She did not like this cold, sly old man, but she could not doubt his dreadful agitation, his agonized sincerity, and, convinced of the truth of what he said, there was only one course she could follow. Never in her life was Catherine to prefer her own interests to the interests of her dynasty. Now as the old man's stumbling words opened to her the pit above which she had been walking, now that she saw for a moment what life was like in courts, the hidden motives, the crooked dealing, the schemes, the intrigues, here unsuspected in her own household, she felt foolish and unarmed, but also braced and unafraid. She sat down and took pen and paper. "Tell me," she said, "what I must write." [11]

Somehow, using Catherine's letter, De Puebla managed to defeat the Manuels' intrigue. Henry was too cautious to risk an interview on unstable ground, particularly with a ruler like Philip who did not seem to know his own mind. Uncertain what sort of double game all these Spaniards were playing, or just what use they were trying to make of him, Henry hesitated, drew back, and Rimbre returned to Flanders, having achieved as little as Savage. The chief result of the incident was at Durham House. In the discovery of her duenna's treachery Catherine suddenly came of age. Neither Catherine nor Doña Elvira ever cared to record the scene which only they two shared, but the accompanying explosion of the famous Trastamara temper so echoed through Durham House that years afterward Don Alonzo de Esquivel still remembered with a shudder "that terrible hour" in which Doña Elvira departed for Flanders. Thereafter, she and the Manriques remained among the Castilian exiles at Philip's court, and Catherine never spoke of her again. Thereafter the Princess was mistress in her own house.

Catherine might have trusted De Puebla more, but for one of the consequences of Doña Elvira's departure. Mistress now in her own household, the Princess herself had to grapple with the problem of how fifty needy Spaniards could live and keep their wonted state on nothing a year. She consulted De Puebla, and De Puebla consulted Henry. Henry agreed that something would have to be done. But, he pointed out, since Catherine had no money of her own, surely the great establishment at Durham House was somewhat excessive. It would be easier to make ends meet if she dismissed some of her servants, and came to live at court with his daughters. In fact, now that there was no lady of a suitable rank and age to chaperon the Princess, Doña Elvira having gone so unexpectedly to visit her brother and showing no signs of returning, it was highly irregular for Catherine to live alone, exposed to the dangers and temptations of the world. His mother, the Countess of Richmond, thought it most improper. Really he could not allow it, nor would it be convenient at present to provide the English duenna Catherine had asked for. For a time, at least, Catherine would have to give up Durham House, and come and live at court. De Puebla trotted back with the message, and Catherine, furious at the loss of most of her new freedom, was obliged to submit. But she never forgave the ambassador for failing to support some other solution, and at times she was inclined to believe that the whole imbroglio had been devised by De Puebla to get rid of Doña Elvira and to save Henry money. She felt treachery and conspiracy now thick all about her. If she could not trust Doña Elvira, she could trust nobody.

And in spite of Catherine's sacrifice and De Puebla's machinations, Philip got his interview with Henry after all. What the diplomacy of the Manuels had failed to effect, the winds of the Channel accomplished. Though the negotiations with England had come to no conclusion, though the balance at his court hung undecided between the Castilians and the Aragonese, Philip decided to go to Spain after all. Nobody knew whether for peace or war. Everything was in confusion, the voyage had been postponed and postponed again, the season of the year was most unfavorable, but the petulant Philip suddenly insisted on sailing as soon as the fleet could be prepared. At dawn on January 8, 1506, the whole armada, bearing a court which numbered almost a small army, and several thousand *gens d'armes*, pikemen and gunners besides, weighed anchor at Arnemuiden in Zeeland. At dusk the high-sided ships passed Calais, shooting great guns, and with torches in the bows. Rounding Ushant the weather still held so fair that the courtiers laughed at the long faces of the shipmasters, laughed even when the wind died to a whisper and fell silent. Towards evening, straggling across an oily sea, the fleet rolled helplessly, its sails flapping.

Darkness had fallen when the great gale the sailors had smelled came roaring out of the southwest. The light on the masthead of King Philip's ship went out in the smother, and each of the clumsy, creaking hulks, with their burdens of frightened horses and drenched and panicky noblemen, fought alone against a black, howling universe. Forty-two hours the gale blew, scattering the Flemish fleet along the Channel, and driving it towards the English coat. In sight of breakers the King–Archduke's ship dragged her anchor; later, trying to claw off she lost a mast and nearly capsized; for a time a fire in the forecastle threatened a second danger. The Burgundian nobles, huddled on the poop, swore vows they would later grin at, and Philip himself promised two statues of silver, each of his own weight, to Our Ladies of Montserrat and Guadalupe if he came alive out of the tempest. Only Queen Joanna, crouched at her husband's feet, her arms locked tightly about his knees, seemed calm, almost exultant, throughout the worst of the danger. Finally, on January 13, battered and leaking and partially dismasted, King Philip's ship worked its way at high water into the shallow harbor of Melcombe Regis, near Weymouth in Dorset. Later, two others straggled in to join her, and another, waving helplessly, was driven past. All along the coast from Falmouth to the Isle of Wight others of the fleet took refuge. The Venetian ambassador found himself in the harbor of Plymouth in a ship which he did not think would stand the battering of the sea another six hours. Two great ships and several smaller craft foundered or broke up upon the sands. At one place a few bedraggled Flemings came ashore in their shirts, at another only the bodies of the drowned.

The ships of the foreigners had created an alarm all along the coast; some said they were Scotch or Danish pirates, some that the

French were landing, and at Melcombe Regis Philip's ship was greeted by a hasty array of tenantry with bills and bows prepared to defend the foreshore. The appeals shouted from deck were taken for threats, and answered with sullen defiance. The impasse gave Ayala and Fuensalida their last chance to prevent the interview the fates were forcing; they argued before a hastily called council that Henry should not be notified, and Philip should not land, but up-anchor again and make for Plymouth where it had been agreed the fleet should rendezvous in case of misfortune, there to refit and sail for Spain as soon as possible. The gale still roaring up the Channel, and the angry white water on the bar, were unanswerable refutation. Philip longed for solid ground under his feet, and the shipmaster announced that refitting would take help, and at least a week. On shore had appeared a young sprig of the local gentry, whose family's future fortunes were founded on the circumstance that he alone at Melcombe Regis could speak and understand French. Grasping the situation, he dispelled his countrymen's suspicions, assured the King–Archduke of the hospitality of England, arranged for the accommodation of the distinguished visitors, and hurried off a courier to the King.

Henry was not ill pleased. He sent Sir Thomas Brandon with a dignified following to escort Philip to Windsor, and prepared to receive his unexpected guest with all the pomp he knew so well how to display when occasion demanded. The story has grown up that Henry took advantage of the casting of the King of Castile on his shores to hold him a virtual prisoner until he had extorted from Philip a commercial treaty (so unfavorable that the Flemings cursed it as the Evil Intercourse, *Intercursus Malus*), and obliged him, against his honor, to surrender the rebel Duke of Suffolk. It makes a good story, illustrative of Bacon's conception of Henry VII as the ideal Machiavellian prince, to whom honor and hospitality meant nothing as against the winning of a point. Only it happens to be contradicted by every contemporary witness.[12] Philip of

Castile was the prisoner in England, not of its king, but simply of bad weather. The storms of the Atlantic often thus interrupted communications between England and Spain from December until April, making it impossible, not merely for such great flotillas as Philip's to cross, but even for bold individual captains, with staunch ships designed for the purpose, to get through with dispatches. Philip had been foolish to attempt to sail during the winter months. We have the evidence of Quirini, who remained with the fleet at Falmouth, that an earlier sailing from England was out of the question.

In fact, the treaties between Philip and Henry took up remarkably little time. The two kings met at Windsor on January 31. During the next ten days they settled all the details in private conversations, and had the treaties drafted and sworn to by February 9, a testimony to the slightness of the grounds which separated them, and to the wisdom of De Puebla in seeking to prevent a personal interview. On February 15 Philip gave instructions for Suffolk to be surrendered to Henry, as a free act of gratitude and loyalty to his new ally. The commercial treaty was no doubt as unfavorable to the Netherlands as the Flemings later represented. Philip's Burgundian counselors would not have agreed to it, had they not thought that its enforcement could be indefinitely obstructed. The marriage arrangements pleased both sides. Maximilian, who was under no duress, ratified them all, and was genuinely anxious to marry his daughter, Margaret of Savoy, to Henry VII, though the reluctance of the lady proved insuperable. The groundwork was laid for the betrothal of Henry's daughter Mary to little Charles of Ghent, and perhaps for that of the Prince of Wales to Philip's daughter Eleanor, as well. But the really important treaty was the secret one sworn to February 9. In this, the parties agreed to an unlimited alliance of the closest sort, binding themselves to be friends of friends and enemies of enemies without excepting any prince in Christendom, and notwithstanding any alliance previously contracted. In particular Henry bound himself not to assist in any way the enemies, foreign or domestic, of King Philip, his heirs and successors, and undertook that, if any person should invade the dominions which the King of Castile then possessed, or which he or his heirs and successors in future should have a right to possess ("*vel in futuro possidere debet*"), or should any person attempt to disturb him in the possession of such dominions, then the King of England would at once come to his assistance with whatever force might be necessary. In other words Henry promised not only to guard the Netherlands and keep open the road by sea while Philip was in Spain, but to help him conquer Castile by force if necessary.[13] The Treaty of Windsor countered the Treaty of Blois, and the realignment of Europe was complete. Henry's last tie with Ferdinand was broken, and De Puebla, who could only guess that the worst had happened, sent a frantic warning to his master. For such a diplomatic triumph Philip probably counted the sordid gains of the Flemish burghers and the life of a broken English exile a light price.

Philip, indeed, was in the highest spirits. There were pomp and revelry, feasting and jousting and dancing, wrestling and tennis and high play, and all the pageantry the Burgundians loved, while ever and anon the two kings would slip away to talk in some corner, finding each other apparently the most congenial company, and loath to part even at night, so that they walked back and forth together arm in arm between their separate lodgings, and were seen deep in converse over a candle while all their suite slept. It was an ill day for their enemies, Henry was heard to say exultantly, and in future men would talk of the table about which they sat as they talked of the Round Table at Winchester. There was, in fact, a sure bond between them: They both hated the King of Aragon.

Catherine had her revelry after all. We catch glimpses of her with jewels in her hair, dancing Spanish dances with two of her ladies in the great hall at Windsor, while all the court applauded, or coquettishly taunting Philip with being a sailor, not a gallant, because he preferred hobnobbing with Henry in the chimney corner to dancing with her, or listening while little Mary showed her skill with the lute, a skill Mary had learned, in part, from Catherine herself. But the chief thing to which Catherine had been looking forward was a grave disappointment. Her sister Joanna did not come to Windsor with Philip. She did not reach there until the tenth of February, and Catherine went back to Richmond with Mary on the eleventh. She can hardly have seen her sister alone. And she did not see her again, for when Philip rejoined the royal party on the fourteenth Joanna had been sent back towards Plymouth in a litter, and she was not present at the junketing in London. Nor did Catherine see the Joanna she remembered. Instead of a laughing, high-spirited girl, this was a white, silent, frightened woman, easily moved to tears, sunk in melancholy self-absorption, so wrapped in brooding on the obsession of her life, the faithlessness of her gay, handsome husband, that she had no ear for Catherine's troubles.

The years had dealt more hardly with Joanna in Flanders than with Catherine in England. It is hard to lose a husband through death, even if one has not learned to love him; it is infinitely harder to lose the husband one loves, and to know him completely and forever lost while he sits at one's table and shares one's bed. From her first arrival in Flanders Joanna was desperately in love with her husband, and that blond, smiling, dull-witted athlete was first flattered, and then bored, then annoyed and perhaps a little frightened by this intense, possessive passion. Philip's idea of life was to spend his days in hunting and drinking with his male companions and his nights in the bed of some complacent and unexigent female, lady of quality or kitchen wench, who would take him as lightly as he took her, and not disturb too much his emotions or his slumbers. Joanna's stormy jealousy, her unending demands, chilled and embarrassed him. She was jealous of every minute spent away from her, not only of his women, but of his drinking companions, his counselors, his very hunting dogs. When she upbraided him with his infidelity he was callously brutal; when she sank into stony despair he took it for mere sulking and left her severely alone; when, at last, she flew at one of his mistresses with scissors, he declared that she was out of her wits and ought to be locked up, and have the devils beaten out of her.

Had Joanna not been Queen of Castile in her own right, and had Philip not been anxious to take advantage of her love to win her kingdom for himself and his greedy flatterers, perhaps he would have locked her up and treated her frankly as a madwoman. And perhaps she was already beginning to be mad. She had always been high-strung, ill-balanced, excessively responsive to affection or ill-treatment. Now under the strain of her grievances, real and fancied, her personality was beginning to break up: brief, hysterical outbursts of weeping or anger alternating with long periods of silent melancholy. But the disintegration was by no means complete. While some observers at the Burgundian court found her behavior inexplicable, others were impressed by her grave, graceful bearing, her queenly manner, her courage and dignity and wit. At Windsor, she was shaken by her recent terrible experience at sea, a trial in which she had borne herself bravely enough, and hurt by Philip's neglect and by the completeness with which she had been shouldered out of the celebrations for the royalty she conferred, and the discussions of the fate of her kingdom. But though Catherine found her sadly changed she did not find her mad. And Henry VII was curiously stirred. He had asked for her presence; he regretted having so little of it. He thought her – as many people thought her – beautiful. He was sincerely sorry for her. When Catherine was writing to her sister soon after her departure he suggested that she add that the King of England had been very pleased by her brief visit, and was deeply sorry that it had been no longer.

Much of Catherine's fate sailed with Philip and Joanna from Falmouth. Their voyage was prosperous. They made port at

Corunna on April 26, 1506, and moved slowly into Old Castile, receiving the allegiance of towns and noblemen. Since for reasons of policy Philip had to be more often with his wife than had been his habit, Joanna, for a time, was almost happy, though his recurring neglect – and no reasons of policy could keep Philip attentive for long – soon brought on her fits of silent sulking. Somewhere on the borders of Aragon, Ferdinand was rumored to be collecting men, and no one knew how many of the noblemen and counselors who came to pay homage to his daughter and her husband were really in his pay. No one knew whether it was peace or war, and many said it was lucky that Philip had not landed at Laredo, where Ferdinand was expecting him; but the Aragonese party in Castile seemed stunned or disorganized, and already the Flemings and the Castilian exiles were beginning to quarrel over the spoils.

Ferdinand's own messages were all sweetness. He was impatient, he wrote, to embrace his son-in-law, and to offer him a father's affectionate counsel. Though Juan Manuel warned Philip that many kings had found Ferdinand's embraces more deadly than his enmity, Philip advanced slowly towards the meeting, too undecided to avoid it altogether, too insecure to seek it confidently, surrounded by an army, and taking all the precautions of war. Suddenly, near Villafafilla, there rode into the middle of Philip's host a little knot of men whose peaceful cloth and ambling mules looked odd among the steel and the war horses – Ferdinand of Aragon, slightly accompanied, come to throw himself upon the bosom of his dear son, and to silence the slanderous tongues which hinted that there could be any division between them. Unable to wait for a confidential talk, Ferdinand dismounted and drew Philip after him into a little chapel, to give thanks for their fortunate reunion. They stayed a long time within; the courtiers could hear two voices – one earnest, pleading, impassioned, one reluctant, perplexed, then more and more convinced. Philip emerged, persuaded that he had misjudged his father-in-law. The complete and touching confidence with which his supposed enemy had placed himself in his power proved that Ferdinand had never meant him any harm. Ferdinand was eager, Philip found, to agree to everything he demanded, even to go beyond his wishes, and to give him much excellent advice. All Ferdinand wanted was to leave for Italy, sure that Spain was quiet, and in good hands. Surprisingly, he quite understood about Joanna. She might not be exactly mad, he agreed, but she was certainly unfit to rule Castile. Philip would have to assume all her duties, act, in fact, as regent. And it would be a good thing if it were signed and sealed between them that each should act as the other's executor and regent of the other's realms in the interests of their common heir, Philip's son, Charles. Of course he, Ferdinand, was getting to be an old man, and Philip was a young one. Philip signed and sealed. Three months later he was dead. An Italian suggested that he had "eaten something," but Italian diplomats notoriously thought the worst of everyone. Two physicians, one of them Ferdinand's own, who just happened to be at Burgos, certified immediately that the King of Castile had died a natural death, caused by overexertion after a meal. Ferdinand had actually sailed for Italy; would he have done so, the Aragonese asked, if he had anticipated Philip's death and the resultant confusion in Castile? It was only his far-sightedness which had provided his party with instructions against such an emergency, and given Cardinal Ximenez the power to act, virtually, as his viceroy. It was only his good fortune that Castile slipped back under his rule, more securely held even in his absence than it had ever been since Isabella's death.

In this process Joanna neither helped nor hindered. She had been almost cheerful during Philip's brief illness, watching constantly at his bedside, giving vigorous orders for all the remedies the science of the time suggested, feeding the sick man with her own hands, seeming, indeed, to recapture some of the poise she had known when they faced danger together on the Channel, as if only moments of peril made her sure that Philip was hers. When he died her weeping was like any normal woman's weeping. But later, when his body lay in state at Burgos and masses were being chanted for his soul, she resumed by the bier the vigil she had kept by the bedside, fixing the coffin with anxious, unwavering attention. When she was asked to sign orders for her husband's funeral, and to attend to the details which his death threw upon her alone, she did not answer, hardly seemed to understand. But any attempt to separate her from her husband's body aroused such fury that finally her puzzled counselors took advantage of a moment when she slept upon her knees to remove the coffin almost by stealth to a near-by convent. Thither, as soon as she learned where the body was, went Joanna, ordered the coffin opened and stared for a long time upon the dead face. She would give orders about that, but she would give no other orders, not though the factions in Castile were arming, and archbishops and dukes pressed problems and documents upon her. Suddenly she took alarm. With a little, worried suite she appeared at the gate of the monastery, beat down all objection, had the coffin removed and raised on the shoulders of bearers, and, as night fell, like a thief stealing a holy relic, she was off through the mountains towards distant Granada, a few alert counselors spurring anxiously behind her. Thereafter, from time to time, astonished peasants saw from their mountain fastnesses a weird procession winding through the night: monks chanting a Miserere, a wavering line of torches, a horse litter with sable plumes, and behind it, swathed in black, a solitary figure. Whoever liked, whoever was strongest, might rule now in Castile. Joanna had only one thought. She would never be parted from Philip again.

Chapter Four

ONLY FRAGMENTS of Joanna's fantastic story drifted to England. In July it was known that Ferdinand and his son-in-law were reconciled, in October that Philip was dead. From Spain the disappointed Flemings trooped back to Brussels, laden, so Aragonese partisans declared, with every article of value they could carry off, even to the trappings of the dead king's hearse. The irreconcilable Castilians, still led by Don Juan Manuel, scurried after them, to resume at the court of their chosen prince, little Charles of Ghent, their endless plotting. One heard that Queen Joanna was mad with grief, and that Castile was being governed by regents of the King of Aragon; that she was sane and in full control, government activities being merely suspended for a period of mourning; that she was sane, but a prisoner in the hands of Ferdinand's jailers, who gave out that she was mad. From the malcontents in Flanders rumors spread of feudal conspiracies, rebellious grandees, mutinous towns, all waiting for the signal to rise and free their queen. From Ferdinand came only the most brief and enigmatic letters. The less certainty there was about the affairs in Spain, the less clearly would the lines be drawn, and the more time he would have to strengthen his position.

Catherine's only certainty was that her own position was growing worse and worse. The fifteenth birthday of the Prince of Wales, the twenty-ninth of June, 1506, which should have been her wedding day, came and went, bringing nothing except Ferdinand's tardy excuses for the nonpayment of her dowry. No money at all came from Spain, hardly any news. What was left of her Spanish suite huddled and hid their rags from a court daily more negligent and contemptuous, in whatever lodgings the King of England chose to provide: some outbuildings at Greenwich, the rooms over the stables at Richmond, a decaying manor house at Fulham. There was no money for her servants' wages, no money for new liveries or new dresses, not always enough money for food. Juan de Cuero no longer resisted the Princess's attempts to break into the hoard of her plate and jewels. People must eat. Now and then Henry allowed her an odd sum, once a hundred marks, once seventy, once, in a rush of generosity, two hundred pounds, but never enough to meet current expenses, let alone pay back debts, and never with any regularity, or without some insulting reminder that it was charity. For almost five years altogether, nothing came from Spain, and when in July, 1507, Ferdinand at last sent 2,000 ducats, it was all flung into the pit of Catherine's debts, to pay which another three thousand would not, by then, have sufficed. In mere self-protection from so bad a risk as the marooned Spanish princess, the London goldsmiths felt obliged to charge the highest rates of interest, even when the loan was covered by the most satisfactory tangible security. Sixty-five thousand ducats, even if Ferdinand should ever send them, would not make up Catherine's dowry now. Piece by piece the jewels and plate meant to furnish the remainder were disappearing into strongboxes along Lombard Street, so the forlorn Spaniards might cling to their post, and to some fragments, at least, of their pride.

Catherine, in charge of her own destiny, was as reluctant to part with the earmarked treasures as Juan de Cuero had been. Every driblet of plate she pawned set her marriage that much farther in the future, and before every loan she wrote three appeals to Spain. She had snatched a moment during Philip's visit to Windsor to describe her plight to her old friend Don Pedro de Ayala, in terms so piteous and convincing that Don Pedro risked his own advancement to plead her case with Ferdinand. She wrote later that her people were so desperate they were ready to ask alms on the street, that the liveries and hangings and linens of her household were all in tatters, and she herself without a dress fit to wear in public. Juan Lopez, the principal trustee of Queen Isabella's estate, saw some of her letters, and wrote to Ferdinand that such a state of things reflected dishonor on the memory of his dead queen and on the living King of Aragon, and that, if no other funds were available, he, Lopez, would authorize the sacrifice of some of Isabella's jewels to meet Catherine's needs. But Ferdinand was not tender-minded. He told the English ambassador that Catherine's dowry was a charge on the treasury of Castile and would never be paid from Aragon, and wrote his daughter that God alone knew his sadness when he thought of her trying life, that King Philip's recklessness had been the cause of all her troubles, that she was to be patient, on no account to touch the plate, and to look to the King of England for wherewithal to live. But Henry was not tender-minded either. No one knew the value of a penny better than he, and he was not investing another in Spanish friendship. Let Ferdinand pay for his daughter.

It never occurred to Catherine to blame her father or her father-in-law for this extraordinary contest of meanness. It was fixed in her mind that the cause of her griefs was the laxity and venality of Dr. De Puebla. He had readier access to the King than she. It was his business to see that her interests were properly looked after, and the prestige of Spain preserved in England, but to save himself trouble, and because he was paid by the English, he wrote nothing but lies to Spain, and made no effort to protect her from poverty and ignominy. In every letter Catherine exhorted her father to disregard his ambassador's reports, call him back to Spain, punish him for treason.

Poor De Puebla's influence had long waned. He still dined at court whenever he could, because that saved money, and not a *maravedi* of his back salary had come from Spain for three years.

The 2,000 ducats Catherine disdained would have seemed a fortune to him. The little bits of property he owned in Spain had all been sold long ago to stave off his creditors, and satisfied them so little that only the King's favor kept him from arrest for debt. He and his staff lived as meanly as he dared, meanly enough to expose them to the ridicule he dreaded, scraping along on the fees he collected from Spanish merchants for legal help and for special trading licenses from the English council. His bare livelihood had come to depend on the friendly tolerance of the English court.

Nevertheless, the little Doctor did his level best for his Princess. Many of his letters survive, and there is not a word in any of them unfavorable to Catherine's interests, none of the lies she felt sure he was writing. He pleaded her cause with Henry and with Ferdinand, urged repeatedly that her dowry be sent and her debts be settled, struggled manfully to hold together the shreds of Anglo-Spanish friendship. Short of quarreling with Henry, a futile gesture, De Puebla neglected in his efforts to help the Princess none of the dodges learned in a long experience of diplomacy. It helped very little that he was still received by the King of England. The two shrewd old egotists understood, and in their cold way, liked each other. But though Henry still consulted him sometimes on European problems, even granted him an occasional small mark of favor, De Puebla knew very well that the King was the last man to let such mild sentiments influence his statecraft. There was nothing to be done for Catherine. She must wait out the doldrums like other people.

The ambassador was growing old and tired. More clearly than Catherine, he saw the dwindling of Spanish interests, the gradual undoing of a life work. He was so ill he had to be carried to court in a litter (the only fact of importance which his letters suppressed) but though he knew it was futile he continued to go there. When Catherine stormed at him his eyes filled with tears – the Princess was no longer moved by his tears – and his gouty old hand trembled so afterwards that his always crabbed handwriting became almost illegible. But Catherine mistook helplessness for indifference or treachery. De Puebla's slackness, she wrote her father, was the cause of all the trouble. Someone must find out what King Henry meant, and tell both sides of the truth.[1]

Ferdinand's answer was to send his daughter formal credentials as his ambassador, to write her fully his side of the diplomatic tangle, his reasons for delaying the payment of the dowry, all the information he had previously sent through De Puebla, and to instruct her to communicate with Henry and make what she could of him. Ferdinand knew that De Puebla was not to blame for the state of affairs, but at least his credentials to his daughter regularized somewhat her anomalous position and her intervention could do no harm. His relations with England could hardly be worse.

Catherine had thirsted for action. She seized the formal appointment as an outlet for pent-up energies, worked at it as seriously and energetically as if not only her own fate but that of Spain depended on her efforts. She took a line quite apart from De Puebla, sought independent sources of information, arranged for her own couriers, demanded and got a separate cipher, and spent laborious hours coding and decoding dispatches. She saw Henry as often as she could, presenting her father's excuses and apologies, and coming to use herself, to evade a final explanation, the dodges she had previously blamed. She collected every scrap she could of political gossip, and learned slowly to weigh men and events, to understand in part the seamy side of court intrigues and the complications of European diplomacy. She learned, too, though this was a hard lesson, to keep her head and her temper, to be patient, wary, closemouthed, to endure without a sign insult, humiliation, open rebuffs and sly persecution, to be spied upon and lied to, and browbeaten without betraying herself, without abandoning for an instant her sense of the larger issue, her relentless pursuit of her one aim. Her father had told her that on her marriage to the Prince of

Wales depended the friendship between England and Spain, perhaps the very safety of her house. If the driving force of a single will could achieve that marriage, Catherine would do it.

Not the least queer of the queer shifts to which Catherine had recourse during her two years as ambassadress was her part in Henry's negotiations for the hand of her sister Joanna.[2] While her dowry remained unpaid, while Maximilian continued to tempt Henry to share with him the spoils of Castile, and Ferdinand clung to the humiliating alliance with his old enemy, France, the bait of marriage with Joanna came to seem to Catherine, as it had to De Puebla, almost the only way of keeping Henry's interest. For Henry was definitely interested in Joanna. His senses had been stirred by his brief glimpse of her at Windsor; now his avarice and ambition were aroused, as well. The crown of Castile was reputed to be wealthy, and though Henry could hardly hope to swallow so big a prize by himself, he could, once married to Joanna, make Ferdinand, or the Habsburgs, or whoever was in power, pay high for his friendship. He still hoped also, a hope in which his council encouraged him, to beget more sons. Joanna had borne several healthy children, a good reason to suppose she could bear more. As for her madness, De Puebla wrote that the council did not consider that an insuperable obstacle; it was likely that in new surroundings and under the affectionate care of a husband Joanna would recover her wits, and anyway her misfortune did not seem to affect her children. The observation in its context is not so callous as historians have found it. The best medical knowledge of the period, and the most read fiction, took a view of madness not incompatible with what De Puebla was instructed to write. But actually the council was saying, in diplomatic language, that Henry did not believe what Ferdinand constantly hinted but would never flatly assert, i.e., that his daughter was mad. The belief that the widowed queen was sane, but a prisoner, increased Henry's eagerness to marry her. He remembered Joanna as he had seen her at

Windsor, isolated, pathetic, proudly silent. Now those haunted eyes, that slight, tragic beauty had passed from the keeping of a callous husband to that of an unnatural father. Somewhere in Spain Joanna was confined, lied about, ill-treated, for Ferdinand's advantage. The thought that she might be rescued, that she might not be ungrateful to her rescuer, quickened all that was left of Henry Tudor's chivalric youth. In Henry motives of greed and policy were oddly mixed with motives out of French romances. The obstinacy with which he pressed his suit for Joanna throughout the remainder of his life, his refusal to accept a final rebuff, the agents he sent to Castile, the plots he wove, all show that the deliverance of the Spanish princess had become a kind of obsession. Ferdinand came to wish he had never baited his diplomatic hooks with Joanna's name, and as Henry saw his suit put off with one shift after another, his disappointment and his indignation at what he believed to be Ferdinand's heartless conduct swelled the score of his old grievances to a bitter hatred. He began to cast about for some means of teaching the old fox beyond the Pyrenees a lesson.

The means were at hand. In the years just after Philip's death Ferdinand was absorbed by his plans to marry again, and beget a new heir to the multiple crowns of Aragon. He was ready to risk dividing the heritage of Isabella's children if he could be sure of spiting the Habsburgs, and prevent Spain from becoming the tail to the Austrian kite. In consequence, the Emperor Maximilian, furious at the thought that the motto of his house, "Let others wage wars, thou, happy Austria, wed," might for once be balked of fulfillment, was ready to promise anything to anybody who would help him drive Ferdinand out of Castile. He sent Sigismund Frauenberg to England, instructed to point out that the government of Castile, Leon and Granada descended of right to Isabella's grandson, Charles of Ghent, the Emperor's grandson and ward. Frauenberg was to invite Henry to join in an invasion of Castile, and to offer three marriages to bind the alliance: little Charles to Henry's small daughter, Mary; Margaret, the Emperor's daughter, to Henry himself; and Charles of Ghent's sister, Eleanor, to Henry's only son, the Prince of Wales. Maximilian, through whose head the grandest schemes of European domination chased in rainbow glory while he dodged from one German town to another to avoid his creditors, was never niggardly of promises. Within a year Frauenberg had a treaty of close alliance between Henry and the Habsburgs, a treaty repeating many of the clauses of that of 1506, and definitely, though silently, aimed against Ferdinand. He had also completed negotiations for the marriage of Mary to Charles as soon as the bridegroom reached fifteen.[3]

Catherine had received her credentials as ambassadress while the negotiations with the Habsburgs were still in their preliminary stages, and she soon came to understand, what De Puebla could have told her at the outset, that these negotiations were a hundred times more important than unpaid bills. As she learned to gauge the drift of English policy, as she began to see that what she had taken for irrational vexations and humiliations were mere surface signs of deep, hostile movements, she grew more and more alarmed. Her little artifices and formal arguments beat in vain against the set of this current; while Henry was certain of the Habsburgs, she wrote her father, he felt no need of Spain. But though her exertions as ambassadress had failed to improve matters in the slightest, had failed even to relieve her own desperate poverty, she did not despair. The right person, she felt sure, could find the right word, the right touch to set things straight again. She was only a woman, ignorant and hampered by her anomalous position. De Puebla was but a poor creature. Even if he were honest – and Catherine was still unconvinced of his honesty – his poverty and his consequent semi-dependence on the English King told too heavily against him; he could not be expected to muster the energy and courage to carry through her great affair. A strong, dignified, independent ambassador was needed, one who would speak firmly to the King. Otherwise, with the Habsburgs gaining ground every day, and with the Prince of Wales growing towards the age when he would surely be married, all might be lost. Catherine hoped that her father would send her old friend, Don Pedro de Ayala, but anyone with the proper rank, experience, loyalty, and courage would do.

ii

Ferdinand finally responded to his daughter's pleas. Don Gutierre Gomez de Fuensalida, Knight Commander of the Order of Membrilla, met all the specifications laid down in Catherine's letters.[4] His family was ancient and wealthy; he had proved his courage in the civil wars and the campaigns against Granada, and his loyalty during ten years' service as ambassador, first at Maximilian's court, then at Philip's, where, though a Castilian, he had steadfastly co-operated with Ayala in opposition to Juan Manuel and the exiles. During his service in Germany and the Netherlands he should have learned all about relations between the Habsburgs and England, and he had twice visited England on special missions long enough to give him some familiarity with affairs there. As for firmness, Fuensalida was stiff-necked enough to satisfy anybody. His habit of standing strictly on his dignity and telling unpleasant truths at all costs had got him cordially disliked at Maximilian's court. In Flanders he and Ayala had made a good team, but the tact and subtlety and suppleness had all been Ayala's; honest, zealous Fuensalida wore no velvet gloves. Ferdinand might have been warned by a phrase in one of Fuensalida's old reports. "These people," he had written from Brussels, "are only docile when they're treated roughly." [5] Said of the proud Burgundian nobility by a man who had spent three years among them, the judgment reveals a certain insensitivity. But Ferdinand may have been willing to accept his daughter's opinion that the quality most needed in England was firmness.

Against an excess of that quality, Ferdinand took what precautions he could. Fuensalida would have Catherine's advice, and the assistance of De Puebla, who was supple enough for two. The King of Aragon had by now consolidated his position in Castile, and could offer a better bargain in international affairs. Best of all, he was now able to spare the money for his daughter's long overdue dowry. Fuensalida was given bills of exchange for sixty-five thousand ducats of Aragon, a coin worth slightly more than the *escudo* of Castile in which Catherine's dowry was supposed to be paid, and very conciliatory instructions. He was to complete the payment of the dowry, arrange all outstanding disagreements, reconfirm the treaty of amity, and not to haggle over details. He was to follow Catherine's advice, and to make whatever use of Dr. De Puebla he saw fit. In this connection, Ferdinand gave him alternative letters, one confirming the Doctor as resident ambassador, and directing him to give Fuensalida every assistance; the other removing De Puebla from his post, and ordering him back to Spain. But Catherine and De Puebla together did not make one Ayala. Catherine lacked the necessary tact and patience to manage the headstrong Knight Commander, De Puebla the necessary social position. Neither was the sort of person from whom Fuensalida would accept advice. A veteran diplomat, a nobly born knight of the great crusading orders of Castile, did not need a green girl and a sniveling Jewish lawyer to teach him how to talk to kings!

Fuensalida reached London on February 22, 1508, and marched straight on his objective. When Dr. West told him that it was contrary to etiquette for an ambassador to visit any member of the royal household before he was received by the king, Fuensalida made no attempt to communicate with Catherine. De Puebla, who was confined to bed with the gout, sent his son to warn the new envoy that the matter he had come about had got into a very complex and difficult state and the English would try to delay its solution, but Fuensalida made no effort to sound his predecessor further. He shared Ayala's view of De Puebla. Instead he sought out Francesco Grimaldi, the agent in London of the great Genoese banking firm who were to negotiate his bills, and heard from the banker his views of English politics, and such stories of De Puebla as he could not bear to write.

Thus armed, Fuensalida went to his first interview with Henry. Henry had been ill most of the winter, and his physicians would not let him talk long, but he received the new ambassador almost benignly. He spoke of his dear brother, the King of Aragon, with affection, and expressed his pleasure at the news that Ferdinand was now able to meet his obligations. As for the Princess Catherine, she was as beautiful as she was virtuous, said Henry, he loved her like his own daughter, and would prefer her for his son to any lady in Christendom. Long ago he had given his word that his son should marry her, and he never broke his word – although, he added reflectively, he had had many better offers. Fuensalida foresaw no difficulties.

Four days later, he was formally received by the council; Dr. Fox, Bishop of Winchester, Dr. Nicholas West, the Earl of Surrey, Somerset and others, and met his first obstacle. He had come, he announced, to pay the final installment of Catherine's dowry and to claim the fulfillment of the marriage treaty. The council said they were glad to hear it, and Fox asked when and how the dowry was to be paid. At once, said Fuensalida, sixty-five thousand crowns in cash, the balance in jewels and plate. That, Fox said, should be quite satisfactory. Had the ambassador brought the jewels and plate with him? Fuensalida took alarm, and when alarmed he blustered. The council knew very well, he shouted, that the Princess brought the jewels and plate with her in 1501. No, said Fox, softly, the council had not known that. They had assumed that Catherine's personal ornaments and household goods had been her own property when she married Arthur. After that, of course, they would belong to her husband, and consequently, on Arthur's death, revert to Henry as Arthur's general heir. Naturally, though, Henry had permitted the Princess to use the jewels and plate as her own, and so, they understood, she had done. Nicholas West added slyly that either Ferdinand had sent his daughter into England naked and unfurnished, or else he was now trying to pay her dowry with Henry's property. Either way, it almost seemed that Ferdinand should be ashamed of such unkingly behavior. Fuensalida cried out that if Catherine had broken into the jewels and plate, she had been driven to do so by Henry's meanness, and it was for the English to be ashamed. The meeting broke up in a furious squabble.

On this point the negotiations stuck. Fuensalida knew no tactics but bluff and bluster. The council, not unwilling to prod him into making a fool of himself, were gentle, as a rule, but firm. Henry was too ill to be disturbed. After two weeks of futile wrangling, the council handed Fuensalida a formal protest that they would accept no part of Catherine's jewels and plate in satisfaction of the dowry, and that further discussion was useless unless their view could be met. Meanwhile Fuensalida had discovered that the jewels and plate had been seriously depleted. Instead of bringing thirty-five thousand crowns on the London market, they might not bring twenty thousand. In his dispatches, outbursts of generous indignation at the straits to which the Princess had been reduced alternate with lamentations over her improvidence.

So far Fuensalida had cold-shouldered De Puebla, but the impasse drove him to seek the old man's advice. De Puebla said calmly that the English would have to take the jewels and plate unless they meant to repudiate the treaty. He had drawn the treaty, and he had seen to that. On the other hand, any deficit in the valuation on the London market would have to be made up in cash. That was in the treaty too. He had often warned Ferdinand that the plate was being depleted, though he had not been able to find out by how much. As for the present tactics of the council, De Puebla said, there were several things the English hoped to gain by delay. They were determined to secure Ferdinand's consent to the marriage of his grandson, Charles, to the Princess Mary. Henry, himself, still hoped to marry Joanna. Besides, they wanted to avoid committing themselves until they saw the result of Maximilian's invasion of Italy. That mercurial sovereign, now Henry's ally, expected to bring the King of Aragon to his knees at last. If his trumpeted expedition really menaced Spain, the English hoped to make a better bargain. Only time, the old ambassador counseled, could remove some of these obstacles. They would have to be patient. Anyhow, it would be better to wait for warmer weather, when Henry's health was always better. When the east wind stopped, the King would be more accessible and in a better temper. Dr. De Puebla had spent twenty years over this question of the marriage. It had been six since Arthur died, two since the date set for Catherine's remarriage. In twenty years De Puebla had waited out many storms, learned that things were rarely so hopeful or so hopeless as they looked. He knew the English, and the Habsburgs, and every comma in all the treaties, with a weary knowledge. What he said was sound and shrewd: they must wait and see. Boiling with impatience and suspicion, Fuensalida was obliged to accept the veteran's help and advice.

The advice proved sound. The Emperor who set out to conquer Italy could not even beat the Venetians, and the ridiculous and humiliating breakdown of his campaign removed any immediate danger to Spain. In the same letters which reported Maximilian's failure, Ferdinand told Fuensalida to encourage Henry's suit for Joanna, and to assure him that he should marry her if anybody did. Ferdinand also enclosed a draft for ten thousand ducats to make up the deficit in the plate. Meanwhile De Puebla, after a series of confidential talks, got the English to admit their obligation to take at least a part of the plate and jewels, and assured Fuensalida that the rest of this disagreement could be compromised. But although

De Puebla had won the only success so far, Fuensalida kept him in the background as much as possible. He went alone next time to the council and got involved in another silly wrangle about Henry's obligation to provide for Catherine; lost his temper, exposed his ignorance of the law (of which he was rather proud), and gave the English an excuse to break off the conversations in real or pretended anger. When De Puebla offered to smooth things over with Henry, Fuensalida haughtily forbade it. Only when it was quite clear that alone he could not even get in to see the King, would he agree to use his colleague. Again De Puebla pulled his wires, and Fuensalida was granted another interview at Greenwich. There he learned the accuracy of De Puebla's warning that Henry was most interested in marrying Joanna. To Fuensalida's suggestion that probably Joanna would never be able to marry anybody, Henry countered directly: "Tell me, ambassador," he said, "is the Queen such as they say she is? If what they say is true, God defend that I should marry her for three kingdoms such as hers, but there are those who say it is your King who keeps her shut up and spreads this rumor about her. Indeed I have had reports from Spain that she listens and replies rationally and seems quite normal. When I saw her two years ago, her husband and some of his council were giving it out that she was mad, but at that time I saw her speak and act rationally and with great grace and dignity. I thought her sane then, and I think her so now. On your honor, is she not such as her husband would desire?" [6]

Put upon his honor, Fuensalida could not say. Probably he had not thought her mad in 1506, and since Philip's death he had hardly seen her. Ferdinand, for his own purposes, had involved the question of his daughter's sanity in such confusion that not only his enemies but his ministers were uncertain what to think. The most tactful evasion that Fuensalida could muster was the remark that whatever the Queen's health, surely Henry himself was too old to think of marrying.

Henry let that pass, though the deep-set eyes glared dangerously. He turned to the question of Mary's betrothal to Charles. Here, too, Fuensalida had been instructed to temporize and hold out hope. His idea of doing so was to let Henry see that Ferdinand had no real intention of confirming the betrothal and that he, himself, was eager to keep the two questions separate. Henry returned to his suit for Joanna, arguing, wheedling, almost pleading, dangling the hope that a favorable reply would solve all the difficulties about Catherine. Stubbornly Fuensalida repeated that the two proposals were not on a common footing; Henry was bound by treaty to marry his son to Catherine, whereas –

"My son and I are free," Henry cut in, and the interview was over. When De Puebla called that evening to hear how things had gone, Fuensalida would not even let him see the last dispatches from Spain. He would tell him what was decided, he said, after he talked to Henry again. Glumly De Puebla predicted that he would not see Henry again for another fortnight. That proved correct, and Fuensalida's conviction that the former resident was in collusion with the English was confirmed. He felt that no ambassador should be on such good terms with the English King and his ministers. Old and ill as he was, De Puebla seemed to flit about like a shadow. Every whisper of palace gossip came to his ears. Even without dispatches from Spain he still knew more of what was going on in Europe than Fuensalida did, and he could predict uncannily what the English would think and do next. All this scurrying, and tattling, and backstairs intrigue revolted Fuensalida. That De Puebla could outguess these inscrutable islanders made it plain that he was in league with them. Fuensalida ordered De Puebla to accompany him to the meeting of the council next day, and the fact that under the old man's experienced touch the discussion really moved a fraction forward deepened Fuensalida's certainty that De Puebla could do still more. Instead of praising his colleague after the meeting, Fuensalida berated him. It would take years to settle matters at this rate. All this legal hair-splitting, these endless technicalities, were nonsense. De Puebla must see the King tomorrow, and tell him to order his council to come to terms at once. In an anguish of vexation the old man screamed: "I can do no more! No more! I can't twist the ears of the King of England!"[7] Thereupon Fuensalida carried out his oft-repeated threat; he handed over Ferdinand's letter of dismissal and told De Puebla that he was a Spanish ambassador no longer. Twisting a king's ears was just what Fuensalida conceived an ambassador's function to be.

The old man wrote one last letter to Spain, a pathetic reminder of his long and ill-paid service, an earnest warning that affairs were going badly and were full of danger. Then he took to his bed and stayed there. For the next ten months, slowly and with cunning delays, as he had always done everything, De Puebla was dying. As time went on the attitude towards him of the two who, between them, had shouldered him out of his long-held post, softened. When it was too late, Fuensalida began to appreciate his advice, even to seek his help. He wrote in De Puebla's behalf to Spain, and perhaps would have reyoked him in their uncomfortable double harness if he could. Catherine sent the old man her own physician, and before long was comparing him very favorably indeed with his successor. But although he just managed to live to see the end of Fuensalida's extraordinary comedy, De Puebla had drafted his last treaty.

iii

Fuensalida went about his self-appointed task of twisting King Henry's ears with righteous thoroughness, undismayed by danger. De Puebla had warned him, Catherine had warned him, the Spanish ambassador in Flanders had warned him that Don Juan Manuel was moving heaven and earth for a military alliance between Henry and Maximilian and a joint invasion of Castile. Emissaries of the

Castilian malcontents, slipping back and forth between Spain and Flanders, usually stopped in London for a conference with Henry's counselors or with Henry himself. In Spain the agents of sedition had got the ear of Henry's resident ambassador, John Stile, and filled him with tales of the unpopularity of Ferdinand, the ill-treatment of the imprisoned Joanna, and the strength of the opposition to the King of Aragon. Fuensalida's notion of countering this devious intrigue was to try to seize the person of one of the Castilian plotters, the Bishop of Catania, who was in London, incognito, and send him back to Spain as a rebel, meanwhile declaring loudly that John Stile was an abominable liar who ought to be tried for treason. The Bishop of Catania was arrested at the ambassador's instance and lodged in the Tower, but instead of being handed over for extradition he was escorted to Greenwich, sumptuously entertained, granted a long private interview with Henry, and sent on his way with honor to Flanders. And Henry and his council, though they may have noted that Fuensalida had no idea of respecting in others the sacred character of an ambassador, continued to believe John Stile.

Fuensalida did not even know of the most serious threat to his mission. George van Theimseke, Provost of Cassel, Maximilian's new ambassador in London, had been given secret instructions that the betrothal of Eleanor, Charles of Ghent's elder sister, to Henry, Prince of Wales, was to be pushed at all costs, and secured by any reasonable sacrifice, or almost any promise. At first Theimseke was pessimistic. But Fuensalida's indiscretions lightened the Fleming's task. After the stormy interview with Henry on June 21, 1508, following which De Puebla had been sacked, Theimseke found Henry raging against Ferdinand and ready to listen to anything. When Theimseke cautiously broached the subject of an alliance against France, Henry cried out that there was not a better Frenchman in Paris than the King of Aragon. The way to strike at King Louis was through Ferdinand. If the Emperor would agree to invade Castile in the name of his grandson, Charles, Henry would support him to the limit, and both Ferdinand and Louis would be brought low. Theimseke was naturally delighted.[8]

During the last year of his reign, Henry VII was moody, irascible, easily roused to violent gusts of anger from which not even his favorite daughter, Mary, was safe. His foreign policy was becoming the sport of his rheumatism and his nerves. The most tactful ambassador would have found him hard to handle. Fuensalida was about the least tactful, always fancying slights to his dignity, and proud of his techiness. The most frequent remark in his letters is "*Yo no puedo esso suffrir con paciencia*" (I could not bear this patiently). He was quick and rather effective in his angry retorts, and could make even the Bishop of Winchester lose his temper. His interviews with the council invariably degenerated into furious, aimless quarrels, while, before long, the mere sight of the Spanish ambassador jangled the nerves of the ailing king.

Everybody was aware of Fuensalida's failing except the ambassador himself. After the disastrous colloquy on June 21, Fuensalida was refused an audience with Henry for more than a month. When he was finally granted one, De Puebla, Catherine, even Bishop Fox, all begged him to be careful this time. To them all Fuensalida replied airily that he knew how to talk to kings. This he proceeded to prove.[9] Henry received him almost jocularly. He said he heard from Stile that Ferdinand was holding high festival at Burgos, and he supposed the newly married King had had no time to attend to state affairs. Fuensalida replied that Ferdinand never let pleasure interfere with business; he was strong enough to attend to both. It was too bad, he added, that Henry was not. Henry controlled himself, and continued more gruffly on the subject of Joanna. He did not believe she was mad, he repeated, but saw clearly that she would not be permitted to marry, though Ferdinand might yet find he would need all his friends. Fuensalida took this as a threat. His master, he answered proudly, was so great a king he feared no enemies in the world. "We'll see," said Henry sourly and the conversation continued in increasingly acid tones. Fuensalida did not know how to do anything but oppose blunt refusals and make blunt demands. Henry met his insistence that a date be fixed for Catherine's public betrothal with stony contemptuous silence, and a few minutes later, gave him a curt dismissal. He did not see the King again for six weeks.

Late in September Fuensalida heard again from Spain. Alarmed by English coldness, by Fuensalida's lack of progress, Ferdinand was yielding to the extreme English demands. He groaned against Henry's covetousness; he protested that he had done nothing to deserve this implacable enmity; he declared that in dealing with persons of no honor and indifferent character one must take every precaution; he expressed the fear that once the money was in England Henry would have Catherine poisoned. But he ordered Fuensalida to pay the full dowry in cash if necessary, and inclosed a draft for thirty-five thousand crowns, and a free deed of gift of the jewels and plate to Catherine. By yielding gracefully now he had the power to do so, Fuensalida might have won an important point, but he could not forbear representing the whole transaction as a free act of generosity on Ferdinand's part, reopening all the old arguments, and pressing Henry to accept at least a part of the plate.[10] Henry contemptuously agreed, and asked for the document renouncing Catherine's dower rights. Now this point had been conceded in 1504. Fuensalida knew nothing whatever about it, but he had no hesitation in replying that such a demand was outrageously unjust. Henry dropped the subject, but Fuensalida could see he was growing angry. How, Henry asked next, about Ferdinand's consent to the betrothal of Charles and Mary? That, said Fuensalida, might come later. Henry cried out furiously that he had been deceived about Joanna and would not be deceived again about his daughter. The strain of talking to Fuensalida was telling on his nerves. The ambassador, calm for once, said that the two negotiations were quite separate. One ought not to impede the other. Henry had been growing "more yellow than ever." "But they do," he spat out, "you shall not have the one without the other," and flinging over his shoulder that he must consult his council, he stalked off.

The worst of the quarrel had not come. Fuensalida, very proud of his firmness, went to tell Catherine how he had sped, and on leaving her room met Henry.

"I thought you had gone," the old man snapped. "Now come in with me. The Princess shall see how you handle her affairs."

Henry began an account of his conversation with the ambassador. Before he had gone very far, Fuensalida interrupted, contradicted him. Henry jumped "like a singed cat." He could not deal with such a man, he cried. He would marry Mary to Charles without Ferdinand's consent. Thereupon Fuensalida began the tale of the crowns which such an act might lose the couple: Aragon, Valencia, Majorca, Sardinia, Sicily, Naples, Jerusalem –

"You honor your King with many crowns indeed," Henry cut in, "but for years he hadn't a hundred thousand to pay for his daughter's dowry."

"Señor," said the ambassador, "the King, my lord, is equal in fame and glory and power to any prince in Christendom. He does not lock away his gold in chests, but pays it to the brave soldiers at whose head he had always been and will always be victorious."

At this taunt, Fuensalida records with satisfaction, the King was speechless for a moment, and then "grew so angry with me that it was marvelous to behold." Naturally it was some time before the two met again.

Almost the only qualities of a successful negotiator which Fuensalida did not lack were courage and pertinacity. There was another interview and another, each time ending in furious recriminations. After one such row which broke out in the presence of the full council, Henry flung himself out, declaring that never in his life had he wrangled so with anyone and been so braved, and Bishop Fox, who had tried in vain to keep the discussion on a reasonable level, turned to Fuensalida and said:

"You know, ambassador, he is a bad cook who spoils good food with unpalatable sauce. Most ambassadors try to present things as pleasantly as possible, and keep the good will of him to whom they are sent." One does not know which to admire more: the obtuseness which could so thoroughly deserve the criticism, or the honesty which could record it.

All this time the discussion turned on the betrothal of Charles and Mary, and in vain. Fuensalida would not make the least concession. His behavior made it plain that Ferdinand had instructed him to prevent the match. The Flemish ambassadors had come. The date for the ceremony was set. Henry announced, finally, that he would dispense with Ferdinand's consent; he merely asked the Spanish ambassador to attend the public betrothal. But Fuensalida would not recognize the betrothal in any way, and even forbade the Princess Catherine to be present. This was the last quarrel. When next Fuensalida rode to court, the guards seized his bridle and forcibly ejected him from the palace precincts. He never saw Henry again.

iv

Within six months of his arrival, Fuensalida broke with De Puebla and with the line Spanish policy had followed in England for thirteen years. Before another six months he had broken with Henry, and nullified the last remnant of Spanish influence in England. Shortly after, he broke with Catherine, and was left thereafter stranded, useless, pouring out in letters to Ferdinand his bitterness, his forebodings and his guesses. At first, Fuensalida's relations with Catherine had been extremely cordial. She was pleased by the arrival of a Spaniard of her own class, someone she could trust and talk to. She was warmed by the indignation he showed at her treatment, and by the bluff, wholehearted way he assumed her championship. A very different person, she thought, from the miching De Puebla. For his part, Fuensalida was charmed by Catherine's beauty and spirit, touched by her patience in adversity, and infuriated by her ill-treatment. He recognized, of course, that in these complex affairs the Princess was at sea. She had been foolish about her money; she was foolish about her suite and her relations with the English. But he found her impracticality rather charming. His reports of her condition are a torrent of indignation which, though directed against Henry and the English, spills over upon his own king. His sense of her wrongs, and his desire to impress them on all and sundry, stiffened his back at the council table, occasioned, in fact, his loudest, bitterest quarrels there.

As his partisanship grew more raucous, Catherine's esteem for him diminished. She had been through a hard school in England, learned hard lessons. Fuensalida saw on her table stinking fish "such as he would not give his horse boy." But Catherine's household had long bought its fish where it was cheapest. She was shifted arbitrarily from room to room of the palace, and lodged in the hottest weather directly over the stables. The King's servants ignored her or were insolent. When, in September, the court suddenly removed from Richmond on a rumor of the plague, Catherine and her household were abandoned there without horses, and left to follow as best they could. Fuensalida was afraid that her health and sanity might break under such treatment. But for more than three years Catherine had not lived differently. She was inured to pinpricks and petty persecution. What she wanted from Fuensalida was not sympathy, but action.

She was far from being the charming little ninny that Fuensalida thought he was protecting. "They tell me nothing but lies here," she had written to her father with hard-won pride, "and they think they can break my spirit. But I believe what I choose and say nothing.

I am not so simple as I seem." What Catherine wanted was not revenge for the past, but assurance for the future; her business in England was the same as Fuensalida's – to make a safe alliance between her house and Henry's. As she saw that Fuensalida's indignation at her wrongs was obscuring the issue, she confided in him less, and spent her conversations with him in warnings not to irritate the King, not to rake up old quarrels, not to be led astray by trifles. His complaints of her treatment in his letters to Spain were promptly relayed back to England by John Stile and did her more harm than good; his insistence that she stand always upon her dignity in matters of precedence was a needless provocation. She was beginning to lose patience with her champion.

She lost it altogether when he told her she must absent herself from the ceremonies for the betrothal of Mary to Charles of Ghent because the place assigned her was not sufficiently honorable. She told the ambassador that he might attend or not, as he chose, though she advised him to do so, but as for herself she would be present in the place assigned to her. She had no wish to offer gratuitous insults to Mary, and to the English King. She had consulted her confessor on the point, and her conscience was clear.

Probably the reference to the confessor was tactless. Fuensalida had already clashed with Fray Diego Fernandez and decided that there was no one in Catherine's suite he liked less, had already, in fact, complained to Ferdinand that this young man out of nowhere exercised an undue influence on the Princess, ordered her about in a peremptory and unbecoming fashion, wheedled her into selling her plate to buy him books, and encouraged her to disregard the advice of abler and more experienced people. The tactlessness of the Princess's reference was pointed by her choice of the confessor himself as the bearer of her message, and Fray Diego's manner in delivering it seemed so insolent that only his habit, Fuensalida wrote furiously, saved him from a beating. Stung by Catherine's flat refusal to follow his advice, Fuensalida poured out his wrath on her counselor. The friar, he wrote to Ferdinand, was a light-minded young jackanapes, overbearing in his conduct and scandalous in his way of life; he roistered in the city in secular attire; he domineered over Catherine's household and squandered her money; he was ill bred, he was a nuisance, he was unfit to be anybody's confessor, and ought to be removed. And carried away by rage, Fuensalida so far forgot himself as to try to get the English authorities to arrest Fray Diego and ship him out of the country, a move which, when Catherine heard of it, widened the breach between them.

There is no doubt that Catherine was attached to Fray Diego, regarded him as providentially sent her by God in her hour of need. After her old confessor and tutor, Alessandro Geraldini, had been sent back to Spain in 1502, Catherine had confessed to Doña Elvira's private chaplain who was thereupon breveted to the chaplaincy of Durham House. When Doña Elvira departed for Flanders in 1505, Catherine was left without any spiritual director. She found it impossible to confess satisfactorily in cold, formal Latin or in her stumbling, imperfect English, and the lack of religious guidance and consolation during the period of her poverty, illness and discouragement was one of her severest trials. For a long time her repeated appeals for a Spanish-speaking confessor went unheeded in Spain. Then, sometime before April, 1507, she found Fray Diego Fernandez. He was a member of the very order to which she, like her mother, was most attached, the Observant Franciscans. Like most of the Observants he was of humble birth, but he was a Spaniard of the Spaniards, a native of Old Castile, and he had studied at Salamanca, and was able to share her intellectual interests. He had been long enough in England to speak English and knew something of the islanders. And whatever his motives – and we know nothing of the motives of Fray Diego – he proved himself loyal and devoted. Before long he was the only person in her household on whom Catherine felt she could rely.

She needed someone. Poverty and isolation had thoroughly demoralized her little suite. They were divided as ever by jealousy and backbiting, but on one point they were almost all united. They wanted to go back to Spain. The two chief gentlemen of her household, now the Manriques were gone, Juan de Cuero, the gray-headed treasurer, and Alonso de Esquivel, the master of the hall, were perpetually suspicious of each other, hardly on speaking terms, but they both resented their exile, both agreed that Catherine's position was untenable and thought only of making good their retreat. Even Catherine's own ladies in waiting were no longer thoroughly loyal. Inez de Venegas and Maria de Salinas would stay with their princess to the end, but even Maria de Rojas was weakening. Her Stanley suitor had married elsewhere; after Doña Elvira's treachery young Iñigo Manrique was impossible; and no one any more, in Spain or England, looked to the ladies of Catherine's suite for brides. It was hard to grow old in England without present gaiety or the promise of future security, among the shabby, neglected vestals of a vain devotion. It was hard even for Maria de Salinas, the bravest and most loyal of them all, who was bound to her mistress by more than common ties of affection; it was harder for the others. Next to Maria, Catherine had always been fondest of Francesca de Carceres, the gayest, the most vivacious and spirited of her maids. But it was hardest of all for Francesca, and she had become the most active intriguer of the cabal who wanted to get back to Spain. No wonder Catherine turned from them to her confessor who, alone, never faltered, who told her with a voice which seemed like an echo of her own conscience, to trust in God and stay at her post.

The clique who hoped to induce Catherine to give up the battle were not slow in identifying Fray Diego as an enemy. His encouragement of the Princess in her foolish stubbornness was Juan de Cuero's chief count against him, and Francesca de Carceres regarded him as the chief obstacle to her campaign to get the whole suite out of gloomy, hopeless England. Francesca was the source of

Fuensalida's information. The ambassador was lodging at the house of Grimaldi, the Genoese banker, which the relaxed discipline of Catherine's household permitted Francesca to visit. Francesca had about made up her mind that a rich, elderly Italian merchant who was infatuated enough to marry a noble young lady without a dowry, and even without her family's or her mistress's consent, would be no bad substitute for the noble suitors she was missing. Always provided, that is, she could not get back to Spain. But she preferred to return to Spain, and with that in view she instilled into the ambassador the notion that Catherine's stubbornness was all owing to Fray Diego's bad influence. If Fuensalida could get the confessor removed, she hoped to establish herself in his place as Catherine's chief confidante.

Instead, Fuensalida's attack on Fray Diego drew down Catherine's fire on Francesca. She was thoroughly scolded as a gossip-monger and a malicious, disloyal intriguer, and warned against further interference in the Princess's affairs. In particular, she was not to see Grimaldi or Fuensalida again. Frightened by the anger she had provoked, despairing, perhaps, of ever regaining her lady's favor, Francesca fled by night to the house of her elderly lover, and was married to him before Catherine discovered her whereabouts. Nothing could have been better calculated to add fuel to Catherine's anger. Francesca's flight was a confession of her past intrigues, and thoroughly identified Fuensalida in Catherine's mind with the clique in her own household who wanted her to admit defeat. To Ferdinand, Catherine stigmatized Fuensalida's conduct as disloyal and scandalous. He had not only encouraged dissension among her servants, she wrote, but had engaged in a vulgar intrigue with one of her waiting women, whom he had carried off and married to his landlord as a cover for their disgraceful amours. Probably Catherine believed what she wrote; to her aristocratic prejudices an affair with a Knight Commander of Membrilla would be the only conceivable reason for a De Carceres to marry a commoner, even if that commoner were one of the Grimaldi to whom the crown of Aragon owed the better part of two years' revenue.

Close upon Francesca's flight, Catherine discovered that the ambassador had given up all hope of her marriage, and was sending her dowry money out of the kingdom. This was the ultimate treachery. Her worst suspicions of old De Puebla had never gone half so far. In words of fire Catherine warned her father that they were both betrayed.

Ferdinand, in fact, had already been informed of Fuensalida's action. The ambassador had convinced himself, not only that the marriage was utterly hopeless, but that Henry meant war, and soon. The scheme, he wrote, was for the Emperor to give Henry his power of attorney to act as Charles's guardian in Spain. Henry would then invade Castile while Maximilian, aided by English money, attacked the French. Matters had not really gone quite so far, but Henry's ambassador in Flanders that autumn was urging a not dissimilar scheme; the chief interest of the English diplomats at the congress of Cambrai, which opened in December, seemed to be the organization of a European coalition against Ferdinand; and there was much justification for Spanish alarm. In September Fuensalida wrote asking for a ship in which he and Catherine might withdraw with honor. In November he noted the presence of warships in the Thames, and a general bustle of preparation, inspections of arms and artillery and mustering of men. He felt sure he would be arrested on the outbreak of hostilities, asked for his passports, and was in a fever of anxiety because they had not come. Grimaldi recommended, as a reasonable precaution, getting Ferdinand's money out of the country. The banker was able to arrange for its transfer, piecemeal, by the purchase of bills of exchange on Bruges, an operation for which his Most Catholic Majesty, on Fuensalida's authority, paid a heavy discount, and the house of Grimaldi realized a neat profit. That was better, however, thought Fuensalida, than having the English seize the lot.

That Fuensalida's maneuvers to get her and her father's money out of the country were dictated by an honest anxiety for their safety, and that her years of waiting had ended in failure, Catherine simply could not admit. She had written long ago that she would rather die in England than go back to Spain without achieving her marriage, and, whoever deserted, she was determined to stand firm and trust God to achieve for her the apparently impossible. Her simple faith in the special interest of the Deity in her family made it easy for Catherine to see her own duty; and she was not one to forgive those to whom duty is less clear. If Fuensalida flinched from the plain way, it must be because he was a scoundrel. "Your ambassador here," she wrote her father tersely, "is a traitor. Recall him at once, and punish him as he deserves." [11]

She had never been more alone. Most of her household were, by now, in almost open rebellion against her stubbornness. At the English court no one dared show her a friendly smile. The little Princess Mary and Princess Mary's suite held her responsible for the delay in the betrothal to Charles of Ghent and went out of their way to show their dislike of her. The old Dowager Countess of Richmond, more powerful than ever now that King Henry's health was failing, had never approved of her as a bride for the Prince of Wales and treated her with open hostility. Everywhere the partisans of the Habsburg alliance were triumphant; everywhere people were saying that before long the false French and their Aragonese allies would know the weight of English might. When he thought of the King of Aragon, old Henry's pain-wracked face became a frozen mask of hatred. Revenge on Ferdinand had become an obsession with the dying king.

That Henry VII was dying was, in fact, Catherine's only real hope. On his death, her fate would be in the hands of his son, the prince who would be Henry VIII. She had seen the tall blond boy but seldom of late years, but he always looked at her kindly. She put her trust in the Prince of Wales.

Fuensalida knew of that hope, but he was inclined to discount it. He admitted that he knew little of the Prince, because of the precautions of his guardians, but what little he knew was not encouraging. The boy was not likely to have a will of his own. He was kept in closer seclusion than if he were a nubile girl. He was never permitted to go out of the palace, except for exercise through a private door leading straight into the park. At these times he was surrounded by the persons specially appointed by the King as his tutors and companions, and no one else dared, on his life, to approach him. He took his meals alone, and spent most of his day in his own room, which had no other entrance than through the King's bedchamber. He was in complete subjugation to his father and his grandmother, and never opened his mouth in public except to answer a question from one of them. To sum up, an ambassador had as little chance to talk to him as a woman had. Later Fuensalida noted the Prince's robust good looks, his skill in horsemanship, and his fondness for expensive presents, but to Ferdinand's suggestion that Catherine seemed to think that things would be better when young Henry was king, Fuensalida only replied, "Please God they may, but I see no likelihood of it." [12]

Old Henry was dying at Richmond. He was settling his affairs, drawing up his will, pardoning prisoners accused of violation of the unpopular trade laws and those arrested for debts of less than fifteen pounds, spending much time with his mother and his confessor, while his council sat late debating the problems a new reign would bring. Echoes of their conference drifted to Fuensalida. There was a pro-French party, it seemed, and a pro-Habsburg party. French partisans were urging that the new king should marry Marguerite d'Alençon, sister of the lad who would one day be King of France unless Louis XII had a son – a fine girl, people said, and one to whom her cousin, the King, glad to secure English friendship, would give a rich dowry. Habsburg partisans put Eleanor first, but suggested as a second choice the daughter of Duke Albert of Bavaria, whom Maximilian himself had proposed as a substitute should the young prince not wish to wait three or four years for Eleanor. Most people felt that it would be better if the new king married soon after his father's death. But Fuensalida could hear of no Aragonese party, saw little hope that Catherine would be seriously considered, and less still that the Prince of Wales would intervene in her favor. All Fuensalida really hoped was that the change of government would delay matters long enough for him to get Catherine and the rest of the money out of England.

On April 21, 1509, Henry VII died. Next day the young King came from Richmond to the Tower of London. He was a youth of gigantic size, people noted, with a ruddy countenance as soft and sweet as a woman's, a mass of red-gold hair, and a bearing like a young Saint George. He freed prisoners, arrested the most unpopular of his father's officials, proclaimed a general pardon (with the customary exceptions) and ordered that those who had been injured by the crown should hasten to inform his council, all amidst the greatest popular rejoicing. There was to be an end at last of prying and whispering and hoarding, an end of senile avarice and senile caution. People could say what they liked now, and eat and drink and wear what they liked, and drive their bargains as best they could, without fear of a sudden descent of the King's officers and a thumping great fine. There would be gaiety again at court, music and jousting and feasting, and young country gallants spending their money along Cheapside. There would be great deeds, perhaps, and conquering armies loaded with French spoil returning to London's welcome, as it had been in the old days. There was a young king on the throne again, a king of the right royal blood, a king who looked like a hero. The winter of the old reign was passed. Spring promised to be glorious.

To Fuensalida, writing to Ferdinand on April 27, the change boded no good. Two members of the council had told him that on his deathbed Henry VII had assured his son that he was free to marry whom he chose. One of them (was he Warham?) added that the young King would probably make a scruple of marrying his brother's widow. If Ferdinand sent the consent to Mary's betrothal at once, Fuensalida would make one more effort; Henry was reputed to be very fond of his sister. But probably, he added glumly, nothing would be any use.[13]

The ambassador had hardly sent off this gloomy report, when to his astonishment he received a summons from the council. They were surprised, they said, that Fuensalida had not communicated with them. What was he doing? The King was anxious to serve the Princess; he would be glad if the ambassador would hasten matters. Fuensalida had not been daunted by failure, but the prospect of success unnerved him. He was doubtful and hesitant when he appeared before the council,[14] began a long-winded defensive speech, rehearsing all the old difficulties: Ferdinand's delay about Mary's betrothal, the nonpayment of the dowry, Catherine's renunciation of her dower rights – Ruthall, returning from a colloquy with young Henry, who was waiting in another room, interrupted. Fuensalida's assurance that Ferdinand did not intend to obstruct Mary's betrothal was perfectly satisfactory, Ruthall said. The King – he reminded Fuensalida that he must speak of the former Prince of Wales as king now, not prince, – the King said Catherine should do whatever she liked about her jointure. The royal generosity would be her best safeguard. Dazed, Fuensalida took up the question of Catherine's plate. Ruthall cut him short. The council, he said, could not waste time over trifles; the question of the plate (question over which Fuensalida and the whole council had spent months of weary wrangling!) was quite without importance. Thereupon he read the bemused ambassador a long, prepared harangue on the danger to Europe of the overweening power of France, and the advantage of a triple alliance of the King of Aragon, the Emperor, the King of England, to bridle French ambition.

Fuensalida could not believe his ears. He stammered and checked; his complete unpreparedness for this turn of events was obvious. Let him take time, then, Ruthall said, to consider these grave matters; meanwhile the King trusted him to hasten the details to be arranged before the wedding. As he withdrew, almost in a trance, Fox took his arm and began to tell him all over again, in a soothing tone, what had happened. He himself, the Bishop of Winchester assured him, and the majority of the council favored an immediate marriage; they would do everything to make Fuensalida's task easy. They hoped to begin work at once on a treaty of friendship and alliance which the King wished to be as close as was fitting between father and son. Still bewildered, Fuensalida asked whether he might see the Princess. That, Fox laughed, was for the Princess to say. She is mistress in England now. "Your best advocate to her," he added, "will be the King. I, myself, will ask him to intercede for you. Write the Princess a letter, and when the King speaks in your favor I think she will not be too hard on you."

As Fox advised, the ambassador wrote to the Princess, wrote in a strain of abject apology and received a formal note. The Princess accepted the ambassador's assurance that he had acted loyally, and in the belief that he was serving her best interests. She was very busy, but she would be willing to receive him whenever the settlement of her affairs required. She was very busy. Too busy to bear malice. If Fuensalida said that he had been a fool, not a knave, probably it was so. She had no need of his championship, or anybody's championship, now. All Fuensalida had to do was to repair the minor consequences of his folly.

Even that proved unexpectedly simple. Grimaldi had transferred nearly fifty thousand crowns to Bruges and getting them back cost so much that Fuensalida had to write to Spain for more money, and scurry about arranging loans and making unpalatable explanations; but the English council now took everything with the greatest good humor. Genoese and Spanish merchants and bankers in London competed for the privilege of making up any temporary deficit, or of supplying anything the Princess might need against her wedding. From a knight in armor, fighting the battles of his ungrateful Princess against frightful odds, Fuensalida found himself transformed into the likeness of a fumbling man of business whom people bustled and prodded and absent-mindedly encouraged to get on with his petty tasks while they went about their more serious affairs. To be whisked thus from the hopeless morass in which he had floundered for fourteen months to the crown of a broad highway was almost too much for the Knight Commander's nerves. As soon as his Princess was married he would be going home to Spain, and his final letters sigh with relief at the prospect of escaping from this mad country.

There are two accounts of the reason for the peripetia which had taken Fuensalida so completely off his guard. One of them, given at great length and with much circumstantial detail in his dispatches, is Fuensalida's own. It ascribes the whole astounding reversal to the dramatic intervention of the young King, and though Fuensalida may have been mistaken, his explanation does fit all that we know from other sources of the diplomacy of the last year of Henry VII's reign. The other explanation, offered by Henry VIII himself to Margaret of Savoy in a letter announcing his wedding, is the one historians usually follow. His marriage to Catherine, Henry wrote, was dictated by his regard for treaty obligations, and for his father's dying wish. On his deathbed, his father had enjoined him to marry Catherine at once. Such a wish no pious son could fail to respect.

On the face of it, Henry should be the most reliable witness. It may be, of course, that Fuensalida was deceived, that in his relations with the Spanish ambassador old Henry was merely acting an elaborate comedy designed to screw better terms out of Spain, that he always meant his son to marry Catherine. If so, he was a consummate actor, and carried his histrionics to extraordinary lengths. Or it may be, that, seeing his time so short, the old king repented of his malice towards Ferdinand, returned to a simple respect for the spirit of his engagements, and wished his son to repair his wrongs to Catherine. There is no way to be sure. Henry VII died as he had lived, ambiguous, enigmatic; in death his lips remained sardonic, his eyes veiled. He was a king who kept his secrets. But if Henry did repent, we must believe that there was someone on the council who meant to go on with his game, and who thought it would be useful to lie to Fuensalida.

On the other hand, the bland phrases of Henry VIII's letter to Margaret of Savoy are rather pat.[15] Few deathbeds are as pious or as edifying as those of princes must always be represented. And how does one explain to a lady whose chief characteristic is her family pride that one has suddenly jilted her niece? It was a situation not without its ticklish side, especially at a time when the new King's policy was to use his good relations with the Habsburgs to engineer a rapprochement between them and Ferdinand. If, in drafting the difficult letter to Eleanor's aunt, Henry and his council used a little diplomatic prevarication, we may be sure the cynical ghost of Henry VII would not have resented the liberty they took with his name.

What Catherine thought of her triumph, we can judge only by a brief note to her father, the curt announcement that the game was won. But we can be sure she felt the victory was hers alone. Hers, or God's rather, who would not desert Isabella's children. God had strengthened her heart, given her the courage to say that she would die in England but not give up this marriage. She had had no help from her father, who had accepted Fuensalida's frantic warnings, acquiesced in the transfer of her dowry to Flanders, and begun to prepare for war; she had had no help from his ambassador, or, as far as she knew, from anyone. The English had spied on her, lied to her, almost starved her. But she had endured through seven long years, endured in the face of humiliation and discouragement, endured when far wiser people were ready to give up the game. Endured and won. Later she would need to remember that endurance, that eventual triumph against all probability and all advice. Those seven years of widowhood, while she grew from a girl to a woman who had learned to fight her hardest battles alone, formed a durable core to Catherine's character, a core of iron self-reliance, lonely stubbornness, not without consequence to the history of England.

PART II
ENGLAND'S QUEEN
(1509–1527)

Chapter One

LATER CATHERINE might need to remember the lesson of her widowhood, but in that glorious springtime there was no need or leisure to remember. On May 10, 1509, the body of the old king was laid beside that of his wife in the vault beneath his unfinished chapel at Westminster, to dwell "more richly dead than he did alive in Richmond or any of his palaces," and as the last strains of the requiem died away, and the herald of the Garter cried *Vive Henry le huitiesme, Roy Dangliter*, a door seemed to clang for Catherine on the long, gloomy tunnel of the past. As soon as the funeral was over, they went, she and her youthful lover, to Greenwich, whose sunlit windows, pleached alleys, and broad lawns stretching down to the Thames were dear to Catherine ever after, and there, Henry's impatience having contained itself for quite six weeks, they were quietly married at the oratory of the Franciscan Observants just by the palace wall. It was time, for Henry was determined that his bride would share his coronation, set for Midsummer's Day, and to keep custom the King and Queen must lie the night before at the Tower. So the Londoners first saw their new Queen borne from the Tower to Westminster, sitting in a litter of cloth of gold slung between white palfreys, clad, herself, all in white satin, the costume of a virgin bride, with her gleaming hair "hanging down her back, of a very great length, beautiful and goodly to behold."

It is hard to imagine Henry and Catherine at their coronation. Their images are pale as ghosts beside their later selves, the strangely matched antagonists whose domestic quarrel stamped them indelibly in history: the Catherine Shakespeare wrote of, a dumpy, melancholy little woman without charm except for the low sweet voice and the unshakable dignity; the Henry Holbein painted, a terrifying tyrant, balancing a massive bull's torso on legs like pillars, the head thrown up in the bull's gesture of challenge and defiance, the heavy, bearded jowl, the self-indulgent mouth, the small predatory nose, the flat hawk's eyes gleaming with malice and alertness. That was not the Henry Catherine married. The body was already huge, towering above big-limbed courtiers, deep chested, with shoulders wide as a door, but it was an athlete's body, flat stomached and clean limbed, the body of an indefatigable dancer, tennis player, wrestler and horseman, magnificent in action and repose. The face above it was the face of an angelic adolescent, round apple-blossom cheeks, just touched with golden down, a crown of ruddy gold hair above features engagingly immature, reminding observers of a cherub in an Italian church. As for Catherine, old Sir John Russell remembered her as one who, when she was first Queen, was not easily paralleled for beauty. She was small and daintily made then, with a dancer's grace and rhythm of movement. Her portrait by Master Michiel Sittoz, taken in 1505, shows fine eyes, hair shot with golden lights, a fresh, delicate complexion, an expression full of sweetness and winsome dignity. The Londoners thought her bonny, so did the ambassadors and the court, Henry thought her bonnier than any. His letter to Ferdinand, replying to his new father-in-law's thanks and congratulations, boasts of his sincere love for her, sings the praises of her virtues, and winds up with the tribute: "If I were still free, I would choose her for wife before all others."[1]

Catherine was more restrained. "Among the many reasons that move me to love the King, my lord," she wrote her father tactfully, "the strongest is his filial love and obedience to Your Highness." But triumph and happiness shine through her formal phrases. Impossible not to be touched by the adoration of this magnificent youngster, who had laid his whole kingdom at her feet with a gesture out of the French romances. "The news here," she notes, "is

Henry VIII

that those kindnesses of Your Highness [it will not do to overemphasize the courtly Spanish phrases] are in great points, and entertain much love to the King, my lord, and to me. Our time is spent in continual festival."

In "continual festival" the new King opened his reign. Henry was like a boy just out of school. Since his mother's death his father's court had become very grim, as old Henry's humor had sunk deeper in sordid greed and unreasonable suspiciousness. Besides his father, only his grandmother, Margaret, Countess of Richmond, had charge of young Henry's upbringing, and, from what we know of her she was not likely to indulge overmuch the lighter side of a boy's nature. Even the jolly poet John Skelton, who had taught the infant Henry to spell, had been packed off to a rural parsonage lest he teach his pupil less seemly things. A series of graver instructors took his place, their supervision unrelieved by any such circle of young nobles as had formed a schoolboy court around Catherine's brother Juan. Perhaps isolation was meant to teach the Prince what his father had learned a harder way, that a King is always alone. But it was a dull life for a boy. As he studied and exercised alone in the center of a watchful ring of tutors and guards, or passed from them to the seclusion of that inner room, accessible only through his father's bedchamber, young Henry must have known hours of purest boredom.

Now suddenly the world was at his feet. He seemed to be in haste to recoup himself for the lost years of his boyhood. Brought up in a household that saved candle ends and turned its doublets, he would see the use of blazing lights, rich food, and gorgeous new clothes. Secluded in his teens amidst gray beards and wrinkles, with no more chance to talk to a girl than to an ambassador, he hastened to surround himself with reckless young men and lovely, laughing ladies, among whom he basked in a pleasant atmosphere of gregarious excitement. All his life had been planned for him along the rigid lines of duty; now he was free to plan for himself whatever pleasures he liked. And he knew what he liked.

that these kingdoms of Your Highness [it will not do to overemphasize the courtly Spanish phrase] are in great peace, and entertain much love to the King, my lord, and to me. Our time is spent in continual festival. . . ." [2]

In "continual festival" the new King opened his reign. Henry was like a boy just out of school. Since his mother's death, his father's court had become ever grimmer as old Henry's humor had sunk deeper in sordid greed and unreasonable suspiciousness. Besides his father, only his grandmother, Margaret, Countess of Richmond, had charge of young Henry's upbringing, and from what we know of her she was not likely to indulge overmuch the lighter side of a boy's nature. Even the jolly poet John Skelton, who had taught the infant Henry to spell, had been packed off to a rural parsonage lest he teach his pupil less seemly things. A series of graver instructors took his place, their supervision unrelieved by any such circle of young nobles as had formed a schoolboy court around Catherine's brother Juan. Perhaps isolation was meant to teach the Prince what his father had learned a harder way: that a king is always alone. But it was a dull life for a boy. As he studied and exercised, alone in the center of a watchful ring of tutors and guards, or passed from them to the seclusion of that inner room, accessible only through his father's bedchamber, young Henry must have known hours of purest boredom.

Now suddenly the world was at his feet. It would take him years to recoup himself for that boredom and that loneliness. Brought up in a household that saved candle ends, ate porridge and turned its doublets, he would never tire of blazing lights, rich food, and gorgeous new clothes. Secluded in his teens amidst graybeards and wrinkles, with no more chance to talk to a girl than to an ambassador, he hastened to surround himself with gay, reckless young men and lovely, laughing ladies, among whom he bustled in a pleasant stir of gregarious excitement. All his boyhood had been planned for him along the rigid lines of duty; now he was free to plan for himself whatever pleasures he liked. And he knew what he liked.

He stated his preference forthrightly in perhaps the earliest and certainly the best of the songs he wrote for his own lute and his own voice: —

Pastance with good company
I love and shall until I die
Grudge who will, but none deny,
So God be pleased this life will I
  For my pastance,
  Hunt, sing, and dance,
  My heart is set;
  All goodly sport
  To my comfort
  Who shall me let?

Youth will needs have dalliance,
Of good or ill some pastance;
Company me thinketh best
All thoughts and fancies to digest,
  For idleness
  Is chief mistress
  Of vices all;
  Then who can say
  But pass the day
  Is best of all?

Company with honesty
Is virtue — and vice to flee;
Company is good or ill
But every man hath his free will.
  The best I sue,
  The worst eschew;
  My mind shall be
  Virtue to use;
  Vice to refuse
  I shall use me.

Indeed they were innocent enough, these pastimes into which the young King threw himself with such defiant and tireless avidity. Hunt, sing and dance . . . who shall me let? Hunt from dawn till dark, dance from dark till dawn, feast five hundred persons and fill the night with music, build elaborate structures for a single entertainment and throw handfuls of money to the gaping populace, and no one at all to offer let or hindrance, though behind the King's back the older counselors might shrug and look down their noses as they counted the months old Henry's household could have lived on the cost of one of young Henry's sprees. But the well-stuffed treasury the father's parsimony had provided gave the illusion of illimitable wealth, and behind the deep filled chests were wide, well-administered crown estates whence flowed a steady revenue, and behind those again a loyal, prosperous land that was enjoying the contrast of an open-handed king. There was no occasion for serious protest.

Two sorts of pastimes Henry loved especially: tournaments, and masks, followed by dancing. Sometimes in the middle of a banquet the King and some of his companions would disappear, and presently a party of Turks or Moors or Germans in glittering disguise would intrude upon the company, with one towering, especially resplendent figure in their midst, demanding to dance with the ladies, and expecting to astonish them. Once when the court was at Greenwich, a party of masked outlaws, all in Kendal green, burst into the Queen's apartments, conveniently followed by a band of music. The Queen and her ladies, the chronicler assures us, were surprised and terrified by the invasion, but courteously danced with the outlaws instead of calling the guards, and were duly amazed and delighted when the King and his nobles unmasked. However often Henry metamorphosed himself in quaint and gaudy raiment, Catherine never disappointed him by suspecting that the gigantic Muscovite or wild man or Saracen was really her husband, or by failing to be completely surprised when he revealed himself. Catherine herself donned no disguises. Her part in these amusements was that of audience.

She was essential as audience, too, for the other sport in which Henry chiefly delighted, the tournament. In mimic combats, afoot or on horseback, he excelled all his subjects, and he was indefatigable in devising the pageantry with which this diversion was adorned. Sheathed extravagantly in German or Italian plate armor more cunningly jointed than a lobster's mail, fluted and braced and inlaid with gold, he would thunder down the lists on a magnificent stallion, the Duke of Mantua's gift, plumes flying, a very god of battles. One hears the splinter of lances and the roar of applause from the long, packed tribunes as some courtier acknowledged the superior prowess of his king. It was amazing good fun. Henry sometimes ran a dozen such courses in a morning and was ready for more exercise in the afternoon, combats on foot perhaps with blunted weapons. The huge frame cased in massive plate was as agile as if in smallclothes (refuting those Italian theorists who held that a knight should be of rather less than middle height or the weight of his armor would encumber him unduly); the powerful arm could swing the heaviest sword like a wand, and deal a blow with it that would stun an ox. And so, while less lucky contestants rubbed themselves ruefully, to supper with a hundred knights and ladies in costly attire and the Queen on his right, smiling and murmuring that there was none like him in the lists (indeed there was not) but he ought to be more careful, and not run such risks. There would be musicians in the gallery, and dancing after supper, and the King would dance on and on, long after the Queen had stopped to watch and rest, leading out lady after lady, and leaping and capering higher and more tirelessly than any of the carpet knights who had not sat a horse that day.

Let the psychologists murmur sourly of exhibitionism and the escape mechanisms of dressing up and playing at warfare. Male children of all ages, at all periods of history, have loved to dress up and to play games, and above all to triumph over their fellows, and have that triumph observed. At no period was the dressing up so gorgeous and so costly, at no period were the games so elaborate and so solemnly played as in this high noon of the Renaissance in which Henry and Catherine lived. Let us note only that Henry played at everything with an especial earnestness, with the wholehearted absorption of a child. There was not an ounce of malice or meanness apparent in that great body, not a hint of cunning or indirection. The arrogance and display, the generosity and selfishness, were all equally unself-conscious. The great laugh that echoes down to us from that old festivity is the hearty, carefree laugh of a schoolboy on a holiday.

ii

A youthful, holiday-minded court echoed the laughter. To be handsome, to wear fine clothes with an air, to be witty and affable and accomplished, to be lusty enough and gusty enough to keep pace – or try to keep pace – with the royal dancing and drinking and dressing up, the royal jousting and tennis and other rough sports, was a way, if not to fame and fortune, at least to the easy good graces of the King. For the first time in years pleasure as well as duty drew men about the King; the older nobility, and especially the younger scions of old houses, were in frequent attendance, and the new men, young squires from families new risen or new refurbished by a wealthy marriage, found, if their wits were sharp and their purses full, a welcome also. Courtenays and Nevilles and Staffords, Howards and Percys and Talbots, rubbed elbows with Comptons and Bryans and Boleyns and men of other names hitherto unknown to the court chroniclers. The landed families who ruled England began to feel drawn together in a unified society with a center and a leader.

It was saved, this court, from vulgarity, in spite of its mixed crowd, its boisterous revelry and naïve ostentation, by its genuine, youthful freshness, and its genuine regard for learning and the arts. The last and perhaps the greatest generation of English medieval craftsmen worked for it, side by side with artists from Italy and the Low Countries, and though much of their best talent was squandered on gawdy, perishable toys, what they have left is precious, and we have the word of foreign judges that the standard of taste which controlled them was not inferior to that in countries thought less barbarous. The English school of music bloomed, and Italian virtuosi hurried towards a land where excellence was rewarded with a fortune. The King himself was a passionate musician, played the organ and the virginals, was a master hand on the lute, and composed some charming pieces. He was a keen, discriminating, sometimes relentless critic of every kind of musical skill, capable of rewarding real talent with kingly generosity and a glowing enthusiasm that was almost better than gold, or of turning a bored shoulder on an indifferent performance, no matter how high the reputation of the performer. To get the best voices and the best masters for the children of his chapel was his constant care; to bring to his notice a new organist or a new composition worthy of his standards was a sure way to his favor.

At first the burly young men who thronged about the King wrote neither music nor verses, nor much of anything else save their names to the notes which city merchants cashed for them to help pay for new clothes and fine horses. Youths of breeding did not frequent the universities, or go much, as yet, to Italy, or find any tutors save in the bower and the tiltyard. Lord Mountjoy knew one bluff knight who would as soon see his son hanged as reading books, and Italian observers found the English nobility more given to dicing and drinking than to the beautiful letters which every Italian gentleman made at least a pretense of knowing. Lord Mountjoy, himself, the Queen's chamberlain and her chief friend among the barons, was singular in his friendship with humanists like Colet and Linacre, and his patronage of Erasmus. But the stir of learning was in the air. Warham, the Archbishop of Canterbury, encouraged scholars; so did Fox, the Bishop of Winchester. Lady Margaret, the King's grandmother, had been generous to the universities. In and about London, there were, Erasmus thought, at least half a dozen men who were the equals of any Italian in their command of the new learning. Soon there were to be more, and gathered more and more closely about the court.

For the King was on the side of the scholars. Thomas More, the brightest genius among the younger English humanists, who had been so discouraged in the last year of the old king's reign that he was thinking of leaving England, abandoned the idea, to greet the new king and his bride with a volley of Latin verses. Lord Mountjoy wrote to Italy to the rising chieftain of the northern humanists: —

O, my Erasmus, if you could see how the world here is rejoicing in the possession of so great a prince, how his life is all their desire, you could not contain yourself for joy. Avarice is expelled from the land, liberality scatters riches with a bounteous hand, our King does not desire gold nor gems, but virtue, glory, immortality. The other day he said to me, "I wish I were more learned than I am." "That is not what we expect of your Grace," I replied, "but that you should foster and encourage learned men." "Yea, surely," said he, "for without them we should scarcely exist at all." What more splendid saying could fall from the lips of a prince? [3]

What indeed? It was just what the humanists had been telling princes for a century, and finding, as a rule, no more than very qualified agreement. Such sentiments, combined with a noble scorn for gold and gems, formed a conjunction too rare to be overlooked. Erasmus packed his saddlebags for England. And though Erasmus was to find that very little of the lifegiving golden flood which

Henry tipped out of his father's treasury overflowed as far as the parched fields of Apollo, even that trickle was enough to nourish a new crop.

If the tireless, versatile, young King was the center of all this bustling life in England, its center and focus for Henry was Catherine, the chief trophy of his new reign, the necessary audience for all his triumphs. He defied custom by wearing her favors in the lists, by inventing allegorical devices and high-sounding pseudonyms to proclaim his utter devotion to her, by accepting the meed of his prowess only at her hands. He was always seeking her out to show off a new present or a new musician, or to share with her the latest book from Italy or the latest budget of news from his ambassadors. "The Queen must hear this" or "This will please the Queen" were often on his lips. All the entertainments he delighted in devising were duly set down in the accounts as "for the Queen's pleasure." No doubt he thought they were. It would not be odd if the princess he had rescued and set upon his throne was Henry's first love; if he never felt for any other person in his life a deeper or more lasting emotion.

At ease at the center of the court, Catherine fulfilled and complemented all the King's tastes. Her tranquil grace was the best foil to his exuberance, her effortless dignity the right touch in the center of his flamboyant effects. And she had a natural buoyance and high spirits of her own, and in the first flush of her victory almost an equal relish for entertainment and magnificence. She loved jewels and fine dresses and rich blazing colors, and to have everything about her seemly, her women the prettiest and best dressed, her liveries and hangings the most splendid, her service the neatest and best ordered. She loved music and dancing as much as Henry did himself, and her skill in both was almost as notable as his. She was passionately fond of hawking, and – though she could not always keep pace with her husband's mad gallops – she rode fearlessly and well. She bore a merry part in all his prankish entertainments, and managed, besides, to draw about her a circle of the older families, links with the great past and her especial friends, who gave the court a tone it might otherwise have lacked.

She shared, too, tastes of her husband's into which few of his courtiers could enter. Like Henry she was an eager reader of devotional and theological books, and she had an equally meticulous piety. If her humanistic education of late years had been less strenuous than Henry's, she had had a better start, and tutors at least as good, and the seclusion of Durham House, where one of her few extravagances had been for books, had given her much time for reading. She was at least as quick as Henry to appreciate the new learning; in the early days she and her chamberlain, Mountjoy, must have been almost the only persons not ecclesiastics to whom Henry could talk of it. Her influence, as much as Henry's, drew more and more humanists around them.

In addition, she was the only person in those first years to whom Henry could talk freely about kingcraft. On his accession Henry had been wise enough – or perhaps merely diffident enough – to keep the courts of pleasure separate from the courts of business, retaining most of the old council. William Warham, Archbishop of Canterbury, and Richard Fox, Bishop of Winchester, led the churchmen on it, with Nicholas West and Thomas Ruthall their industrious seconds. Thomas Howard, Earl of Surrey, and George Talbot, Earl of Shrewsbury, were the chief barons, supported by such tried administrators as Sir Edward Poynings, of Irish fame, now Controller of the Household and Warden of the Cinque Ports, Sir Thomas Lovell, and Sir Harry Marney. The last three had fought beside Henry Tudor at Bosworth, and all, laymen and ecclesiastics, had been props of his throne and sturdy wheel horses of his government. But young Henry was not comfortable with them. He could no more share their thoughts and views than he could their memories of the blood-stained, uncertain days when Richard of York was king, or of the rebellions that had shaken his father's throne before he was born. Of them all he trusted most Richard Fox, perhaps because that wily prelate had the reputation of having been Catherine's partisan on his father's council, perhaps merely because the Bishop of Winchester was the ablest and the most assiduous; but even of Winchester Henry could say that he trusted to his peril one whom everyone thought so well-named Fox.

Henry needed, however, to trust someone. Behind his bluster there was still the timidity, the uncertainty of a boy who has seen little of the world, who wants to be reassured, to be encouraged, to be told delicately and tactfully what he ought to do next. He never quite outgrew the need for someone to lean on, some affectionate, admiring mentor and guide to protect his self-esteem, and help him to his desires, someone who, living only for him, would enhance his sense of life and still his inner doubts. He was to turn to one such image after another for most of his life, only to fling away from each in outraged indignation when he found the image had a life of its own. That was a great part of his tragedy.

In the first flush of his kingship he found Catherine, and for a while it seemed the quest might end at its beginning. From the guarded eyes and careful tongues of his father's councilors, who met his every wish with bland agreement while they measured the strength of this young whelp they would have to manage, he turned to the quiet, wise, admiring wife to whom he could pour out his whole heart. To confide in Catherine compromised neither his dignity nor his independence; her womanly dependence appealed to his boastful young strength, her inner strength complemented his secret weakness.

Catherine accepted the responsibility as a matter of course. She had a clear, level head, never much troubled by any sort of doubt. In the seven years of her widowhood she had learned to rely on herself, make her own decisions, keep her own counsel. She had always had the same exalted views of royalty as her husband, and her early education had stressed the duties even more than the prerogatives of kings. She had acquired by hard experience a sort of competence in business, and a habit of making prompt, definite decisions. Even before her marriage, when the old Countess of Richmond fell ill and some member of the royal family had to attend to details of the funeral and the coronation, Catherine had calmly added these preoccupations to her own. She worked over the lists of the King's suite and of her own, on which the names of her friends at Ludlow naturally appeared. After her marriage she continued to keep under her hand a great part of that business of the royal household which was so inextricably entangled with the government of England. More and more the young King found in those first months that her realism and practicality, her knowledge of affairs and placid confidence, could be relied on to smooth his path. And she did everything so unobtrusively and tactfully that it was just as if he were doing it himself.

iii

The best evidence of her unobtrusive tact is in the field of foreign affairs. When Catherine married Henry she was her father's accredited ambassador at the English court, as much trusted as Ferdinand ever trusted anyone, possessing from his confidential letters and instructions a certain insight into his real views, his immediate aims. For five years after her marriage Catherine continued to be the real ambassador of Spain in England, the real agent on the ground of Spanish policy, and all that time the government of Henry VIII followed with almost comical precision the steps laid down for it in Spain. Yet, though one or two of the shrewder members of the English council and the watchful Venetian ambassador had some inkling of the real extent of Catherine's influence, it was exerted with so little ostentation that even the official Spanish ambassador who arrived early in 1510 was largely unaware of it, and one is inclined to wonder how much of it Henry himself suspected.

Catherine's chief task was made easier by the simplicity of her husband's views. Henry had no doubt that a king of England was bound to reconquer France, his rightful heritage, usurped for the moment by the house of Valois. It was a notion born of youthful brooding on the past glories of Cressy and Agincourt, and of unlimited youthful ambition, self-confidence, and ignorance. France was a powerful nation of perhaps twenty million people, prosperous, united, bristling with fortresses, ruled by a king whose absolute power to tax made him the richest and hence the strongest monarch in Europe, commander of a veteran professional army, so formidable that it took the combined strength of the rest of Europe to keep it from overrunning Italy. England was a little island with less than four million people, whose only military experience in the past sixty years had been acquired largely in fighting each other, so that while the art of war in Europe had been revolutionized, and continental armies were composed now of trained professionals who won their successes by combinations of heavy cavalry, artillery, and disciplined infantry equipped in part with firearms, the only army that could be raised in England was still a feudal militia, armed, as their grandfathers had been, with bows and arrows, and probably less efficient than the archers of Agincourt. The English had no guns or gunners worth mentioning, and had ceased to have any heavy cavalry fit for foreign service. In all his reign Henry VIII did little to modernize his archaic levies; he left England's armies farther out of date than he had found them. Yet those who, in view of the obvious disparity of forces, conclude that Henry could not have thought of conquering France, credit the King with more realism than he showed. The dream of Agincourt obsessed him for years; he abandoned it only when his domestic involvements had made any sort of foreign adventure unsafe, and then only partially and reluctantly. It was hard for Englishmen to realize that the Hundred Years' War was irrevocably over.

This romantic obtuseness inspired the first act of Henry's reign, the harangue calling for a European coalition against France which, when Ruthall read it to him, had so staggered Fuensalida. Its purport proved to suit exactly the views of Fuensalida's master. The King of Aragon was the ally of the King of France, but he did not intend to remain so long. At Cambrai, just as Henry VII lay dying, the European powers had agreed to put aside their quarrels long enough to combine in despoiling the weak, wealthy Republic of Venice. In the summer of 1509 French armies were overrunning the Venetian mainland. But Ferdinand, though willing to let Louis XII do the lion's share of the fighting, meant to cheat him again out of the lion's share of the spoil, just as he had done over the partition of Naples. Once his own pockets were lined, the King of Aragon would be ready to abet Pope Julius II's change of sides, and encourage the Pope's effort to drive the French barbarians back across the Alps. Then, while the French were busy in Italy, he would help himself to the little, neutral, French-protected Kingdom of Navarre. In this realistic plot, England had its place.

Without knowing all her father's purpose, Catherine was ready to encourage her husband's hostility towards the Valois. England had not been included in the league formed against Venice at Cambrai. Under Catherine's tutelage Henry VIII discovered that England and Venice were old allies, and that England had a vital interest in the preservation of Venetian independence. As the last Venetian posts in Naples surrendered to Ferdinand, the Venetians began to be aware of English sympathy, the first encouraging sign they had found in a hostile Europe. English diplomats were instructed to explain to the Pope, to the Habsburgs, to anybody who would listen to them, that the destruction of the Venetian Republic would be a catastrophe to Christendom and that the overweening power of France should be checked. Thus, without compromising himself prematurely, Ferdinand was able to advance his schemes under the cover of English diplomacy.[4]

The King of England was as mettlesome as a young colt – a description Ferdinand frequently applied to him behind his back – and breaking him to diplomatic harness was a delicate task. If he bolted out of hand, and scared the French too badly with his bellicose antics, they would come to terms with Venice and prepare to defend themselves. Therefore Ferdinand warned his daughter that the greatest care must be taken not to arouse French suspicions before an unpleasant surprise had been prepared for them. The warning did not come too soon. At his first interview with the French ambassador, Henry listened to the Frenchman's suave opening phrases with a face like a thundercloud. "I ask the King of France for peace?" he had broken in. "I ask for peace?" he shouted at his embarrassed councilors. "Who dares to say so?" But someone calmed him down. Someone explained to him the place of guile in the game of power. He let his councilors negotiate a treaty of peace and intercourse with France. This stroke of diplomacy in Ferdinand's own vein pleased the pro-French party in Henry's council, secured solid advantages in trade, insured the payment of the next installment of the "indemnity," the blackmail which France paid England for peace, and best of all it lulled the suspicions of Louis XII. Meanwhile Henry VIII was collecting arms and mustering men, the lines of a grand alliance against France were being formed, and Anglo-Spanish co-operation was growing into reality under Catherine's competent direction. When Ferdinand's new ambassador arrived in London,[5] most of his work had been done in advance.

Not that the magnificent Don Luis Caroz ever suspected his indebtedness to the Queen of England. Ferdinand had sent to Henry's court a nobleman who would spend his own money in making a show there for the honor of Spain. He did not have to look about for a nobleman with both wealth and brains; he already had a representative in Henry's household who would do all the thinking necessary. Caroz was intended to impress the English with the splendor of his suite, and exerted himself so strenuously that even amid the glitter of that splendid court he usually wins separate mention from the chroniclers. He impressed himself with his own cleverness without a struggle. He wrote Ferdinand stirring accounts of the obstacles he had overcome, and the cunning with which he had twisted the English to his purpose. He was too much of a tyro to notice that difficulties which normally would have taken months to unravel became straight and smooth at a touch. He was not even surprised that the tentative draft of the treaty of alliance which the English councilors showed him at their first meeting, corresponded in every important particular with the terms for which Ferdinand had instructed him to ask.

Why should it not? Catherine had spent months of patient toil upon it. She had been in close touch with her father about every paragraph. Before Caroz had even sailed from Spain, she had sent Ferdinand an outline of the best terms she thought the English could be induced to offer. That was the paper Caroz carried with him.

Ferdinand had not enlightened Caroz as to the identity of the real Spanish ambassador in England, and Catherine did not think it necessary to explain. She had more serious preoccupations. The first duty of a queen was to bear children. Within a few months of her marriage, Catherine was pregnant. The birth of an heir to the English throne, born to Catherine and Henry, would, in the dynastic politics of the century, consolidate Anglo-Spanish friendship more surely than any treaty. The same post that told Ferdinand the treaty was signed brought him also a short note from his daughter. Some time before its signing she had been delivered of a baby girl, born dead. The juxtaposition of the signed treaty and the stillborn child was an ill omen.

Catherine's first diplomatic triumph and her first domestic misfortune both came in the early months of 1510. Not long after the news of the signing of the treaty on May 24 Ferdinand heard that his daughter was again pregnant. On New Year's Day, 1511, while the war with France was still hanging fire, waiting for Ferdinand to be ready to support the Pope, who had already attacked the French, Catherine's second child was born. This time the infant was a boy, alive and apparently healthy. Guns boomed from the Tower; joy bells pealed; the streets of London blazed with bonfires and ran with wine; couriers dashed off to announce the King's good fortune to all Christendom. Henry's subjects rejoiced with him that the continuance of the dynasty was assured and the kingdom would be spared the threat of the civil strife that would surely engulf it should anything happen to the only male Tudor. For weeks the court had been astir with preparations; now Richmond palace blossomed in new hangings and fresh ornaments. With the greatest possible splendor, the most moving ceremony, the infant was christened Henry. Twelfth Night passed; the King, too impatient to stay until his wife could leave her bed, rode to Walsingham to offer to Our Lady there his thanks and that of his people; then, when Catherine could rise, the whole court moved to Westminster where a tournament, intended to surpass anything the reign had yet seen, celebrated the birth of Henry's son. The Queen, the diplomatic corps, all the nobility were in the tribunes, and the King himself was chief of the defenders in the jousting, entering in a pavilion sprinkled with golden H's and K's, and announced, by way of compliment to the Queen, as "Sir Loyal Heart." Nothing marred the merrymaking, not even the fact that the rude people broke into the festivities before they were ended and rent, tore, and spoiled the pageant by snatching the gold letters from the spangled cloth; and later, when Henry offered to the company the golden ornaments on his own clothes, mobbed him also, stripped him to his doublet and hose, stripped one of his courtiers who tried to get away to a less decent state, and ripped the gold lace from the ladies' dresses, until the King was obliged to call the guards, and the laughing beef-eaters thrust the cockneys out of doors with the butts of their halberds. A tattered court sat down to supper, but the King's high spirits and the Queen's amusement "turned all these hurts to laughing and game." On so happy an occasion Henry would have given the shirt off his back "for honor and largess." But as the court feasted, the baby at Richmond was fighting for its breath. The nobles who had come for the tournament remained to bury a royal child who had lived just fifty-two days in an uncertain world.[6]

The baby's death was a terrible blow to both parents, a terrible blow to the nation. Henry was so grief-stricken that ambassadors dared not even offer their condolences. For the first time fate had struck at him, hard, and he could not altogether understand it. Nor could Catherine, though she asked enlightenment through many weary hours on her knees. Yet the fatality was only too common in those days, in every walk of life. We have no means of knowing what infant mortality was among the lower classes in the sixteenth century; only that it must have been appalling. Among the royalty and aristocracy, it has been estimated, of every five children born alive at least two failed to live out their first year, and at least one more died before reaching maturity. The figure is probably conservative. Of the eight children of Henry VII and Elizabeth only three survived their parents. Isabella not unluckier than most queens reared five, but lost at least five others by stillbirth, late miscarriage, or death in early infancy, and saw two of the five who passed childhood die in youth.

Henry had seemed more deeply sunk in grief than Catherine; he rebounded more quickly to the surface. Vain regret was never a thing on which Henry wasted much time. He left the Queen still kneeling in her chapel while he busied himself with ships and armaments and fresh amusements. He and Catherine were both young. Next time the child would live.

iv

Don Luis Caroz, the King of Aragon's magnificent ambassador, made up for his negligent and unprofessional accounts of diplomatic negotiations by the avidity with which he collected scraps of court gossip. In his infrequent letters, sandwiched between his complaints of the terrible expensiveness of the English court and his complacent references to the figure he was cutting there, are anecdotes in which he let it appear that Ferdinand's daughter was behaving unwisely and would be better off if she took his advice. In particular, Caroz thought, Catherine let her confessor, the Franciscan friar, Diego Fernandez, exercise far too much influence in her household. Like Fuensalida, Caroz had a low opinion of the friar, a vulgar, meddlesome fellow. It was Fray Diego, Caroz thought, who kept the Spanish ambassador from seeing the Queen as often as he would have liked. Fray Diego's word was Catherine's law, he intimated, and Fray Diego even interfered between husband and wife. Caroz hinted at no graver impropriety, but his letters display an oddly feminine anxiety about the minutiae of Catherine's connubial conduct, an anxiety not unmixed with a curious cattiness.

The explanation appears when we learn that Don Luis Caroz' chief informant was a young woman not actually attached at the moment to the court, though devoted to the person of the Queen, a lady of many virtues, the wife of the Italian banker, Grimaldi. This would be Fray Diego's old enemy, Francesca de Carceres, who had already got one Spanish ambassador into trouble and was now intriguing with another. Francesca's purpose was simple. By the narrowest of margins, for want of the patience to endure two scant months more, she had lost the glories of her mistress's marriage and all the subsequent merrymaking. Had she held out a little longer she might have married one of the greatest lords in England instead of an elderly moneylender. Even now, she imagined, were it not for Fray Diego she might win back the Queen's affection. And Catherine's affection, or at least tolerance, some corner of the splendor she had missed, was what Francesca wanted most in the world. She never got it. She had charm and plausibility, and was apparently an indefatigable schemer. But though she subjugated Caroz completely, though Fray Diego was finally sent back to Spain, though she later enlisted no less an advocate than Margaret of Austria, Catherine's former sister-in-law, in her cause, Catherine never took her back. Catherine rarely trusted a second time where she felt she had been once betrayed.

One morsel of gossip which Francesca de Carceres fed to Don Luis Caroz concerned two sisters of the Duke of Buckingham, both married and both young. One sister was a great favorite of the Queen's; the other was being courted by the King's boon companion, Compton. But gossip said that Compton was only a stalking horse for the King himself. Whether out of loyalty to her Queen or to her family, the elder sister alarmed her brother, who surprised the gallant Compton in the younger's chamber. Buckingham was furious. Women of the Stafford family were no game for Comptons, no, nor for Tudors either. He would see that his careless sister had time to meditate her folly away from the temptations of the court, and that very night the lady's husband hustled her off as if in flight, hardly pausing until he had her in the safety of a convent some sixty miles away. Meanwhile Compton had gone straight to Henry, and Henry had sent for Buckingham, and broken on him such a storm of wrath that the Duke had rushed out of the presence exclaiming that he would not pass another night under the palace roof. Next morning Henry abruptly ordered the Queen to dismiss from her suite the elder Stafford sister, whose gossip had precipitated the scandal, and Catherine sulkily complied. Members of the older families looked daggers at the upstarts who backed Compton and the King, and it was obvious to all that Catherine and Henry had had a furious quarrel.[7]

Most of the story seems probable enough. A young man in

Henry's position may be expected to have a roving eye. If Catherine made a scene over this affair, that was the only one for such a cause recorded in the first eighteen years of their marriage. But there is no doubt that, like other queens, she had to learn to shut her eyes to royal infidelities. In fact, the honeymoon was over. Catherine's business in life was to bear children. During the first nine years of her marriage Catherine ended one pregnancy only to begin another. Naturally her intimate association with her husband was interrupted for long periods. Naturally, Henry turned to other pastimes, other company, other women. It was the custom of the time. Catherine's own father had begotten and acknowledged several bastards during Isabella's lifetime. Every king, practically every member of the ruling feudal aristocracy anywhere in Europe, took mistresses. Marital fidelity was not expected – or rather it was differently interpreted. According to the standards of the age, Henry was an unusually faithful husband. Caroz' story has no sequel for the first four years of Henry's marriage. Thereafter, if he now and then amused himself with casual lights of love, no one, Catherine least of all, did anything to draw attention to the lapse. Henry, for his part, continued to treat his wife with every mark of tenderness and respect. That was the most that could be expected of a king.

Indeed, Henry did more than could be expected. Custom did not require him to link Catherine's initials with his own in every corner of his apartments and on every sleeve he wore, to receive ambassadors by preference in her chamber, to run to her with every new announcement, every new toy, to wear her colors always in the lists, and proclaim himself to Europe as the Knight of the Loyal Heart. No doubt these were his ways of telling her that whoever might take his fancy, she had his heart and his trust. For her part, though she began to drop out a little from some of his tireless rollicking, Catherine was still much by his side, gracing his most splendid feasts, loyally applauding his pasteboard triumphs.

Chapter Two

SOMEWHERE in the background of those triumphs, inconspicuous at first, but always edging nearer the King, the burly figure of a clerk begins to shoulder forward into history: Master Thomas Wolsey, the King's Almoner. The new reign was beginning to find the new men to suit it, and in Master Thomas, the King was beginning to realize, he had a man in a million. It was true Thomas Wolsey was a vulgarian; his father, men said, had been a butcher at Ipswich, but he had proved himself at Oxford a notable scholar and the tonsure should make all men equal. When one listened to his honeyed voice, one forgot, in admiration of the clearly ordered sentences, the common accent and the coarse red face. Sitting as a judge in the King's cases no one reasoned more subtly and precisely, or with a greater command of all the intricacies of the law; no one decided more frequently and firmly in the interests of the crown. At the council table, to which he had been recently admitted, others might raise objections or see difficulties or lose themselves in a maze of alternatives; Master Thomas only wanted to know one thing: what was the King's will? That declared, Master Thomas would undertake to carry it out, and the most obstinate barriers dissolved at his firm touch. Let the labor be his – such men as he existed for labor, as kings existed to command. Henry was delighted to find a counselor whose notion of royal duties was so clear and definite, who never burdened him with details or demanded his attention for long at a time, who never lacked an expedient, and for whom no business was too troublesome or too exacting. Master Thomas could be trusted for anything, and the more that was entrusted to Master Thomas, the more time the King had for his own amusements.

As for Master Thomas, himself, his whole being turned with a kind of tropism towards the power that radiated from the throne. He had known penury and the rebuffs which the well-born reserve for poor men's sons; he had been a tutor at Oxford and a chaplain in a gentleman's household; he had changed his patrons more than once, and found his feet slipping on the upward climb, before he had secured a royal chaplaincy and finally managed to take the notice of the old king. Now in the new reign he was rising fast. The new royal absolutism had need of such men as Wolsey. The great nobles on the royal council had always their own interests to consider, and loyalties to their caste and family and position; the older style churchmen could be more safely trusted with power, but even they thought sometimes of the Pope, and sometimes of the Church, and sometimes even of their Maker. But Master Thomas, whose grandfather might have been a serf, and who could see in the King's service endless perspective of power, was ready to give the King such a single devotion as a saint might give to God.

Such devotion could have none of those doubts about the war with France which troubled Archbishop Warham, and Poynings and Lovell and even Wolsey's immediate chief, Bishop Fox. Master Thomas was glad to be busy with details of musters and armaments, and with whatever matters of high policy Fox would trust him with, welcoming the chance to prove himself as competent at war as at every other department of government, particularly since such activity would win him the approval of the Queen. When Don Luis Caroz rashly reposed confidence in an Italian rascal, Giralmo Bonvisi, Wolsey's alertness rescued the ambassador from the worst consequences of his folly and saved the alliance with Spain from shipwreck or premature exposure. When a document had to be drafted, or a ship provisioned, or a special courier dispatched, Master Thomas was always ready to add the task to his other occupations. Catherine could congratulate herself on one able and resourceful, if humble, ally in pushing forward the alliance and the war.

ii

Henry chafed to begin his conquest of France. All through 1511 he waited impatiently for his father-in-law to be ready, giving tokens of his martial ardor by sending some archers to annoy the French in Flanders and others to help Ferdinand against the Moors. At last, in November, Ferdinand gave the signal for Don Luis Caroz to sign a treaty for the joint invasion by English and Spanish troops of Gascony the following spring. Lest any of Henry's council should think the Basque frontier an odd starting point for the conquest of France, Ferdinand pointed out that England had an excellent claim to the adjacent duchy of Guienne, and solemnly assured his daughter that the citizens of Bordeaux yearned to resume the English yoke which they had cast off some sixty years before. He did not tell her that he was going to snatch the undefended neutral kingdom of Navarre, and wanted an English army to hold the French at bay while he made off with spoils. When Catherine passed her father's arguments on to Henry, he accepted them without suspicion. So far he had learned his geography and politics mostly out of Froissart and Malory. It did not surprise him that the Aquitanians preferred him to the King of France. If France was to be conquered, the great point was to begin at once; Ferdinand might know best where.

July, 1512, therefore, saw ten thousand English archers sweltering in idleness at San Sebastian between the mountains and the Bay of Biscay, while beyond the shallow Bidassoa puzzled parties of French horse scouted cautiously, and more and more French troops, iron clumps of lances, quick-stepping regiments of Gascon infantry, sweating columns of gunners with their long, wicked-looking bronze guns, concentrated at Bayonne. Meanwhile, off to the right, the reinforcements for which the English were waiting, seventeen thousand Spanish horse, foot, and artillery, under the Duke of Alva, had turned aside and were streaming up through the valleys of the Pyrenees into the little saddlebag kingdom of Navarre. The Navarrese, having relied for safety on their declared neutrality, and on treaties with both belligerents, could offer only an unorganized show of resistance. They called loudly on the French for aid, but the French commander clearly could not uncover Bayonne or divide his forces while an English army of unknown strength and intentions lay directly in front of him, nor could he risk attacking the English while the Spaniards were on his flank.

The English commander, the Marquess of Dorset, was as puzzled as his adversary. He had no cavalry, not even any draft animals or enough mounts for the gentlemen of his command. He had no artillery worth mentioning. When he asked when he might expect the reinforcements and supplies he needed, the cavalry and guns without which it would be madness to advance on Bayonne as he had been ordered to do, Alva replied only by suggesting that the English make themselves useful by helping chase the Navarrese out of their mountains. In San Sebastian the idle English clamored for the blood of Frenchmen, and swigged the potent, harsh red wine of the country as if it were Kentish ale. In three months their sole exploits were the ferocious sack of one undefended French town, and a series of unlicensed raids on the villages of their allies, raids which so exasperated the tough Basque mountaineers that they began to cut the throats of any straying Englishmen, and to intercept the infrequent mule trains of supplies. By September the English army was rotten with fever, dysentery, and insubordination, and clamoring to go home. The Marquess of Dorset, a worthy gentleman, whose chief qualification for high command was his illustrious birth, wrote piteously to Henry, who promptly sent a herald to tell the whole army that they must winter in Spain. But the army was sick of foreign countries, of garlic and hot wines, fleas and Spaniards. Why should they perish of the flux in this God-forsaken land to please the King of Aragon, they asked each other. They shouted down the herald, and crowded about their leaders, crying, "Home! Home!" Since the men were obviously going home, their officers, glad to escape from the riot with their lives, went with them.[1]

From the English point of view, the campaign was unmitigated disaster. To the loss of two thousand men by disease and two hundred thousand ducats wasted was added the unprecedented public scandal of the unrepressed mutiny of an entire army, practically in the face of the enemy. Henry's shame and humiliation were spectacular. In May he had watched the embarcation of this force at Southampton, and written to his ambassadors abroad that he had never seen a finer army. In December, as the ragged scarecrows straggled off their hired transports, he was ready to improvise gallows enough to hang the lot of them, their officers first and highest.

From the Spanish point of view the campaign had gone splendidly. While Dorset's army had immobilized the French, Ferdinand had taken possession of Navarre with a minimum of fighting and expense. The subsequent mutiny had relieved him of the presence of unwelcome guests, and freed him from his promise to undertake a doubtful and profitless invasion. He could have afforded to be generous. Instead he chose to rub salt into his son-in-law's smarting wounds. He sent two special envoys to complain that Dorset's army, which had lain idle all summer while the Spanish did the rough work of securing their flank, had stampeded at the moment the main operations were to begin, thus preventing the conquest of Guienne. Under the circumstances, Ferdinand said, he had been obliged to conclude a six months' truce with France for fear the French would invade England, which such troops could hardly be relied on to defend. He would not, Ferdinand assured Henry, consent to consider Dorset's disgraceful performance characteristic of English valor; no doubt, in time, if properly led and properly equipped, the English might yet make soldiers not inferior to those of other nations; but for the present he must refuse to have any more of them in Spain. If Henry still wanted Guienne, he, Ferdinand, would conquer it for him, provided England would contribute the pay for ten thousand German mercenaries. No series of taunts and insults could have been better calculated to find the tenderest spots in Henry's vanity.[2]

Ferdinand could afford to behave as if he were sure of his hold on his son-in-law. Catherine accepted her father's version of the 1512 campaign at its face value, and saw to it that her husband accepted it too. She interceded to prevent Henry from hanging Dorset and his captains – she had many friends among them, and such summary vengeance would have had a bad effect in England – and persuaded her husband that the best way to wipe out the disgrace at San Sebastian would be to show that England was still to be feared. She even managed it so that Ferdinand's most impudent suggestion, English payment for ten thousand German mercenaries on the Pyrenees frontier, appeared as a spontaneous offer on Henry's part, an amends for Dorset's misconduct. Ferdinand's special envoys, for their part, showed that they knew who was handling the interests of Aragon in England. Ignoring Don Luis Caroz, they went straight to Catherine for instructions, followed the steps she had planned, and found their path marvelously smooth. Giustiniani, the shrewd Venetian ambassador, also knew the secret of Spanish influence. The disaster at San Sebastian, which many people did not hesitate to attribute to Ferdinand's deliberate treachery, had emboldened the peace party on the King's council, a party led by Warham, Archbishop of Canterbury, and including most of the older and more experienced officials. But Giustiniani wrote that as long as the Queen was for war, war it would be.[3]

War it was. On the terms that Ferdinand's envoys brought, a new treaty was drawn up, providing that Ferdinand, aided by a subsidy of a hundred thousand English crowns, was to invade Guienne and keep the seas as far as Finisterre, while an English fleet swept the Channel, and an English army, commanded by Henry in person, issued from Calais to duplicate the feat of Agincourt. Once diplomatic preliminaries were out of the way, Catherine plunged into the details of war, interviewing the Venetian ambassador herself about hiring galleys to strengthen the Channel fleet, checking over muster rolls and lists of camp equipment with the indispensable Thomas Wolsey. But while she fulfilled efficiently the role her father had designed for her, she was far from knowing all his mind. All over Europe Ferdinand's ambassadors were clamoring for a grand alliance to crush the French. Meanwhile a Spanish friar was discussing peace terms with Louis XII at Blois.

Ferdinand played that game like a master. He used what his daughter wrote him about English plans to frighten the French into increasing their offers for peace, and then used hints of what the French offered to stir up Henry to increase his bid for war. With Henry's new offers he went back to the French and raised his price again. The goings and comings across the frontier alarmed the English ambassador in Spain, but how could Henry believe his warnings when Catherine was so confident of her father's good faith, and Caroz so eager to sign the treaty for the joint attack on France? On April 18, 1513, Don Luis solemnly swore to the treaty in a public ceremony at London. But on April 1 – appropriate date – Ferdinand's commissioners and those of Louis XII had already signed at Orthez in the Pyrenees a complete truce for one year, excepting only the endless war in Italy. Ferdinand virtuously included his son-in-law.[4]

When Ferdinand's desertion was known, the whole brunt of English rage and indignation fell on Don Luis Caroz. Ferdinand wrote to everyone concerned in strains of outraged pathos. His incompetent ambassador had put him in the position, he protested, of appearing to break his royal word. After this unbelievable misunderstanding, who, he asked sadly, would believe him again? Caroz had misinformed him about negotiations in England, and misinformed the English about affairs in Spain. Caroz had mistaken his instructions and exceeded his powers. Caroz had betrayed two honorable kings, but with Christian forgiveness Ferdinand conceded that he might have done so through ignorance rather than through malice. The bewildered ambassador, convinced by the universal storm of condemnation that he really had been at fault, was grateful to Henry and Catherine for preserving his life from the infuriated English nobles, and apologized abjectly to everybody, to Fox, to Catherine, to Henry, to Ferdinand – especially and repeatedly to Ferdinand. Ferdinand finally forgave him and continued him at his post. A dupe of his proportions could still be useful in England.

Catherine also was bewildered, but loyal. She was so used to understanding her father at half a word that perhaps this time she really had misunderstood. She had worked quite independently of Caroz, relying on hints and veiled messages, intelligently anticipating her father's wishes. She had not even seen most of Caroz' correspondence. It was easier to believe that Caroz had been stupid than that her father had been false, and she urged this view upon Henry and made the best of all Ferdinand's excuses, his promise to press the French hard in Italy where he was still at war with them, his good wishes for the coming campaign, his promise to conquer Guienne for Henry next year. Henry agreed to accept Ferdinand's explanation, and carry on for the present without him. That was what his father-in-law wanted. He had duped Henry twice, and meant to dupe him again.

iii

There was no leisure in England that spring to abuse Caroz properly; everybody was too absorbed in the final plans for the invasion of France. Henry himself was going at the head of his army, with a forest of gold-embroidered tents, a wardrobe of suits of armor, a stable full of magnificent horses. With him were going all his glittering young men, Brandon and Compton and Bryan and the rest, and his faithful almoner and familiar shadow, Thomas Wolsey, into whose capable hands had somehow fallen all the real management of this war. Herbert and Shrewsbury and that grim old captain Sir Rhys ap Thomas were already in France with fourteen thousand men, and most of the nobility and gentry who were not with them were going with the King and the main army. So in the last days of June, Catherine accompanied Henry by slow journeys to the sea, and Kentish roads were gay with the new green and white liveries of his yeomen of the guard and the nodding plumes of his untried knights as the procession moved to Dover where four hundred ships waited to convey their sovereign to the scene of his prospective victories. Not for more than a hundred years had such a host sailed from an English port. Henry V had led to Agincourt a force less than half as numerous and incomparably less gaily dressed. No one would set a limit to the triumphs which might be expected.

On Dover strand Henry had Catherine proclaimed Governor of the Realm and captain-general of the forces for home defense. A skeleton council headed by the Archbishop of Canterbury and old Sir Thomas Lovell were left to advise her, and the seventy-year-old Earl of Surrey, choking with rage and grief at missing the triumphs in France, was ordered to remain to guard the north. As Catherine rode back to Greenwich between Lovell and Surrey, perhaps she felt proud to have been trusted with unprecedented powers in her regency; perhaps she only reflected that all her subjects seemed to have tonsures or gray beards.

From Calais Henry's main army moved towards his rendezvous with his remaining ally, Maximilian, under the walls of Thérouanne. In certain respects the alliance with the Holy Roman Emperor

Elect had also been disappointing. Max had been obliged to explain that an empty treasury and heavy obligations made it impossible for him to furnish the contingents agreed on. But the King of England could have all the German *Lanzknechts* and Burgundian cavalry he could pay for, and a fine train of artillery at a very low figure. The Emperor himself would be proud to serve under the King of England's banner at a mere hundred crowns a day for his personal expenses, plus, of course, the hire of his household troops. And Henry could have free the benefit of his experienced advice. On the borders of Artois, which belonged to Max's grandson Charles, Prince of Castile, the French held two strongly fortified towns, Thérouanne and the city of Tournai, the points of two awkward salients jutting into Habsburg territory, menacing the trade routes of the southern Netherlands. Inspired perhaps by Ferdinand's success in persuading Henry to begin conquering France on the borders of Navarre, Max pointed out that really the best beginning would be the reduction of these fortresses on the frontiers of his family's dominions, and, again, Henry accepted experienced advice. When, clad in simple black, Max rode into the camp before Thérouanne to pay his respects to his young commander, the glow of having an Emperor in his pay quite reconciled Henry to a few minor infractions of a treaty, a few thousands more of expense.

It was a delightful campaign. King Louis, it is true, proved recreant. He had had losses in Italy which he still hoped to recoup, and his generals were instructed to observe the English and reinforce the border fortress, avoiding a pitched battle. And Henry missed the nub of the most exciting action, an exhilarating gallop in which the English and Burgundian horse chased for miles the flower of the French army (which had orders not to fight) and captured enough prisoners to dignify the cavalry skirmish with the name of a battle. But Henry saw all the pageantry of war: villages burning, and towns invested, and entrenchments pushed forward. He fired a cannon against Thérouanne with his own hands, and knighted his subjects on the field of battle, and held solemn councils of war with the Emperor and his captains. He received the illustrious French prisoners as his due – after all he paid Maximilian's wages – and sent them home to Catherine quite in the style of a knight in a romance. We catch glimpses of him amid the smoke of a bombardment, paying no more heed to the French shot than if they were bird-bolts, or riding about the camp all night in his armor, encouraging his soldiers, and astonishing the Venetian ambassador with his courage and endurance. Military exploits were pleasantly diversified by softer amusements. We see Henry being received by the Emperor's daughter, Margaret of Savoy, and passing a month of feasts and revels while the rain fell on the trenches around Tournai; we hear of a fair Belgian lady to whom he promised many fine things, chiefly a dower of ten thousand crowns when she should marry.[5] Altogether, war was more fun than tournaments, though a good deal more expensive.

Meanwhile Catherine applied herself, energetically and unobtrusively, to the business of ruling and guarding England; no light responsibility, for no sooner was Henry well across the Channel than the Scots began to move. It was axiomatic that the Scots always attacked England whenever the English were busy in France, but Henry had a treaty with his brother-in-law, the King of Scots, was still a great believer in treaties, and was reluctant to put off his glorious conquests any longer. Or perhaps Catherine convinced him that she and Surrey would be equal to anything the Scots could do. The old Earl went to raise his tenantry, the borders were warned, and Catherine drove her council to the double task of supplying the army in Flanders, and preparing for invasion from the north. Commissions of array were issued, musters were held, the towns were assessed for special taxes. In the midst of signing writs and warrants, Catherine found time to keep up a stream of letters to the camp in France. She arranged to write once a week, and to have every courier bring back a letter, at least from Wolsey if Henry was too preoccupied with war. She worried about Henry's rashness in battle, and his tendency to get overheated and catch cold. As one woman to another, she begged her former sister-in-law, Margaret of Austria, to send the best physician she could find to look after him. She pestered Wolsey about her husband's health, and remembered to send fresh supplies of linen for him. She was relieved to hear that Maximilian had joined him, "for by the Emperor's good council, His Grace shall not adventure himself so much as I was afeared of, before," and she was overjoyed at the famous cavalry victory, "the greatest that ever was heard of," though she was a little embarrassed as to how to take care of the princely prisoners Henry sent her. About her own preoccupations she was more reticent. The council had all been very diligent, and she hoped Henry would commend them. She confessed to Wolsey that she was much encumbered with the war, but as for the Scots, Henry was not to worry about them. She and all his subjects at home were glad to be busy with them, taking it for a pastime. Her ladies were horribly busy making standards, banners, and badges.[6]

The first to be ready of her knights and captains were hurried northwards to reinforce Surrey, and whether or not Catherine made them the ringing patriotic oration which her old schoolmaster, Peter Martyr, set down in his letters, the sentence about God's hand being over men who fought for their homes and the reminder that in valor the English had always excelled all other nations sound as if they might be hers. There is no doubt that she was the center and soul of the defense, busy, now, with forming a reserve army around London. As August ended sweating couriers brought word that James of Scotland with a force variously estimated at forty, sixty, a hundred thousand men, an enormous army anyway, splendidly equipped and trained in new tactics, had crossed the Tweed. The walls of Norham Castle crumbled in five days before James's French siege guns; there was skirmishing at Chillingham and elsewhere, then the fog of war closed over the north. Thomas Ruthall, Bishop of Durham, counted one of the coolest heads on the council and specially charged with the northern defense, was near panic at the contradictory rumors filtering through from the front, but Catherine was calm. Along the roads that led to Buckingham levies from as far away as Wales, and from all the southern and western counties, were pouring to form a reserve army of sixty thousand men, which she, herself, meant to lead to York. Early in September she rode out of the City at the head of the gentlemen and yeomen of the home counties, a stout band of Londoners, the cannon from the Tower. If Surrey found the Scots too strong for him, he could fall back on this support. If he fought and was beaten, the Scots would still find a powerful army between them and the south.

By September 14 Catherine was at Buckingham. But already, on the afternoon of the ninth, the Scots, burning their camp behind them, had marched down from their strong position on Flodden Edge to try conclusions with Surrey in the open field by Branxton Brook, already English bows and bills had made havoc of their close-packed ranks, and the last stubborn ring of spearmen had fallen round the dead body of their king. Flodden was the bloodiest battle of Henry's reign, the only one the English fought comparable to such pitched fields as Ravenna. Beside it the Tournai and Thérouanne campaign was a mere exercise in mass maneuvers. While Henry had been picking roses in Hainault, the laurels had been gathered in the north.

iv

No word in Catherine's letters about Flodden pointed the current jests about her victories and her husband's. The taunt that she was sending Henry a king for his duke existed only in the imagination of the gossips in Flanders. What she did write was: "You see I can keep my promise, to send for your banners [the banners taken at the "Battle of the Spurs"] a king's coat. I thought to send himself to you, but our Englishmen's hearts would not suffer it." But the victory she spoke of as the King's, given him in his absence by his subject's valor and God's grace, "the greatest honour that could be" to him and to all the realm, more than if he should win all the crown of France, but as much his, by God's gift, as if he had been there in person. "And with this," she wrote, "I make an end, praying God to send you home shortly for without (that) no joy can here be accomplished, and for the same I pray, and now go to our Lady at Walsingham that I promised so long ago to see."[7] The touching reference was for Henry alone. He knew when it was that she had promised to see our Lady at Walsingham: on the day he had left her to give thanks at that shrine for the birth of his infant son. Before Catherine could fulfill her vow, the baby had died. "Until I can give you a son," her letter meant to say, "take, meanwhile, this victory."

We may be sure that Henry had no misgivings about taking the victory to himself. Flodden, like the Battle of the Spurs, was his triumph, another evidence of God's favor to an orthodox king, the defender of the Pope against the schismatic French and the perjured Scots, a token that England would be safe while he resumed his conquests. So far those conquests had netted him only the dubious privilege of garrisoning Tournai and Thérouanne, "ungracious dogholes" a bitter member of Parliament later called them, of no possible value to anyone but the Netherlanders. But they were the first French towns to fall to an English king for nearly a hundred years, and Henry felt that the French had shown they dared not meet him in the field. Already foreigners were talking respectfully of the renewal of English might. Ferdinand, who had sent only regretful messages in answer to Henry's appeals for help, now sent a special envoy to draft plans for a grand joint invasion the next year. This year, Tournai, next year, Paris! Henry boasted. His ally and employee, the Emperor, grinned covertly. He and Ferdinand had not survived a generation of cutthroat diplomacy by conquering other people's kingdoms for them.

In England, Catherine worked loyally to forward her husband's plans. Scotland had taken a stunning blow, and there was always a party in Henry's council, a party with strong backing in the country, which felt that Scotland would be a conquest easier and more valuable than France. This seemed a time to push the northern war home, and make an end of the Scottish menace forever. But Catherine realized that England could not afford two simultaneous campaigns of conquest. Promptly on the news of Flodden she began to disband the reserve army, and to arrange to decrease Surrey's. At the same time she wrote Lord Dacre that she would gladly send someone "to comfort the widowed Queen of Scots." Margaret, after all, was Henry's sister, and if she would rule Scotland in the interests of the Tudors, alliance would be cheaper than conquest. Before Henry recrossed the Channel a Franciscan friar charged with Catherine's comfortable messages was on his way to Edinburgh. Margaret was assured that while she kept the peace her brother would support her regency in Scotland. The letters exchanged between the two queens looked to a permanent peace.[8] Catherine's prompt steps to end the Scottish danger as much as her courage in opposing it showed her complete fitness for the hard task Henry had left in her hands.

By late September the last banquet and the last tourney in the Netherlands were over, the last promise to meet again in June exchanged, and the English army was being ferried back across the Channel for the winter. Henry, suddenly impatient to be home, slipped across to Dover, lightly escorted, and galloped like the boy he still was for Richmond where the Queen waited, and where, says the chronicler, "was such a loving meeting that every creature rejoiced."[9] Europe rang with Henry's praises. He could lay this time at the Queen's feet no mock trophies, but the keys of two proud cities, an earnest of greater glories. In November the Parliament, with less grumbling than usual, would vote him a hundred sixty thousand pounds for his march on Paris. Now Henry could begin to be the king he had dreamed of being. And Catherine was glad to exchange her regency for her husband.

There were some shadows on that homecoming. It was said that, in September, before Henry returned, Catherine had lost another child by miscarriage, the same price that her mother, Isabella, had more than once paid for a victory won by her exertions. London was plague-ridden, and the celebrations for the returning army were less splendid than they would otherwise have been. A cousin of Lord Mountjoy's, one Bessie Blount, took Henry's eye at the New Year's revels, and it is unlikely that the King was so discreet that Catherine could not note that soldier habits had not made him a more faithful husband. She may have noted, too, how much more often than of old Henry leaned on Thomas Wolsey's arm and whispered with him in the embrasure of a window away from the ears of the court, how it was Master Almoner that Henry now sought out first when dispatches came from abroad and Master Almoner who was most often quoted at the council table. Bessie Blount was not her first rival in Henry's bed, but Thomas Wolsey was the first to threaten her ascendancy in his confidence. There is a Spanish proverb that the light of the sun and the favor of the king are not for any one alone. When, in February, Henry was seriously ill, with what some described as measles, others as smallpox, and what was, perhaps, the greater pox which was beginning to scourge Europe, and Catherine sat by his uneasy bedside, and changed the cold cloths on his forehead, that disillusioned tag may have been some comfort.

By March Henry was up and about again; as spring advanced, the tempo of military preparations quickened. No one in England suspected, as yet, the threads of intrigue that had been shuttling back and forth from Spain to Flanders all winter. The treaty of Lille, binding Ferdinand and Maximilian to join Henry in invading

France, had been signed on October 17. Ten days later Ferdinand opened secret negotiations with France, negotiations in which Maximilian soon joined him. He and Maximilian had in common two promising grandsons. The elder of these, Charles of Ghent, affianced for the moment to Henry's youngest sister Mary, would one day inherit the realms of both his grandparents. The game was to carve a kingdom in Italy for the younger, using the threat of English invasion to bluff the King of France into relinquishing his claims there, for that purpose.[10]

Ferdinand chuckled over the limitless uses to which one could put a complacent son-in-law; and the Emperor, with a hundred twenty thousand English crowns in his pocket and those awkward salients on his frontier rubbed out, understood his partner at a wink and a nod. The young colt, they agreed, wanted bridling. It would be a mistake, they agreed, to let their victim suspect anything until he had been neatly fleeced. They vied with each other in protesting their martial ardor to Henry, while they dickered with the French for a treaty of peace from which England was to be excluded unless it accepted harsh and humiliating terms. All the diplomatic phrases with which these two elderly sharpers perfumed their scheme are not enough to exorcise its aroma of primitive skulduggery. They might have been planning to lure Henry up an alley to be slugged and sandbagged while they went through his pockets. France was to do the strong-arm work, and to pay handsomely for the privilege.

In April, while London buzzed with warlike preparations, strange portents began to disturb King Henry's council. Don Luis Caroz, the Spanish ambassador, had not yet been authorized to ratify the treaty which Ferdinand had signed in December. There were few signs of readiness for war in Flanders, and when Maximilian was asked about the approaching marriage of his grandson Charles to Henry's sister he was curiously evasive. Then, suddenly, the cat was out of the bag. From Paris came advance news that

Ferdinand had agreed to extend the truce along the Pyrenees for another year, and a broad hint that there was more in the wind than that. Though it was becoming clear that Maximilian, too, was deserting his ally, the tempest of popular indignation was directed solely at the King of Aragon. It made last year's storm seem a zephyr. Poor Don Luis Caroz, again his master's dupe in duping the King of England, hardly dared face the council, begged, this time, to be allowed to come home. He was like a bull in the ring, he wrote, at whom everyone throws darts. In the streets people were saying that this time the King of Aragon had gone too far. He was worse than the King of France. The time to settle with him was approaching, and the score would be a long one.

No doubt Ferdinand relied on his daughter to smooth things over in England as she had done before. But whether it was in Catherine's power to undo the harm was not to be tested. On two occasions she had been able to blind herself to her father's treachery, and to persuade herself to accept his excuses so that she could persuade Henry to accept them. This time she could not. She had married in England to serve Spain, but not to be a partner in swindling her husband. She let her humiliation at the part she had played, her disappointment and indignation be clearly apparent. She told the Spanish ambassador, coldly, that she had nothing to discuss with him, did not wish to see him, and refused to intervene in any way in Spain's behalf. If she wrote any line to her father, it was not a message Ferdinand cared to keep. "Her confessor," wrote the helpless Caroz, using the customary diplomatic periphrasis for blaming a daughter to a father and one member of a royal family to another, "her confessor has persuaded the Queen to forget Spain, and gain the love of the English." [11] One doubts that Catherine needed such advice from Fray Diego. She would never forget Spain, but she had now lived thirteen years in England, five as England's Queen. In the seclusion of her widowhood she had preserved much of her Spanishness, but her life since had opened new windows. There were only a few Spaniards left in her suite; except for her confessor and her favorite lady in waiting, Maria de Salinas, most of her daily contacts were with the English. Though she never lost a faint trace of foreign accent, she was beginning to talk, write, think like an Englishwoman. For five years she had devoted herself wholeheartedly to the activities and interests of her husband's land; she had made a widening circle of English friends, and during the last year she had felt the thrill of national leadership in a crisis. It still pleased her, on occasion, to talk Spanish and to hear news of her native land. She had believed, she was to believe again, that the true interests of England and Spain were one, and that in fostering the alliance between them she was serving both. But she was Queen of England; she had no doubt, she was never again to show any doubt, where her final allegiance lay.

v

During the summer and fall of 1514 that allegiance was put to its first test, for under the impact of Ferdinand's treachery English foreign policy made a sharp change of direction. Louis XII, the elderly King of France, was able to appreciate the feelings of one who had been duped by Ferdinand. It is of Louis that the story runs that he sent an ambassador to complain to his fellow monarch that the King of Aragon had deceived him twice. "He lies, the sot," cackled Ferdinand in high good humor, "I have deceived him five times!" In the negotiations of 1514, however, Louis had out-foxed his foxy adversary. Louis had no intention of surrendering his claims on Italy, and no desire to be involved in an aimless war with England. He wanted nothing from England except a benevolent neutrality while he pursued his continental aims, none of which ran counter to any real English interest, and for that neutrality he was willing to pay as before. Consequently, by spinning out the arguments over his new treaty with them, he had lured Ferdinand and Maximilian into showing their hands, and he was ready to make a strong bid for peace with England the moment the disclosure of Ferdinand's treachery produced a favorable state of mind. He was ready to offer a permanent, favorable alliance, and to bind it by making Henry's younger sister Mary, whom Maximilian had rejected for Charles of Ghent, his bride and queen of France.

The moment was well chosen. Henry's faith in his father-in-law was destroyed, though his faith in himself was unshaken. "I do not see," he told the Venetian ambassador superbly, "any faith in the world save in me only, and therefore God Almighty, who knows this, prospers my affairs." His immediate affair, as he did not conceal from anyone, was to make Ferdinand suffer for deserting him. In that determination Thomas Wolsey, his new chief minister, a man quite free of any aristocratic prejudice against the French, was quick to encourage him.

Fifteen-fourteen was Wolsey's year. It found him simple King's Almoner and Dean of Lincoln. It left him Bishop of Tournai, Bishop of Lincoln, Archbishop of York, and well on the way to his first grand goal, the cardinal's hat. It found him a new figure on the King's council. It left him so dominant there that the other councilors sat like dummy directors, waiting until the Archbishop pulled the strings. One by one those who might oppose him – Archbishop Warham, Buckingham, Surrey, Shrewsbury, even his old master Fox, the Bishop of Winchester – were shouldered aside and reduced to silence. It was the triumph of audacity and unrivaled competence. No burden of business could stagger Wolsey; no problem was too hard for him to solve. The chief law courts, the treasury, war, the church, foreign affairs – he took them over, one by one, arranged their tangled controls neatly on the busy switchboard of his brain, and drove them all at the fierce acceleration of his own restless, dynamic energy. He was the one, a shrewd

Courtesy of Houghton Mifflin Co.

Henry VIII

brain among his enemies admitted, who knew more and could do more than all the rest of the King's council put together.

Henry, himself, abetted this unparalleled assumption of power by his servant. Thomas Wolsey professed himself so entirely the King's creature, was so eager to anticipate the King's slightest wish, existed so exclusively as a mere engine for carrying out the King's directions, that to center every department of government in Wolsey's hands gave Henry the thrill of absolute, personal rule, without the tiresome necessity of interrupting his amusements to see to the details.

There was a moment when the Queen might have challenged the minister's supremacy. Wolsey was eager for the French alliance, because the King favored it, because the Pope favored it and Wolsey hoped for favors from Rome, and because Wolsey was bent on dazzling Europe by appearing as the diplomatic arbiter of its destinies, a vanity he never outgrew. Catherine seemed the logical person to oppose the new alignment, as her father and the frantically anxious Spanish ambassador hoped she would do. Some members of the council were dismayed by Henry's aggressiveness, thinking that peace with France was one thing, marriage and an offensive alliance were another. Had Catherine taken the lead in opposition, powerful elements would have rallied to her support: the conservative, anti-French nobility, the merchants who traded in Flanders, and the people who hated the French, all the members of the council who resented Wolsey as a plebeian upstart. She might even have found an ally in one of the persons most concerned, Henry's favorite sister Mary, who, at a full-blooded eighteen, was pardonably unenthusiastic at the prospect of a battered bridegroom of fifty-two who was said to look and behave like a valetudinarian of seventy. Had Catherine summoned all her powers for the thrust, she might have upset Wolsey's unprecedented policy.

She did nothing of the sort. Her manner towards Wolsey was

unchanged; she gave no sign to Caroz. Somewhat to their surprise, the French ambassadors, when they came, found her perfectly cordial. She appeared as a matter of course at all the ceremonies connected with the signing of the treaties and the delivery of the bride, and helped Mary prepare for her duties as Queen of France. It was as if she wished to mark by her actions that her father's duplicity had relieved her of any obligation towards Spain, or any interest in English foreign policy other than a dutiful support of her husband's views. Without a struggle she surrendered to the new minister her place in her husband's councils, and deliberately withdrew from the sphere of high politics.

It has been suggested that at this moment Catherine's own position was seriously endangered, that, in fact, for some months Henry thought of divorcing her and taking a French wife. Venetians at Paris and Rome heard the rumor, and there is an odd note in an index to the archives of the Vatican. If there was any substance to the rumor, we should have to anticipate Henry's interest in a divorce by thirteen years. But the rumor must have been the idlest gossip, born of the wishful thinking of allies of France who feared Catherine's pro-Spanish influence, and did not know that she refused to exert it. In England there was no sign of any breach between the King and Queen. There can have been none. The grounds for the divorce were said to be Catherine's failure to bear an heir to the throne, but in the summer of 1514 Catherine was actually expecting another child. In June, when the French ambassadors came, she was visibly pregnant. Soon new curtains and new linen for the Queen's bed were being ordered, and Henry was writing the joyful news to all the courts of Europe. Louis XII was asked to be the godfather. To suppose Henry VIII capable of planning a divorce under such circumstances is to accuse him of a baseness beyond anything his subsequent conduct ever suggested. It would be unlikely in the embittered tyrant of twenty years later – unthinkable in the still hopeful, ingenuous young king of 1514.[12]

In December the child was born – dead, the Venetian ambassador thought. But more likely this was the second of Catherine's male children born alive, "a boy who lived not long after." For Catherine it must have been the blackest disappointment of all that gloomy year.

Her father had betrayed her; her confessor, Fray Diego, had got himself into a scrape and gone back to Spain under a cloud; her favorite and friend Maria de Salinas, the last of her Spanish maids to leave her service, had married an Englishman, Lord Willoughby, and was no longer at court; Henry reserved his embraces for Bessie Blount, and his confidences for Thomas Wolsey. But none of these things would have mattered if she could have borne him a son.

Chapter Three

CATHERINE'S SERVICES to her father were not quite over. The passage of the months brought a lessening of her bitterness at Ferdinand's treachery – brought, too, a change in relations with France. Catherine had no intention of helping Ferdinand to play any more tricks on her husband, but in Henry's own interest she might do something to mollify the rage and injured vanity which insisted on hurting Spain even at England's cost, particularly since Ferdinand, now thoroughly alarmed, made what she was willing to do easier by his anxiously conciliatory attitude, and his skillful choice of a new ambassador.

"Men of the sword for war, men of the robe for peace," the sixteenth century said. Bernardino de Mesa, Bishop of Elna in Roussillon, was very much a man of the robe, a meek little Dominican friar whose demure downcast look masked one of the shrewdest intelligences in the Spanish service. De Mesa had been the principal go-between in the Franco-Spanish truce, and before that he had been useful at Rome where his inconspicuous, black clad figure had flitted through most of the labyrinth of Roman intrigue and gone ferreting after half the plots in Italy. He was just the man to deal with the new English Cardinal whose aggressive self-importance was soothed by De Mesa's bland humility and whose hard-won respect was engaged by the little friar's easy familiarity with papal politics, the one mystery in Christendom of which Wolsey stood in awe. De Mesa was just the man, too, to re-establish relations with Catherine. He knew how to make more out of a word dropped in an antechamber, or a few sentences in private from the Queen's physician, than Caroz could have made of hours of explicit conference and piles of substantiating documents. With Catherine's indirect help De Mesa, in a few months, was better oriented in England and on better terms there than any Spanish ambassador had been for a long time, the better because he took no pains to call attention to his influence with the Cardinal and the help he got from the Queen.[1]

Just as De Mesa was establishing his ground, events in France came to his and Ferdinand's aid. The marriage of May to December had lasted less than three months. An old man at fifty-two, gouty and feeble before his time, Louis XII had long accustomed himself to the plainest meals, the mildest exercise, and decently restful hours of sleep. But no true Frenchman will prefer his comforts when a gallant gesture is called for, and Louis' court saw him dance, who had not danced for years, and ride out hunting through the cold November drizzle, and yawn over his supper at an ungodly hour. For a little while the brave spirit sustained the aching joints; then the King collapsed. Propped on a couch he watched his young heir tilting in honor of his marriage and grumbled, "That big youngster will ruin everything." He was too tired to care. As the year closed, he died.

The big youngster, Francis of Angoulême – Francis I, now, of France – was ready to comfort the widow. His long sharp nose, like a humorous fox's nose, poked into her darkened bedroom, his bold, sly eyes appraised the form huddled under the counterpane while the skillful tongue mingled jest and irony with admiring wooing. An English alliance and a dowry like Mary's would be the best of starts for a reign which he meant to make more exciting than old Louis'. Some women already had found the swaggering high-colored youth irresistible; now that he was the greatest king of Europe a great many more were to do so; but Mary, cowering in the great bed, equally miserable with fright and a toothache, clung desperately to plans of her own. When Mary had consented to marry the aged and sickly Louis, she had extorted from her brother the promise that next time she might marry where she liked. Henry's council were already debating the advantages of France as against Austria or Savoy, in fine oblivion of that promise, but if Henry did not mean to keep it, he should not have sent the Duke of Suffolk to bring Mary home.

The eighteen-year-old princess had already set her heart on her brother's friend. Of all the circle of boisterous young men whom Henry had gathered about him, Charles Brandon had come the farthest, and he was to go farther still. It is hard, now, to say why. He had not Frank Bryan's wit and gaiety, nor Will Compton's brains and address, nor any other qualities that anyone remembers except a kind of loud joviality and beefy good looks. But he had the good luck to have had a father killed on the right side at Bosworth, his brawn and good humor and submissiveness succeeded with Henry, who had raised him from a simple squire to be Viscount Lisle and then Duke of Suffolk, and something about him succeeded with the ladies. He had married – more or less – three of them, and his domestic entanglements in 1514 were of a fascinating complexity, but neither that nor his anguished reluctance to risk Henry's displeasure made any difference to Mary Tudor. She insisted that he marry her at once and take her away. King Francis, not sorry to play a mischievous trick on his brother of England, since he was not to have the lady himself, lent his gay connivance, and Suffolk, shivering with apprehension in every nerve of his big body, consented.

Both the culprits were convinced that Henry would be in a dangerous mood, and that the council would clamor for Suffolk's head. They lingered timidly in France writing piteous letters to the King, and to the two persons they thought might be willing to help them, Wolsey and the Queen. Before Henry let his anger cool, and agreed to be satisfied with stripping his friend of most of his wealth, and his sister of her dower rights, without insisting on their heads as well, the culprits had needed, or so Wolsey's letters assured them, both their intercessors.

Probably Henry's real wrath was directed more against Francis I than against Mary and Suffolk. He considered that that young man had played him an unfair trick, and the more he heard of the swaggering youngster across the channel, the less he liked him. That circumstance made De Mesa's task – and Catherine's – easier. Ferdinand had learned from his daughter that the best salve for Henry's wounded feelings would be a handsome present. Fear made him lavish, and Catherine congratulated her father upon the effect.[2] Before the summer was over De Mesa and Wolsey were drafting a new Anglo-Spanish treaty of alliance and consulting with Henry on how to keep Francis from invading Italy and upsetting the delicate balance of European peace.

Henry was confident that the King of France would not be mad enough to take the offensive in Italy while his relations with England were unsettled. "Tell your master," he directed De Mesa grandly, "that the French will not attack Milan without my leave." But to make assurance doubly sure he consented to hasten the signing of a defensive alliance in which the Habsburgs were to be included. When, in the midst of these negotiations, the French army with its young king at its head streamed into Lombardy, defeated the Swiss in a battle of giants, occupied Milan, and resumed a position of dominance in northern Italy, all with a most pointed disregard of English wishes or threats, Henry's council was thrown into a kind of panic which almost halted the progress of the treaty with Spain. Catherine's experience again came to her father's aid. The English, she wrote, are always unduly elated at small successes and unduly cast down by small misfortunes.[3] With Spanish gravity she regarded the islanders as an excitable, mercurial race; but she had lived among them long enough to know how to handle them, and the treaty of alliance with Spain was signed after all.

It was a good treaty, she wrote her father, because the commitments on both sides were definite and limited, and the advantages were mutual. Ferdinand could be sure of English friendship as long as he promised nothing that he would not or could not carry out. It was, indeed, a sensible treaty, and Catherine's satisfaction with it marks another stage in her development in statecraft. A solid peace with Spain, solid, understandable commercial advantages on both sides – these were better than risky schemes of conquest.[4] Having satisfied herself that De Mesa's treaty assured these things she withdrew from the field, leaving to the ambassador the ordinary conduct of Spanish affairs in England.

ii

When the treaty of 1515 was signed, Catherine was again noticeably pregnant. The court was less hopeful, this time, but on February 18, 1516, at Greenwich palace, the child was born alive. It was a baby girl, baptized Mary three days later at the same altar of the Observant Friars where her mother and father had knelt in marriage almost seven years before. Everyone had hoped for a boy, but a healthy girl was something, and Henry was not too much cast down. "The Queen and I are both young," he told the Venetian ambassador (Henry was just twenty-five, Catherine still only thirty-one), "and if it is a girl this time, by God's grace boys will follow." Meanwhile even a girl was some excuse to strut his fatherhood. The fluff of hair was the true Tudor red; one might almost fancy, in the round baby face not unlike Henry's, the jut of the true Tudor nose. Henry was persuaded of his daughter's uniqueness. "*Per deum, domine oratore,*" he told the Venetian ambassdor earnestly, "*ista puella numquam plorat.*" "By God, Mr. Ambassador, this baby never cries."

As for Catherine – perhaps she was as disappointed as her husband that the baby was not a boy, though girls were more predictable and likely to be a greater comfort. Undoubtedly she hoped that boys would follow. But one could not expect Isabella's daughter to agree that women might not govern kingdoms. As the years passed and no second baby lived, she began to train Mary for the scepter more thoroughly than even she herself had been trained.

The birth of Mary marks another step in Catherine's settling down to an unexciting place as Queen Consort of England. Wolsey had taken her place as her husband's adviser in statecraft, and she had long since ceased to be the one woman in Henry's heart. Elizabeth Blount was still, in so far as any such position existed in England, *maîtresse en titre;* in 1519 Henry proudly exhibited to the court a son she had borne him, and Catherine, with who knows how much – or how little – bitterness in her heart, dutifully attended, at the manor house Henry had built for Lady Tailleboys, the festivities in honor of the child named Henry Fitzroy, Henry King's son. If there were other more casual lights-of-love, that was something for Bessie Blount to worry about. It did not concern the Queen.

The disparity in age between Catherine and her husband was beginning to show itself. "The King of England is young," Francis I said brutally, "but his wife is old and deformed." [5] She was not quite that, but a Venetian who saw her for the first time in 1515 described her cautiously as "rather ugly than otherwise." [6] Repeated pregnancies had spread and loosened the once girlish figure; the hair had lost its golden lights and darkened to a muddy brown; the skin had taken a sallow tinge, so that later observers tend to speak of Catherine as a brunette. The eyes, the voice, the little hands and feet, these alone still suggested the girl who had come to England, the young beauty Henry had married.

Catherine's tastes were changing, too. In public she and Henry were still much together; always the Queen made a splendid and dignified appearance beside the King on occasions of ceremony, when foreigners noted the magnificence of her gowns and jewels and the charms of her ladies in waiting, "such beautiful young women as there might be in paradise"; often she received ambassadors with Henry, sometimes she rode hunting with him, and now and then she still danced – once with Wolsey. We catch a glimpse of her being affable to the French ambassador while Henry showed off his fleet in the Thames, though her figure is eclipsed by that of the King, clad in a sailor's smock and trousers all of cloth of gold, and blowing on a silver whistle "so loud it was like a trumpet." We see her leading out her maidens from Greenwich to gather May-dew and blossoms in the dawn, or receiving garlands of silk roses, red and white, with which to deck the victors of a tournament. But more and more Henry's more raucous revels seem to have done without her. "The Queen withdrew early," "the Queen, who was sewing amongst her women," "the Queen, who had just come from hearing mass," "The Queen, who was in her chapel," "the Queen, who has gone on a pilgrimage" – these begin to be the phrases ambassadors throw her in their reports. Henry was a devout monarch and regular in his attendance at divine service, but Catherine heard three masses to his one, and prayed at all the famous shrines of the home counties while her husband killed stags in their forests. It was probably about this time that she began to wear, under her handsome dresses, the coarse habit of the third order of Saint Francis. The strain of piety which had made Isabella's last years seem those of a crowned nun was beginning to show in the daughter.

Not that all her time was spent in devotions. She still had a large share in the management of the royal household; a thousand things, from the care and embroidery of Henry's linen and the provision of the small personal comforts he had come to expect to the general supervision of the officers in charge of hall and wardrobe, kitchen and buttery, were largely in her hands; and the seemly management of the court at Richmond or Greenwich or lumbering from one country manor house to another through the summer and early autumn owed much to her vigilant eye. She had, also, her own estates, wealthy and widely scattered, calling for a whole machinery of supervision culminating in the Queen's council, a group of clerics and officials who met regularly for the discharge of business, and over whose deliberations Catherine regularly presided in person. She had the right of presentation to this living and that abbey, the rights of forest and meadow in this or that manor; and in the margins of documents we find her busy pen now querying the price of hay and now the virtue of pretendant abbess, characteristically insisting on the last fraction of her rights and performing with exactness her remotest duties.

iii

Among those duties her charities took up more and more of her time. The poor, it has been noted, are a persistent phenomenon, but there were beginning to be more poor than usual in sixteenth-century England. In spite of the extravagance of the court, and an extravagance in scattering subsidies abroad which made the most lavish domestic amusements seem penny-pinching, taxation was light and the realm prosperous. But prosperity, as usual, failed to distribute itself evenly. Wool prices were especially good and the market for unfinished homespun cloth excellent, so, as the merchants of the Staple chinked Flemish gold and the clothiers began to look for more looms, the country gentry began to keep more sheep, fencing in waste and common, pulling down cottages, stopping plows to provide grassland. Thus, a thoughtful Englishman noted, "one covetous and insatiable cormorant may compass about and inclose many thousand acres of ground; the husbandmen to be thrust out of their own, either by coveyn and fraud or by violent oppression; they must needs depart, poor, silly, wretched souls, men, women, husbands, wives, fatherless children, widows, woeful mothers with their young babes, and their whole household, small in substance, much in number. . . . Away they trudge, out of their known and accustomed houses, finding no place to rest in. What can they do but steal and be hanged, or else go begging and then be cast in prison because they work not, whom no man will set to work? For one shepherd is enough to eat up that ground with cattle, to the occupying whereof with husbandry many hands were requisite."[7] For various reasons many persons besides Thomas More were alarmed by the increasing drift of homeless, penniless vagabonds about the English roads. Cardinal Wolsey even appointed a commission to look into it, and a few hedges were uprooted. But little could be done against the solid opposition of a landlord class who found that sheep doubled their revenue, and the idle thousands continued to starve. Economic historians tell us that the extent of the inclosure movement in the early part of the sixteenth century has been exaggerated, and, indeed, compared to what happened to the peasants and yeomen of England when landlords were really in the saddle, it seems mild enough. Perhaps no more than five per cent of the arable land in England was affected. But even much less than five families out of every hundred turned adrift in an economy which has no means of absorbing them may produce an appalling lot of misery.

Catherine did what she could. As a member of the third order of Saint Francis she had a special obligation to charity; as Queen she had a duty to the whole people of England. The few scattered papers that survive give us little insight into just what measures she took. There was an official called the Queen's Almoner, and apparently the funds at his disposal were increased, and an effort was made to see that they were expended wisely. A number of the indigent aged were at her constant charge, and on some, at least, of her manors regular reserves were set aside for charity. In addition, so her earliest biographer records, she always had inquiries made into the needs of the poor in whatever neighborhood she was living; and used, herself, to spend much time in visiting them unostentatiously, garbed perhaps simply as a lay sister of her order. Hundreds of poor families were to remember that they owed to her money and clothes and food, fuel in the winter cold, and clean linen against childbed.[8] The deep affection which the poor commons of England showed for the Queen in her adversity may have been grounded, in part, on the memory that she had not forgotten them in theirs. Her worst enemy said of her that the English poor loved Catherine only because she fed them.

Such relief for the poor as Catherine could manage out of her personal estate had necessarily the defects of all medieval charity; it was designed to give temporary aid to the specially unfortunate, not to meet a widespread, persistent dislocation of the normal ways of getting a living. In a static agricultural economy in which there was work, however hard, for every pair of hands, and coarse, plain food for every mouth unless crops failed, there was need for little more. But the economy of Europe was entering a dynamic phase, and Catherine's charities, even if her example roused some of her subjects to imitation, could make little impression on the mass of destitute vagabonds which change had thrust out on the English roads. Catherine never showed any genius for social generalization; she was wedded to the old ways; but she had a deep sense of duty and a keen sense of fact. She read, as all educated Europe was reading, Thomas More's *Utopia*, and we know she delighted in More's conversation. Did she discuss with him how far the practices of his fantastic Nowhere might solve in England the practical problem with which they were both concerned? We know she discussed it with another humanist of genius, her countryman, Luis Vives. When Vives came to write his book, *De subventione pauperum*, the earliest treatise on poor relief which can be described as modern and scientific, he was thinking primarily of the problems confronting Bruges and the wool-working cities of Flanders, but he was conscious that these formed only one aspect of a wider problem, and more than once in his pages we catch the echo of Queen Catherine's questions.

iv

Her charities were not Catherine's only connection with the commons of England. A persistent tradition attributes to her initiative the spread of lace-making in the midland shires [9] and another credits her with doing much to improve English gardening, bringing in new varieties of fruit trees from the Netherlands and introducing superior salads. The best-grounded tradition of all has it that it was she who saved the 'prentices of London from hanging for their part in the Ill May Day of 1517.

The Ill May Day was long remembered as the most dangerous riot disorderly Tudor London saw. More and more English were crowding into the warren of mean streets that ran down to the Thames, and while they begged at the doors of rich men's houses they saw the Italian merchants go by in silk and velvet, and the fat Germans of the Steelyard bulging with good eating, and the skilled Flemish artisans busy in their shops with leather work and jeweler's work, with armor and felt hats and fine textiles which might have kept busy many pairs of English hands. Resentment swelled into occasional violence which, awkwardly suppressed, grew to a general tumult; the old cry of "Prentices and Clubs" was raised on a morning when every brisk London youngster was early abroad, and instead of ransacking the neighboring fields and woods for May blossoms, the 'prentices, re-enforced by beggars, vagabonds and sanctuary men, ransacked the shops of the foreigners, set some houses alight, burst open the jails, and, before they were overawed by men in armor and shotted cannon, gave London the look of a city in the hands of a hostile army. When the insurrection was suppressed thirteen of the leaders dangled from gibbets in the city streets and four hundred young men, scared and puzzled at what they had done, were led with ropes about their necks before the King. To pardon them was good policy, and the official version recorded that the 'prentices owed their lives to Henry's clemency and Wolsey's advice, but as the Londoners remembered it, it was Queen Catherine who, with her hair loosened in the traditional gesture of a suppliant, knelt before the King for the lives of the young men whose riot had spilled the blood of her Spanish countrymen.

> For which, kind queen, with joyful heart
> She heard their mothers' thanks and praise . . .
> And lived beloved all her days.

Whether it happened quite so or not, the ballad, current more than half a century later, guarantees the truth of its own last line.[10]

𝔳

If time and the partisan bitterness of a revolution have dulled the memory of Catherine's relations to her poor commons, they have also almost obliterated the traces of what was perhaps the most important service of all her peaceful years as Queen: her encouragement of the new learning, and fostering care for the classical Renaissance in England, so short-lived. Her patronage of learning was not ostentatious, and much of it was bestowed indirectly, through her husband; the plant she was nurturing was of slow growth, and never bore the fruit she hoped for; it seems hopeless now to attempt an accurate estimate of the nature and extent of her influence. Nevertheless any record of Catherine's life must set down somewhere the scattered clues to what she did for learning in England, and what she tried to do. We can know enough of Catherine's character to guess that whatever she did was done consistently and seriously and with a settled purpose, and this at least the clues verify. Although they become more frequent as her daughter Mary grew older, these clues are scattered all through the whole record of her active life in England and they all point the same way.

As has been said, the months of Henry's accession were marked by a fresh interest in humanism at the English court, an interest soon announced to Erasmus by his friend, William Blount, Lord Mountjoy, the only English nobleman who, at that time, took a serious interest in scholarship. Mountjoy had just been appointed chamberlain to the Queen; later he married one of her Spanish maids of honor, Inez de Venegas, and he was long one of her most intimate friends and a link between her and the humanists. In writing to Erasmus it is Henry's interest in letters that Mountjoy stresses, and indeed Henry, who at the age of nine had written a boyish epistle to the prince of humanists, may be assumed to have had such an interest, independently of Catherine. But there is reason to believe that it was neither as deep nor as well grounded as his queen's. Henry's own education, if one can judge by his Latin writings, particularly by his *Assertio septem Sacramentorum*, must have been more influenced by the schoolmen than by the humanists, and his attitude towards the new learning was always, to say the least, erratic. Catherine, on the other hand, had begun her education at a court where the encouragement and purification of the new learning was a serious object, and she had since developed an independent taste for that sort of reading. It is noteworthy that to Erasmus, among others, her scholarship seemed more impressive than Henry's.

Next to Mountjoy, the key figure in the first connections between the humanists and the court was Thomas Linacre. Now, prior to 1509, Linacre had received but one transitory mark of royal notice. Although a man of fifty, he had published by 1509 only one small book, and his real merits were known to few. But in 1501, influenced perhaps by the economy of combining the functions of tutor and physician in a single person, Henry VII had appointed

Linacre to the household of Prince Arthur. He cannot have taken up his duties much before Catherine's marriage, and after Arthur's death he dropped back into complete obscurity. It is reasonable to suppose that his prompt appointment as royal physician immediately after the young king's coronation owed something to Catherine's recollection of him from her days at Ludlow. Certainly she took a lively interest thereafter in his distinguished career. Her physician, Dr. Fernando Vittoria, himself something of a humanist, was associated with Linacre in founding the Royal College of Physicians, and it was to Linacre the Queen turned first for a tutor and a plan of study for her daughter Mary. The Latin grammar which the famous physician wrote for the little Princess became one of the famous textbooks of the century.

Soon Linacre's friends began to find places in the royal circle: John Colet, before long the favorite preacher of the King and Queen, by royal favor made Dean of St. Paul's and helped to found a famous school; Thomas More, whose conversation set a standard of wit and elegance more nobly born courtiers could not hope to equal. On his return from Italy another young humanist, Richard Pace, whom, for learning, wit, and sweetness of temper his contemporaries thought comparable to More, gravitated naturally into Catherine's orbit. The lines are sometimes almost obliterated, but there was hardly an Englishman of learning or promise in the two decades after 1509 but had some special connection with the Queen, from Richard Whitford, for the sake of whose pious scholarship the Queen was a frequent visitor at the monastery of Sion, to young John Leland, later the famous antiquary, who, at Greenwich and Richmond, had the run of her books.

Catherine's patronage was not confined to humanists of English birth. The chief of European humanists, Desiderius Erasmus, followed his own eccentric orbit, and never revolved long around any royal luminary, but he, too, must be counted as a visitor to her sphere. Whether she had anything to do with Mountjoy's invitation to him in 1509 we do not know, but we do know that she was active in trying to keep him in England and later in trying to lure him back. We know that she respected his genius, enjoyed his conversation, read and treasured his books. For his part, Erasmus often referred to the Queen's exceptional learning – and in terms far more enthusiastic than he ever used of Henry's – and repeatedly acknowledged an especial indebtedness to her.[11]

After Erasmus, perhaps no humanist of the period was more gifted, more prolific, or more distinguished than Catherine's countryman, Juan Luis Vives, whom she was instrumental in drawing to England and setting on the path to fame. When Catherine first heard of him, possibly from Thomas More, possibly from Erasmus himself, Vives was twenty-nine, married and living in relative obscurity at Bruges. He had published little and was known to few, though he had already outgrown the instruction at Paris as he had that of his native Valencia, and had studied Greek for two years with Erasmus at Louvain. Catherine sent him a purse and a letter of encouragement, soon followed by the gift of a regular pension. Thus encouraged, he dedicated his long studied *Commentaries on Saint Augustine* to Henry VIII, and was called the next year (1523) to lecture at Wolsey's new college at Oxford. He brought with him to England the finished manuscript of his first famous book, *De institutio Christiana feminae*, "the education of a Christian woman," which Catherine had commissioned him to write for her. For the next five years, Vives spent some part of every year in England, lecturing eloquently at Oxford, spending much time at court, and writing joyously on such a variety of subjects that Thomas More professed himself quite abashed before the performance of the younger man. These were the years in which Vives' own reputation was chiefly made, and during which his energies did much to fill the gap made by the deaths of Linacre and Colet, and to carry forward the standard they had raised.

If Catherine's motives in patronizing scholars had been like those of the Italian princelings, to foster an empty Ciceronian elegance designed solely to secure the immortality of the patron by enshrining his name in aureate verse and ornate prose, we might now have more solid evidence of their indebtedness. But the next world was too real to Catherine's medieval temper for her to be much concerned about fame in this one; in her letters there are many references to the judgment of Heaven, a few to that of her contemporaries, not one to that ubiquitous will-o'-the-wisp of Renaissance minds, the judgment of posterity. Following her mother's bent, Catherine approved and did what she could to strengthen the serious, reformist tendencies of English humanism. "The end of right learning is right living; the foundation of sound faith is sound knowledge." Such maxims required that scholarship should be diffused, not hoarded, and pointed to a reform of teaching in the schools and universities as the essential beginning of a reform in the Church and in the lives of ordinary Christians. Consequently Catherine took a lively interest in English education. She contributed to lectureships at Oxford and Cambridge, maintained a number of poor scholars at both universities, and kept herself informed of their progress. When the battle of the Greeks and Trojans was raging, the struggle to introduce the new Hellenic studies against the opposition of the schoolmen, the Queen was definitely on the side of the Greeks. However strongly she might disapprove of some of Wolsey's policies, his suppression of decayed religious houses to endow his new colleges at Ipswich and Oxford, a course which horrified thoughtless conservatives, drew no protest from her. On the contrary she continued to sympathize with his aims and to demand news of their progress, even when she and the cardinal were most bitterly at odds. It was in accordance with this interest that in 1518 she combined a pilgrimage to the shrine of St. Frideswide with a tour of the colleges of Oxford, dining at Merton, and being received everywhere with "as many demonstrations of joy and love as if she had been Juno or Minerva." [12] It is noteworthy that on this occasion Henry remained at Abingdon, not far away, absorbed in his eternal hunting. In spite of his frequent presence in the vicinity, the royal patron of scholars seems never, at any time, to have had curiosity enough to visit the most famous place of learning in his kingdom.

vi

As her daughter grew older, Catherine's interest in education began to focus more and more on a single problem. The little Princess was educated by her own parents far more than was usual, but while Henry sporadically supervised her music, beating time for her practice on the virginals, setting her fingers on the frets of the lute, and boasting of her musicianship to anyone who would listen, it was Catherine who taught her her A B C's, guided her childish pen, ordered her reading, and corrected her Latin exercises. It was Catherine, therefore, who had to grapple with the momentous question of a general plan for her daughter's studies.

The question of the proper education of a prince was much to the fore in those early days of the northern Renaissance. The philosophers of the new learning did not expect to become kings, but they did not despair of making some king a philosopher, hoping that when the new learning captured the new absolutism, the philosopher king might yet prove the savior of society. There was still an immense faith in the power of merely literary propaganda, and contact with Greek thought had given some of the best minds among the humanists a fresh confidence in human nature, a belief that a virtuous education would produce a virtuous man, and that a king who had been immersed in the study of Plato and the Bible, the moral philosophers and the Christian saints, could not fail to appreciate his responsibilities and to introduce the reign of peace and justice upon earth. When Erasmus wrote *The education of a Christian prince* he was engaged on no mere humanistic exercise, but on a serious piece of literary engineering, which, he and his fellows felt, might have the most tremendous consequences.

But how if the prince be a woman? There were not wanting theorists to maintain that the soft stuff of the female mind, given naturally to levity, and meant for blind submission, was unfit for the rigors of philosophy, and there were many scholars to regard women who talked Latin with the tolerant surprise they accorded performing animals. Though the late middle ages and the Renaissance had not prevented a few women from becoming learned, no generally accepted theory of their education beyond obedience and needlework had developed. Isabella's daughters, and the few Spanish ladies who had imitated their queen's enthusiasm for the classics, were exceptional; and even Isabella, a queen and ruler in her own right, had differentiated between the training of her girls and that of the son who was to wear the crown. But Catherine's daughter Mary seemed more and more likely, as her infancy passed, to be the only Tudor of her generation, destined to rule England if any of her family did. How far could a woman be educated for such responsibilities, and more generally, – this was the nub of the whole problem, – how far were women capable of the same kind of education as could be given a man? Catherine felt the need of guidance or perhaps only of reassurance, on this point, and invited Luis Vives, as his first task in her service, to consider it.

The conclusions which Vives set forth in the book [13] he presented to the Queen seem trite to the twentieth century; in the sixteenth they were so advanced as to be almost revolutionary. The difference between the sexes, he decides, being functional, dictates a difference in education, but it does not – and here he musters a sheaf of ancient and modern instances – imply a necessary difference in intellectual power. Every tutor must judge the aptitude of his pupils from his own observation of them, remembering that an intelligent girl may go farther in grammar and philosophy than a boy less intelligent. Therefore Vives recommends, in general, a program modeled, so he says, on what he had learned from Catherine of her own education. A young lady, even of the highest rank, should be taught the special skills of her sex, needlework and embroidery and all the more strenuous parts of housewifery, even to spinning and weaving in wool and flax, "two crafts left us from the old innocent world." But she should also pursue, with equal vigor, grammar and rhetoric, Scripture and moral philosophy, up to the full extent of her ability, unobstructed by any preconceived notion of an essential difference in the intellectual capacity of the sexes.

This was what Catherine wanted to hear. For if a woman's mind could be trained like a man's, why should not a woman govern a kingdom as well as a man? As her mother Isabella had done, for instance? As soon as he came to England, Vives was engaged to act as Mary's tutor, and the reading list he presented to her in his *De ratione studii puerlis* shows what he and her mother hoped her capacity would be: The New Testament, night and morning, much history, especially Plutarch and Livy, and for moral and social guidance, besides Seneca and other standard authors among the ancients, and the fathers of the church, the pacifist tracts of Erasmus, and two dangerous models against which to measure any actual social system, Plato's *Republic* and Sir Thomas More's *Utopia*—the ideal reading list for that ideal prince for whom the humanists were always hoping, liberal, pacific, benevolent, a Christian philosopher devoting his life to the material and spiritual welfare of his subjects.

Once Catherine took up the theory of female education, she did not limit herself to its reference to her daughter. She began to form around Mary a school for the daughters of noblemen, on the pattern of that for noblemen's sons once formed around her brother Juan, and she even persuaded a number of the older ladies of the court, notably her sister-in-law, the Duchess of Suffolk, to resume the study of Latin and take up a course of serious reading. She turned over a copy of Vives' treatise to Thomas More, whose own

Thomas More

daughters were probably the best educated young women of their class in England, and urged him to translate it into English, or to get it translated, so that its ideas might be available to everybody who could take advantage of them. It is almost as if she dreamed that this Christian Renaissance for which the humanists were working and which the men were bungling so badly might be saved by the intervention of a sex whose thoughts were not given over to senseless aggression and military pride.

It was a vain dream, a lost cause. While the humanists planned the regeneration of society by reason and knowledge, the education of rulers to peace and charity, the spread of grammar schools and colleges over the land, and the consequent reform of the abuses in the Church and in the world, once clergy and laity alike were trained in a strengthened and purified Christian doctrine reinforced by the best wisdom of the ancients – while men talked hopefully of these things, the forces were gathering which were to hurl all their work in ruin and confusion. The first boys who entered Wolsey's new colleges would live to see a year in which no student proceeded to a degree at either university, when the schools were wrecked and empty, and scholarship had degenerated into snarling dogmatism settling its arguments with the gibbet and the stake. The dawn of reform merely heralded, in a style that became, in time, tiresomely familiar, the whirlwind of revolution. Much of the best of the old was to be lost, or to become, in the effort of self-defense, something less good than it had been; much of the best of the new, which had seemed so nearly within grasp, was to be achieved at last only by generations of slow rebuilding, or never to be achieved at all. The hopes of the humanists proved liars; only their fears were surpassed.

We can smile now at the humanists' crude faith in the most persistent of human delusions, the idea that men can somehow lift themselves by their own bootstraps. They really believed, these friends of Catherine's, that princes and magistrates would grow wise and virtuous by reading rhetorical commendations of wisdom and virtue, just as their contemporaries, Luther and Tyndale and the Protestant reformers, really thought that plowboys, when they had enough verses of the New Testament by heart, would behave better than bishops. Our own delusions about the magic of education are much less obvious than that. But unless we have abandoned all delusions but the last and deadliest, – the delusion that human life and history are as mechanically fated as the falling of water or as mechanically indifferent as the falling of dice, – we cannot afford to smile too scornfully. They were wrong, these humanists, but they were nobly wrong, and their error inspired them to efforts not wholly without consequence. The culture of following generations in England, as elsewhere, was different because of their work, and even though it often differed in ways they had not foreseen, they would have recognized some increments with satisfaction. Perhaps no honorable cause is ever altogether lost.

Just what increment there was from Catherine's share in this lost cause, it would be hard now to say. Her interest in the education of women was probably not wholly without results. In the society in which she lived royal example was particularly potent, and though her influence was cut short it had already begun to take effect. We may admit that the times were favorable to feminine participation in learning and still suppose that had she not begun Mary's education so carefully, Henry's younger daughter, Elizabeth, might have escaped some part of her rigorous training, noblemen's daughters like Lady Jane Grey might have been less learned, and their daughters in turn, the bluestockings for whom Edmund Spenser and John Lyly wrote, might have afforded the great Elizabethans a less appreciative public. Sidney's Stella and even the Countess of Pembroke herself were not precisely the kind of women Catherine was looking forward to; nevertheless she contributed to forming the standards which produced them.

Chapter Four

CATHERINE ALWAYS THOUGHT it her first duty to advise her husband, and her absorption in charity and education did not mean that she had abandoned an interest in foreign affairs. But she was beginning to share the pacifist views of More and Colet and Erasmus, and she could not approve the schemes of aggression with which her father began to tempt Henry as soon as the treaty of 1515 was signed. After Ferdinand's death, January 23, 1516, news of which reached England only a few days before her daughter Mary was born, Catherine had less motive than ever for abetting Henry's itch for meddling in the affairs of the Continent.

The one counselor Henry listened to was Thomas Wolsey.[1] England was dominated by the scarlet figure of the King's great minister. Archbishop of York, Lord Chancellor, Cardinal of the Roman Church, he wielded by delegation all the powers of the King and many of the powers of the Pope, and yet never felt that he had power and responsibility enough. His grasping fingers seized one after another upon all the lines that controlled Church and State in England, gathering them with ruthless efficiency into a single set of reins which the King might take over whenever he liked. But for the moment only Wolsey's broad shoulders and sinewy hands seemed equal to the strain, and both the English, who raged at his overbearing pride, and the foreign ambassadors, who described him as "*alter rex*," the real ruler of the kingdom, thought of his master, the King, as no more than an idle passenger in the coach of royal absolutism. In this the observers may have been somewhat mistaken. The letters that passed between Chancellor and King show Wolsey always in the attitude of the adoring, obsequious servant, eager only to carry out his master's will, all his greatness the mere reflection and acknowledgment of royal splendor. And Henry did not leave everything to his minister. A considerable number of documents passed under the King's own eye, or at least under his pen. Sometimes he scribbled comments in their margins or interlined them with expansions and alterations. Intermittently he felt the tug of the reins in his own hands. But when the ambassadors wrote: "the King pays little attention to business," "the King is away, hunting, while everything here is managed by the Cardinal," "the King takes his pleasure, and leaves to the Cardinal the whole government of the realm," they cannot have been wholly wrong.

Henry could leave the details of driving to Wolsey because they were at one about the manner of it: magnificence at home and abroad, a pompous show of absolute power, and a spirited foreign policy, asserting the greatness of the English King, and giving him a voice in all the affairs of the Continent. Henry and Wolsey were alike in their need to dominate and dazzle their contemporaries. While they could do so, the dangers of the road only heightened their excitement, and the exhilaration of their speed made it unnecessary to ask just where they were going, or why.

In this spirit, after Ferdinand's death, they looked about for accomplices. There were only two Continental powers worth backing, France or the Habsburgs, and Francis I, whom Henry disliked anyway, having just conquered the duchy of Milan and come to a satisfactory agreement with a thoroughly frightened Pope, felt no need of England. Of the Habsburgs, sixteen-year-old Charles of Ghent, lord of the Burgundian Netherlands and now, as Ferdinand's heir, King of all the Spains, needed peace with France. But his grandfather, the penniless Emperor of the Holy Roman Empire, was always available for an adventure if someone else would pay for it, and was involved already in the intrigue cut short by Ferdinand's death. Henry and Wolsey therefore engaged the Emperor to drive the French out of Milan with an army paid by English gold. As had happened before, the foreign princes pocketed the winnings and England paid the bills. "*Mon fils*," old Maximilian had beamed to his grandson in the thick of the plot, "*vous allez tromper les français et moi, je vais tromper les anglais*." When Max sold his Italian conquests back to their former possessors while his grandson, after borrowing from Henry the price of his passage, made a treaty with the French and set sail for Spain without so much as a bow to his English uncle, Europe tittered. Once more Henry and Wolsey furiously changed their tack, swung in the summer of 1518 to an alliance with France, and decided to seal it this time by the engagement of the two-year-old Princess Mary to the French king's infant son.

Although her nephew, Charles of Habsburg, was now King of Spain, and had continued her friend De Mesa as Spanish ambassador in London, and although De Mesa was active in promoting Maximilian's swindle, Catherine lent the Habsburg maneuvers no aid, and when her husband turned to the French she made no objection. De Mesa was alarmed, and the court at Brussels made a desperate last-minute effort to break up the negotiations, but Catherine was affable to the French ambassadors, complacently showed off her infant daughter, and appeared with composure at the public ceremonies. She was pregnant again – it was to be her last pregnancy – and pathetically hoping that the birth of a son would make Mary's engagement of less importance. Moreover, the negotiations in London were taking a turn which greatly appealed to her. A mere defensive alliance with France, likely to be directed sooner or later against Spain, she might have opposed, but Wolsey was planning much more, a general guarantee of European peace, and all the hopes of peace and progress which she had learned from the humanists stirred her to support the project. Through her partisanship of the idea it embodied she was drawn back to another effort to influence Henry's foreign policy.

ii

To understand the appeal of Wolsey's project, one must remember that, even at the end of the middle ages, the peoples of western Europe still thought of themselves as belonging to a single community. After the disillusionment of the religious wars, Europeans were glad to forget ideals which they had so painfully failed to reach, and Niccolo Machiavelli found a posthumous revenge in providing the sole terms of appraisal for the century which had ignored him. Yet the Renaissance was, perhaps, not more Machiavellian than other ages, and at the moment of its dissolution medieval Europe had a fleeting vision of the unity in which it had been born.

As the grave logic of Saint Thomas and the music and passion of Dante remind us, the first Europeans never doubted that they were members of one body, and spent their earliest self-consciousness in exploring the contradictions between a unity based on force, the Roman Empire, and a unity based on faith, the Roman Church. By the fifteenth century the Holy Roman Emperors had become little more than the shadow kings of an insubstantial German nation, and the Popes of Holy Rome hardly distinguishable from other petty Italian princes, but the two ruinous institutions had created between them an idea stronger than either, the idea of Christendom, the *res publicae Christianae*, the commonwealth of Europe. Long after papacy and empire had destroyed each other's claims to its exclusive headship, the idea of Christendom was still strong enough to call forth the great church councils which for a time promised Europe a central deliberative assembly and supreme court, and though that hope failed, Christians continued to think of war among themselves as abnormal and internecine, and the soberest lawyers wrote of the powers of the greatest dynasts as if they were sometimes subject to a higher power. Christendom clung to its hope that someday the rule of law might be substituted for the rule of force.

In the fifteenth century, two forces were working to revive the unity of Christendom. One was a light from within. The humanists had rediscovered in classical culture a bond even older than Christianity. Their pacificism was based on the sentiment that a common origin and a common culture implied a common destiny, a sentiment reinforced, particularly among the serious northern humanists to whom the New Testament was a document not less important than the dialogues of Plato, by a new feeling for the universality of Christ's teaching. Their pens had called forth a new reading public throughout Europe, and labored to create in it a sense of common interests and responsibilities. Both as Christians and as classicists their allegiance turned to Rome, and the best of the popes, by drawing the humanists about them, were seeking to regain their old leadership by means of primacy in the new cultural and intellectual synthesis.

The other force driving Europe together was a threat from without. Christendom had been born in the Crusades; without a new crusade it seemed likely that Christendom might perish. Out of the steppes of Asia had moved a race of military conquerors whose disciplined Moslem fanaticism, more dangerous than the wild Arab flame, menaced not only Christendom, but any culture which the heirs of Greece and Rome and Judea could possibly understand. The Turks were not so much a people as a nomad army, living on the populations of Anatolia and the Balkans as they had lived on the mutton and horseflesh of Turkestan, and using their hordes of disciplined military slaves as a herdsman uses dogs. In slow, terrible waves their conquests lapped westward; the horse tails of their sanjaks floated now in Thrace, now in Macedonia, now by the shores of the Adriatic and at the edge of the Hungarian plain, and though there might be pauses in their advance, the next wave would surely follow, for the nature of Turkish institutions demanded war, and the health of their state required the constant enslavement of fresh peoples. In 1516 it was clear that a new wave was gathering. After a sleepy sultan, a new conqueror, Selim the Grim, had taken Syria and Egypt and pushed his eastern boundary through Azerbian to the wild Iranian highlands. When he turned westward the two keys to Europe, Rhodes, the guardian of the Mediterranean, and Belgrade, the gate of Hungary, both weakly held, would be menaced by the two wings of the Turkish host. When those fortresses fell, it was hard to see what would keep a flaccid Germany, a war-weary, disunited Italy, from succumbing to the Turk.

His Holiness, Pope Leo X, was not unaware of the danger, or the remedy. The first Medici Pope displayed all the Renaissance variety of responses to the world, all the subtle, skeptical, unfixed intelligence, all the fierce appreciation of the immediate moment in all its facets and aspects, which made northerners speak of Italian levity and fickleness. He could neglect business for the antics of buffoons or the pleasures of the hunt, squander fortunes for trifles, and set all Italy by the ears for the sake of half a dozen villages to add to a Medici dukedom, but a fresco by Raphael or a brown Greek manuscript could bring the tears of gratification to his eyes as easily as could a bawdy jest; and his eye took in the whole perspective of world politics as clearly as it did the minutiae of Italian intrigue. When the Turkish banners were planted in Cairo he mobilized all the skill of his chancery and the eloquence of his humanist allies, and sent his legates throughout Europe to urge a five years' truce among all Christian powers, and union for a belated crusade against the Turk.[2]

One of the most skillful of papal diplomats, Cardinal Lorenzo Campeggio, brought the Pope's proposal to England at the very moment Wolsey was dickering with the French. Wolsey saw and seized his opportunity. Under Leo X's tentative opportunist plea lay the great idea which, by a stroke as bold as it was simple, could change the negotiations at London from ordinary dynastic haggling to a solemn refounding of the unity of Christendom, an act commanding forever the applause of humanists, the wonder of statesmen, and the gratitude of the Church. By proposing this union, his master, the King, would become the leader and would remain the arbiter of the princes of Europe, and though the Pope would enjoy the headship of the resulting league, all Europe would know that he, Wolsey, was its real architect. The vision captured his daring imagination, challenged all the resources of his energy and skill.

The preamble of Wolsey's treaty[3] recited the Pope's bull asking for peace among Christians and union in opposing the Turk. Therefore, the King of England and the King of France concluded a permanent peace with each other, agreed never again to attack each other, and to give each other assistance against any aggressor. So far we have only an ordinary defensive alliance. But all the sovereign powers of Christendom – they are carefully listed – were to be invited to adhere to the treaty at once, and to share fully and equally its privileges and responsibilities. All treaties contrary to this fundamental act of union were declared abrogated; the Pope was to be president of the perpetual league thus formed, and all the member states were to guarantee its provisions. All disputes were to be submitted to peaceful arbitration, and any violation of the non-aggression pact was to be punished by the united strength of all the signatories. Thus simply was effected a permanent league of Christendom to end war forever among Christian powers and provide for defense against the Turk, a task in which Henry protested his eagerness to do his share. If the skill of draftsmen and signatures on paper could save the peace of Europe then, once the enumerated powers had signed this treaty, Europe would have peace.

In fact, the Treaty of London, ratified by all the greater powers before the end of 1518, kept the peace of Europe for thirty troubled months. It was the prelude to thirty years of the bitterest and most widespread war that Europe had ever seen, and even before it was signed, a Wittenberg professor, posting on a chapel door the announcement of ninety-five academic theses offered for debate, had laid the train of an explosion which was to blow the idea of European unity out of all practical discussion. But historians who, in the light of later disillusionment, discount its promises as so much cynically empty verbiage, risk a grave misunderstanding of how the treaty affected the minds of its contemporaries. Its phrases did not seem empty to Queen Catherine. Here in the realm of the concrete was the dream of her humanist friends; here, extended and perfected, the work of her mother Isabella, union of Christians against the enemies of the faith; here was the purpose of her own life, the preservation of peace between England and Spain and the checking of French aggression, achieved not while an uneasy dynastic alliance lasted, but forever. Her friend, Bernardino de Mesa, had been startled and alarmed by a development so far beyond his instructions. Viewing any treaty in which the French had a hand with the deepest suspicions, he had taken no part in the preliminary discussions. But gradually, urged perhaps by Catherine, he came round to the view that the treaty meant what it said, and, so far from being dangerous to the Habsburgs, was, since it freed them from the onerous obligations of their past treaties with France, and guaranteed them the peace they needed, highly advantageous. Though he had no powers to ratify, he was present at the solemn ratification in St. Paul's by England, France and the Pope, wrote warmly in favor of the treaty to Maximilian, and hurried himself off to Spain to persuade young Charles to ratify at once.[4] With him he took a warm message from Catherine. Her husband's new foreign policy was again one which both her sympathies and her conscience could thoroughly approve, and while Spain abided by the Treaty of London, the new King of Spain could count on his aunt's support.

Catherine of Aragon

[illegible]

iii

That autumn of 1518 the Emperor Maximilian was hunting in his favorite Tyrol. In that high, sharp air the battered adventurer recaptured more fully than elsewhere the ardent zest of his youth; always an incorrigible optimist, among his beloved mountains his hopeful imagination roamed like the chamois, soared like the eagle. Max knew, well enough, that when his grandson Charles tried to succeed him in his Austrian lands and his imperial dignity, such an unparalleled concentration of dynastic power would provoke powerful resistance, severely testing the guarantees of the Treaty of London; but he was confident of his ability to secure the election for his grandson when the time came. With Charles, Maximilian reflected, the house of Habsburg would really enter upon its destiny, really rule from Sicily to the Baltic, from the Pillars of Hercules to the borders of Poland, as no emperor had ruled since Charlemagne. But that was years away. First there would be this crusade the Treaty of London promised. With all of Europe to be levied on for funds, Max would lead an army down the Danube that would scatter the Turks like chaff. Once in Constantinople he might stop to assume the crown of the Emperor of the East, but it would surely be wrong not to push on with his victorious Germans through Asia Minor to the rescue of the Holy Land and the recovery of the lost imperial province of Egypt before returning to Rome for his triumphant coronation. It seemed almost lucky now that he had never had the money before to go to Rome to be crowned; it would have been a pity to have anticipated any part of the splendor of his reception there as restorer of the Roman world. Then he might think of raising Charles, as Caesars had done of old, to a share in his dignities, might even abdicate in his favor, like that other restorer of the empire, Diocletian. And become a hermit? Why not become Pope? Could the savior of Christendom, the refounder of the circle of the Roman world, the liberator of the Holy Sepulcher, expect less? For future ages Saint Maximilian would quite eclipse Saint Constantine, and his descendants would have to adore him in his place among the saints, as the first line of emperors adored the divine Julius. Max grinned as he elaborated the idea for the benefit of his daughter. Fantastic? Perhaps not so fantastic as Margaret's sober sense would make it. Julius Caesar was no youngster when he conquered Gaul, and as old as Max was now before he overthrew Pompey. Max himself had never felt better, more equal to dominating diets and leading armies; the long days hunting in his wintry mountains would put him in perfect condition for a summer's gallop down the Danube. It was January, but he paid no heed to the chill one long day's hunting cost him. A few days later he was dead, leaving to his heir his dreams, his debt-burdened estates, and his family's claim to a tumbledown empire still in the same confusion that for twenty-five years he had been always just about to remedy.

The death of Maximilian sharpened the international crisis which diplomats had seen coming for a decade. There were now only three monarchs of the first importance in Europe: Charles, King of the Spains and heir to the heterogeneous Habsburg land; Francis I, King of France and Duke, by conquest, of Milan; and – very far the third in everyone's eyes but his own – Henry VIII, King of England. To point the struggle, the highest title in Christendom, that of Holy Roman Emperor, was vacant and would have to be filled by election. In the contest for that office the rivalry of the three kings began.

Unlike the other kings of Europe, the Emperors of the Holy Roman Empire had never been able to convert their monarchy from an elective to a hereditary state. Their feudal vassals were no more stubborn than feudal vassals elsewhere, and even the strain of trying to rule both Germany and Italy might not, in itself, have been fatal, had not the unique dignity of the imperial office made it unthinkable that it should be handed down like ordinary heritable property, or bestowed in any fashion less solemn and hallowed by tradition than formal election. Therefore, since every election had to be bought by the concession of new privileges, the empire, instead of becoming a powerful dynastic state, had remained a crazy, ramshackle feudal structure, in which the actual power of a number of new territorial states grew almost unchecked.

Nevertheless, the Emperor's shadowy title remained the greatest in Christendom, men still believed that a strong ruler might convert the shadow into substance, and the fear that the leading candidate to succeed Maximilian might prove strong enough to make the empire a reality aroused bitter opposition. At nineteen, Charles of Ghent was still an unknown quantity, but the extent of his inheritance gave him, even without the imperial title, unprecedented territorial sway; Pope Leo X feared it might enable him, if he became Emperor, to reassert the old imperial claims in Italy, and reduce the popes to the dependence from which they had only escaped once before after centuries of struggle. Francis I, seeing his boundaries ringed by Charles's inheritance, and knowing that his conquest of Milan could only be confirmed by the emperor, needed no urging to contest any extension of Habsburg power. Henry VIII could not admit that any king could be more worthy of imperial honors than himself. In the spring of 1519 French agents and English agents were bidding against the Habsburgs and each other at the courts of all the prince electors, while papal agents, hoping to evoke from the confusion a compromise on a minor German prince, impartially encouraged all opposition to the leading contender.

The rivalry of the three kings did not seem absurd to their contemporaries. The Empire was not a national state, even in the sense that England and France were becoming national states, and in the sixteenth century, though the idea of the nation was taking root among the gentry and the bourgeoisie, the higher feudal aristocracy and their chiefs, the princes, still lived in a single society, Christendom. It seemed natural and right that the three greatest of them should contest its chief dignity. Charles was not really much more German than Henry or Francis, and even now it is not clear how much his rather dubious claim to be the national candidate helped him, and how much he owed to the shrewd diplomacy of his Spaniards, Burgundians, and Austrians, and to the handsome bribes which an Augsburg banking firm was induced to underwrite, less because they were patriotic Germans than because they saw no hope of collecting Maximilian's old debts unless they lent something substantial to his heir. In the end only one elector held out for Francis, and none even mentioned Henry. Henry, who had begun to recognize that he had only an outside chance, and who had protected his vanity by announcing that in default of his own election he preferred Charles to Francis, was able to carry off his failure gracefully. But for Francis I, whose envoys had unwisely assured him that the empire was within his grasp, defeat was intolerable. Most men knew that the herald who, in the Romerplatz at Frankfort on June 28, 1519, proclaimed Charles V Holy Roman Emperor elect was proclaiming the beginning of a struggle to the death between Habsburg and Valois. In the approaching clash Wolsey's Treaty of London, on which Catherine had based such hopes, was to meet its first test, and the strain was certain to be felt first in England, for in all Christendom now there was no one except the King of England who could hope to hold the balance between the two powerful rivals.

iv

There were some signs that he would not tip the balance in favor of the French. Charles's election was celebrated in London with flowing wine casks and blazing bonfires and a solemn mass at St. Paul's attended by the King, the Queen and the Cardinal. London streets echoed with cheers for the new emperor, for England

and Burgundy, and when, a little later, the young men of the King's chamber, who had been so noisily pro-French in November, even the King's boon companions Bryan and Compton and Carewe, were packed off to the country, or to distant posts in Ireland or the Calais pale, and their places filled by reverend seniors like Sir Richard Wingfield and Sir William Kingston, known imperialists and friends of the Queen, Londoners, whom sentiment and interest combined to make pro-imperialist, rejoiced that French influence was on the wane.[5]

Catherine, however, was not so certain. She cannot have been sorry to see the backs of the young men, and she made an extra effort that summer to create at court an atmosphere of gaiety in which Henry would not miss them, but she knew that the person whose influence had really profited by their dismissal was the Cardinal, and that whether England held the neutral position dictated by the Treaty of London, or wandered off on some adventure in alliance with France, depended almost entirely on Wolsey. There were reasons to distrust Wolsey. Catherine, by this time, knew something of the Cardinal's restless itch for activity and power, and something of the view common among diplomats in London that he could be bribed. He was already drawing a pension from France which he would be sorry to lose, and since the French, holding Milan and allied with Venice, could, if they won England, close every route between the Emperor's northern and his southern domains, they would bid high. Unless her nephew Charles could match their bids, Catherine did not trust Wolsey to abide by the treaty he himself had drawn.

In Catherine's view, any danger to peace, for the time being, could come only from Francis I, and if he were convinced that Henry would enforce against him the non-aggression clause of the treaty of London, he would not be inclined, Catherine thought, to break the peace. It was clearly her duty, therefore, to prevent as long as she could any sinister understanding between Henry and

Francis. That meant backing her nephew, Charles, to the limit, and returning to the old game of supporting Spain, but since, this time, she had reason to believe that Charles really wanted peace, and since it was certain that, although the Cardinal might profit by helping the French, England could not, her natural inclinations merely reinforced her sense of duty.

She was hampered at first by the absence of her friend De Mesa, and by the confusion in Habsburg policies, but she could at least warn her nephew that he must look to his diplomatic fences in England. The French were proposing that the new treaty of peace be celebrated by a meeting between Henry and Francis, somewhere near Calais. The proposal seemed innocent enough; Wolsey favored it, and Henry, curious to see for himself the reported magnificence of the French court, to match his taste for extravagant display against the Frenchman's, and to measure himself against the young king whose military reputation already surpassed his own, agreed enthusiastically. The Emperor's advisers, once they were warned of it, saw all the dangers of such a meeting. It would be bad enough to emphasize the friendship of England and France at a time when English neutrality was the chief stabilizing factor in a world balancing precariously on the edge of war. Moreover, it was at just such personal interviews that the kings of the age were wont to reach sweeping secret agreements, revolutionizing international policy. The French were already boasting that acceptance of the interview proved that alliance between England and France was the real nub of the Treaty of London, and that once they met, the two kings would "give laws to Christendom," quite ignoring the Emperor. The mere appearance of close friendship with England, of an intimacy from which the Emperor was excluded, would be of enormous advantage to French diplomacy throughout Europe, and there was always the graver danger that unless Charles could make counter proposals equally attractive, the French might tempt the Cardinal, and through him his master, to acquiesce in their contemplated aggression, or even to join them in it. Such an outcome would make a sad mockery of the Treaty of London.

Such an outcome Catherine was determined to prevent.[6] She no longer objected to a policy of friendship with France, so long as England's friendship with Spain – that meant with the Emperor – was equally strong. But she was ready to join battle with the Cardinal himself to hold him to his policy of peace. Her warnings brought her old friend De Mesa hurrying from Spain, with a request which Catherine seems to have suggested. The Emperor hoped soon to leave Spain to take up the crown of Germany at Aachen; he asked permission to stop in England to pay his respects to his aunt and uncle – if they could manage to see him before they left for France. De Mesa had also thought up an alternative proposal: How about postponing the meeting between Henry and Francis until Charles could take part in it? Then most of the questions vexing Europe could be solved once for all, and the three chief signatories of the Treaty of London could decide how best to execute it, and what steps to take towards the Crusade. Wolsey, himself, the author of the peace, and the Pope's legate *a latere*, would naturally preside over the meeting of monarchs. It was a shrewd trap for Wolsey's vanity, and that he found the strength to refuse showed his determination not to play the Emperor's game. Catherine had more confidence in her own modest plan. She anticipated that Henry would find the flattery of an imperial visit – an event unprecedented in English history – almost irresistible, particularly as the Emperor would be coming to him almost as a suitor, and she saw more clearly than De Mesa that the crux of the problem was to appeal not to Wolsey's vanity, but to Henry's.

After failing with Wolsey, De Mesa returned to Catherine's idea, but even the interview in England was beset by a thousand difficulties. Wolsey was frankly cold to it; Henry feigned to be coy. At an awkward moment, Charles chose to stand on his dignity and nearly wrecked the whole scheme. The place of the interview, the protocol to be observed, the safeguards to be required and given, the outstanding disputes with the Netherlands which Wolsey arbitrarily insisted on settling in advance, all gave occasion for endless wrangling, which tried even De Mesa's patience, and reduced his imperialist colleagues sometimes to despair. Worst of all was the fixing of the date. Charles, involved in difficulties with his Spanish subjects, could not promise to reach England until some indefinite time in the spring of 1520; the French advanced plausible arguments against any postponement of Henry's promised arrival in France before the end of May.

To court circles the whole question assumed the aspect of a tug of war between the Queen and the Cardinal. It is hard now to read Wolsey's motives. Perhaps he was influenced by the fact that papal policy seemed to incline towards France. Perhaps he was, as cynical persons believed, bought by French promises of support at the next papal election, and by the musical clink of cash down. Perhaps he was just anxious to keep a free hand, and feared that should Henry see Charles before he went to Calais, he would be too bound by prior commitments to profit by the second interview. Perhaps he was just being coy, to increase his own importance. Whatever his motives, he behaved in a most discouraging manner, constantly raising new difficulties, emphasizing to Italian diplomats Henry's sympathy with the French, and even, on the rumor of a league concluded between the Pope and Francis I at Rome, officiating himself in honor of the event at a special High Mass at which the nuncio and the ambassadors of France and Venice occupied places of honor, while De Mesa and the other imperialists were left to be jostled among the ruck of the courtiers in the chancel. Henry proved almost as trying as Wolsey. When, on hearing about the proposed interview with the Emperor, the French ambassador reproachfully suggested that Henry might not keep his engagement with Francis, the King swore a great oath that he would not shave again until he had embraced his brother of France. Sure enough, his previously hairless chin began to sprout a reddish fuzz, and the royal jowls to be framed in a sparse growth of whiskers. For three months the beard grew, then one morning, after a hitch in the conversations with France, Henry's jaw jutted naked as of old. People attributed the unexpected harvest to the influence of the Queen, and the French diplomats looked gloomy. A week later the beard was growing again – because the Queen found she liked it, after all, the imperialists said. Because the French had won, the Venetians retorted. Daily the court observed the barometer of the King's whiskers, and the French pointed to their increasing luxuriance as a sure sign of victory.

Having set imperialist diplomacy in motion, Catherine contented herself for a while with keeping in touch with De Mesa's progress through Dr. Vittoria, her Spanish physician, dropping an occasional line of advice and encouragement to Margaret or Charles, and exercising in private her influence on her husband. But as spring of 1520 approached, and the negotiations for the interview with Charles neared a crisis, she took a more active hand. In her own apartments, in the presence of the imperial ambassadors and a number of nobles and counselors, she fell on her knees before her husband and declared that the greatest wish of her heart was to see her nephew, the successor to her father's kingdom. Henry raised her at once and assured her that he would do everything in his power to satisfy her wish. Perhaps the scene was prearranged. But her next and bolder step was sprung as a surprise. She was in the midst of a routine discussion with council, a body which included a number of distinguished persons, when Henry happened to enter the chamber. The topic before them was preparations for the meeting with Francis I at Calais. On Henry's entrance, Catherine swung suddenly into what was apparently a prepared speech, a daring and well reasoned criticism of the whole negotiations with France, and a vigorous argument against any French alliance. Her councilors, taken unprepared, and perhaps feeling that the Queen would not have spoken so vehemently without Henry's approval, did not try to conceal their agreement, or their delight that the national distaste for this coquetting with the ancient enemy had found a voice. Henry, somewhat embarrassed, contented himself with commending his wife's eloquence and the force of her arguments, but the court, when it heard of the incident, buzzed with excitement, and Wolsey, De Mesa thought, was alarmed and shaken.[7]

Catherine undoubtedly staged the scene to apprise her husband of the strength of the anti-French feeling in his entourage, but without hope of preventing the French interview. What she was really counting on was the scheme, as elaborated by De Mesa, to nullify the diplomatic effect of the meeting at Calais by bracketing it between two interviews between Henry and Charles, the first in England before the Calais meeting, the second at Gravelines in Flanders immediately afterwards. Aided by Catherine's open advocacy the imperialists finally got the treaties for these two interviews signed, but even then, except for Catherine, the first interview might never have taken place. June 1 was the latest possible date for the French meeting, and Henry planned to be in Calais well before that time. But the fifteenth of May went by, and the Emperor did not come. Wolsey opposed further delay, and Henry was in a fidget to be off. The court moved down river to Greenwich, and then to Canterbury on the road to Dover, while all the channel ports bustled with embarkation of thousands of mules and horses, the lading of the mountains of provisions, the forest of tents and pavilions, the collapsible wooden houses that made the impedimenta of this merrymaking expedition as cumbrous as the baggage of an army. It was not until the evening of May 26, 1520, that the Emperor's fleet dropped anchor off Dover, and had not Catherine's repeated pleas kept Henry waiting until the last moment, it was likely, De Mesa thought, that the King of England would have already set sail, and the two monarchs have missed each other by a few hours.

Of the three great world rivals Charles V, in his twenty-first year, was by far the least prepossessing. Henry VIII and Francis I looked like kings, but the young Emperor looked like a backward, handicapped boy. His legs were too short for his body, and a little bowed from overexercise on horseback, forced on a delicate child by the convention which demanded that a king excel in the sports of his nobility; his face was too long and too pale, and his lower jaw so undershot that his teeth would not meet, and his mouth usually hung a little open. In other circumstances he might have grown up a typical Flemish country gentleman, phlegmatic, conscientious, conservative, a little suspicious of strangers and of innovations, absorbed in hunting and the placid supervision of his fields. Indeed, his early education had scarcely fitted him for more, and only since his sixteenth year had he begun to learn with pain that the inheritance of half the Christian world meant a daily burden of decisions which he hated, a constant traffic with subordinates whom he did not understand or trust, the study of languages, which came slowly to his tongue, and long hours of tiresome, sedentary indoor work. To balance all the brilliant qualities of his rivals, Charles had only two: an inbred sense of responsibility which never let him shirk a task, and the aristocrat's unshakable confidence, so bafflingly like stupidity, in himself and his place in the world. Since his place happened to be the first in Christendom, Charles was to spend his life in flogging his mediocre mind and body up to its level – making out of unlikely material, by sheer tenacity of purpose, one of the ablest soldiers, statesmen and diplomats of his age, capable of holding his own with men a hundred times more gifted by nature. His visit to England was to be the first triumph of his peculiar powers.

By advice, or shrewdness, or sheer good luck, Charles took the line best calculated to win his tremendous uncle. He landed at Dover under the black eagle of the Empire, surrounded by a glittering suite, amid the salutes of the Castle guns and the answering thunder of all his navy; but he made no effort to shine thereafter.

When he came stumbling out between his guards to greet the King of England on the stairway to his chamber at Dover Castle, Henry could not divine that only a complete inner security could so easily dismiss the forms of precedence and ceremony; their later conversations did not lead him to suspect that his nephew's slow hesitant speech with its trace of lisping stammer hid reserved judgments and secret purposes, and that behind the pallid vacuous face, with its prominent light-blue eyes, lurked a mind as cold and formidable as an iceberg. As they rode together towards Canterbury, Henry all voluble good humor, Charles all deference and attention, the King of England felt a glow of protective sympathy for his diffident, pliable, rather stupid young relative.

On the note of familial intimacy and avuncular patronage thus happily struck, the interview continued. When, on the edge of the town, the Queen and her ladies met the royal cavalcade and Charles came forward murmuring shyly some phrase of courtesy and thanks to be swept into his aunt's embrace, there was a moment warm as a genuine homecoming between the youth who had scarcely known father and mother, and the matron who embraced, in the head of her father's house, her sister Joanna's son. Catherine's tears sprang partly, perhaps, from relief and thankfulness at a hard task achieved, but partly, too, from the love of her own kin that was almost her deepest emotion. In his aunt, Charles had an ally from the start.

Not even Wolsey sat down with the three at breakfast that morning, and not even Wolsey was present at two of the long talks they had before Charles rode back to his waiting ships. Secretaries and ambassadors, prowling hungrily outside that closed family circle, could catch no phrase of what went on, and not until the imperial court had reached Flanders did the Emperor's most intimate counselors get anything like a full account. Only Charles and his aunt and uncle ever knew all that was said, and we are left to conjecture, from words they let fall afterwards, the course of that friendly family council, in which Henry and Catherine listened to their nephew's slow account of his aims and needs and perplexities, and Henry pronounced judgments on his advisers and opponents, told Charles how to deal with Spain and Germany, Italy and the Low Countries, and as difficulties were proposed, grew fertile in devising expedients. Catherine would have played the woman's part, listening quietly, now and then throwing in a word of sympathy or the hint of a solution. We only know that Charles told his uncle that he wanted peace, and counted on the Treaty of London, and Henry assured him he should have peace through the treaty. We can be sure, too, that it was agreed between them to meet again near Gravelines after Henry had seen Francis, and to lay their further plans in the light of what might develop in the meantime. But more was spoken – or at least tacitly implied. Wolsey felt that the conversations limited him thereafter. Charles later spoke with more than his usual emotion of the inestimable debt he owed the Queen, his aunt, and wrote gratefully to Henry of "the advice you gave me like a good father when we were at Cantorberi."

"Like a good father." Perhaps that was the real nub of the matter. Catherine had never been able to like the French marriage proposed for her daughter. Henry knew that most of her subjects shared her distaste. Mary, it is true, was only four, and his nephew Charles was twenty. But royal marriages are arranged early, and between fourteen and thirty is no great gap. One might almost say that the two were just the right ages for one another. To Catherine, nothing could be more satisfactory than that her daughter should carry on her work, linking England, Spain, and now Burgundy–Austria into one family, perhaps even one dynasty. To Henry it was clear that his daughter could not make a more glorious match. And since Charles had no father of his own, and turned so naturally and deferentially to his uncle for advice, it would be specially flattering to Henry's vanity to stand *in loco parentis* to the Emperor of the World. Nothing was concluded, of course. Perhaps nothing was said in so many words. But in the familiarity of a family discussion a half-word may be enough. The thought was certainly in the minds of all three when they parted.[8]

Charles's fleet had hardly weighed anchor for the Netherlands before Henry and Catherine embarked for Calais, to find, in contrast to the domestic intimacy and frank, informal conversation at Canterbury, a round of pompous ceremony, hollow gaiety, and mutual distrust. The Emperor had come simply to his uncle's house without a thought of safeguard. The monarchs of France and England approached the Field of Cloth of Gold warily, the captains on each side eying the strength of the other as if preparing against ambush, the groups of French and English closing ranks instinctively whenever they came near each other, and fumbling at their sword hilts. In the midst of the festivities the English were alarmed by a rumor that the French were moving against Calais; another time an armed French party made ready to rescue Francis, captured they believed by the English. Even the elaborate entertainments which the kings provided had an air of rivalry, of matching against each other the wealth which the magnificence of the booths and tents, the gilt, the embroidery, the damasks and the cloth of gold implied.

Francis, himself, did his best to break the atmosphere of constraint. He was genuinely anxious for English friendship, and he wanted the party to be a success. The prettiest ladies of France had been mobilized, the best cooks, the most skillful artists. The swaggering gallants of the court and the hard-bitten veterans of Italy had been sharply warned to offer no provocation and to notice none that was offered. Their king gave them an example of smiles and flattery, was profuse in his admiration for English feats in the list and for English splendor in display.

It was no use. No use though Catherine, reassured by Canterbury, was at her most gracious, and played her part in the most genuine and friendly scene of the whole meeting when she and the French Queen, ccming to kiss the pax and each holding back to yield precedence to the other, suddenly both laughed and kissed each other instead. No use though Francis, when he sensed his guests' suspicions, had ridden almost unattended into Henry's camp, surprised his royal brother in bed, and offered gaily to act as his valet, proffering the morning cup and handing the royal shirt. He was too tall, this *grand gaillard*, a shade taller than Henry himself, most people thought, too broad in the shoulder, too sure of himself for all his courtesy. His seat in the saddle was as firm as Henry's own, and he was as tireless as Henry at leaping and dancing. The kings had the good sense not to run against each other in the lists, where they gloriously broke their spears against all comers, but no one could say that one had done much better than the other, and there was one perilous moment when the rivalry each felt almost flared into something uglier. In the midst of the festivities Henry, with boisterous joviality, had seized his royal brother by the collar, shouting "Come, you shall wrestle with me!" Francis was taken off guard; to the horror of the watchers there was a grim moment of writhing strain, a sudden twist, and the majesty of England measured his length on a carpet. People simply did not throw Henry. He rose, pale eyes dangerous, a dark tide of red rising from his neck, squared himself and grunted "Again!" Had the tact of the queens not intervened, and a rush of babbling gentlemen not come between the two, there was no telling what might have happened. It was an incident to undo a week's geniality, though perhaps Francis did not know it.

What he did know, and this was as disconcerting to Henry as the unlucky wrestling match, was his own mind. He was not in the market for advice. He intended to attack the Emperor, and soon, before the unwieldy forces of the Empire could be mustered to attack him. He would be delighted with English alliance, and was prepared to bid high for it; he would be glad of English neutrality, and for that also he would bid. But blow whatever winds might blow, Charles of Ghent was his enemy and should rue it. If the English considered themselves slighted, Francis would have to risk their hostility too.

All in all, the English were glad to turn their backs on the Field of Cloth of Gold. Henry had parted from Francis with the greatest show of cordiality, but he could reflect that a king with that fierce, bold, mocking face, those swaggering shoulders, would never make a comfortable partner. Wolsey had settled with Semblançay some details about French pensions, not altogether to his own disadvantage, and calculated that if this magnificent interview had cost his master as much as the taking of a city, it had certainly cost the French no less, and they were probably even shorter of money. But the main matters of negotiation had advanced no inch. The nobles and gentlemen of England breathed more freely out of sight of the French lines. "By God," cried one of them, "when I meet those Frenchmen again I hope it may be with my sword point!" and Lord Leonard Grey brandished a dagger and swore that if he thought he had a drop of French blood in his veins he would hack it out on the instant.

After the play-acting at Guisnes, the meeting with the Emperor at Gravelines took place in a burst of genuine good feeling. "The emperor," Hall records, "made such semblant of love to the English court that he won the love of the Englishmen. All sorts of Englishmen from the highest to the lowest were so cheered and feasted that they much praised the emperor." In the intervals of cheer and feasting Wolsey and the imperialist diplomats, aided by the assiduous De Mesa, blocked into shape the agreements sketched so informally at Canterbury.

𝔟

Having made Henry and her nephew friends, Catherine yielded the initiative to the professional diplomats, and Wolsey promptly began to recover what was left of his liberty of action. He soothed and flattered the French; he asserted that England was not bound by the informal understanding reached at Gravelines, and he struck a sudden blow at the conservative, pro-imperialist nobles who were the chief threat to his own power. The victim was Edward Stafford, Duke of Buckingham, first of the English nobility, and one of Catherine's oldest and closest friends.

No family in England was more illustrious than the Staffords or bound more closely to the House of Tudor. Of Plantagenet blood, they stood next to the throne, and by a descent unblemished by the imputation of bastardy. The old Duke had died in Henry of Richmond's cause, and the present Duke, in his youth, had been the most brilliant figure at the court of Henry VII, adding to its prestige and security by his mere presence, even if his abilities added nothing. When Henry VIII and Catherine first came to the throne, no one seemed closer to them, and though he had been less often at court in recent years, there had never been any question of Buckingham's unwavering loyalty. But everyone knew that the Duke could not stomach the upstart Wolsey. There was a story that after Wolsey became Cardinal Legate, and had taken to dining like a king, with the ranking nobleman present holding a silver ewer for him to wash his hands, Buckingham had marked his distaste for the office by pouring the water over the Cardinal's shoes. Perhaps Wolsey thought it more serious that many of the older nobility looked to the Duke as their natural leader, rejoiced in his outspoken condemnation of Wolsey's dalliance with France, and might form behind him a dangerous opposition if ever the Cardinal's shifty policies should go awry.

It was not hard to trap the rash, muddle-headed Buckingham, to twist his outbreaks against the minister into treason towards the master, to find among his servants those who could be bribed or bullied or tortured into remembering more treasonable matters, among them that, on the prophecy of a soothsaying monk, the Duke had boasted that Henry would die without issue and Staffords be kings of England. To speculate on the death of the King was legally high treason, and the particular twist of the speculation flicked Henry's rawest nerves. Only his own life and that of one girl-child barred the fulfillment of the prophecy. Perhaps Wolsey pointed out to his master that soothsayers had been known to be poisoners also, and from wish to deed was sometimes a short step — that Buckingham was indeed next in the succession, the richest subject in the kingdom, and with friends and relatives ready to push him higher. When frightened, Henry could be merciless.

Buckingham was tried in May, 1521, before a jury of his peers, on evidence that now seems a farrago of nonsense, malice, and surmise. But a man accused of treason stood little chance under the absolutism Wolsey had been so busy strengthening, and one by one the peers responded "Guilty" to the Earl Marshal's query, and the barbarous sentence was read: "To be drawn on a hurdle to the place of execution, there to be hanged, cut down alive, your members to be cut off and cast in the fire, your bowels burnt before your eyes, your head smitten off, your body to be quartered and divided at the King's will, and God have mercy on your soul." The King's mercy permitted a more seemly execution, but no more. Catherine begged in vain for the life of the old friend who had welcomed her to England in her girlhood, and danced and jested at her first faraway wedding, who had sent her fruit and venison in the days of her adversity, and whose head was forfeited now, in part at least, because his sympathies were like her own. If she guessed that Wolsey's ferocious spring had been meant as a warning for her, too, she gave no sign; but the nobles of England quivered like cattle who scent the wolf, and the commons were appalled. As for Henry, he was surprised how easy it was to kill so great a man. "If the lion knew his strength," said Sir Thomas More, "hard it were for any man to rule him." Now the lion, prodded on by Wolsey, had tasted the best blood of his kingdom. He would not forget that the ax is a sharp conclusion to any argument.

Foreign observers, however, who concluded from Buckingham's fall that the French had triumphed in England, proved mistaken. Events, stronger than French bribes or imperialist pressure, forced his hand. Even as Buckingham was led from his trial with the ax's edge turned towards him, French men-at-arms were pouring through the passes of the Pyrenees into Navarre, crossing the frontiers of the Empire at Sedan; a year later, in spite of all Wolsey's conferences with both sides, his proffers of mediation, and his desperate postponements of the sanctions called for by the Treaty of London, the Emperor was again in England, and England was at war with France.

Cynical people held that, in the auction of the Cardinal's favor, the imperialists had outbid the French. Others noted that the pro-imperialist sympathies of nobles and people, the powerful influence of the Queen, and the fact that Leo X had thrown in his lot with the Emperor, all created a current difficult even for Wolsey to resist. Some held that Henry, urged by Catherine and spurred by a reviving lust for conquests in France, spoke the decisive word. But it would be charitable to remember that a simple observance of Wolsey's Treaty of London forced England to declare against France.[9] Though Francis I had done his best to cloud the issue, no reasonable man doubted that the French were the aggressors, and Wolsey's conferences had proved that they would not surrender the fruits of their aggression. The time had come when peace had to be fought for; the treaty obligations of England were clear. Wolsey may have postponed but, in the end, he did not evade the responsibility.

It was clear to Catherine, at least, where England's duty lay. She could not have approved a war of simple aggression against France. She was coming more and more to hope for peace among Christians and unity against the Turk. But when the hirelings of France launched a double attack upon the Emperor she despaired of peace until the aggressor was punished. Her conviction was strengthened by the fact that Francis had chosen a moment when the danger from the Turk was more serious than ever, and when the Emperor was just engaged in meeting, at Worms, a new danger, a heresy which, by denying the supremacy of the Pope and the validity of the Sacraments, threatened Christendom from within as the Turk threatened it from without. However sympathetic she might be to reform, Catherine's every instinct was shocked at the suggestion of heresy; though English theologians might shake their heads, Catherine, at least, thoroughly approved the extreme statement of papal supremacy which her husband had written into his book against Martin Luther. She rejoiced that her husband would fight side by side with the Emperor as the champion, not only of the peace and unity of Christendom, but of its orthodoxy as well. During the year of hesitation – May, 1521, to May, 1522 – she worked with De Mesa, her nephew's ambassador, to bring Henry and Wolsey to a sense of their duty. She welcomed Charles's return to England, even though it meant war. Martin de Salinas found Catherine a sympathetic listener when he told how the Turk had taken Belgrade and now menaced Rhodes and Hungary, but when he proposed patching up any sort of peace with France to meet the eastern danger, she could only shake her head. "The King of France is the greatest Turk," she told him. Until the French were beaten there could be no other crusade.[10]

That conversation took place in June, 1522, during Charles's second visit to England, a visit which lasted more than a month, and made up, by the splendor of its pageants and the thoroughness of its diplomatic arrangements, for the hurried informality of the first. Charles saw Greenwich and London, where the citizens gave him an enthusiastic welcome, Richmond and Windsor, and journeyed down to Winchester, the traditional capital of Arthurian Britain, before he set sail from Southampton. All the way was punctuated with banquets and tourneys and processions, and interspersed with confidential discussions with Henry, while picked committees of diplomats worked at the drafting of a series of treaties designed to tie Charles and Henry into double harness forever. There was a permanent treaty of peace and friendship, commercial intercourse and mutual aid, and a whole series of minor agreements, including a substantial loan from Henry to his nephew, leading up to a great enterprise for the joint invasion, complete conquest, and final partition of the entire kingdom of France. The whole was crowned and cemented by the betrothal of the Emperor to Henry's daughter, with definite arrangements for dowry and delivery of the bride, and the provision that the eldest male child of the marriage should, unless Henry had a son, inherit the crown of England.

During all this visit Charles bore himself so as to confirm and extend the good opinion the English had of him. From the moment when, with a graceful Spanish gesture, he fell on his knees before his aunt to ask her blessing at their reunion, the common people took him to their hearts. He laughed but little, and his tongue was always guarded, but his modesty and courtesy were unfailing, and Henry found him as deferential as of old, eager for advice and full of expressions of gratitude. He applauded the graces and talents of his six-year-old fiancée, subtly flattered the greater English nobles, told Wolsey he trusted him as a second father (Henry was the other "father" he trusted) and completely charmed his aunt. If English interests were being identified with his to an almost unparalleled extent, why he was almost a member of the family already, and Henry felt confident that his nephew and prospective son-in-law would never serve him as he had been served by other monarchs in the past.

Catherine must have hoped not. The alliance between England and the Emperor had grown far beyond anything the Treaty of London called for, into something perilously like the old alliance with Ferdinand, which had turned out so badly. And again, she had engaged all her influence in the venture, though this time, older by a decade, and less sure of her husband, she had not only his wrath to fear in case of failure, but the fury of the Cardinal, for whom failure might mean ruin. A good deal depended on her nephew's good faith, and on the success of the war.

vi

The war went very well at first, then not so well, then better, then very badly indeed. As Christmas of 1524 approached and the third year of the war was half over, not a foot of French soil had been conquered for Henry, though he had sent two invading armies into France and paid part of the expenses of two others. The Emperor had done somewhat better at first, pushed the French out of Italy, and straightened his frontiers in Spain and the Netherlands; but the chief hope of the allies, a feudal insurrection in France headed by the Duke of Bourbon – a project on which Henry had spent a lot of money – had come to nothing, and an imperialist invasion of Provence in 1524 had ended in disaster. In September of that year, Francis himself, turning his back contemptuously on the idle English, had led a great army into Lombardy. As winter approached the imperialists found themselves clinging desperately to a few fortified positions in northern Italy, deserted by their Italian allies, even by the new Pope, Clement VII, whom their influence had helped to elect, and with not only their positions in Lombardy, but Charles's Kingdom of Naples as well, in serious danger. By every courier Charles told his ambassador in London that, without more help from England, troops in the north, and an important sum of money, the whole game might be lost. But Wolsey was already laying his plans to cut the losses of an unprofitable enterprise, and make a separate peace with France.

From Wolsey's own point of view it was high time. It was not merely that his personal hopes from the imperialist alliance had been rudely disappointed, though the thumping pensions promised him were two years overdue, and he had twice seen the papacy, which also had been promised him, go to another imperialist nominee. Henry had been equally disappointed; instead of the promised prompt repayment of the sums advanced in the past, and the "indemnity" which was to compensate Henry for the loss of French tribute, nothing had come from Spain except appeals for more money, so that Charles now owed in England nearly half a million crowns. It was possible to represent all of Charles's successes as due to English aid, and to blame all the English failures on lack of co-operation by the Emperor, a view Henry was naturally prone to take. When Henry also began to take the view, popular throughout the country and beginning to be heard more and more often at court, that the King had been seduced into this war solely by the insatiable ambition of the Cardinal, it would be all up with the great minister.

For Wolsey had no support except his master. Most of the courtiers had always hated him and were eager to believe now that he was bilking them and their master, while he pocketed the Emperor's gold. Most of the clergy hated him for his pride and avarice, and, even more, for his efficiency. And the common people hated him, in spite of the cheap and speedy justice he had given them, because, being no better than themselves, he had made himself like a king in pomp and splendor, and because they never thought to blame the expensive tastes of their popular sovereign for higher taxes and oppressive fines, but only the minister who ruled under him. The war had brought all these hatreds to a head. The bottom of Henry VIII's treasury had been scraped at last, and Wolsey, having exhausted the arts of bullying and cajolery in wringing a grant of money from Parliament, had driven the country to the verge of rebellion in an unsuccessful attempt to collect what had been granted. Ballads were sung against him in the streets, and in every tavern men grumbled that the Cardinal had sold them to the Emperor. Whatever Wolsey's motives and responsibility at the beginning of the war, he had dipped deep in his own pocket to support it, and had worked for its success with the furious energy of ten ordinary men, wearing out relays of subordinates and dispatching mountains of business, even when he lay stricken by disease in a darkened chamber, half-blinded, apparently three-fourths dead. He knew that no such considerations would save him if the alliance proved disastrous. He knew, also, that if he broke it clumsily or if the breach turned out to be unfortunate, his enemies would be equally eager to seize that excuse also for his ruin.[11]

Wolsey had to move with care. He had already been in touch for months with a French agent, half spy, half unofficial envoy whom he kept close in the house of one of his servants in London, and saw privately for hours at a time at Hampton Court. But he had been unable to conceal the intrigue from the Queen and the Emperor's ambassador; and he was perhaps uncertain how far Henry, who still thought longingly of French conquests, would support a change of front. With his enemies on the council licking their lips at the prospect of his downfall, he dared not risk a showdown with the imperialists until he had made sure of his bargain with France. Characteristically he considered how to anticipate and paralyze the opposition.

For the moment the Cardinal dared do no more against Catherine than try to cut her off from communication with her nephew, and to watch for some false step that would place her in his power. He had his own spies among her ladies, and, as she realized, he read her correspondence. He prevented her from ever seeing the Emperor's ambassador except when he, himself, was present. He probably knew that her relations with the new ambassador, a Flemish nobleman, Louis de Praet, were not as close as they had been with old De Mesa, and he must have known, also, that she was from the first dubious of the ambitious schemes Henry and Charles had elaborated, and that for over a year her only messages to her nephew had been to beg him to be completely open with her husband, to say frankly whether he was able to carry out his past promises, and to promise nothing in the future that he did not intend to fulfill. But correct as her conduct was at the moment, and little as she liked the objectives of the war, she would be outraged by Wolsey's scheme for an alliance with France, and if her resentment became active Wolsey did not doubt her power to make it felt. She had a better brain and more experience of diplomacy than any of the pro-imperialist nobles on the council, and she was their chief link with the Emperor. She had proved that she still had more influence with her husband than anyone, except, possibly, Wolsey himself. If it came to open hostilities between them, Wolsey wanted every advantage he could lay hold of.

With the Emperor's ambassador, Wolsey could be more abrupt. Louis de Praet was no fool, but a poor choice to succeed the subtle De Mesa. He had a soldier's impatience with the guile of the clergy, and an aristocrat's contempt for Wolsey's lowly origins. He reluctantly admired the Cardinal's ability, but he never attributed to him any but the lowest motives, and since the coming of the French agent it had been almost open war between them. Conducting the rest of the duel not unskillfully, de Praet had made one grave mistake. In default of couriers of his own he sometimes entrusted his letters to the English master of the posts. The letters were sealed, of course, with the imperial seal, and written in a private cipher, but seals are only wax, and de Praet's alphabetic cipher will yield to a few hours of patient substitution. Couched in it, Wolsey could read besides unflattering descriptions of himself, and a painfully accurate estimate of his predicament, the repeated advice to the Emperor to make a separate peace with France before Wolsey anticipated him, along with other matter enough to make the Cardinal sure that judicious excerpts from such letters, read to Henry, would close de Praet's career in England. He could read, also, enough of de Praet's determination to attack him openly, rather than suffer an English understanding with the French, to convince him that he must deal with the ambassador without delay.

Since it would be embarrassing to admit having read letters entrusted to the English Master of the Posts, for Henry's benefit, and perhaps for the Emperor's, Wolsey arranged a little comedy. He delayed de Praet's next courier until the city gates were about to be closed, then when the foreigner tried to pass, the watch arrested him and took his letters to a royal officer who laid them before Wolsey. Wolsey opened them – to assure himself that the man was what he pretended to be, and not a French spy – and found in them words so insulting and treasonable that he felt obliged to lay them before Henry at once. The first de Praet heard of the fate of his courier was when he was called before the privy council forty-eight hours later to be told that his efforts to destroy the good intelligence between the King of England and the Emperor were tantamount to treason, and that he was hereafter forbidden to communicate either with his own government or with the English. A last desperate effort to lay the whole cause before Henry in person, and to expose Wolsey's dealings with the French, was unavailing. De Praet found himself isolated and helpless, with guards at his door, practically under arrest. The stroke at de Praet, like the stroke at Buckingham, was meant to intimidate the imperialists, and clear the Cardinal's path.[12]

The result, however, was not what the Cardinal expected. The Emperor refused to be taken in by Wolsey's comedy, reiterated his complete confidence in de Praet, and protested vigorously at the violation of his seals. And though the way was cleared for bargaining with the French, and though a solemn French embassy appeared promptly to close the deal, Wolsey made no use of his freedom. The French ambassadors were preparing to ride in state to Hampton Court, when a sweating courier was admitted to King Henry's bedchamber. On February 24, 1525, eleven days after the break with de Praet, at Pavia in Lombardy, the French and imperialists had fought, and the French had been utterly beaten. Their army was destroyed and Francis himself was a prisoner. Henry heard the messenger with shining eyes, all his old misgivings about alliance with France confirmed, all his old dreams of conquest reawakened. "You are as welcome as the angel Gabriel was to the Virgin Mary," was how he put it to the courier, and he sprang from bed to tell Catherine the news, and to sit down with her to write congratulations to their nephew. Now that the French are prostrate, Henry wrote, is the time to finish them. Let us begin the invasion of France at once and divide the kingdom between us.

The French ambassadors, on their way to the palace, were stopped by a messenger from Wolsey. Henry would not be seeing them that day.

But also Henry had refused to see de Praet, who after waiting three months left England. So the only result of Wolsey's blow at de Praet was that, at a moment of great importance, the Emperor had no direct representative in London, and not only was Catherine cut off from any channel through which she could advise her nephew, whose affairs in England were handled as badly as possible, but Wolsey himself was at a serious disadvantage in trying to repair the breach. The interruption lasted for twenty-two months, through a time fatal to the good understanding of Charles and Henry, fatal, too, to Catherine, and in the end to the great Cardinal as well.

vii

Even had Henry been able to find the money for another invasion of France, – and in a few months it was clear that not all Wolsey's arts could raise the necessary sum, – his dreams of conquest there would have been disappointed. Charles had no money either; his victorious army of Italy remained unpaid, and troops in the Netherlands were being discharged for the sake of economy. Meanwhile the Turk, having taken Rhodes while the Christians fought each other, was known to be preparing an invasion of Hungary; the French, less disorganized than anyone had thought possible by the capture of their king, were rallying to make a stiff resistance, and – as a consequence, people said, of Luther's teachings – all Germany was aflame with a revolt of the peasants, which for a moment threatened to overturn the Empire. Now that he could hope to extort advantageous terms from his captive, Francis I, Charles had no more desire than he had means to continue the war. He could promise his uncle to include him in the peace, but that was all.

One tie still held between the Emperor and Henry. They might quarrel, as relatives quarrel, but as long as Charles remained betrothed to the Princess Mary, the interests of Habsburgs and Tudors moved on surely converging lines. Mary was nine, now, a pretty and intelligent child if the reports of ambassadors may be trusted, the joy and pride of both her parents, anyway, and the only child, they had come to realize, that they would ever have. In five years she could be married, and she would transmit to her eldest son the crown of England, the lordship of Ireland and Wales, and the English claim on France. That his eldest grandson would also inherit Austria and the Netherlands, Naples and Sicily, the Spains and their dominions in the New World, and would wear, in due course, the imperial crown, helped enormously to reconcile Henry to the reflection that there would be no more male Tudors. London could never be that grandson's chief capital, but Paris might be, if the English claim could be asserted, and it may be that the dream of handing on to the future Emperor of the World the solid core of the future Empire stirred Henry's desire for the conquest of France quite as much as his own ambition for martial glory. He was always reminding Charles that any land conquered in France would revert to their mutual heir, and on the last occasion when they corresponded on the subject he proudly promised to bring his daughter to the Emperor *dans son lit à Paris*.[13]

Catherine shared her husband's dream, and knew its paramount importance to him. In the months when the war was going badly and ties with the Emperor were strained, she kept repeating one thing to de Praet, to the papal nuncio, to Charles himself: "As long as our nephew keeps his promise to marry our daughter, the alliance will remain unbroken; as long as the marriage treaty stands, he may be sure of England." [14]

Because Wolsey had cut her lines of communication, she had no means of knowing of the danger or repeating the warning when the crisis came. Mary was nine and Charles was twenty-four. Charles had another cousin in Portugal, a slim dark princess just the right age to be married, and enthusiastically desired as their queen by the estates of Castile. Isabella of Portugal would bring with her nine hundred thousand golden ducats in ready money, while Mary's dowry would be mostly paid by the return of certain slips of paper on which the Emperor had acknowledged loans from her father. Charles was anxious to be married at once, so that he could leave his Empress to rule Spain while he attended to the demands of the rest of his Empire. Perhaps he thought he could dispense with England, or perhaps he merely hoped his aunt and uncle would not be unreasonable. He might not have jilted Mary so gracelessly had his diplomatic lines in England not been snarled by Wolsey's quarrel with de Praet.

In April, 1525, Charles sent a worthy, ineffectual dignitary, the Knight Commander Peñalosa, to explain all his difficulties to Henry, and to intimate that unless Mary could be sent to Spain at once, and with her some part of her dowry in cash, it would be an act of friendship to release him from his engagement, so that he could marry the Portuguese cousin. Peñalosa was to say nothing until he handed de Praet, in London, a ciphered letter the contents of which were to be a secret between the Emperor and the resident ambassador. Then Peñalosa and de Praet were to consult Queen Catherine and rely on her advice. But de Praet had left England before Peñalosa's arrival, and since the rather incompetent Flemings whom Margaret of Savoy, Charles's aunt, acting for him as Regent of the Netherlands, had sent as stopgaps had failed to retain their predecessor's secretary, there was no one in London who could even read the important ciphered letter. The Flemings had failed also to establish any communication with the Queen, and Peñalosa never saw her except at his public reception and did not tell her a word of his real mission. Worst of all, when Peñalosa had passed through Brussels, the Regent Margaret, for once at cross-purposes with her nephew, and anxious about the outcome of some petty disputes over commerce and fisheries which her envoys were arranging with the English, had deleted from his ordinary instructions every hint that Charles wanted to be released from his promise in order to marry elsewhere. In consequence Henry found what was left of Peñalosa's message impertinent and unintelligible, and was left to learn from his own ambassadors in Spain that Charles was making terms with the French, had no intention of waiting for Mary, and expected to marry a Portuguese princess as soon as possible.[15]

The treachery seemed blacker than any Ferdinand had ever perpetrated, an affront so deadly that reproaches were out of the question; the only possible response was a contemptuous acquiescence. In his letters to Spain Henry took that attitude, coldly informed the Emperor that he would make no difficulties about the Portuguese marriage, but expected the immediate repayment of the moneys due him, and considered all the treaties between them void and at an end. But Henry was determined to show the Emperor that he and his family could not be jilted and snubbed with impunity, and his silent rage was more dangerous than the noisy outbursts of 1514. Wolsey was instructed to hasten the separate peace with France, and in two months had signed and sealed with the

French envoys at his house of the More a treaty which, for all its slippery phrasing, was a sword-point directed against the Emperor. All over Europe that autumn Wolsey's agents were busy stirring up a great league to overthrow the victor of Pavia. The year 1525 repeated the pattern of 1514 and 1518. Repeated disappointments and betrayals left Henry with little of the trusting humor in which he had begun the game of diplomacy. He had learned all its lessons, except the important one – that he did not have to play it. He was as wary and as tricky now as any of his fellow monarchs. And his trickiness was edged by an angry bitterness, an indignant resentment, as of personal injury and humiliation, which more disillusioned players of the game usually managed to escape, even in defeat.

This time he vented some of his resentment on Catherine. Elizabeth Blount's child, little Henry Fitzroy, was six. He had a decent allowance, but the world had seen little of him. Peñalosa had been gone for no more than a few days, and the last dispatches from Spain had been opened but a few hours, when the court received summons to Bridewell Palace to see the knighting of Henry, the King's son. After the knighting, the little boy was led out of the presence to return between two earls to be created a peer of England, Earl of Nottingham. Hardly had he made his bows and been drawn away, while the chamber buzzed with talk, when he appeared again, supported by the two remaining English Dukes, Norfolk and Suffolk. When he rose from his knees this time there was a third, Henry Fitzroy, Duke of Richmond and Somerset. The titles pealed like alarum bells; from Richmond, Henry VII had made one step to the throne. And before the ceremony was over the significance had been underlined unmistakably: the little boy was proclaimed Lord Admiral of England, Wales, and Ireland, of Normandy, Gascony and Aquitaine, Knight of the Garter, Keeper of the City and Castle of Carlisle, and first peer of England. Nothing was wanting except Mary's title of Wales, and it seemed clear to most that, if his father could manage it, Bessie Blount's child would be the next King of England.

Catherine's outspoken indignation at the insult to herself and her daughter only rebounded to her harm. Wolsey, more surely in the saddle than ever, since revenge on the Emperor was wholly in his hands, had a commission to reorganize the royal household, and took the opportunity to dismiss from Catherine's suite those of her waiting women who were not tools of his own. When Catherine protested against their dismissal, the Cardinal told Henry that it was these women who had prompted the Queen's outburst against the little Duke of Richmond, and Henry brusquely rejected her pleas for the continued companionship of her friends.

The third blow was shrewdest of all. Henry summarily ordered Mary, aged nine, to go to Ludlow Castle and take up her duties as Princess of Wales. For the first time Catherine was to be separated from the child whose studies and whose every step she had always overseen. Perhaps the Queen found the fact that her daughter was to have a suitable household, and her friend, the Countess of Salisbury, for governess, some consolation. The appointment showed, at least, that Henry had not quite made up his mind about the succession. At any rate, Catherine protested no further, and her reply to Mary's first letter from Ludlow shows sorrow at the parting, but no darker foreboding: —

I pray you [she wrote [16]] think not that any forgetfulness hath caused me to keep Charles [the courier] so long here, and answered not your good letter, by the which I perceive you would know how I do. I am in that case that the long absence of the King and you troubleth me. My health is meetly good, and I trust in God, he that hath sent me the last dooth it to the best, and will shortly turn it to the first to come to good effect. And in the mean time I am very glad to hear from you, especially when they show me that ye be well amended. I pray God to continue it to his pleasure.

As for your writing in Latin, I am glad that ye shall change from me to Master Federston, for that shall do you much good to learn by him to write aright. But yet some times I would be glad when ye do write to Master Federston of your own enditing when he hath read it that I may see it. For it shall be a great comfort to me to see you keep your Latin and fair writing and all. And so I pray you to recommend me to my Lady of Salisbury. *At Woburn, this Friday night. Your loving mother. Katharine the Queen.*

In the letter there was resignation touched with sadness, like the autumn that was closing round her. She had never been separated from Henry for so long a time; she had never been so cut off from the world, almost as if she were getting ready to leave it. Her health was only "meetly good" – earlier in the year she had been moved to settle some of her affairs and to write to Wolsey of "when God calls me," and there were rumors abroad that she was dying. But autumn was to have its St. Martin's summer. Henry rejoined her at Richmond, apparently appeased; they read Erasmus' latest book together, and Henry received in her chamber as of old. Her high hopes had been disappointed, so might her fears be too. Perhaps she had been too greedy of power for herself and her daughter, too sure she knew God's plans for the world. Her husband would surely not put their daughter aside, and, married to the little King of Scots, a boy just two years older than she, Mary might bring England the peace and security that was better than world dominion. Meanwhile, for Catherine herself, there were her books and her charities, and a not unpleasant drifting in the chill November sunlight.

One afternoon she went by barge from Richmond to pray, as her custom was, at the house of the monks of Sion, taking Luis Vives with her for the charm of his thoughtful tongue. As they came back with the late afternoon tide, the slanting rays of the sun catching now and then a glitter on lazy oar-blades, and the green and gold landscape mellowed by a golden haze, Vives fell to talking of the tides in men's lives of good and bad, and the inscrutable turns of Fortune's wheel. As for herself, Catherine said, she had experienced many kinds of fortune, but now she preferred a moderate and steady lot to dramatic ups and downs. If she had to choose between the two extremes, she went on, she would choose the saddest lot rather than the most flattering, for in the midst of the greatest unhappiness there is always consolation, but judgment and a sense of measure often disappear from those giddy with prosperity.[17] Vives agreed, reflecting perhaps that he was unlikely ever to talk with one who had experience of greater changes of fortune than this placid, soft-voiced woman; and Catherine, sighing a little, may have thought, as she watched the brown-backed river slide past, that, after all, it was good to know that all one may expect is a middling fortune, without the triumphs of the past, without the adoration of a young king and the sense of the destinies of Christendom in one's hands, but without dangers or trials or disappointments, either, or anything except the mild autumn that slips imperceptibly towards winter.

PART III

THE DIVORCE OF HENRY VIII

(1527–1536)

Chapter One

THE LAST COMMUNICATION between the magnificent Seigneur Louis de Praet and the Queen of England was at the time of the Christmas revels of 1524. When de Praet's successor kissed the Queen's hand at Richmond, the Christmas revels of 1526 had begun. Less than a month before, Catherine had written to Charles a brief note, her first since her congratulations after his victory at Pavia, between the lines of which one can read sadness and anxiety. At that time she had not heard from him for two years.[1]

The sadness and anxiety were mostly on his account. In the autumn of 1525, after the unpleasantness over little Richmond had worn off and Mary had departed for Wales, Henry had rejoined Catherine, and they had kept their accustomed state as usual. True, the King was less often in the Queen's company, and her personal and political importance was diminishing. Catherine's last pregnancy had been in 1518, and the English council had faced the disappointing fact that the Queen, in her forty-first year, was "long past the usual age of childbearing."[2] Just when Henry began to think so, and to lose the last flicker of interest in his wife as a woman, is a matter about which his later confused and defiant statements still leave us guessing, but surely it was before 1525. Catherine did not complain. She had passed a crisis in her physical health, which was definitely better after the autumn of 1526, and if she had lost Henry forever as a lover, she had seen too many of his casual infidelities to be alarmed for her position as his wife, the woman who had most of his confidence, the greatest share in his life. They read and even hunted together, as of old, and presided together over banquets and tournaments and receptions to foreign notables, and whatever frail ladies took Henry's fancy did not disturb the Queen's placidity.

Although the proposal to declare Richmond Henry's heir had subsided, and nothing more was heard for the present of the suggestion that he be married to his half-sister Mary so that they might inherit jointly, Catherine was still disturbed about the King's illegitimate son, for there was still some talk of finding him a royal bride abroad, and of erecting for him a separate kingdom in Ireland, a scheme which, people said, would make Ireland a greater nuisance than Scotland had ever been. But Richmond's prospects caused Catherine less uneasiness than Wolsey's foreign policy. To that, Catherine attributed all Henry's coldness and abstraction: the blank look and mumbled word with which he greeted her after long conferences with the Cardinal; the restraint and even the suggestion of friction which was creeping into their less frequent conversations. Knowing she would disapprove, Henry told her very little of English policies abroad, and not all he told her, she suspected, was true. As for Wolsey, she knew that he barely troubled to dress up his lies for her benefit, that he still made spies of her waiting women and opened her correspondence, that he was careless whether she noticed the malevolent watchfulness which would be quick to pounce on any opening she gave him.[3] More arrogantly than ever the Cardinal moved through the court, the unwieldy hulk of corrupted flesh bearing perilously the supple, powerful brain, a demoniac incandescence of ambition and pride driving and lighting from within the bloated, rotting body. Seeing upon her, wherever she moved, that eye, – like a wet brown stone except for the red spark burning deep behind it, – Catherine was coming to believe that Wolsey had always hated her; she was about convinced, too, that she had always hated Wolsey.

She more than half believed him responsible for all the pother about Henry's bastard; she knew his foreign policy was wicked.

It was he, more than anyone else, who had tempted the King of France to break the word plighted at Madrid, plunging Europe again into war. It was he, she was now convinced, who had ruined the alliance, by withholding aid from the Emperor in his need; and he who had seduced the Pope and the Italian states. Deeply as her nephew had injured her by jilting her daughter, she was inclined to forgive him (it was hard to bear a grudge against Spain, and she understood, better than anyone else in England, the clamor there would be in Castile for a Portuguese marriage), and to score that disappointment also against the Cardinal. If Henry was irritable and abstracted, Wolsey's policy was to blame. God would not uphold oath-breakers and liars against His Emperor and Spain; the affairs of the French and their allies, the Italian league, were going badly, and the deeper Wolsey drew England after them, the greater Henry's losses would be. With all her heart Catherine longed for peace, not for another bout of war on Charles's side – just for peace and an end to this French entanglement. If only her nephew were not so distant and so negligent, if only he had someone at her husband's court, someone like De Mesa for instance, to keep him informed of what was going on, to soothe and reassure Henry, to bribe or frighten Wolsey, and to settle all the petty irritations which had accumulated through the lazy indifference of a succession of Margaret's slow Dutchmen, something might be done.

Catherine would have been surprised had she known how warmly Henry and Wolsey would have agreed. They knew better than she how badly for the French and their allies the war in Italy was going. Actually France was almost less at war with Charles than England was; there was still an imperial ambassador at the court of Francis I, though there was none at Henry's, and Francis seemed to pay less attention than Henry to the beating his Italian champions were taking at the hands of the Emperor's mercenaries. What Henry and Wolsey wanted, now Henry's anger had somewhat cooled, was to act as arbitrators, and draw a neat profit from rewriting the

Treaty of Madrid in London. But Charles had not been very pleased by their abrupt cancellation of the Treaties of Windsor, their treatment of de Praet, their encouragement of the French. Francis might accept their mediation, but unless Charles would, they would have to come out in open support of the French, since it was unthinkable to take no hand at all in the game of shifting boundaries. "I shall count Your Grace happy if you can escape this alliance," Wolsey wrote.[4] If you *can* escape. For the Emperor remained aloof, and the net of the French alliance was closing round them.

That autumn of 1526 the imperial ambassador for whom Wolsey as well as Catherine was looking so anxiously, the ambassador who might bring the word that would prevent the French alliance, was cooling his heels in a French prison. After months of deliberation, Charles, who had too many more serious troubles to bear much malice against his uncle, had decided to send someone to England with conciliatory instructions. Several months more had gone by in picking out the man, a fifty-year-old political ecclesiastic of high family and sound judgment, Don Iñigo de Mendoza; five weeks more in drafting Don Iñigo's instructions; and with no more than the proverbial slowness of Spain, the ambassador had reached the Pyrenees by the end of June, 1526, a month after the League of Cognac, intended to drive the imperialists from Italy, had been signed. France did not look safe for Spaniards, but Don Iñigo's instructions, made out in April, said *Go through France*, and after waiting in vain for a counter order from Madrid through weeks in which France moved steadily nearer war, Don Iñigo had taken the plunge. Apprised of his mission, the French had played cat and mouse with him, promised him a safe conduct, made him wait for it, told him he could safely go on without it, let him get nearly to the Netherlands frontier, and then arrested him as an enemy spy.

So Mendoza spent the autumn in the damp confinement of the fortress of Arques, until the French judged it time to express cour-

Charles V

teous surprise and regret that the sacred person of an ambassador had been molested by ignorant and overzealous underlings. He did not reach London until December 26, 1526, with instructions which might have been appropriate and useful eight or nine months before.[5]

He was too late. While he played for time, wrote desperately for fresh instructions, and cursed the Biscay storms which cut him off from Spain, Henry and Wolsey were turning to the French. A great embassy headed by the Bishop of Tarbes arrived in February, armed with promises of pensions and tributes, to discuss a close alliance against the Emperor, sealed by the marriage of the Princess Mary to a French prince. On April 30, Mendoza still without instructions, still fighting for delay, the English and French delegates signed the treaties which made war with the Emperor inevitable.

Mendoza and Catherine had been able to co-operate only with difficulty. At their first interview he had hardly advanced to greet the Queen before a messenger from Wolsey dragged him off elsewhere. His subsequent attempts to see her alone always met with some neatly devised obstruction, and Catherine, herself, sent word to him that it would be useless and even dangerous to persist in them without the Cardinal's permission. Her countryman's presence emphasized what Catherine had felt before: that in her own palace she was virtually Wolsey's prisoner. But the Queen was not without resource. Her confessor and her physician, Spaniards both, could not be prevented from calling on the new ambassador, and Wolsey could not put off forever granting Mendoza's formal request for an audience with the Queen whose mother's page he had been, and in whose own train he had once ridden years ago, from Granada to the sea. At the reluctantly granted audience Don Iñigo kept carefully to recollections, messages, and news of old friends, welcome enough to bring a light to Catherine's eyes, though not what she most wished to hear. Even so, a few minutes of unintelligible Spanish were all that Wolsey, standing watchfully at the

Queen's elbow, would permit, and with bland incivility he swept the ambassador off to look for the King. Later, however, while Wolsey and Henry were closeted with the French, the interrupted interview was resumed, in privacy. They wasted little time on reminiscence. Don Iñigo gave Catherine a rapid résumé of the Emperor's actions, plans, and offers to England, and as he watched the surprise, pleasure, and confirmed suspicion cross her face, he decided that she had been much misinformed. When Catherine spoke it was to ask shrewd questions about the Emperor's willingness to accept a negotiated peace, and the exact extent of Mendoza's lamentably obsolete powers and instructions, and to offer a few warnings and suggestions too delicate to be trusted to a go-between. She hardly needed to confirm Mendoza's judgment that the Cardinal was bent on the French alliance, and that the Cardinal, for the moment, was all-powerful. "She will do her best to restore the old alliance between Spain and England," the ambassador concluded from the interview, "but though her will is good, her means are small."

Small, perhaps, but not altogether negligible. When the French ambassadors called at Richmond a few days later for their first glimpse of the Princess Mary, who was back at court for that very purpose, Catherine used a mother's authority to say that Mary could not be disturbed, knowing well that the streets of London would buzz before nightfall with her opposition to the unpopular match. When, finally, Henry introduced the ambassadors to her, and discussed the approaching treaty, alluding to the former one with France in which she had so willingly concurred, Catherine said she was glad to hear that peace was to be restored to Christendom, asked just how it was to be accomplished, and delicately pressed Grammont, the head of the embassy, until his embarrassed admissions made it clear that what was brewing was not an offer of peace to the Emperor but an ultimatum. Thereupon she froze into silence. She could not prevent the signing of the treaty, and the betrothal of her daughter, but she could underline the unpopularity of the French connection, and repeat to Mendoza, when she let him know that the treaty was signed, Warham's word that, whatever was concluded, it would not be easy to bring the country into war.[6]

Perhaps she knew how dangerous a game she was playing, but she could not have guessed what the counterstroke would be. On the night of May 18, as Mendoza was drafting his rueful report to the Emperor of his failure to prevent the Anglo-French alliance, an agitated caller knocked at his lodgings, a caller who would not admit he came from the Queen, and begged for anonymity even in cipher. His message, couched in Mendoza's words, was brief: "The Cardinal, to crown his iniquities, was working to separate the King and Queen, . . . and the plot was so far advanced that a number of bishops and lawyers had already gathered secretly to declare her marriage null." In fact the plot was at least six weeks old, and before Mendoza sat down to begin his letter, Henry had heard from the eloquent Dr. Wolman that he had been living for eighteen years in sin with his deceased brother's wife.[7]

ii

So, in the conspiratorial secrecy of the King's collusive suit at Westminster, began the resounding case which custom obliges us to call "the divorce" of Catherine of Aragon. While royal officials swore each other to silence, and frowned and denied knowledge of it, and referred to it obliquely as "the king's great matter" even in their most private correspondence, all London buzzed with the open secret; on the morrow all Europe would ring with it. The tiny splash which Mendoza barely heard would send ripples widening and swelling higher, until the quiet cells of scholars, the innermost rooms of chanceries, and the daily life of a whole people rocked with its commotion, until its center became a vortex sucking ancient institutions into its abyss, and its subsiding waves stirred armies and launched navies from Lisbon to the Baltic. Men would die because of it, in battle, on the scaffold, at the stake, long after the last participant had ceased to plead; and the scholars who wrote mountains of books about it for three hundred years would find their eyes blurred by the ancient fury, and dip their pens in bile. Whether the great case itself was the mine which wrecked the unity of Christendom, or only the spark which fired the train, its battle cries became the shibboleth of partisans, and its events marked the line of the watershed between the old way of life and the new, so that even today it is hard to find men to write or speak of it without prejudice or heat, and many of its features are still obscured, as much by passion as by the erosion of time.

For instance, it is still hard to find any agreement about the origin of "the king's great matter." At the first alarm, Catherine jumped to the conclusion that Wolsey was the instigator, Mendoza concurred; the Emperor found it plausible, so did Reginald Pole; the Catholic controversialists of the next generation adopted the view, and Catholic writers ever since have inclined to defend it.[8] But that was not Henry's own account, nor Wolsey's. Protestant writers, of the orthodox Anglican variety, have usually stood squarely on the King's own assertion that a scruple of conscience led him to separate from the woman he had believed to be his wife, and the most respectable modern historians have accepted Henry's initial responsibility, though they emphasize motives of statecraft rather than of piety. The cynical soon began to say that neither statecraft nor piety, but desire for another woman, was at the back of Henry's mind; and their voices are not yet silenced.

Catherine's judgment that Wolsey was the instigator of her troubles should have due weight. She was not inclined to hysteria, and the discipline of more than twenty years' experience of court and diplomatic intrigue, acting on an intelligence naturally strong and alert, had given her an insight into character and motives unsubtle, it is true, but usually sound and shrewd. She should have known both Wolsey and Henry better than anyone else. She believed that Henry would never have thought of a divorce if Wolsey had not suggested it, and that the expedient had occurred to Wolsey as the best method of safeguarding his pro-French policy by removing from Henry's side the Emperor's chief friend in England and substituting a French princess. Catherine's view, shared in 1527 by most of the diplomats in London and generally by the court and the city, has much to recommend it. Wolsey was committed to the French alliance, and he did hope to arrange a French marriage. He had every reason to fear Catherine, and for more than two years he had shown that he knew it. She was strong-willed, patient, intelligent; she could be an implacable enemy; as long as she remained at the King's side, sooner or later the shove of her resentment would dislodge him from favor. And Wolsey knew the popular fury that awaited him once he lost the slippery favor of the King. To meet such a danger by a bold counterattack was thoroughly characteristic of his temperament. The dreadful risk appealed to his gambler's instincts almost as much as the possible gain. If he failed his own ruin was sure, and a grievous loss of power and prestige to the Church of Rome, to which he was devoted, only too probable. But if he brought off this tremendous *coup*, Henry's dependence on him, and on the Pope, would be more complete than ever. When he told Clement VII that by pronouncing Henry's marriage null he would confirm forever the power of Rome in England (and that meant the power of Rome's representative as long as Wolsey lived) Wolsey named stakes worth playing for.

About Wolsey Catherine may have been mostly right. About Henry she could be wholly wrong, was to be wrong about him, repeatedly and pathetically, for the next nine years. Always, if it was possible to invent an excuse to clear Henry of any shadow of blame for anything whatever, Catherine invented it. In her mind the picture of the chivalric youth who had rescued her and married her in a springtime now eighteen seasons cold always obscured the thick-necked egoist her husband had become. She never understood that Henry was not a boy to be scolded or indulged or managed for his own good; a little wild perhaps, a little willful, and too easily led astray by designing companions, but fundamentally a good boy, who could be trusted to leave off his follies once he was brought to see them, and to do the right thing as soon as the bad influences about him were removed. One of Catherine's partisans could be angry enough, three centuries after the King was dead, to call him "a spot of blood and grease on English history." No one who ever lived, not Henry himself, would have repudiated that judgment more hotly than Catherine. Her loves and loyalties were more lasting even than her hatreds, and though she might scold her husband to his face, and try to shame him before the world, and long to see him disciplined (not too severely, only enough to make him understand), to others she would always be his apologist. Across the centuries, her letters invite our charity for Henry, make us wonder if she did not see in him something that nobody else ever saw. But no one was less likely to see all the King's complex character. If we want to thread the dim jungle of his motives we must take another guide.

Even his warmest admirers admit that the King himself is not a thoroughly reliable guide to that jungle, although his own account of his decision to separate from his wife has the virtue of being even simpler than Catherine's. Someone – the Bishop of Tarbes in one version, his confessor Longland in another – suggested to him, after he had been married about eighteen years, that perhaps his marriage was not legal, being contrary to the law of God. He looked, and there in the twentieth chapter of Leviticus stood the dreadful text: "And if a man shall take his brother's wife, it is an unclean thing . . . they shall be childless." It was true, he and Catherine were childless, or as good as childless, having only one daughter. So, fearful that he had sinned by living with his brother's wife, Henry had called upon the lawyers and theologians to decide whether he was truly married.

Henry repeated this account of his conscientious scruples over and over again to his loyal subjects, to the Pope, to all Christendom, until no doubt he came to believe it firmly. He must have believed it; it was impossible for him to think of himself as acting from any but the highest and purest motives, of playing any but the noblest and most heroic role. He could even believe that his daughter was not legally his daughter, since it would be more pious and convenient to believe so. Others might be faithless and unscrupulous, those who opposed him invariably were, and the longer he lived the less he trusted anyone, but he never saw cause to modify his earlier announcement: "I, alone, have acted with the purest faith, and therefore God favors my designs." His peculiar partnership – almost, scoffers might say, his identity – with the God he worshiped became the chief article of Henry's creed.

Yet the timing of his access of scruple still needs accounting for. Catherine's marriage to Arthur had not been kept secret from him, and it is hard to imagine so enthusiastic an amateur theologian failing to notice that text in Leviticus before. Everyone else in England and Spain had canvassed it exhaustively, and the bull of Pope Julius II, the basic document in the file of papers about Henry's own marriage, was specifically designed to remove the impediment which Leviticus imposed. Because his wife had failed to give him a male heir, Henry said, he had come to believe either that the dispensation was defective, or that the Pope had no power to dispense, since God, Who favored him in everything else, would not deny him a son unless he had somehow offended. To his subjects he explained that his desire to spare them the dangers of a disputed succession weighed with him as much as his scruples of conscience. Some of his subjects thought that bastardizing the accepted heir, even if she was a girl, was an awkward way to begin establishing a secure succession. If there was any doubt about Mary's right to mount the throne after her father,[9] the best solution would be to marry her to the next in the legitimate line, her cousin, James V of Scotland, who was just the right age for her. That way, there would be no dispute about their joint right, the old running sore of border warfare would be healed, and when the two kingdoms were united, the greater, as Henry VII had foreseen, would draw the less, particularly if young James came to finish his education in England. The Scottish marriage had many partisans; [10] forward-looking men in both countries were eager for it; in 1524 the Scottish envoys would have been glad to arrange it, and in 1527 his alliance with France put it again in Henry's reach. He did not consider it. Nor did he consider that if he bastardized Mary, and then failed to have a son by his new wife, a failure against which no sanctions of the Church could insure him, the succession would be confused indeed. His mind had no place for such thoughts; the spur to his awakened conscience had a keener point than anxiety about his heir.

He was infatuated with the younger sister of his cast-off mistress, Mary Boleyn. When Anne Boleyn came back from France late in 1521, Henry had paid her little attention, though some of the gentlemen at court, her cousin, the poet Thomas Wyatt, and mooncalf Harry Percy, heir to the border earldom of Northumberland, had not taken long to find her attractive. Attractive she must have been, though later observers were puzzled to discover the exact secret of her power. Her figure was unremarkable, her complexion sallow, her neck somewhat too long and slender, her mouth wide but sly rather than generous or frankly sensual. She had masses of black hair and almond-shaped black eyes which some found beautiful, but they alone were not enough to distinguish her among the beauties of the court. One distinguishing mark she had, a rudimentary sixth finger on her left hand, a mark to make the pious cross themselves to avoid the evil eye, and the more superstitious still to

Anne Boleyn

whisper of devil's gets and the sure sign of a sorceress, but it was only a tiny blemish, and she had learned to manage so well with gloves and the folds of her dress that many people never noticed it at all. Her birth and accomplishments picked her out as little as her appearance. The Boleyns had risen from a London mercer's shop, – new men for the new times, – but wealth had enabled them to mingle their tradesman's blood with the blood of Hastings and of Ormonde-Butler even before Anne's father married a daughter of the Howards, just as the solid merits of a conscientious underling had advanced Sir Thomas Boleyn in the King's service, even before the complaisance of his daughter Mary hastened his elevation to the peerage. Anne's education had been partly in France, but she spoke no better French than many a court lady, and time has left us no record of any special skill of hers in music or dancing, of any erudition above the common, or any taste in poetry or the arts. If she was able to fire the King's blood, that was no more than other ladies, her sister among them, had done before her, and others were to do after. But in one thing she was uncommon. Having started the King in pursuit, she had calculation and dexterity and nerve enough to continue to evade him. To be denied something he wanted was a bewilderingly new experience for Henry; disprized, or too accurately prized, love roused a pounding in his veins so furious that no wonder he mistook the tumult for the pangs of an awakened conscience.

Time has spared a little bundle of yellowing letters from Henry to Anne,[11] setting forth his ardors, his impatience, and his sufferings. Perhaps they are not very different from the love letters of a poet or a man of genius; they are not very different, either, from the embarrassing revelations so often read out in divorce courts, and breach of promise cases. If they tell us nothing else about Henry, their mixture of bribes and threats, cajolery and supplication, transparent efforts to drive a cunning bargain, and frank confessions of helpless longing tell us that the man was desperately in earnest, too far gone to match wits with a greedy, commonplace slip of a girl who could keep her head; one can almost feel sorry for that majestic rage, thrashing so hopelessly at the end of a delicate silken line. If we could know for certain when Henry wrote the first of those letters, if we could know when his cheerful pursuit of a new quarry turned to a blind besotted passion, we would know enough about the origins of "the king's great matter." When, at the Mardi Gras revels in 1526, Henry mounted the motto "Declare I dare not" (he had long since forgotten "The Loyal Heart"), was the covert declaration aimed at Anne or another? All we can say is that in May, 1527, if Catherine knew of his pursuit of Anne, she thought no more of it than of similar affairs in the past; but by July all the court knew that this was something different.

iii

Catherine's first reaction to the news that her marriage had been called in question was uncomplicated by any suspicion of Anne Boleyn's part, but it could hardly have been more violent had she known all about it. Nor, indeed, other circumstances remaining the same, could it have been much different. How Catherine would have responded had Henry laid before her without concealment his scruples of conscience, his fears for his dynasty, his desire to marry again, one can only guess. But anyone who knew her at all should have been able to predict her response to a surreptitious, conspiratorial attempt to declare her marriage null from the beginning, herself, consequently, no wife, and her daughter a bastard, an attempt launched without a word of prior warning or the slightest opportunity for her to enter her defense. The whole nature of the proceedings marked the case as prejudged and the court as hostile. She met the emergency as boldly as she had always met personal attacks. Her first message to Mendoza was that the Emperor and the Pope should be informed at once, and immediate steps taken at Rome to admonish Wolsey to abandon the case, and to prevent its being tried in any English court.

The object of the secret collusive suit at Wolsey's palace of York House, before Wolsey, as legate *a latere*, and William Warham, Archbishop of Canterbury, was to get the dispensation of Julius II pronounced invalid, the marriage annulled, and the King declared a bachelor, after which he would be free to marry again, although it would be wise for him to procure a bull at Rome, confirming the judgment. Henry's brother-in-law, the Duke of Suffolk, had employed a similar device to get rid of one of his wives, and the technique had the merit of being simple and expeditious. The cast of the comedy was carefully chosen among Wolsey's most trusted underlings; Henry, presumably an innocent offender, was summoned to appear in the archiepiscopal court to answer the charge of living in sin with his brother's wife, and, after the charge was heard, Dr. Bell, his attorney as defendant, put in an elaborate justification, to which Dr. Wolman, as promoter or prosecutor, replied. Presumably the King was prepared to bow to the decision of the court and consider himself free, but somehow no such conclusion was reached. Archbishop Warham was old and timid. He was very much in awe of his royal master and of his masterful colleague the Cardinal legate. Perhaps he had, himself, some genuine doubts of the validity of Catherine's marriage, though of that we cannot be sure. But he was as honest a man as any Tudor official was likely to be, and he may have been reluctant to pronounce judgment in so difficult a case, one in which not only the law but the facts might be called in question, without hearing the other party concerned. Moreover, while his court was sitting, news reached London that Rome was in the hands of an imperialist army, and it seemed risky to assume that Clement VII would confirm the annullment of Catherine's marriage while he was the prisoner of the Queen's favorite nephew. So the court found only that the marriage seemed open to doubt, and merited the strictest examination by canonists and theologians. Before the case could be terminated as the King desired, two things would have to be done: the Pope's consent must be secured, and Catherine would have to be told. Wolsey charged himself with the first, and prepared to set off for France to begin liberating the Holy See from oppression by the Emperor. The second task he left to Henry.

Henry evaded it for three weeks. Finally he sought out Catherine in her closet, with a speech prepared to break the news to her gently. Learned and pious men, he told her, had advised him that their marriage was defective, that they were, in fact, living together in sin. In all conscience he could not continue to be her husband. They must separate. He would be glad to have her select some place of retirement, away from court. Where would she like to go?

Catherine stared at him, all sorts of emotions fighting for utterance: disappointment that he could thus callously blacken her good name and wreck their daughter's hopes, grief at the memory of a dead love, anger at an unprovoked, unjust attack, and perhaps not a little pure exasperation at the connubial blindness which could assume that she had not known what he was up to. For a moment her mouth worked dumbly, then she burst into uncontrollable sobbing.

Her tears unnerved Henry completely. He babbled. She must not cry. It was not that he had ceased to love her, it was only this doubt . . . this doubt . . . his conscience troubled him . . . He had to be sure . . . after all, nothing was settled . . . things might come out all right . . . there was no hurry . . . she could take her time. . . . Meanwhile all this was secret . . . a great secret . . . say nothing to anyone . . . a question of his conscience. . . . The storm of tears did not abate, and Henry rushed away from them, defeated.

Probably no one in England but Henry believed that his marital perplexities were still a secret. They were canvassed in every tavern on Cheapside, and Mendoza could have learned from apprentices and sailors, had he not had surer sources of information, how the pleadings at York House had run, how Wolsey had scowled and Warham fidgeted, and what Dr. Wolman had said and what Dr. Bell, how the Princess Mary, God bless her, was to be declared a bastard, and the Queen's grace clapped into a nunnery or sent home to Spain, and the wicked Cardinal, whose plot all this was, should go to France about the freeing of the Pope, and bring back a French princess for the King's new wife. They did not like such goings on, the seamen and apprentices, or the honest merchants who were their masters, and they grumbled and talked big, and passed about handbills denouncing the Cardinal and the French, and drank the Queen's health with ostentatious truculence, so that the King's council and the Lord Mayor were disturbed for the peace of the city, and some people thought it might come to a general uprising, though the Spanish ambassador, with an aristocrat's contempt for the humors of the herd, was certain that unless some gentlemen put themselves forward as leaders, it would all end in smoke.[12]

The murmurs of the city had penetrated the walls of York House, and Catherine knew of them as well as Mendoza, but the use she meant to make of them was her own. The storm that overpowered her when she tried to speak to Henry passed, and to the royal councilors who timidly approached her she made her position perfectly clear. The King might be disturbed by doubts about their marriage; if so, it was right those doubts should be set at rest. As for herself, she had none. She knew that she was Henry's wife, and that she had never been the wife of any other man. The boy Arthur had never been her husband except in name, so the question of the Pope's power to dispense the solemn prohibition in Leviticus simply did not arise. She had been married to Henry at God's altar with the management and approval of the wisest men of two kingdoms, and publicly crowned Queen in the sight of all England. Married and Queen she would remain. She would live wherever her husband commanded, but she did not fear the embarrassment of publicity entailed by remaining at court; she had nothing to be ashamed of, her place was at her husband's side, and unless he publicly ordered her to leave him, she would stay where she was. But wherever she lived, she would be his wife and England's Queen. Meanwhile, since legal matters were afoot, she would be grateful for legal counsel.

For Henry and Wolsey, Catherine could not have taken a more embarrassing position. The question of a place of retirement for the Queen was simply dropped. Whatever was done now would have to be done under the stare of the public. Moreover, by denying that she had ever been married to Arthur, Catherine had cut to the heart of the question. Wolsey saw that to meet her on that ground would mean a public examination of the facts, an open trial and a questionable verdict. It would be better, if possible, to find a technical defect in the bull; a sharp lawyer might do much with the objection that, on Catherine's own showing, her marriage had been not completed in the sight of God, but only *in facie ecclesiae*, in the eyes of the Church, and from this impediment the bull had not dispensed. Or perhaps, oldest trick of the canon lawyers, it could be shown that because the grounds for the application had been misrepresented, the bull had been surreptitiously procured. Meanwhile, before he left for France, Wolsey did his best to make sure that Catherine should get no legal advice, in England or anywhere else.

To Catherine, as to Mendoza, the Spanish ambassador, it was clear that whatever help she could expect must come from Spain; Spanish lawyers would not need to fear the wrath of the English King; all the documents in England about her marriage were in the hands of her enemies, but in Spain there might be other documents; and from Spain, her nephew the Emperor could put pressure on the Pope, a necessity if Giulio de' Medici was to be expected to inconvenience himself in another's cause. Her first step then, Mendoza agreed, was to appeal directly to Charles, and see that he was fully informed of all the facts; her first difficulty was how to smuggle such a message out of England.

Among the few remaining Spaniards in her suite was one who had served her faithfully for twenty-seven years, her sewer, once her page, Francisco Felipez, a gentleman no longer young, but tough and resourceful. A fortnight after Henry's interview with Catherine, Felipez applied to the King for a passport to go to Spain, where, he said, his old mother waited to give him her dying blessing. Catherine, on being consulted, said she did not believe Felipez' mother was sick, and saw no reason for his going except that all her servants would want to leave her, now the King was displeased with her. Henry, more compassionate, granted the necessary license. In relating the incident to Wolsey, Dr. Knight chuckled at how neatly the King had met Catherine's transparent stratagem. Felipez was an old ally of hers, and knew all her counsel; he would be going post-haste to the Emperor's court to bear tales and make trouble over the divorce. But the King had blandly agreed with him that he should hasten to his mother's side, and since the quickest way would be through France, had given him a special safe conduct for the route. Other precautions were to be taken, but to make doubly sure Wolsey might see that Felipez was arrested by the French, or make any other suitable arrangements, so long as Felipez never reached the Spanish border, and the King's servants were not too openly connected with whatever accident befell him.

Felipez must have gone by France and ridden hard, but whatever accidents occurred on the road to Pamplona, he was not their victim. When Dr. Knight wrote on July 15 Felipez was still in England; less than two weeks later a grizzled, dusty Spaniard, battered but jaunty, was seeking audience with the Emperor at his castle near Valladolid, to be conducted, once his mission was known, to the Emperor's private closet and kept there all day long in conversation, while grandees and the English ambassadors kicked their heels in the antechamber. Catherine had trusted but the briefest of lines to paper, all the rest Felipez' memory transmitted to Charles so faithfully that by evening the Emperor had a full account of his aunt's predicament, her plans, and her requests.

Catherine asked three things of her nephew: to expostulate personally with Henry, to rouse the Pope and persuade him to advoke her case to Rome, and to begin efforts to get Wolsey's legatine authority revoked. Charles had troubles of his own, and must have been reluctant to involve himself in any more unpleasantness with his uncle Henry; he certainly felt for his aunt very little of the spontaneous affection she had given him, and she was no longer much use to him. But he had a strong sense of family honor and of obligation, and it never occurred to him, then or later, to avoid this new responsibility. Next morning he wrote in his own hand a shocked, plainly worded letter to his uncle, and inclosed it in one to Mendoza in which he directed his ambassador to assure the Queen of his devoted support. He was sending at once, to carry out her instructions at Rome, Cardinal Quiñones, the General of the Franciscans, the ablest canonist and most experienced Roman politician in Spain.[13]

Charles did not mention some other representatives of his in Rome. On May 6 the half-mutinous army of Lombardy, dragging with it its reluctant generals, had stormed the ruinous walls of the Eternal City; and since that time, while drunken Germans made targets of monks and auctioned off nuns and cardinals, Clement VII, cowering in Castel' Sant' Angelo, had had ample time to repent the folly which had led him to join the League of Cognac and oppose his strength to a victorious Emperor's. Charles had not exactly wanted Rome to be sacked, and even now the Pope was not exactly a prisoner, but Clement had had a salutary lesson, and Charles could reflect that he would be unlikely to refuse a reasonable request.

iv

It was the presence of the Emperor's troops in Rome that was taking Wolsey to France.[14] If he had suggested or encouraged Henry's scruple of conscience with the idea of fostering the French alliance, he had achieved his object with a vengeance. Now no alliance except with France was possible, and on Wolsey's success in persuading the French to "liberate" the Pope, and on their ability to do so, depended the fate of the King's case and the Cardinal's whole future. He was sending agents to Rome, but he did not imagine that they would be successful without the success of French arms. The idea of transferring the Pope's powers during Clement's "captivity" to a commission of cardinals, a commission which he had no doubt of his own ability to dominate, fascinated him, but the best chance was a French victory in Italy reversing the decision of Pavia.

Either chance was slim, but difficulty and danger merely stimulated Wolsey. To the onlookers, to members of his own suite like his gentleman usher Cavendish, even to experienced foreign diplomats, the Cardinal never seemed more impressive than on that mission to France. He had crossed the Channel with a train like a King's, and like a King he was everywhere received. The French lackeys might steal the plate from his dressing room, and vulgarians who suspected that his coming meant more taxes and more French bones rotting on the plains of Italy might scrawl insults on the walls opposite his lodging, and inscribe rude sketches of a Cardinal's hat surmounted by a prophetic gallows on his very window panes, but the French court was the pattern of cordial hospitality, and Francis and his counselors were eager to alter their plans to meet the Cardinal's suggestions. It proved impossible, however, to find more than three or four cardinals willing to give even the most dubious assent to his proposal that the Pope be declared incompetent during his captivity, and that his powers be assumed by a committee of the curia, sitting at Avignon or somewhere else in France. And, though effects of penury were unnoticeable in Francis I's daily life, the French treasury was said to be empty, so that before the plans to liberate the Pope were completed, the financial advantages of the last treaty had melted away, and England was again paying the piper. But this time, Wolsey could proudly assure his master, England was also calling the tune. Lautrec, the French commander, was to be reinforced and ordered to abandon his Lombard campaign. He would march the length of the peninsula and sweep the Spaniards out of Naples, freeing Rome completely from the Emperor's threats. His success would establish that French domination of Italy which Henry and Wolsey, in the past, had spent so much money and energy to prevent; but in return, Henry was to have his divorce.

Meanwhile, in his great minister's absence, Henry had thought of a cheaper and quicker scheme. Wolsey already had agents in Rome badgering the distracted Pope for a decretal commission which would give him full powers to try the King's case in England and pronounce sentence without fear of reversal. Henry now sent an agent of his own, the serviceable Dr. William Knight, who was by no means to let the Cardinal know that he was to ask the Pope for several quite different documents. Of these the most interesting were two: First, a license to commit bigamy, replacing an old, barren wife with a young fertile one in the manner of an Old Testament patriarch. Second, a dispensation for the new marriage to be valid even within the first degree of affinity. The embarrassing fact was that since Mary Boleyn had been Henry's mistress, he was related to her sister Anne, under the canon law, in the same degree that he was to Catherine if she had, indeed, been Arthur's wife. But Henry was so anxious to marry Anne, and soon, that he was careless of admitting that the Pope had exactly the dispensing power which it was part of his case to deny. Anyway, if he got the license to commit bigamy, the validity of the first dispensation need not be questioned. When Wolsey squeezed the story out of Knight at Compiègne, he did not know whether to be more vexed at the crass stupidity of the King's amateur maneuver, or alarmed by the intention it disclosed.[15]

At least the first shock prepared him for the second. During his absence the King and Anne had given up all circumspection, and the friends of the Boleyns were openly boasting that once the King was free of his old wife, Mistress Anne would be queen. When, on his return from France, Wolsey hurried to Richmond, and sent, as his custom was, to know when and where he might have audience, his messenger found Henry with his new lady. The messenger had hardly finished before Anne cut in, in her best imitation of a regal manner: "Where should the Cardinal come except where the King is?" and though the liberty was one which Catherine would never have permitted herself, Henry was too besotted to countermand the affront.[16] So the tired, travel-stained old statesman sagged through his first account of his dealings and triumphs in France under the malicious eye of the young lady in waiting whom (it was fresh in both their memories) he had once bullied and humiliated as if she were a too frisky servant girl. At least Wolsey knew at once the worst that could happen to him. He was to help turn out Catherine so that her place might be filled, not by the pliable and respectable French princess he had hoped for, but by a young woman of no name and doubtful manners, whose influence with the King was greater than Catherine's had been these ten years, who hated him with a personal vivacity which made the Queen's distaste seem pale, and who would probably observe few of the laws of honorable war. Following in her train, less calculable because more unscrupulous than Catherine's alliance of foreign dignitaries and stiff old aristocrats, he could sniff a hungry gang of the new men, men he had despised and used for fifteen years, and who had come together while his back was turned, to push this sly wench in between him and the King. Anne had made him feel at once, she was to make him feel again and again, the completeness with which she had cut him off from Henry. In serving his master, he had earned the hatred and envy of most of England, and he knew, as he stood in his muddy riding boots, his manners as bland, his voice as round and bell-like as ever, but feeling old and sick and weary, and with God knows what terror gnawing at his bowels, that he could not count on that master's gratitude, or even on his pity. There was only one resource left him. He was still, for the time being, indispensable.

"The Cardinal," wrote the French ambassador M. du Bellay in February, 1528, some four months after that inauspicious return from France, "is playing a terribly dangerous game.[17] He alone seems in favor of the war." The preceding month that game had led to a joint formal defiance of the Emperor by the heralds of England and France at Burgos; by February, 1528, trade with the Netherlands, on which half the population of the kingdom were said to live, had dwindled to an illicit trickle, and, England's earliest capitalists, the merchant clothiers, having been quick to pass on their losses by refusing to buy cloths, by dismissing their workmen, and by telling all who complained that it was because of the Cardinal's war, the murmurs in London and the countryside had swelled to a roar of rage and hatred. It was the Cardinal's fault, too, that the bad harvest of the year before had left a shortage of corn and meat and cheese, and certainly the Cardinal's fault that the Antwerp market was closed, and food supplies were not to be had in France even for famine prices. It was the Cardinal's vanity and greed that routed monks from their peaceable monasteries to build new colleges, and the Cardinal's rank pride and ambition that worked to estrange the King from the Queen, make a bastard of the Princess, and drag the country at the heels of France. Du Bellay did not really like Wolsey, but again and again he was constrained to praise the courage which could ignore so many and such manifest dangers, and the invincible energy and will which crashed through every obstacle.

Wolsey knew better than M. du Bellay, who had no inkling of all the smoldering animosities at court, what a terrible game he was playing, but he played as he had never played before. Defeat was certain ruin, and victory might mean ruin not much less certain, but while the game lasted, the joy of mastery and power was there. After Wolsey's hands were once more on the reins there were no more silly blunders at Rome and, thanks to Wolsey's arrangements, the wily Dr. Stephen Gardiner, whom Wolsey selected to repair Knight's errors, found smoother going. As long as the arguments of the Emperor's advocates were backed by the eloquent glitter of pikes in the Roman sunlight, Clement would sign nothing he might promptly regret. Even from the comparative safety of Orvieto, all he would give Knight was a commission, skillfully nullified by its own phrasing, all he would offer Wolsey's agents was the indirect suggestion that a really impatient lover would marry a second wife and trust the future for the Pope's understanding forgiveness. But Wolsey's terrible game was paying. All England might curse him, tremble on the verge of insurrection, and obstinately refuse to be flogged into war with its best customer, but Lautrec's army was marching through Ancona. As the imperialists fell back to their defenses in the south, Clement fell back on technicalities of phrasing, conceding points as he heard of fortresses lost; and when the Emperor's broken, plague-ridden army crowded into Naples for a last desperate stand, and Doria's galleys swept in from the sea to shut the trap on them, the Pope, tears running down his beard, crying dramatically that he had ruined himself forever with the Emperor and had no hope now save the King of England's love, flung his arms wide in a gesture of surrender, and practically invited Gardiner to write his own ticket.

When it came to the final drafting, the concession was not quite so sweeping as it sounded, and, from Wolsey's point of view, the documents left something to be desired; but Cardinal Campeggio, who would bring them and sit with Wolsey in judgment, had another secret and more potent document, and altogether Wolsey thought he could manage. He was still alone in a ring of watchful, sullen faces, and even after he and Campeggio had pronounced judgment there would be narrow bridges to cross, but he could talk to his faithful usher of the time when he had settled the "king's great matter," given peace to Christendom and reformed the English church, and could turn to the peaceful cares of his province of York and some thought of his soul's salvation.

𝔳

If there was anyone in England more alone than the Cardinal through the long months of the diplomatic battle at Rome, and in the following summer of 1528, while Campeggio came slowly northwards, it was the Queen. Once the first agony of the interview with Henry was over, she found the courage to go about her duties with her usual placidity. She directed the household as always, and appeared as carefully and magnificently dressed as ever at public ceremonies and court entertainments; she read and sewed and listened to music, and joined her maids at cards and similar amusements, even though Mistress Anne Boleyn was among them. Later one of her women remembered seeing her at cards with Anne in an alcove, hearing her say calmly when Anne had dealt: "You have good hap to stop at a king, my lady Anne, but you are not like others, you will have all or none." But if she paid that one jest to gossip, the hungry watchers detected no other sign.

All that winter of 1527–1528 she shared the royal apartments with Henry, while Anne, in apartments of her own near by, bore herself ever more bravely, and the buzz of whispers, which died at the first sight of the Queen's slow passage through the corridors, sprang up redoubled when she passed. In June, 1528, the court broke up at the threat of a recurrence of the English plague, the sweating sickness. "One has a little pain," wrote Du Bellay, "in the head and heart. Suddenly a sweat breaks out, and a physician is useless, for whether you wrap yourself up much or little, in four hours, sometimes in two or three, you are despatched without languishing." Irregularly the sickness had revisited England, coming usually with warmer weather, sometimes more, sometimes less severe, ever since men could remember. It terrified Henry, who had more than the normal horror of a full-bodied, athletic animal for the mysterious visitations of disease. At the first rumor of its coming, though the rumor included Anne among the first victims, he stampeded out of Greenwich, taking a reduced household to Eltham, then to remoter places. It was bad that summer. Eighteen persons died at Warham's house within four hours; and at the More and at Hampton Court, where Wolsey was grimly working through the summer months as usual, the Cardinal's suite was decimated. The Duke of Norfolk came down with the sweat, but recovered, and three of the King's old companions, Carey and Poynts and Compton, were left to die in manors Henry successively abandoned in his scramble for safety. He shifted his dwelling every few days, always with a smaller suite, always farther from London. Anne's first illness had not been the dreaded sweat, but she got no word to rejoin the court, though Henry did send her his second-best physician; and later on she had to struggle through a severe genuine bout with only epistolary comfort from her royal lover. He was a jelly of fear, keeping his physician at his elbow, confessing his sins daily, receiving communion often, and dividing his time between prayers and experiments with nostrums. For one who was so sure of their partnership, Henry was notably reluctant to interview his Maker. But his terror brought no pains to his remarkable conscience. He took time off from his devotions to write to Anne of his yearnings for her body, and to lecture his sister Margaret on the scandal of her divorce and the mortal sin of adultery. His conscience told him he was a bachelor.[18]

Catherine had never paid any particular attention to the "English sweat," and the dwindling of the court could not increase her loneliness; she had a graver threat to herself and her daughter to outface. She got little help from her council. Old Archbishop Warham, whom no fear of sickness could turn from his duties, went in terror of his King. "*Indignatio principis mors est,*" he muttered when she asked his advice, "the wrath of the king is death," and turned away his head. The honest Englishmen from whom she could expect counsel were silenced by fear, others proffered glib, specious traps. Don Iñigo de Mendoza freely confessed that he was no canonist and no theologian, and the legal aid for which he appealed to Spain and to Flanders was unaccountably delayed. Even Luis Vives had left her, partly upset by a rough grilling at Wolsey's hands which he shared with the less easily frightened Francisco Felipez, partly disgusted because Catherine would have none of what advice he could offer.[19] His opinion was the same as that of the one Englishman who had the courage to advise her. John Fisher, Bishop of Rochester,[20] had been specifically warned by Wolsey not to meddle in the King's great matter, but ignoring threats he sent Catherine word to be of good courage. There was no doubt of the Pope's power to dispense; she should stand firmly on Julius II's bull, and apply secretly to the present Pope, for a supplementary bull making good any accidental defects in the first. Mendoza inclined to concur in Fisher's and Vives' opinion, but Catherine, whether she dreaded testing so far the Pope's authority in England, or whether she was simple enough to think that mere truth was the best defense, meant to rest her case on the facts. She had never been Arthur's wife except in name. Along that line, during the plague-sick, breathless months while she waited for Campeggio to come to England, she hammered out her defense, alone.

Chapter Two

SINCE HE YIELDED to Stephen Gardiner's insistence just in proportion to the success of the French army in Italy, Pope Clement VII has been accused of caring only for the victories of Italian politics and the temporal interests of his office and his family. That is not just. Clement VII's weakness was that he was careful of too many things. He cared, of course, about the house of Medici, the responsible headship of which, with its burden of a singularly incompetent and unappetizing brood of nephews and cousins recently ejected by the indignant Florentines from their palaces, now weighed on his frail shoulders. And he cared, perhaps even more deeply, about the temporal power of the Church, which he could never learn to use with Borgian insouciance for the advancement of his family, and if he erred in postulating the interdependence of the temporal and the spiritual power, he erred in illustrious company. As the Pope shivered in the dirt and discomfort of his refuge at Orvieto, the temporal power was anything but free, and how to clear central Italy of the foreign mercenaries tramping over it preoccupied him even more than how to wedge his nephews back into Florence. But Clement VII cared, too, for the interests of the Church beyond the Alps, and there, as in Italy, he found himself the inheritor of weakness, discord, and impending chaos. His lucky uncle, Giovanni, under whose broad shadow he had grown to greatness, had been able to dismiss the mutterings in Germany as a squabble of monks, but Giulio found that the Church was no longer obeyed in more than a third of its wealthiest provinces, where its lands were being confiscated, and its doctrines and authority denied. He had heard drunken *Lanzknechts* shouting for

Pope Luther under the casemates of Sant' Angelo, and had begun to realize that there might be no limit to the spread and danger of the German revolution. A sensitive, delicate, nervous man, with a talent for log-rolling and devious, personal intrigue, and the soul, if not of an artist, at least of a good, second-rate art critic, he was temperamentally unfitted for the dangerous decisions called for by these iron times. No wonder that the King of England's inconvenient scruples, coming just in the midst of all his other troubles, reduced him to a hysteria of terror and exasperation.

The wonder is that he kept his head as well as he did. The nature of Henry's case troubled him more than it would have some of his thicker-skinned predecessors; Clement could appreciate the gravity of an issue involving the sacraments, the supernatural foundation of the common law of Christendom. But to suppose that he stated the case to himself so simply is to underestimate the complexity of his apprehensions. It might be unjust to the Queen of England to declare her marriage null, but sometimes private persons must suffer for the general good, and, if divorcing her would prevent a greater evil, Clement would have sighed and acquiesced. The peremptory demands made on him by Wolsey for a commission which in effect prejudged the case were unusually blunt and brutal, but in other circumstances they might have been met. Wolsey asserted that the whole power of Rome in England depended on the issue, and Clement had seen enough to know that Wolsey might not be exaggerating. But if he could hold England only by losing the Emperor, he might save a part to lose the whole: Italy as well as Germany, and therefore probably all Christendom. It was a painful dilemma, one from which a great statesman, farsighted and daring, might have wrested a double victory, but never a little, cautious, clever man like Clement, anxious only to evade the worse consequences of defeat.

Clement's instinct, in any crisis, was to delay and compromise, to save appearances, avoid irrevocable commitments, and leave himself loopholes for escape. He granted for thc trial of the case in England, first, a general commission to Cardinal Wolsey and Cardinal Campeggio, jointly and severally, to hear the case, declare the marriage null if the facts and the law warranted, and license both parties to remarry. The court was unlikely to be very favorable to the Queen, but at least the trial was to be a full and open one. Such a concession, however, was far from satisfying Wolsey, and Clement granted next, under pressure from Gardiner, a decretal commission which laid down the law in detail, and limited the facts to be inquired into. This commission, Wolsey's idea, practically directed the verdict. Finally, when it looked as if the imperialist garrison at Naples must surely surrender, Clement signed and swore to a promise not to reverse the decision given in England. But the promise, drawn with Roman ingenuity, was less binding than it seemed, the decretal commission was not to be published or to leave Campeggio's hand, and the Roman cardinal had, before he started, explicit instructions to delay all he could, and if he found it impossible to reconcile the parties or arrange any satisfactory compromise, not to take any final action without further word from Rome.

Cardinal Lorenzo Campeggio, to whom these documents were entrusted, was the logical choice in the curia for this delicate mission. He was a distinguished canonist, had been indeed a noted professor of the canon law at Bologna before, a widower with three children, he had taken holy orders. He was a veteran diplomat whose patience, dignity, and tact had been successful in difficult negotiations where flashier qualities had failed, and he had special connections with England, was the official "protector" of England at Rome, had had a palace given him by Henry VII, and was the absentee holder of the wealthy bishopric of Salisbury. At the time of the Treaty of London he had spent nearly a year at the English court, could be said to know Henry and Catherine well, and had proved that he could work with Wolsey.

Englishmen were to find Campeggio's mind circuitous, and, mistaking for an intent to bewilder and deceive his lawyer's capacity to see both sides of every question and to spin endless distinctions out of simple facts, were to charge him with excessive guile; but actually his mental processes, though uncolored by enthusiasm, were direct and precise, and under his lawyer's detachment and caution he had a fundamental honesty, a store of disillusioned sympathy for the infinite varieties of human weakness and folly, even a streak of wry, puckish humor. He was a heavy, tired, sluggish-appearing man, with the face and bearing of a seedy, sedentary scholar, and a body wracked by the tortures of gout, but his wit preserved an astonishing nimbleness and dexterity, and he got through more hard work than most of his colleagues, finding his resources in accuracy, patience, and a spirit salted by irony against the canker of defeat. No saint, no hero, no fanatic, Campeggio was incapable of those passionate counteroffensives which can turn a losing into a winning cause, but he knew how to lose slowly, cannily, methodically, saving what could be saved, and turning the risk of rout and disaster into orderly retirement. He had shown that sort of skill in Germany, and he knew that he had been chosen again for such a rearguard command. The King of England's divorce was a bad business for the Church; whatever was done there would mean a choice of evils with little honor or profit. But Campeggio was prepared to cut the losses in any way that circumstances indicated would involve the least permanent damage. A good deal would depend on how the war went in Italy.

Curial dignity, the confused state of Europe, and recurrent attacks of gout all slowed Campeggio's northward progress. One cannot say that he meant to travel quite as slowly as he did, the shooting agonies which kept him for days in a darkened chamber and made the jolting of his litter torture were real enough, but when he reached Calais towards the beginning of October he cannot have been sorry that he had consumed more than three months in his journey. If the result in Italy was far from clear, it was evident that Wolsey's solution was postponed. As Campeggio sailed from Corneto to Marseilles in July, Andrea Doria had transferred the allegiance of his blockading squadrons from France to Spain, and the port of Naples was again open. The French found the plague an ally less reliable than Doria; their dead were piled in heaps in their stinking trenches, and after Lautrec himself succumbed, the demoralized mob which capitulated to the Spaniards at Aversa was "less an army than a walking pestilence." Genoa fell to the imperialists, and by mid-September the French were once more reduced to the defense of a few posts in Lombardy. Campeggio hardly needed the warning which reached him before he crossed the Channel – to proceed with the greatest caution, and not let any part of the case out of his own hands.

Wracked by gout, he slid quietly into London, disappointing Wolsey's hopes of a pompous ceremonial entrance, and when Wolsey visited his sickroom with a voluble explanation of the need for haste in satisfying the King's demands, he found his Italian colleague blandly determined to do everything in order. The first duty of an ecclesiastical court in such disputes was to try to reconcile the parties; as soon as he was well enough he would see King Henry and urge him to return to his wife.

Henry soon dispelled any hopes Campeggio may have nourished of ending his task so easily. The King listened sourly to the Italian legate's remarks about the sanctity of marriage and the scandal of publicity, and quite ignored the Pope's offer to make good any defect in the bull of Julius II by a new dispensation, as sweeping as necessary. He explained that his conscience compelled him to seek a full investigation of his case, and he left no doubt what result he expected. Campeggio came away to write in humorous despair: "His Majesty has studied this case so diligently that I believe he knows more about it than a great theologian or jurist. He told me briefly that he wished nothing except a declaration whether his marriage was valid or not, always presuming it was not, and I think that an angel descending from heaven could not persuade him otherwise."[1]

Henry brightened up only when Campeggio suggested that the Queen might be persuaded to enter a nunnery, in which case he had discretionary powers to dissolve her earthly in favor of a heavenly marriage. If Catherine would do that, Henry said enthusiastically, he would make any arrangement about her dower rights she liked, and see that Mary was put into the succession immediately after his legitimate male heirs. Catherine would lose nothing except his person by the bargain, and that she had lost anyway. He had not lived as her husband for several years, and, he added viciously, no matter what happened he would never go back to her. But though the arguments in favor of Catherine's retirement were so strong, Henry was not satisfied until he and Wolsey had seen and heard the secret decretal commission Campeggio had brought from Rome. He did not notice how careful Campeggio was to keep the bull in his own hands. Wolsey did.

From the King the two legates went by boat, the only form of conveyance tolerable to Campeggio's gout, to visit the Queen. They had, in all, three interviews. At the first, Catherine, having read the Pope's letters and heard both Campeggio and Wolsey expatiate on the desirability of an amicable, private settlement, asked Campeggio directly if it were true he had come to advise her to enter a nunnery. It was the cue for Campeggio's best eloquence. It lay in her hands, he told her, to compose this matter, by a slight sacrifice, to the honor of God, her conscience, and her fame, without loss in goods or temporal possessions to herself or her daughter, whereas if she fought her case through the courts she would be in continuous trouble and annoyance, would risk, if the case went against her, the loss of her good name and of all her dower rights, and arouse scandal and hostility all round her. He cited the saintly queen of France who had retired to a nunnery so that Louis XII might remarry.

Threats and appeals to self-interest were the wrong arguments to use on Catherine; she only replied that she wished His Holiness to understand the purity of her intentions and the completeness of her obedience, and hoped she might be allowed legal counsel while she considered what she ought to do. Campeggio thought he had impressed her, though he foresaw she would be difficult.

How difficult, he learned a few days later when, by the King's permission, she visited his lodgings to clear her conscience to him in confession. Of what she told him then, Campeggio felt free to repeat that she asserted that from the time of her marriage to Prince Arthur in November to his death the following April, they had slept together only seven nights, and that he had left her, as he had found her, a virgin. She had no vocation, she said, for a religious life, and preferred to remain in the station of matrimony to which God had called her. Campeggio was touched, but not disarmed. He had always found the Queen a wise and prudent lady, but she could hardly understand what trouble she was causing Holy Church. Wolsey was frantic with apprehension of what the King might do if Rome failed him, and Henry had dropped an ugly hint.

The next day Wolsey and Campeggio returned to the charge. They pleaded the peace of the kingdom and the tranquillity of Christendom. Campeggio marshaled his most moving phrases, and Wolsey, in one of those passions of dramatic earnestness into which he knew how to work himself, fell on his knees before the Queen and begged her to save herself, her husband, and her people from an infinity of troubles. Catherine did not budge. She wished to show herself an obedient wife and an obedient daughter of the Church. She would consult with counsel, but on one thing her mind was clear: She had come to Henry a virgin and she was his legal wife; if she were to be torn limb from limb for saying so, and then to rise from the dead, she would die a second time in defense of that truth. Campeggio was in despair. The trial was set for Christmas and he saw no likelihood of a free trial in England. He strongly advised Clement to advoke the case to Rome.

The lonely decision to fight her case to the last was the most difficult Catherine had made since she told Fuensalida, twenty years before, that she would die in England before she gave up her marriage with the Prince of Wales. In its consequences for England and for Christendom it was the gravest she was ever to make, one of the gravest in history. Had Catherine retired in favor of her rival, the separation of England from the Roman obedience would not have come as it did, might have been delayed for years, possibly would never have come at all. Not, of course, that her divorce case was the sole cause of the triumph of Protestantism in England; it was only the occasion. A multitude of forces were converging there, as elsewhere all over Europe, to disrupt the Catholic Church, and with it the unity of western civilization. But the forces of resistance, feeble at the moment, were also beginning to rally; and in England the forces of disruption were weaker than in many parts of the continent, and the crown was stronger. It is almost unthinkable that the Protestant revolution could have triumphed in England without the complicity of the government, and highly unlikely that Henry VIII – intellectually timid, dogmatically orthodox, inordinately vain of his relations with the Pope and the greater sovereigns of the West – would ever have broken with Rome except in a revulsion of bitter disappointment, and under the lash of a compelling passion. Had Catherine retired to a nunnery, Henry would have remained in the Roman fold, and in his time Protestant theology would have found no footing near the throne. As things happened in Europe, that would have made an incalculable difference later on. With English co-operation, the Council of Trent might have had a different outcome; without English opposition, the Counter Reformation might have reunited Christendom. None of the principals could be expected to think of issues so remote, but Catherine knew as well as anyone that her case was loaded with danger for the Church. Campeggio may be forgiven for his exasperation at a feminine obstinacy so understandable, but so disastrous.

Perhaps at bottom Catherine's position was as much the product of blind emotion as her husband's: jealousy of a successful rival, love that the years had not turned into indifference, anguished inability to surrender the place she had held while there was a gleam of hope, all her deepest feelings as a dynast, a mother, a woman — who knows how much each contributed to stiffen her resistance? But her reason did not contradict her feelings. For her to permit the annulment of her marriage would be not only to deny the significance of her whole life, of the aims of her parents, of her long struggle against odds after Arthur's death, of all her years as queen, but to injure, perhaps irreparably, her daughter's chances to continue her work, and to endanger the peace of England, and the whole Tudor succession. Her principles as a dynast, the insights of her statesmanship, her rational fear and distrust of Wolsey's policies, her equally well-grounded fear of the unprincipled greed of the clique behind Anne Boleyn, all confirmed her instinctive resistance. Like Henry, she expressed all these emotional drives, all these reasoned motives, in the language of her conscience. She knew that she was Henry's wife. If she blasphemed against the sacrament she had taken, she would be damning her own soul and consenting to the damnation of her husband's. For fifteen hundred years the Church had struggled to teach its barbarian converts that individual souls were important, that each had an inner voice connecting it with God. Now it was confronted by the stubborn discordance of those voices. Catherine before Campeggio stood as firmly on her inner moral certainty as Luther had stood at Worms.

Campeggio's concern was for the Church. His disappointment in Catherine sprang from her failure to consider in what difficulties she was involving His Holiness. But Catherine had considered. Campeggio unconsciously revealed Clement's chief weakness when he explained that His Holiness had to be careful of many things. Catherine cared for the Church as she cared for the salvation of her soul, but she had the strength of simple faith, so fatally lacking at Rome, to see that it was not necessary to be careful of many things, but only of the one thing needful. A few days before she saw Campeggio she had written to her nephew Charles: "For the present Pope to undo what his predecessors have done, would reflect on his honor and conscience, and bring grave discredit to the Apostolic See which should stand firmly on the Rock which is Christ. Were the Pope to waver now, in this case, many might be led astray into thinking that right and justice are not with him." [2]

"*La Piedra que es Cristo*" – her mother Isabella had been fond of the expression – was Truth, the foundation of the Church. Only on that rock could the Church stand firm. The simple people of Europe expected of their Church an eternal refuge of truth and justice in a slippery, wicked world. On the fight to defend that fortress and to safeguard the sacraments on which the life of the Christian community was based, on the moral leadership of Europe – Catherine could see the issue if Clement could not – and not on the minutiae of Italian politics, depended the authority of the Pope.

ii

Catherine's main line of defense, as she told Campeggio, was the simple plea of her virginity when she married Henry. As a priest and as a man Campeggio believed her, but as a lawyer he felt that her assertion would be difficult to establish in a court of law, particularly in such a court as she would find in England. He agreed with Fisher and Vives that her best plea would be the validity of the bull of Julius II, and from the strictly legal point of view no doubt it was. The advantages of Catherine's contention, other than its truth, were political and strategic. It avoided the question whether the Pope could dispense the positive law of God, a question about which Catherine did not feel too comfortable, and which in these times of attack on the powers of the papacy it was unwise to raise, and shortcircuited the whole vexing theological argument as to whether the verse in Leviticus was abrogated or modified by the one in Deuteronomy (XXV, 5) which, in the case of a childless marriage, enjoined a man to raise up children to his deceased brother. Moreover, the plea of virginity laid the groundwork for Catherine's appeal on a question of fact which it was possible to assert no court could decide fairly in England; and emphasized the function of Rome as a neutral place, standing above all the other courts of Christendom. Catherine wanted the Pope to pronounce, not on the extent of his own powers, but on a question of simple fact; she felt that whatever Wolsey's court held, the people of England, who remembered her marriage to the King in the costume of a virgin bride, and knew something of her character, would believe her. She also cherished the faint, persistent hope that she could establish the truth of her contention in a way Campeggio little suspected.

Catherine had, however, as Campeggio soon discovered, a defensive outwork more troublesome to lawyers than her main line. As soon as Charles got Catherine's message his counselors had set about collecting evidence, examining witnesses who could testify to her virginity, and assembling the relevant documents. Almost at once, Dr. De Puebla's son, now an imperial chaplain, had come forward with his father's private papers, a better file than the government possessed, among them one document of the first importance, a brief of Pope Julius II, bearing the same date as his bull of dispensation, and likewise dispensing for the marriage. The transcript of the brief sent to Mendoza for Catherine's information showed differences in phrasing from the bull known in England.

News of the brief exploded among Henry's legal experts like a bombshell. Until past midsummer of 1528 they had not suspected its existence; all their carefully prepared lines of attack were directed another way. For one thing, the word *forsan* (perhaps), which in the bull seemed to imply some doubt in the Pope's mind about the consummation of the marriage with Arthur, was missing from the brief, which simply assumed that the marriage had been carnally consummated. Another important difference was the inclusion in the brief of the phrase "*his et aliis causis animum nostrum moventibus*" (and moved by these and other reasons) in describing the Pope's grounds for issuing the dispensation. A dispensation must have adequate grounds. Those recited by the bull were to confirm the friendship between Spain and England, and to prevent the danger of war. Stephen Gardiner, now the leading mind among Henry's lawyers, based great hopes on attacking this sentence, intending to argue that the Pope had been deceived about the facts, since there was no danger of war between England and Spain in 1503, and consequently the bull had been procured by what is technically called "obreption" – that is, by misrepresenting the reasons for applying for it. But if the Pope said he had been moved by other reasons as well, without reciting them, no one could say how much the danger of war weighed with him, or whether he might not have heard more cogent arguments, unstated. That the brief existed at all, however, was the chief nuisance. Clement VII's bulls had been drawn without knowledge of it, yet it was a dispensation equally valid, only slightly less solemn and formal, and differing in language from the one under attack. To produce it would be to invalidate the decretal commission, with its rigorous terms, at the outset, and to cast doubt on the whole authority of the legatine court. Unless the English could make away with the brief, or have it declared a forgery, they would have to begin all over again at Rome. Either course was difficult while the original was in Spain.[3] Meanwhile, the opening of the legatine court had to be postponed.

After Campeggio's arrival it had been impossible to deny Catherine legal assistance any longer, and the crown had permitted her a distinguished array of counsel: William Warham, Archbishop of Canterbury; John Fisher, Bishop of Rochester, her bravest and most disinterested defender; Dr. Henry Standish, Bishop of St. Asaph's, an eloquent preacher of her own order of Observant Franciscans; Cuthbert Tunstall, Bishop of London, a distinguished humanist, friend of Erasmus and Thomas More; John Clerk, Bishop of Bath and Wells, and the Bishops of Exeter and Ely; besides four foreigners: two Spaniards, Jorge de Athequa, Bishop of Llandaff, her confessor, a good, simple, timid soul, and Luis Vives, the humanist; and two Flemings, the Dean of Tongres and another, both canonists, whom Mendoza's repeated pleas were at last bringing from Flanders. Actually Vives and the two Flemings, at the moment of their appointment, were still on the road from Brussels, and were so harried after they reached England that they did not long remain, so it was to her English counselors that Catherine handed over the plans and documents of her defense, including the copies sent her from Spain of the bull of Julius II (she had not been permitted to see the original), and of the previously unsuspected brief, the bad news of which they immediately communicated to the King.

What happened next made plain how much Catherine could trust her English advisers. Wolsey had a paper drafted, headed "A devise to be given to the Queen's Grace by her counselors," setting forth that the brief, a copy of which she had given them, was likely to be rejected as a forgery unless the original were produced, that no sort of copy however attested would have any value in court anyway (this was a flat lie), and that her only course "for the love of God and the advancement of justice" was to write to the Emperor asking him "for her sake and her child's" (a nice touch), to take the original from his treasury and send it to her at once.[4] The substance of this "device," drawn by her opponents as a trap for the Queen, was solemnly urged upon Catherine a few days later by her own appointed advocates. Warham and Tunstall were timid men, Clerk, Standish and the rest were to prove themselves typical Tudor officials, but one hopes that Fisher, at least, kept a scornful silence. The first act of Catherine's counselors foreshadowed how the terror of the despotic crown was to poison the wells of justice in England.

It was a pointless betrayal; Catherine simply ignored the advice. She could not ignore what followed. She was sent for by the royal council and threatened with the extremest consequences of disobedience if she failed to send to the Emperor for the original brief. A letter asking to have it forwarded to England was dictated to her, and she was obliged to swear on pain of treason that she would write no other. It was a time for dissembling. Mendoza, the Spanish ambassador, alarmed by a cryptic message from her, managed to smuggle himself into her apartments in disguise [5] – she had been reduced to such lengths to keep touch with the outside world – and the best that they could think of together was to send a verbal message by someone whose word Charles would accept, warning him to pay no attention to the letter.[6]

There seemed to be no one for the dangerous mission but her former messenger, Francisco Felipez. This time Felipez left without license or safe conduct, but not unobserved by Wolsey's spies. A fortnight later he limped ruefully back to court, explaining his bandages by saying, with a defiant grin, that he had broken his arm in a dark alley in Abbéville. Fortunately, he had not had a scrap of paper on him, and the accident was not as fatal as might have been expected, but Felipez could not ride for months, and the Queen would have to find another messenger.

The official messenger had been selected already, Thomas Abell, one of the Queen's chaplains, a convincing bearer for what was meant to look like a confidential personal appeal. Catherine, suspicious of Abell or anyone picked out by her enemies, was driven to committing a brief verbal message to one Montoya, a Spaniard who was accompanying Abell as guide and interpreter.[7]

One would like to know more of this Thomas Abell, whom Wolsey selected for his attempt to impose on the Emperor, and whom Catherine, for all her knowledge of the English, felt she could not trust. A shy, reserved man, one imagines, seeming cold and self-centered, even to those who had observed him casually for years, slow to make up his mind on a difficult question and even slower to speak it, but unshakeable, once his teeth were set, by all the legions of hell. On the outvoyage Montoya must have gabbled to him something of the Queen's secret, and Abell must have seen, what Catherine knew, how leaky a can this courier was. For when they reached the Emperor's court it was Thomas Abell who took full charge of the Queen's interests, drew up a businesslike Latin document setting forth succinctly the reasons why the original brief must be kept safe in Spain, suggesting, what neither Catherine nor Mendoza had thought of, a properly attested notarial copy, valid in any Church court, and summarizing crisply the steps the Emperor could take to prevent his aunt's divorce. He waited calmly, this quiet clergyman, amid the smells and chatter of the strange, foreign city, until his attested copy was ready, and calmly took it back with him, to settle down and write a book against the King's case – a good book, a devastating book, which he published in the teeth of the King's campaign of terror, and for which, and for his obstinate refusal to retract a line of it, he spent the last six years of his life in the Tower, and died, when his persecutors tired of trying to break his spirit, at the hands of the common hangman.

When Mendoza, furious at the behavior of Catherine's counsel, wrote that "in matters of self-interest the English are without conscience or common honesty," he was not thinking of men like Thomas Abell.

iii

Henry's hopes of a speedy trial vanished when Thomas Abell's courage sprang his trap for the brief. His agents in Rome tried in vain, on a dozen flimsy pretexts, to get the brief declared a forgery, but Clement was only too happy to have another excuse for delay, another avenue of possible retreat, and the most he could be persuaded to was a private advice to Campeggio that he might ignore the new document in opening the legatine court, if that seemed expedient.

Campeggio, nursing his gout and his shrinking treasury beside the foggy Thames, was glad of an excuse for not beginning what was so likely to turn out badly. Like Clement, as long as no action was taken he could comfort himself with the hope that something would turn up, "that time would bring forth something," by which he meant that either one of the principals would die, or Henry would lose his head and commit bigamy, or Anne would someday fail to fend him off, and that, once she was his mistress, Henry would lose his eagerness for legal sanctions. Campeggio could feel sorry for Wolsey's predicament, but Henry's fidgeting roused in him only sardonic amusement. Henry had hustled Anne out of London before Campeggio's arrival, then ridden after her, and finally brought her back again with the most transparent show of indifference. He might have spared his subterfuges; Campeggio had known all along about the lady in the case. He found it not a little comical that, although Anne gave herself all the airs of an acknowledged *maîtresse en titre*, Henry apparently had not been able to proceed to "the ultimate conjunction," [8] but was compelled to wait on tenterhooks for the Pope to say the word.

What troubled Campeggio most was the flood of "Lutheran" books in London. He warned Henry against heretics who, on the pretext of denouncing the sins of the clergy, tempted men to steal the goods of the Church, and was not deceived by the King's mealy-mouthed reply. It was Henry's first mild flirtation with heresy. Until the Pope had dared to hesitate in complying with his wishes, Henry had been the staunchest defender of the faith, and particularly of the papacy, in Europe; but people had recently been putting "Lutheran" books in his way, and he had found them surprisingly full of home truths about the guile and greed of churchmen, and the might and majesty of kings. Writers, Henry felt, who took so proper a view of his own exalted position could not be as bad as Wolsey represented. Catherine's friends blamed the Boleyn faction for circulating these heretical pamphlets, and they were probably right.

Whether any of the Boleyn clique, the new men who hoped to shoulder their way into power behind the new queen, were inclined to heresy before 1528, there is no way of telling. Sir Thomas, Anne's father, hardly had enough imagination, or George, her brother, enough seriousness for a religious reformer, and of Anne's own interest in reform the evidence is inadequate. But the Boleyns and their friends needed to make some sort of party for themselves, and the only people they could attract were those willing to condone the King's divorce for the sake of attacking the Church. Moreover, it was amusing to have these sticks with which to prod the Cardinal. For the moment, Henry abetted them.

Some steps had to be taken to change public opinion. Londoners were passing from pothouse orations against the divorce to demonstrations in the streets. Catherine's most casual appearance was enough to raise a cheer, and Wolsey and the French ambassador began to be greeted with jeers and shouted execrations. Campeggio's arrival, and the tale that he had come on behalf of the Pope to order the Queen into a nunnery, raised feelings to such heat that in November Henry summoned the Londoners, the Lord Mayor and the aldermen and the solid burgesses, the gentlemen of the Inns of Court and as many of the meaner sort as could crowd themselves into the doorways and embrasures of his great chamber at Bridewell Palace, and there for the first time unbosomed himself to them about his domestic perplexities. As near as the wit of that staunchly loyal subject, Edward Hall, could carry it away, it was a dignified and moving speech. Henry began by reminding his subjects of the glories of his reign, and of the melancholy fact that he must one day die and leave them. Remembering the horrors of the civil wars between York and Lancaster, he shuddered at the thought of the mischief to them, and to their children, should the succession be unsettled at his death, and told them that, through a doubt suggested by the French ambassador, he had come to fear this might be the case, and having consulted the greatest clerks in Christendom to know whether he were living in lawful matrimony or wicked adultery, he had sent for a legate from Rome to decide. "For this only cause, I protest, before God and on the word of a prince. . . .

"And as touching the Queen," he went on, "if it may be adjudged by law of God that she is my lawful wife, there was never anything more pleasant and more acceptable to me in my life . . . for I assure you that beside her noble parentage . . . she is a woman of most gentleness, of most humility and buxomness, yea and of all good qualities appertaining to nobility she is without comparison as I, this twenty years almost, have had the true experiment, so that if I were to marry again, if the marriage might be good, I would surely choose her above all other women. . . ." And after a mournful but manly reference to his sorrow at the prospect of parting with this ideal helpmate and companion of many years, and another reminder about his conscience and the succession, the King dismissed the citizens, charging them to make known everywhere the true facts of the approaching trial.

So Hall. So also, though more briefly, M. du Bellay, the French ambassador, who was also present, and promptly reported the speech. But M. du Bellay thought he heard another note, a warning that if any man spoke of the marriage other than as he ought, he would learn who was master, and his head should fly, though it was held the highest in the kingdom.[9] Thus, for the first time, Henry wielded for himself the twin weapons of his future despotism, the appropriate weapons, for that matter, of any despotism which seeks to break the pattern of a people's life – cant and terror. By the legal murder of Buckingham, by the abrupt suppression of free speech, enforced by spies and informers so that "every man distrusted other, and no man durst break his mind to another,"[10] Wolsey had already introduced terror. Henry's own instinct led him to cant.

Not that Henry disdained terror. But there were too many heads in London to make fly, and the Londoners were too accustomed to saying what they liked, and though Henry's pathos might confuse them for the moment, it did not, the loyal Hall and the acute Du Bellay agree, arouse any more enthusiasm for his divorce. The grumbling, booing of the cardinals, and the cheering whenever Catherine appeared were as loud as ever. Henry tried, therefore, what terror could do on Catherine. Wolsey was sent to tell her that she was said to be disloyal to the King, and that if any attempt were made on the King's life, or on that of himself and the Cardinal legate his colleague, she would be held responsible. The clumsy threat met the silent scorn it deserved. A more drastic step followed: a committee of the council called on her, charged with a formal reproof which Henry had not the courage to deliver himself. The King, they told her, was disappointed and grieved at her conduct at a time when she should be, as he was himself, sunk in grief and perplexity at the sin they had committed. Instead of showing a proper gravity and contrition, she went about as gaily as ever, and even showed herself more frequently in public than of old, encouraging the ignorant demonstrations of the populace by smiling and nodding and beckoning quite beyond her usual custom. Such conduct under the circumstances was perilously close to sedition, and she was therefore ordered to keep herself in seclusion, and to beware of stirring up the commons.[11]

With this formal order Catherine complied, though the chief effect of her compliance was to draw greater and greater throngs around the palace gates, watching for her rare appearances. The spontaneous good will of the kind, sentimental, muddle-headed people she had so long thought of as her own, had meant a good deal to her, and her response to their acclaim was probably as thoughtless as their cheers, but she was the last person to want to stir them up to anything more serious than noise. What she wanted was justice and vindication before the judgment of the whole world, not the satisfaction of a vulgar riot.

Had anyone wanted a riot, or perhaps some more serious matter, the Spanish ambassador thought it could be had for very little. Someone who knew history had told Don Iñigo Mendoza that six or seven thousand men landed in Cornwall would topple this king from his throne, and merchants, English as well as foreign, assured him that the city was boiling with suppressed revolt. Wolsey's unpopularity was at its height, and the King's popularity, unshakeable until the first rumor of the divorce, was also waning. But Don Iñigo knew of no one who wanted the insurrection he felt so confident of being able to deliver. He had not dared even to mention the subject to the Queen, and all his master, the Emperor, wanted of England was peace. Charles had refused to consider himself at war with his uncle, said plainly he would do no more than stand on the defensive whatever provocation was offered, opposed no obstacles to the resumption of trade with the Netherlands, and instructed Mendoza to give no cause of offense, and to do everything in his power to promote pleasanter relations. So though Mendoza had been arrested and confined by Wolsey's orders when war was declared, and was now free only on sufferance, though no formal peace had been concluded to follow what had been meant for a formal declaration of war, and the French were still being aided by English money and English volunteers, the Emperor's ambassador behaved with the greatest correctness. He refused to have any communication with Richard Pace, who was in the Tower, reputedly for his leanings to Catherine and the Emperor, when that unhappy man sent word to him, and he avoided carefully, though not without a wistful sigh, the Englishmen who wanted to talk sedition. Mendoza foresaw that nothing which could be made to happen in England could prevent Catherine's approaching trial, and since he was no lawyer himself, and Catherine paid even less attention to his suggestions than she did to those of her other advisers, the ambassador begged for his recall. He must have felt galled at the ineffectiveness of his whole embassy, a painful and futile incident in an honorable career. He hoped that his successor would be better equipped to deal with marital disputes, and have better luck.

iv

His recall was granted, and Mendoza had hardly left London – believing mistakenly that, before Catherine could be summoned by the legates, the lawyers so long expected from Flanders would be on hand to advise her, and that probably before the trial started his successor, who he hoped would be an expert canonist, would have arrived from Spain – when Wolsey and Campeggio opened their legatine court at Blackfriars, and issued a summons to the Queen to appear before them on June 18, 1529.

Some time before the day set, Catherine went privately to Campeggio to ask his advice, not as one of her judges, but as a priest and a friend. She was alone and friendless in England, she told him, a helpless and ignorant woman confronted by all the array of learning and ability which the King could command; the counsel appointed for her from Flanders had not come, much of the strength of her case lay in Spain, and she had already lodged an appeal to the Pope. She asked him about the Roman rules *de litis pendentia*, and whether, since her case was pending there, she ought not to ignore the summons to an inferior court. Perhaps Campeggio had heard whether her case had already been advoked?

Campeggio had his own doubts about the indifference of the Blackfriars court, and the honesty and ability of some of Catherine's English counsel, but also he had the Pope's instructions to proceed to trial, – with all possible delays, – and, having exhausted every ruse against the impatience of the English, he was obliged to do so. He had just written to Rome refusing the unofficial suggestion that he delay further by telling Henry that if they went to trial he would be obliged to pronounce against him. In a case before him, he protested, he could not make a statement of that sort until the law had been examined and the evidence was in. Then, if necessary, he would give sentence against the King, even if it put him in instant danger of death, but he saw no need of running any such risk at the moment. Moreover, as he pointed out, though he had destroyed the decretal commission, the general commission gave Wolsey power to pronounce sentence alone if his colleague refused or was unable to do so. To Catherine's embarrassing questions, therefore, he could only reply in his best legal manner, denying that the case would be advoked, advising her to accept the jurisdiction of his court, and urging full confidence in her advocates and in Wolsey. She did not comment, and left Campeggio wondering whether she would take an immediate appeal and on what grounds.

He did not have to wonder long. On June 18 Henry responded formally to the summons by proxy; but Catherine appeared in person, flanked by four bishops, and herself lodged her appeal, choosing all three of the grounds Campeggio had thought of: She protested against the place as hostile, against the judges as prejudiced, and against the opening of the case while it was pending at Rome. The appeal was soundly drawn; Campeggio himself could not have bettered it. If she was the helpless, ignorant woman she said she was, one wonders where she got her advice. She may, of course, have trusted Fisher, concealing her reliance on him to spare him the

King's displeasure. She may have consulted Vives the preceding winter, though Vives, like Fisher, opposed the tactics she adopted. But when Catherine spoke of her helpless ignorance, Christian humility and feminine guile were not absent. She was quite as capable of getting up a case at canon law as her husband, and everything indicates that she, herself, was in full charge of her own defense.

To the surprise of many, in spite of having refused the court, the Queen appeared again, at the first full session at Blackfriars [12] three days later. It was a curious and magnificent spectacle. At the right, under a regal canopy, King Henry was enthroned, then, only slightly lower, the two cardinals in their hats and scarlet robes, and beyond them, a little lower again, the Queen. At their feet were ranged the officers of the court and the whole bench of bishops, with William Warham, Archbishop of Canterbury, in the place of honor; and before them at the bar on either side the counselors of the contending parties, Dr. Sampson and Dr. Bell for the King, and the Bishops of Rochester and St. Asaph's for the Queen. Nothing like it had ever been seen in England, or, as far as men could remember, in Christendom: a reigning king and queen appearing themselves in answer to the summons of a court set up in their own land, to plead like private persons – a spectacle to set people wondering at that power of Rome which had been growing in the land ever since Wolsey was made the Pope's legate. But Henry did not care what glittering climax he had set to the usurpations of the Cardinal, or what admission he made of the Pope's right to set up a legatine court in his kingdom, provided he secured his divorce. All this public magnificence was to be a sounding board for the sincerity of his scruples and the completeness of his triumph. So he heard with equanimity the papal commission read, and when the crier called, "King Henry of England, come into the court," he answered, "Here, my lords," in a clear, round voice.

"Catherine, Queen of England, come into the court."

It was the moment Catherine awaited. Her legal steps had been taken already, but she too could use a sounding board; and there was another, a desperate, faint hope. She arose, and slowly, with everyone's eyes upon her, picked her way round the close ranked bishops, mounted the tribune on the other side, and knelt at her husband's feet.

"Sir," – the intonation was foreign, but the words were clear, – "I beseech you for all the love that hath been between us, let me have justice and right, take of me some pity and compassion, for I am a poor woman, and a stranger, born out of your dominion. I have here no assured friend and much less indifferent counsel. I flee to you, as to the head of justice within this realm . . .

"I take God and all the world to witness that I have been to you a true, humble, and obedient wife, ever comfortable to your will and pleasure . . . , being always well pleased and contented with all things wherein you had any delight or dalliance, whether it were little or much. . . . I loved all those whom ye loved, only for your sake, whether I had cause or no, and whether they were my friends or my enemies. This twenty years or more I have been your true wife, and by me ye have had divers children, although it hath pleased God to call them from this world. . . ." She steadied herself, and her voice was clear when she went on. This was the crucial point.

"And when ye had me at the first, I take God to be my judge, I was a true maid, without touch of man. And whether this be true or no, I put it to your conscience."

She paused. This was her secret trump. She had told the Spanish ambassador that Henry had often said in the hearing of many that she was a virgin at their marriage, and added she was sure he would never deny it. Only in this public fashion could she bring him to the question and put on record his answer.

The King sat silent, immobile. Had she counted on an old love, a youthful chivalry, a simple respect for the truth? The silence in the great hall grew painful. It was clear that the King was not going to say anything, that he was just waiting for her to go on, or go away; only he and she ever knew whether at that moment he was able to meet her eyes.

The rest of her speech was lifeless, hardly worth the trouble, but having to be made: of the wisdom of the kings who made their marriage . . . the want she felt of counsel or justice . . . her own advocates being members of the King's privy council and not daring to defy his will.

"Therefore," she ended, "I humbly require you to spare me the extremity of this new court. . . . And if ye will not, to God I commit my cause."

And with a deep curtsy to the King, and not a look at the two legates or the assembled bishops, she moved slowly towards the door of the great hall.

"Madame," a spectator heard her usher Griffith say timidly, "ye be called again," and indeed the third formal summons of the court crier was ringing from the rafters.

"It matters not," she answered. "This is no indifferent court for me. I will not tarry." And the shadows of the doorway swallowed the stumpy, regal little figure.

After that exit, after that moment of embarrassing silence such a short while before, Henry's prepared speech, a repetition of what he had said at Bridewell about his tender conscience, his affection for Catherine, and his sorrow at losing so good a queen, fell rather flat. So did the bit of play-acting between him and Wolsey.

"Sir," said the Cardinal, falling on his knees, "I beseech your highness to declare before this audience whether I have been the chief inventor or first mover of this matter."

"Nay, my lord Cardinal, I can well excuse you herein. Ye have been rather against me."

Even those who thought the King might be telling the truth must have realized that he could only answer as he did. One of the grounds of Catherine's appeal was Wolsey's initial animus, and the whole standing of the Blackfriars' court depended on the assumption that Wolsey was an indifferent judge.

On the next court day, June 25, the Queen was declared contumacious, and the trial proceeded without her, pushed by the English with indecent haste, Campeggio felt, though a modern reader, turning over the massive bundles of testimony, hardly enlivened by the gossip of prurient beldames, and the boasting of aged noblemen about their youthful prowess in the bed chamber, is apt to find the chief indecency elsewhere. In an effort to establish that Catherine's marriage had been fully consummated, the government raked through enormous heaps of muck, most of it nearly thirty years old, and the ancient stenches steamed up unnoticed under the bored noses of the judges, incurious and unsurprised at the things Tudor gentlemen would swear to at the bidding of their king. Much of the testimony was comically irrelevant, but one witness was not called – Henry himself. Perhaps his odd notions of his relations to the Deity stopped him short of perjury. Or perhaps he had persuaded himself that he must have been mistaken about Catherine when he was married, and found it too embarrassing now to say why.

The dull, one-sided hearings were broken by only one moment of unexpected drama. Warham was droning through a list of the bishops who had put their names to a document endorsing the King's position, a list of all the bishops in England, royal officials and royal appointees to a man.

A tall, emaciated figure, deep-eyed and lantern-jawed, rose suddenly from the listening bench.

"That is not my hand nor seal!" John Fisher, Bishop of Rochester, challenging the judgment of his peers, and the ire of his king.

"You were in hand with me to have my hand and seal," he went on harshly to Warham, "as others of my lords have already done, but then I said to you that I would never consent to no such act."

"True," Warham put in hastily, less abashed to confess forgery than frightened at seeing a man he liked and respected putting his head in the lion's jaws, "but at the last you were persuaded I should subscribe your name for you, and put a seal to it myself, and you would allow it."

"Under your correction, my lord," said Fisher icily, "there is no thing more untrue."

It was a challenge flung down. Fisher followed it later, with a speech for the defense, a blunt assertion of the law, "Whom God hath joined together let no man put asunder," which Campeggio found as eloquent and well reasoned as it was bold and surprising, and in further support of the Queen's cause Fisher handed in a "book," a formal brief or extended pleading, copies of which were soon passing from hand to admiring hand among the learned of Europe. But the other efforts for the Queen were feeble stuff. Standish's brief was drawn with the plausibility of a man who means to lose a case without loss of reputation, and old Dr. Nicholas West, the Bishop of Ely, got tangled in his facts, and could only come back to the bare assertion that he thought the marriage good, and if the Queen said she came to it a virgin, he believed her. The defense was unco-ordinated and unofficial, it called no witnesses and presented no documents, and after the trial had run nearly a month, and people were expecting a verdict, Campeggio wrote that if he had to give sentence on what he had heard at Blackfriars, he would have to find for the King.

He knew, however, that he would not do so. On June 21, the date of the first plenary session at Blackfriars, that inveterate gambler, Francis I, had made his last desperate throw for Italy and lost. The Count of St. Pol's army had been cut to pieces at Landriano, and, as if that were the signal, Clement had come to terms with the Emperor in the Treaty of Barcelona just eight days later. On July 13, the advocation of Catherine's case to Rome had been decided in the *Segnatura* and on the sixteenth it passed the full Consistory. Already the Emperor's aunt, Margaret, Regent of the

Netherlands, and King Francis' mother, Louise of Savoy, were talking at Cambrai about terms of peace. If Campeggio did not yet know what had been decided at Rome, he was skillful in reading the signs in the European heavens.

Henry also was alarmed by those signs, and as Wolsey lay tumbling in his naked bed at York House after a sweaty session at Blackfriars, seeking vainly for a nap in the interval in the hearings, he was roused by a message from the King ordering him to go with his colleague, Campeggio, to the Queen, and make a last effort to persuade her to submit herself entirely to the King's mercy.

The two cardinals surprised the Queen in her apartments. She came out to greet them, making courteous apology for their unceremonious reception, with a skein of white silk, with which she had been sewing, draped about her neck, and the ladies among whom she had been working pushing after her in a curious little crowd.

"If it please you go into your privy chamber," said Wolsey, "we will show you the cause of our coming."

"My lord," she answered, instantly on her guard, "if you have anything to say, speak it openly before all these folks; for I fear nothing that ye can say or allege against me, but that I would all the world should both see and hear it."

Wolsey, with a glance at the surrounding women, began to speak in Latin.

"Nay, my lord," she cut him off, "speak to me in English I beseech you. Although," – with gentle irony, – "*I* understand Latin."

When Wolsey, with some embarrassment, explained that they had come to offer her their secret counsel, and for no other purpose, she softened a little. She was too simple, she said, to reply to such wise and learned men, but certainly a friendless foreign woman should be glad of their advice, and she led them into an inner room whence the straining listeners could at times hear the Queen's voice rising strongly, but could distinguish nothing that was said. Probably the cardinals rehearsed all the old arguments for submission; probably they told her that the case would surely be decided against her, and that this was her last chance to make terms. They might as well have argued with a chunk of Castilian limestone. Catherine's mind was made up, and she said good-by to them both, forever, at the door of her inner chamber, without a quiver. She could even see Wolsey's retreating back with no flare of her old hatred. She knew that, whatever happened to her, she had struck down her first great adversary, and she could watch him going towards his tragedy, dispassionately, almost sorrowfully. Since that moment of shameful silence in the hall at Blackfriars, she had known that it was not Wolsey she was fighting, nor for peace with her nephew, nor even for her own and her daughter's rights that she fought; she was fighting the devil and all his minions for her husband's soul and the souls of all his people.

v

On July 22, a few days after his last failure with Catherine, Wolsey heard that the worst had happened. The Pope had advoked the case to Rome. Campeggio might not know, and in one more session, two at the most, judgment must be pronounced. But next day Campeggio convened the court only to make an announcement. The holidays had begun in Rome; this was a Roman court; therefore the court would recess until after October 1. The last straw Wolsey clutched at had been snatched beyond reach, and, as he turned to face the angry murmur in the hall, he knew what it feels like to drown.

As if fate meant to ruin all at once the man it had raised above kings, the conversations at Cambrai, which Wolsey had repeatedly assured his master could not possibly come to anything, resulted, less than a fortnight later, in the Ladies' Peace. The French king abandoned Italy and settled all his differences with his brother the Emperor; England was contemptuously included in the peace, but neither Wolsey nor the English negotiators on the spot had any part in making the terms, from which Henry derived no profit except the promise of eventual repayment of a part of what he had spent. Francis had deserted Henry as completely and disastrously as Ferdinand, or Maximilian, or Charles had ever done. Wolsey's foreign policy and his ecclesiastical policy ended in simultaneous catastrophe.

For the moment there was no party in England except the party of Wolsey's enemies. It might have been called the party of the dukes, for Suffolk, who had cringed to him, and Norfolk, who had sulkily run his errands, led the onslaught of the pack. It could hardly be called the party of the Boleyns, since there were many in it who hated Anne Boleyn almost as much as they hated the Cardinal, although Thomas and his son bayed as loudly as any on Wolsey's track, and Anne, proud and malignant and openly in power, had drawn the blood whose scent whipped the hunt to fury, and now headed back every double of the Cardinal's towards the only shelter he knew, the shadow of the King he had served and ruled.

There was no place for Wolsey at court now, men hardly troubled to give him news of it, and it was his turn to lament in vain, as Catherine had lamented, that if he could but win back to the King's side for an hour he could silence all his enemies. For a while he still held his head high. His court of Star Chamber was empty of suitors, but he went to it proudly, though in the King's Bench there was already sued out against him a writ of praemunire, a terrible, antique legal weapon found rusting in the arsenal of the royal courts, charging him absurdly with procuring papal bulls to be brought into the country, and setting up therein a court, in virtue of authority from the Pope of Rome, contrary to the peace and dignity of our lord the King. When Norfolk and Suffolk came to take from him the Great Seal, the mystic instrument of his chancellorship, he refused to surrender it until they showed him the King's written authority. The sight of the familiar signature, sprawled at the bottom of the parchment, broke him. He inventoried his goods to be surrendered to the King as if he were going to the scaffold, as indeed the London crowds, watching from Thameside the course of his barge, devoutly hoped he was; and when, on his journey to his desolate country house, Sir Harry Norris brought him a bauble and kind word from the King, he was reduced to maudlin tears and meaningless, half-hysterical gestures. Later he was to recover his dignity, but in his first abject despair there was a depth of abasement more painful than tragedy.

A few faithful servants followed him to the bare manor house where he took refuge, among them his gentleman usher, George Cavendish, a simple man, honest and sweet as a sound apple, a man who, it is good to remember, loved his formidable master. Standing in a window recess at Esher, Cavendish saw another servant, one Thomas Cromwell, a beefy, thick-necked fellow, with a cold slab of a jaw, and eyes like black lacquer, now wet with unaccustomed tears. In Cromwell's hand, of all things, was a prayer book. Every great man keeps one underling to do jobs too dirty for anyone else; Cromwell was Wolsey's. If Cavendish knew anything of the Cardinal's man of business, his queer, shady past and the dark errands he went upon, he must have despised him a little, and been more than a little afraid of him; but now at the man's tears (how was honest George to guess their source?) he was touched.

"Why, Master Cromwell," he said, "is my lord in any danger for whom ye lament thus?"

"Nay," said Cromwell, frankly, "it is my own unhappy case that I am like to lose all I have worked for all the days of my life.

"But," he went on, confessing himself as even the hardest and most cunning of egoists sometimes will to one too simple to harm him, "I intend, God willing, to ride to London, and so to court, where I will make or mar e'er I come again."

Thus, though he did not know it at once, Henry gained one of the tools who were to replace the Cardinal. A little later he met the other – a timid, rabbity little man, blinking nervously and shortsightedly at greatness, the picture of a shabby, retiring scholar, shoved forward by Fox and Gardiner because he had some plan about polling the universities on the subject of the King's divorce. He was promptly attached to the Boleyns, labeled to be kept until wanted. Henry would find a use for Cranmer's hydromedusan plasm as well as for Cromwell's steel.

Chapter Three

MESSIRE EUSTACHE CHAPUYS, the new imperial ambassador, arrived in the breathless September pause after the adjournment at Blackfriars. The Londoners were celebrating the Peace of Cambrai; the King was concealing his chagrin on his usual autumn hunting progress, accompanied by the Queen and the Lady; Cardinal Wolsey still kept his seals of office, though not for long; and his colleague, Campeggio, still nursed his gout in London, ostensibly waiting to reopen the court which everyone knew was closed forever. The new ambassador, cautiously taking his first soundings of the complex situation, was anxious to make this, his first mission in the Emperor's service, a striking success. Messire Chapuys could acknowledge to himself that, though he had come a long way from a modest beginning, he had yet no secure footing in his world, and he was beginning to be a little impatient that learning and industry and constant association with the great had brought him no more rewards than an insignificant benefice or two, the revenues of which political troubles at Geneva were making uncollectable, and the salary of a master of requests in the imperial household. It was something to be in the imperial service at all, but he had arrived there by a series of precarious leaps which left him no way back, and he had no friend or connections at court to defend his mistakes, and no estates or offices to which to retire in case of failure. Instead his kin at Annecy looked to him to establish the family's name, to provide dowries for the girls and honorable employment for the boys, and generally to help them keep the place into which they had recently intruded among the petty nobility of Savoy.

The Chapuys family had been notaries in Annecy for two generations; before that, artisans and peasants of hard-headed, tight-fisted mountain stock, a clannish, unadventurous breed, sticking stubbornly to small gains, pushing their way by inches up the narrow social ladder of their little native town. Eustache's father died when the children were still small, and his mother had emptied the bottom of the stocking and mortgaged a bit of family property to send her eldest son to the little provincial university of Turin. There Eustache had done well, taken a doctorate *utriusque juris*, which was the practical way of advancement, and attracted the notice of the great Prince–Bishop of Geneva. Before he was thirty he was high in the Bishop's service, his vicar for the civil administration of the town, trusted with embassies to the restless Swiss cantons, and able to send money home. Why under such circumstances he should have cultivated the friendship of political firebrands and disreputable humanists, fallen out with representatives of the Duke of Savoy and finally with his own bishop, and thrown over a respectable and promising career to follow the desperate fortunes of the rebel Duke of Bourbon, probably few of his relatives at Annecy could understand. The shortsighted policies of the Bishop of Geneva had, indeed, delivered that town to radicals who would have made short work of his career had he remained there, and though Bourbon's mad adventure had met the disaster it invited, it had landed the son of an Annecy notary in the service of the greatest monarch in Christendom, in a post which bishops and great noblemen had been proud to fill. But there had been more luck than foresight in that consummation. An impatience with fools and hypocrites, a sympathy with the unorthodox and with the victims of injustice, and a liking for long chances and desperate causes made the prudent ways of rising in the world harder for Chapuys than he liked to admit. He knew, however, that he owed his first appointment at the imperial court to the Emperor's reluctance to seem ungrateful to the stranded agent of a prince who had lost his fortune and his life in the imperial cause, and his present preferment only in part to his legal learning. The Emperor needed a man in England who could keep his head. He judged that a Savoyard would be less likely to be carried away by sympathy for Catherine than one of her own countrymen, that a commoner would take a cooler view of a conflict between interest and honor than an aristocrat, and that an untonsured humanist would be less disturbed by an occasional whiff of heresy than a churchman more highly placed or more orthodoxly educated. Chapuys understood what the Emperor expected and was determined not to disappoint him. Chapuys was forty now, beginning to be gray at the temples and stiff in the joints, old enough to appreciate comfort and safety, a little too old to begin again, even if the world offered many chances for a new start. He rather plumed himself on his cynical disillusionment, his hard-headed realism. This time neither enthusiasm nor indignation should tempt him from the safe path.

When he arrived in England his head and his saddlebags were stuffed with instructions about the details of his mission: merchants' claims for damages in the late war to be adjusted, tariffs on wool and corn to be rescaled, indemnity payments left over from the old treaties to be worked out in co-operation with the French, Habsburg jewels to be redeemed, influential persons to be bribed or flattered, or both, pensions to the English nobility to be economically re-allotted, and all the mass of legal and theological and political details that concerned the Queen's divorce, a fat dossier over which he had worked in Spain and on his journey until he knew it backwards and by heart. All of it boiled down to two main points: Since honor obliged the Emperor to undertake his aunt's defense, the ambassador was to place his own legal abilities, the services of the Emperor's agents at Rome, and, in fact, all the resources of imperialist diplomacy at Queen Catherine's disposal; but since the Emperor's responsibilities in Germany and elsewhere made it extremely inconvenient for him to offend the King of England, the ambassador was to do his best to reconcile the King and Queen, and to restore the former good relations between Henry and the Emperor. He was never to forget – this was the recurrent theme of all his instructions – that his mission was one of "*doulceur et amitié*," of sweetness and friendship. Before he crossed the Channel Chapuys assured the Regent Margaret and her council in Flanders that there was nothing at all incompatible in the two parts of his instructions, and nothing in them to embroil Flanders with the English.[1] He felt confident of carrying out both parts to the letter.

After his first month in England he was not so sure. Though he was able to confirm Mendoza's reports that neither the divorce nor hostility to the Emperor was popular in London, and though the Cardinal, whom the imperialists had always regarded as their chief enemy and the Queen's, was certainly out of favor, Chapuys found such courtiers as he talked to shy and wary, and the whole atmosphere of city and court oppressed by an uneasy expectation of great events to come. He was warned not to try to see the Queen until after he had seen the King, and to be careful what he said when he did see her. The account which the Queen's physician, Dr. Fernando Vittoria, managed to give him of Catherine's position and views, an account boldly delivered in rapid Spanish in the midst of a circle of suspicious but uncomprehending English officials, did not reassure him. Nor, when he was finally permitted to ride to Grafton, did his first interviews at court.

His reception was cordial enough, and courtiers vied with one another in expressions of pro-imperialist sympathy, but he noticed that those who were allowed to get near him were nearly all members of the Boleyn faction, that the Lady's father seemed to be assigned as his particular guide and escort – and that except for the Duke of Norfolk, who was, after all, the Lady's uncle and the beneficiary of her feud with Wolsey, most of the persons most in evidence were among those Mendoza had counted as pro-French. When he was introduced to the King, Henry turned on him all the batteries of his famous charm, spoke of his regret at past misunderstandings with his nephew the Emperor, and of the high responsibilities that devolved upon ambassadors to maintain peace and good will among princes, such as he was sure the present ambassador, whom he hoped to see often at court, would work for earnestly. But the climate changed when the conversation turned on the King's great matter. The Emperor had done him a grave injury by retaining that papal brief, Henry complained, and a grave injury to the Queen as well. If he had been able to satisfy himself that the brief was genuine, he would be living with the Queen at this moment, and they would both have been spared months of pain and uncertainty. But the way the brief was guarded in Spain convinced him that it was a forgery. The Emperor's behavior had been most unfriendly; nothing except sending the brief promptly to England and stopping this trial at Rome could atone for it. Chapuys, who disliked having his intelligence underestimated, and who, himself, had spent days over the brief with Henry's agents in Spain, scrutinizing every comma, and letting them compare their attested copies with the original over and over, was surprised to find himself losing his temper, and obliged to struggle for the proper note of cordiality on which to end the interview.

He found Catherine in the center of a watchful circle of attendants towards whom she maintained a determined air of regal indifference. She heard out Chapuys' account of his conversation with her husband as if its subject had been the most commonplace in the world, praising his answers and only adding that the King knew that the brief was not really important, since she had never been Arthur's wife, and the sweeping dispensation it contained was quite unnecessary. She delivered that remark as if she wanted to be sure that everyone in earshot heard it, but Chapuys noted that her one really important injunction, to have nothing to do with Wolsey, was muttered cautiously between stiff, unmoving lips. Even to a less sensitive observer than Chapuys, the sense of strain, of tension about the Queen, was unmistakable. He came away reluctantly admiring her courage and resourcefulness, reluctantly convinced that her defense was going to be much more difficult than he had hoped.[2]

Interviews with the Duke of Norfolk, further details from Dr. Vittoria and other of the Queen's friends, the dribbles of court gossip which he soaked up like a sponge, and the sources and channels of which he was always working to clear and increase, all confirmed his impression. He saw that the French influence at court which he was supposed to counteract was based almost entirely on the hope of French aid for the divorce, and more than one person told him that if the Emperor would abandon his aunt, he could negotiate any kind of alliance he liked in England, – "My King will be the Emperor's slave forever," was the melodramatic way Norfolk put it, – but more and more Chapuys wrote as if the "sweetness and friendship" clause in his instructions was merely conditional, and the defense of the Queen an absolute imperative. He dug from his saddlebags a papal brief, enjoining the two cardinals specifically and all other persons in general from interfering with the Queen's case. Its service in England was a ticklish matter, but when Catherine offered, with characteristic forthrightness, to hand her husband a copy herself, Chapuys dissuaded her, and found a way which involved her less, though the Emperor more. He stretched his instructions to the limit by recommending directly to the imperialist agents at Rome a series of steps to help the Queen and block the English. "The Lady is all-powerful here," he kept repeating, "and the Queen will never have peace until her case is tried and decided at Rome." Except for her optimism about the fundamental goodness of Henry's character, Catherine's views and Chapuys' were becoming indistinguishable. As far as a trusted ambassador could, he mobilized all the resources of imperialist diplomacy in her service. Before he had been six months in England, Chapuys had forgotten all about *doulceur et amitié*, and how much his own career might depend on his achieving them, and within a year he was subordinating every other imperialist interest in England to considerations of the Queen's defense, more zealously than Mendoza had ever done. Had the Emperor been no more scrupulous of his personal honor than Ferdinand of Aragon had been, Chapuys would soon have had to find a new master.

Those first months Chapuys spent in England, the months rumorous with the fall of Wolsey, marked a turning point in history. As long as the scarlet figure of the great Cardinal filled the foreground of the English scene, dominating the state as the King's chief minister, dominating the Church as papal legate, mediating between Church and state as Lord Chancellor, men could not judge how fast the Tudor monarchy was traveling. When the last ecclesiastical statesman of the middle ages fell and the first important parliament of modern times convened, the contradictions which had developed between the dual order of the past which Wolsey as Cardinal and Lord Chancellor had represented, and the new, dynamic, essentially secular and unitary state, which Wolsey's energies had helped to build, became painfully apparent. The knights and burgesses who assembled at Westminster thought they were attacking the Cardinal and his works, the new abuses which his extension of papal power had introduced into the Church, and the old ones which his greed and arrogance had encouraged; actually, they were attacking the constitution under which England had lived as a part of Christendom for five hundred years. The fall of the Cardinal was the prelude to a revolution.

As long as the Cardinal had represented England to Rome, and Rome in England, Henry and Catherine fought their duel in the framework of the past, the framework of the feudal monarchy and the universal Church. But now that royal and papal power had been wrenched apart by the fall of Wolsey, a momentous question was posed: *Is there a human justice in the world to which anyone can appeal when the state refuses justice?* Are there laws superior to the laws of the state, laws resting, that is, on a basis more valid and universal than capricious will imposed by arbitrary force? Since the beginning of Christendom men had never doubted that there were such laws, and the whole constitution of England, as of the other states of western Europe, had been based on their acceptance, and on the dualism which that acceptance implied. Throughout Europe the canon law ran side by side with the laws of each secular community; the Church's courts paralleled the King's courts and locked all Christendom into a common legal unity; right of appeal to the Pope complemented right of appeal to the King. In practice the right might be rarely invoked, and since the rise of the new absolutisms, papal and royal, in the fifteenth century, and the consequent accommodations between Church and state wherever the state was strong, the two systems of justice clashed so rarely that only in unusual circumstances, such as those which had arisen in England, could the question be posed at all. As society was organized, no lay person of less than royal rank was very likely to appeal at Rome against a king, and no subject except one who, like Catherine, possessed independent means of influence was likely to get a hearing. Nevertheless Catherine's appeal at Blackfriars had raised a question more fundamental than that over which the kings and popes of the twelfth century had struggled. Not *Is there a special class of persons — the clergy — not subject to the King's justice?* but *Are there aspects in the life of every person, every layman, over which no lay authority may have final jurisdiction?* If so, then the King, himself, is subject as a Christian to the jurisdiction of the Church. If not, then the arbitrary will of the state is supreme in every department of men's lives, and it is idle to pretend any more that Christendom exists, or that its place in Europe is filled up by more than a jarring collection of independent, arbitrary wills.

No king in Europe had been a more impassioned defender of the papacy than Henry VIII; he owed to his exaggerated partisanship in the papal cause his new, proudly worn title of "Defender of the

Faith." The whole point of the book for which he had received that title was the necessity of an ecclesiastical hierarchy in a society based on the sacraments, and the necessary culmination of that hierarchy in the Pope. To the Pope all Christians, as Christians, were finally subject, and without that final central authority Christendom could not be preserved from heresy, anarchy and ultimate dissolution. Henry had twice, specifically, accepted papal jurisdiction over his own case: in 1527 when he had applied for a dispensation to marry Anne Boleyn, and in 1529 when he had appeared in person before the legatine court at Blackfriars. But then he had felt confident of a decision in his favor. Would he now accept a decision handed down at Rome, where the Emperor was more powerful than ever, and where his own influence, after the complete collapse of Wolsey's foreign policy at Cambrai, was at low ebb? Would he accept defeat?

Catherine thought that he would. Her worst fear had been that Wolsey's court would declare against her, and that Henry would thereupon marry Anne before the Pope could act. Now that the case was advoked to Rome, she breathed more easily. She was alarmed by the unusual efforts Henry's council had made to pack the Parliament with subservient members, and by the hatred of the clergy manifest in that body. She believed the Boleyn faction capable of anything, and knew that their influence, through Anne, on her husband was, for the moment, paramount. Her high respect for the papal office did not blind her to the faults of Clement VII – his love of delay and devious intrigue, his worldly, shortsighted absorption in the temporal affairs of Italy, his natural timidity and the consequent danger that he would oblige the King of England if he could find some way of wriggling out of the responsibility. But she counted on her nephew, the Emperor, to stiffen the Pope's back, and on the solemnity of his office to compel him to a just decision, once he saw that some decision was inescapable. And she counted on the natural conservatism of the English people, and on her husband's conventional habit of mind, to validate the decision once it was handed down. She would wait for justice from Rome.[3]

ii

Henry's words and actions reveal a wavering between opposite pressures. He really did not know what to do next. He toyed with the idea of a "neutral" court at Cambrai. He pushed on with the polling of the universities, the idea he had taken from Cranmer, though once Chapuys had spread the alarm, and the imperialist diplomats swung into action, matching threat with threat and bribe with bribe, it became clear that he was not going to get the unanimous suffrage of the learned. He kept on negotiating with the Pope, and even dispatched an ill-chosen embassy to Charles, himself, at Bologna, an embassy headed, of all people, by Thomas Boleyn, in a desperate effort to persuade the Emperor to take his side of the argument. And he talked of proceeding by his own authority in his own realm, though Parliament, eager enough to persecute the Cardinal and mulct the priests, showed an obstinate unwillingness to take up the divorce, and how he was to proceed without Parliament was not clear.

Meanwhile, at Greenwich, Anne Boleyn had her separate apartments, almost her separate court, and Henry spent much time in her company, fussing about with the anxious, proprietary air of a prospective bridegroom, while in the other wing of the palace Catherine still lived almost as usual, mending her husband's shirts and looking after his comforts, and Henry, out of old habit stronger than affection, supped now and then alone with her before the fire in her chamber, and spent an occasional evening lounging and talking as Catherine sewed. If only his womenfolk would have let him alone, Henry might have been almost content to drift indefinitely in this ambiguous eddy in his life while his case hung fire at Rome, and he avoided, in a way that soothed his self-esteem, the necessity for painful decisions. But between two such women as Anne and Catherine he could not drift for long.

Anne was forever at him to separate from Catherine altogether, and though he would not, at first, order the Queen away from Greenwich, he would not permit Mary to come there; and when Catherine suggested that she would like to see her daughter, he told her brutally that she might go where Mary was whenever she liked. Catherine's calm reply that her place was at his side and there she would remain was not, under the circumstances, placating. A few days later – this was in November, four months after the prorogation at Blackfriars – husband and wife quarreled furiously. Weariness of Anne's complaints, perhaps, drove Henry to Catherine's fireside for supper, to find there no longer the peace he remembered. Catherine greeted him with the remark that she saw him less and less often. He did not sup with her or visit her as he used to, but left her to sit, neglected and forsaken, bearing in loneliness the pangs of purgatory. The sense of her wrongs released a spate of Spanish eloquence, voluble, vehement, hyperbolic, meant to provoke retort. Henry was not hard to provoke. It was her own fault, he growled, if she was neglected and uncomfortable; she was mistress of her own household; she could go where she liked and live as she liked. He was not responsible. He was not her husband, as many learned doctors, including Dr. Lee, his almoner, had told him.

"Doctors!" Catherine cried. "You know yourself, without the help of any doctors, that you are my husband and that your case has no foundation. I came to you as much a virgin as I came from my mother's womb, and you, yourself, have often said so. I care not a straw for your almoner or your doctors. Your almoner is not my judge, thank God, but the Pope. He will decide."

Henry snapped his fingers at the Pope. The theologians and lawyers all supported his view, and he was only waiting until their opinions were confirmed by the University of Paris. "Then," with a defiant flourish, "if the Pope does not decide in my favor, I shall declare the Pope a heretic, and marry whom I please."

Catherine refused to be daunted. "You know best what opinions you have from Paris, and where not, and how much they are worth. And you know, too, that the best lawyers in England have written on my side. Let me but collect opinions as you have done, and for every doctor or lawyer of yours, I dare say I could find a thousand to hold our marriage good and indissoluble."

Really bold opposition always baffled Henry. He glared, speechless, and stormed from Catherine's apartments to rehearse the argument to Anne, and win from her applause the triumph denied him by his wife. But Anne cracked the whip on the other flank. She was beginning to see that this imposing monarch could be driven as well as led. She interrupted his circumstantial report almost scornfully. He ought to know better than to argue with Catherine. Why, he had never won an argument with Catherine in his life! One of these days he would be so convinced by Catherine's arguments that he would go back to her without a thought for the woman who had lost all chance of an honorable marriage while she waited for him. As for herself, said Anne, she saw that her time and youth were wasted and past in vain, and what she was now or what was to become of her, no one, not even she, could say. And she dissolved in tears of self-pity, which all her harassed lover's agitated tuttings and pattings could not abate.[4]

For the moment, Anne's calculated hysterics had their effect. Henry ordered Catherine to go to Richmond, or at least to keep to her own apartments. He conferred the earldoms of Wiltshire and Ormonde on Anne's father, and other titles on her adherents, including the odd one of Lady Anne Rocheford on herself, and celebrated the affair by a banquet and ball at which the Lady, beaming with pride, sat in the Queen's place, above the Duchesses of Suffolk and Norfolk, and nothing seemed wanting to the triumph of the Boleyns, as Chapuys remarked wryly, except the priest and the exchange of rings. Once Anne's temper was appeased, however, word from Rome that Catherine would have to be represented at any trial, and perhaps some hint of how much the older nobility had been shocked by the Boleyns' party, were enough to make Henry draw back, within a fortnight. Catherine presided at the Christmas revels as she had always done, and the Lady Anne Rocheford was kept carefully out of sight.

After Christmas, another reversal. Henry's hopes of his divorce were raised by news from Paris; he hoped also, Chapuys thought, to get Parliament when it reconvened in the spring to act on his marriage and he hoped, absurdly, much from the new Earl of Wiltshire's mission to the Emperor. No doubt, also, he had to atone for neglecting Anne at Christmas. So, before January, 1530, was over, Henry had separated from his wife with every appearance of finality. Chapuys' letters were full of indignant references to Catherine's pathetic plight, and until April Henry kept sternly away from her, treating her meanwhile to a course of petty slights, persecutions and annoyances. But the polling of the universities began to develop into a European scandal. Even at Oxford and Cambridge the King's agents got what they wanted only by steam-roller tactics, amidst popular riot. Parliament was prorogued from time to time and finally put off until autumn, because the King's council despaired, Chapuys thought, of even getting a bill about the divorce introduced into either house; and at Bologna, in March, the Earl of Wiltshire met a sharp rebuff from the triumphant Emperor, and word came that the Pope was preparing another brief, more peremptory than his first, against any attempt to prejudge the case at Rome. Henry was reported to be furious, and Chapuys found the Duke of Norfolk in an ecstasy of rage and alarm. He broke off a tirade against the Emperor to ask, with ill-concealed apprehensiveness, whether Charles would make war for the sake of his aunt. No, Chapuys grinned, but the Emperor could not guarantee his uncle against the rebellion of his own subjects.

Chapuys had come round to Catherine's view that Henry could be frightened. The King's explosion of wrath at the rebuff to Wiltshire had been followed, he noted, not by a worsening of Catherine's position, but by its immediate improvement. In April she was given the means of reorganizing her household and permitted to choose a more suitable residence; in May she was more optimistic than Chapuys had ever seen her; in June, as reports came in of Charles's strength in Germany, and of Anne's unpopularity at court, she was ready to believe that all she needed to win was a papal order to Henry to separate from Anne. Chapuys took the stiffest tone he dared, and when, before July was half over, Henry rejoined his wife for one of their customary summer progresses, the ambassador was almost ready to share the Queen's optimism about her eventual triumph.

More than a year of vacillation had brought Henry no nearer his divorce by October, 1530, than he had been when he first received Chapuys, no nearer indeed than when Campeggio announced that the legatine court would adjourn for the holidays, and Suffolk had snarled at Wolsey that it "was never merry in England whilst we had cardinals among us." On Cranmer's advice Henry had polled the universities, and sent his envoys all over Europe, "fishing needy rabbis out of their ghettos to opine against Deuteronomy at a minimum charge of twenty-four crowns,"[5] only to find that of the diversities of expert opinion there is no end, and that anyone can hire experts. In the manner of Wolsey, and perhaps on the advice of Gardiner, he had obtained the signatures of most of the notables of the realm to a round robin letter to the Pope in favor of his divorce, which resulted only in eliciting the sternest reply Clement had yet penned and after which the very lords who had signed for him had, when approached in Parliament, politely but firmly declined to meddle further with a purely ecclesiastical matter. On Norfolk's advice he had tried packing the House of Commons, and learned that the difficulty with that amorphous mob of burgesses and country squires was to control not their selection but their subsequent behavior. But the chief thing he had learned was that it is easier to break a great minister than to make one.

After the fall of Wolsey he had filled his council with the ablest and most obvious men available, but for all that he found himself surrounded either by fools or – what was just as little to his purpose – by uncomfortably honest men. The Duke of Norfolk could not tell him how to manage his divorce; Sir Thomas More, who had succeeded Wolsey as Lord Chancellor, would not. Stephen Gardiner, royal secretary, of whom Henry had had great hopes, and who had indeed the nearest approach to Wolsey's combination of brains and executive ability, seemed unwilling to propose anything except the routine continuance of the case at Rome, and Sir William Fitzwilliam, a shrewd enough working diplomat, backed the French suggestion that Henry commit bigamy and rely on a future pardon, a course so exactly designed to profit the French, on whom Henry, once he had done anything so foolish, would be obliged to depend completely, that Sir William's colleagues believed Sir William either to be excessively susceptible to the persuasiveness of French gold, or to be getting more of it than they were.

All the Boleyn party could think of was "to declare the Pope a heretic," but though Henry might say, when he was angry enough, that he would do just that, the project was one from which in cold blood he recoiled almost as decisively as the conservatives in his council would have done had he suggested it. Henry was far too much of a conservative himself, far too conscious of the value of traditionally constituted authority, far too sensible of the dangers within and without his realm which such a step would involve, to want to open the floodgates of heresy and rebellion. To flirt with Lutheranism was one thing, to try to establish it in a kingdom where the prince had no standing army, and no power to tax enough to raise one, a kingdom where the prosperity of the people depended on trade with orthodox lands, and the stability of the throne depended on the consent of the people, most of whom were still good sons of the Church, was a more risky matter. Besides he did not know how to go about it. The bishops and the new Lord Chancellor were more active in the pursuit of heretics than anyone had been in Wolsey's time, and the anticlerical Commons showed no sign of disapproval. It would take more than the support of a handful of intellectual radicals at Cambridge, and a few hundred ignorant artisans in London, to carry through any such move as "declaring the Pope a heretic," even if Sir Thomas More and the bishops did not succeed in catching and reconciling or burning all the radicals before the King made up his mind.

To observers about the court it seemed that the King yearned for Wolsey, and indeed it would be odd if Henry did not sometimes regret that prompt energy which needed only a hint to execute his remotest whim, that subtle brain, endlessly fertile in expedients, that courage and resourcefulness which nothing but the King's displeasure ever daunted. Wolsey certainly yearned for the King. He spoke pathetically of his soul's good, and of devoting his last years to his pastoral cares at York, but every mile he retired from court cost him a pang, and each slow withdrawal was compelled only by the menaces of the Duke of Norfolk, who swore that he would "tear the butcher's cur with his teeth" if he did not shog off from London. Norfolk's neck crept with apprehension of the ax at the mere thought that the old magician might again cast his spell upon the King. Even prodded by Norfolk's threats, however, Wolsey did not enter his province until June, and never got nearer York than Cawood.

Meanwhile Wolsey's tireless brain, racing like an engine disconnected, generated the fumes of conspiracy. First the French were approached, then, through Chapuys, the imperialists. Secret letters were got off to the Pope, and the Cardinal's Italian physician, Agostini, slipped in and out of London on mysterious errands. The nub of Wolsey's problem was to get rid of Anne, and his judgment as to means was the same as Catherine's. The two people who knew Henry best both thought he would give way before really vigorous papal action.

To secure such action Wolsey was eager to make common cause with Catherine's partisans, to forget forever his long hostility to the Queen. He knew now of whom it had been prophesied that a woman would give the Cardinal of England a great fall, and though the French turned a cold shoulder on him, and Chapuys gave him only mild equivocal encouragement, – judging that Wolsey's chief aim was to raise such a tempest in the kingdom that Henry would find him the only helmsman who could ride it out, – the old man went on weaving wilder and wilder schemes to ruin his enemy, Anne.[6] A bull of excommunication, an interdict, the threat of deposition . . . Perhaps those vague menaces seemed less alarming to the council than Wolsey's effort once more to get into direct touch with the King. On that threat, betrayed to them by Agostini, they struck, and it fell to young Harry Percy, Earl of Northumberland now, whom Wolsey had once rated for his mooning after Anne Boleyn like a schoolboy caught kissing a waitress, to stammer to the Cardinal the news of his arrest. "High treason," he said, in a voice so faint Wolsey hardly believed it, and went on hoping for some weeks – until the arrival, at the head of an armed guard, of Sir William Kingston, Captain of the Tower, told him his destination.

Kingston had not to conduct him far. Illness which the Cardinal, himself, may or may not have hastened, overtook him, and he chose, rather than a narrow bed in the Tower, to lay his bones among the monks of Leicester Abbey. Perhaps, as he waited for the eighth hour of the eighth day in the bare cell which was so unlike the décor of his life, and for that reason oddly comforting, he really spoke the words his usher Cavendish has made immortal. His contemporaries thought him proud, greedy, overbearing. "In open presence he would lie and say untruth; he was double both of speech and meaning. He was vicious of his body and gave the clergy evil ensample." So a London chronicler who hated him summed him up, and better men were scarcely more charitable: "A crafty, scabby wether," who misled the flock and infected its hale members, "a stinking mass of iniquity and corruption." But a great man, too, with a scholar's brain and an indomitable heart, and to such, even late, may come a moment of self-knowledge, – of wider vision and the words to utter it. "If I had served God as diligently as I have done the King, He would not have given me over in my grey hairs." It was the voice of the middle ages pronouncing the epitaph of a whole period, the architect of the new tyranny perceiving at last, because his roots were in the past, a distinction which was to be increasingly obscure in the future.

The aisle of Leicester Abbey, where the body of Thomas Wolsey was laid near the body of Richard III, popular hatred christened "the tyrants' grave"; and the pious canons of Norwich noted that the great storm which swept over England the night the Cardinal died was such as occurred only when the Prince of Darkness came in person to carry off one of his own. The Boleyns chivalrously commanded a farce "Of the Cardinal's Going to Hell," for the special entertainment of the King; the Lady, herself, was "now as brave as a lion," and her whole party rejoiced, as if the sick, weary old man, stripped of power, broken in spirit, vainly intriguing to regain his lost favor, gave them, merely by dying, a rare triumph. Few that knew him could think of Wolsey as anything but formidable, even in defeat. Even in exile his shadow was heavier than the substance of the little men who tried vainly to fill his place. Only his death seemed to lift the weight which had held back the kingdom from its new course.

iii

Wolsey's death made more difference in appearance than in reality. While the London public and the petty court intriguers still watched that shadow in the north, a few men knew that Henry had at last chosen his course, that he was prepared to go forever beyond the medieval policy of the Cardinal. Among the few who knew was the Cardinal's former man of business, tight-lipped Thomas Cromwell.[7]

On leaving Esher for London where he meant to make or mar, Master Cromwell's first business had been to insinuate himself far enough into the graces of Wolsey's chief enemy, the Duke of Norfolk, to get a seat in the new Parliament. His next had been to persuade his fallen master that the way to save his life, and perhaps his power, was to buy off his enemies with gifts and pensions, a delicate business which Master Cromwell professed his willingness to undertake. Had the Cardinal's judgment not been shaken by his fall, he would hardly have grasped at the hope that a hundred pounds a year here, a lease there, a manor or a field to such a one would appease the enmity of Norfolk and the Boleyns and all the nobles and councilors whom he had snubbed and bullied and mulcted in the days of his greatness. And, perceiving that such sums, though inadequate for such a purpose, would still amply suffice to buy credit for his agent, he could not have failed to fathom Cromwell's purpose. But panic and despair made him pitiably eager to try anything, and if anybody knew how to muster the resources which somehow had not fallen into the King's hands in the Cardinal's general surrender of his property, it would be Thomas Cromwell, who had managed to squeeze so much out of the monasteries Wolsey was suppressing to endow his colleges, and out of the thousand and one other sources of Wolsey's revenue, that the magnificent

Cardinal had never missed the sums which had stayed in Cromwell's own pocket.

For his efficiency in winding up Wolsey's complicated political bankruptcy, in knowing just where this sum or that had slid to and how to recover it, and just what profitable disposition could be made of the leases, rights and pensions which had accumulated in the Cardinal's hands, Cromwell won golden opinions, and also, one may believe, since the practices of Italian banking were among his favorite studies, the usual commissions. Before long Wolsey found himself, in all financial matters, helpless in his servant's hands. The advices Cromwell wrote him grew as brusque as commands, and obsequious deference gave place to an irony in which contempt was scarcely veiled. If he heard, in January, 1530, of Henry's exclamation that he would not lose the Cardinal for twenty thousand pounds, Cromwell would have wondered, not as Cavendish did, at the kindness and generosity of the King, but at the accuracy with which His Majesty estimated what the old man might still be worth to him. By October, however, there was no more hope of the foreign pensions, and though there might still be a matter of some fifteen hundred pounds in money, a few jewels and baubles, and perhaps a piece or two of land, the Cardinal, as far as his devoted servant was concerned, was a sucked orange, a shealed peascod. Neither the King nor Cromwell could get much more out of him; it was high time the ruined man made his final exit. It would not have been unlike Cromwell to hasten that tardy ending.

Just when Thomas Cromwell had his famous interview with the King, and Henry began to see in him a counselor who could solve the knot which had baffled Wolsey, is not clear; nor is it clear from several differing secondhand accounts just what was said. Probably there was not one interview but many, for one of Henry's troubles in 1530 was want of money, and he could not fail to be interested in the man who knew where Wolsey's concealed assets were. And, probably, not a single lucid exposition but a course of insinuation

Thomas Cromwell

led the King to adopt Cromwell's ideas. We now know that the new plan was broached as early as August and developed by October, a month before Wolsey's death, and that all [illegible] the main outline was Cromwell's. Even if George Cavendish [illegible] Cromwell once reading out a passage that was [illegible] which Wolsey's part of business [illegible] [illegible] whether it is [illegible] princes should [illegible] matters.

In one of his moments of [illegible] King's young kinsman, Reginald Pole, [illegible] had helped him to [illegible] how counsellors should [illegible] sovereigns was [illegible] penetrate the disguises under which [illegible] gratify [illegible] religion. The [illegible] ness of the [illegible] than of [illegible] sucked from [illegible] independence of [illegible]

Cromwell [illegible] to the King's [illegible] not [illegible] benefit, saying [illegible] I brought my [illegible] But [illegible] his [illegible] led the King to adopt Cromwell's ideas. We only know that the new plan was broached as early as August and developing by October, a month before Wolsey's death, and that almost certainly the main outline was Cromwell's. For if George Cavendish found Cromwell once reading on a missal, that was not the little book which Wolsey's man of business generally carried in his bosom. He preferred a thin manuscript volume, recently procured for him at Florence, whose rubrics referred to "cruelty and clemency, and whether it is better to be loved than feared," "the way in which princes should keep faith," "the secretaries of princes," and similar matters.

In one of his moments of cynical frankness, Cromwell told the King's young kinsman, Reginald Pole, that his study of this volume had helped him to the conclusion that the schoolmen's debate about how counselors should conduct themselves to bring honor to their sovereigns was vain, and that the great art of the politician was to penetrate the disguise which princes usually throw over their real inclinations, and to devise expedients by which the prince may gratify his appetites without appearing to outrage morality and religion. The little book also contained an exposition of the weakness of the papacy more convincing to Cromwell's practical mind than all of Luther's thunders, and some happy suggestions for the combination of hypocrisy and terrorism. But chiefly Cromwell sucked from it the one heresy likely to appeal to Henry: the more than divine right of tyrants, the absolute sovereignty and unlimited independence of the omnipotent, amoral state.

Cromwell would have known how to dress Machiavelli's maxims to the King's taste, and Henry showed that he had been listening, if not quite understanding, when he Englished one for Cavendish's benefit, saying, "Three may keep counsel if two are away, and if I thought my cap knew my counsel I would throw it into the fire." But Thomas Cromwell was no mere theoretician like the Florentine; his was a severely practical arithmetic. As tout and runner, clerk and solicitor, traveler, factor, merchant, usurer, politician, he had transposed and expanded and studied exhaustively the primary equation of Renaissance politics, money = power. When he told Henry that he could make him in a few years the greatest King in Christendom (greatest = most powerful = richest) he was disclosing the core of his thought, the grand objective, in attaining which the satisfactory settlement of the King's divorce would be merely an incidental advantage.

Only the incapacity of his advisers, Cromwell told Henry, prevented his divorce; they were as timorous and as hidebound as the vulgar mob whose prejudices they shared. By acting cunningly and boldly he could divorce Catherine, marry Anne, and yet disconcert his enemies and avoid the hostility of the orthodox by remaining in appearance a true Catholic. England was at present a monster with two heads; let the King take to himself the supreme power, religious as well as secular, and he would find the clergy, once they realized that they depended on him alone, abjectly obedient. All that was needed was the consent of Convocation and of Parliament to a declaration that the king was Head of the Church in England. In the course of the operation there would be some immediate revenue forthcoming to the crown, but having helped liquidate some little monasteries for Wolsey's colleges, and having estimated wistfully the wealth of the greater ones, Cromwell knew better than anyone that the immediate would be far exceeded by the eventual profits. To convert those profits to the royal treasury, – with, of course, the customary agent's percentage, – to sweep away the ancient, muddled dual constitution with its moldy checks and inefficient liberties, and to substitute a unified, smoothly functioning despotism – since Thomas Cromwell was a man of esthetic as well as pecuniary sensibilities, it would be hard to say which aspect of his scheme appealed to him more.

It was revolution Cromwell was proposing; established rights in law and property would be abolished, ancient safeguards and more ancient sentiments would be violated, force and treachery and ruthlessness would be needed to carry it through. But it would be revolution from above, purely secular in spirit, with no more than the necessary coloring of religious phrases, and no danger of being swept beyond its goal by the rush of popular enthusiasm. For the most part the appearance of law and order and continuity could be preserved, precedents could be dug out of the past, obsolete anticlerical manifestoes like the "Constitutions of Clarendon," disused weapons like "praemunire." Useful institutions need not be endangered; unnecessary alarms could be avoided. And everything could be done step by step, with all due precautions by the way, and no more forward commitments than were absolutely necessary, just like any other complicated, risky, but highly profitable business operation. In that spirit Thomas Cromwell was willing to undertake to destroy the independence of the Church – on commission. If there was a profit in it, he found it unnecessary to ask what else there might be.

The first step was to bulldoze the clergy. Parliament reconvened on January 16, 1531, and five days later, near at hand, in the chapter house of Westminster Abbey, the province of Canterbury met in Convocation, bishops and abbots and representatives of the lesser clergy gathered as ancient tradition directed to legislate for the English Church. Already they knew the threat leveled against them; an information had been laid in the court of King's Bench that they were all in danger of the Statute of Praemunire in that when Wolsey's bulls as papal legate had been procured from Rome "without the King's consent" they had accepted and maintained his usurped authority. "Of this writ of praemunire," Chapuys wrote, after consulting canonists and common lawyers, "there is no one in England who knows anything. Its whole basis is in the imagination of the King, who comments and amplifies it at pleasure, connecting it with any case he chooses."[8] But mystery and unreason only increased the terror of the charge; the penalty was clear enough.

It was plain to Chapuys that Henry was up to something. The papal nuncio, Del Borgho, whom Clement sent to try to arrange some sort of compromise, had been received with a proclamation forbidding the publication of papal bulls in England, and badly frightened when he attempted to present the admonitory brief. Norfolk had been talking big about how England was an empire, a windy disquisition bolstered by references to Constantine and Brennus and King Arthur. Henry had said that to bridle the Pope and take away the temporalities of the clergy would be doing God's work, and when Chapuys had remarked that only a General Council was competent to do that, had retorted that he could reform evils in his own kingdom without any Council at all, since England lay "in a remote corner of the world, cut off by nature from all other kingdoms with whose business he had no mind to meddle."[9] To emphasize the implied threat Henry had paraded his good relations with the French ambassador, and gone publicly to inspect the artillery in the Tower, so that frightened London merchants besieged the imperial ambassador's residence with their anxieties about their goods in Flanders. But though Chapuys felt more uneasy than at any time since his arrival, and felt sure some new stroke of policy was in preparation, he did not fathom the purpose of the charge of praemunire.

Nor did the Convocation. The clergy thought, as Chapuys did, that this new threat of blackmail sprang from the King's old money hunger, and with sighs of resignation offered to compound the absurdly alleged offense by voting the crown a subsidy of forty thousand pounds. That seemed to be not enough. After much going and coming between Westminster Abbey and York House, the thoroughly frightened clergy raised their offer to more than one hundred thousand pounds, though it would impoverish some of the poorer dioceses for years to pay such a sum, and accompanied the extorted ransom by a flattering address, thanking the King for preserving their liberties and property. This the King was graciously pleased to accept, but before he could pardon their offenses, they were told, they would have to insert a clause in the preamble to the address, acknowledging him as "Supreme Head of the Church and Clergy of England."

The bishops were timid men. Most of them were, or had been, royal servants; they owed their places to the King and had only him to look to for future advancement. The abbots were not much braver; and all the clergy were terrified by the outcry against them since Wolsey's fall, by the completeness with which they seemed to be cut off from popular support. But even timid men will make a stand. For three sessions they debated the unheard-of title, and even the King's gracious willingness to accept a modifying phrase, "Supreme Head after God," procured no agreement. That the King was head and protector of the Church of England, anyone was prepared to acknowledge, but the supreme head, in England and everywhere else in the Christian world, was, after Christ, the Pope, the vicar and surrogate of that final, divine Judgment before which all Christians bowed. To vote this preamble would be to transfer to an earthly king, so far as lay in their power, the Pope's justice, cutting off England from the common law of Europe, laying impious hands on the foundation of the universal Church which Saint Thomas of Canterbury had cemented with his blood. While the indomitable John Fisher lashed them with his scorn, not even the Tudor placemen, cowering on their benches in the vaulted chapter house, thinking of their palaces, their revenues, their necks, could concede so much. Wearily at last their presiding chief, the aged Archbishop of Canterbury, proposed that they might recognize the King as Supreme Head "so far as the law of Christ allows," and when no word either of protest or agreement came from the huddled benches, the Archbishop sighed that silence gave consent, and the new title with its awkward saving clause was so entered.

The clergy felt their frightened silence as defeat, but actually the compromise Warham had carried was no great victory for the King. How far the law of Christ allowed any king authority over the instruments of salvation was exactly the point at issue, and until it was settled or shelved Cromwell's clever dodge had failed to provide more than another instance of the crown's power to terrorize a defenseless clergy, with some illustration of the limit beyond which terror might not work.

In Parliament, as in Convocation, the crown encountered resistance. If Cromwell had thought that he could bully the Commons as he had bullied the clergy with the threat of praemunire, he had much to learn of the temper of the House. The bill containing the new title, when it was read to them, received little approbation, not because the Commons loved the clergy, but because they disliked the method used, and were prepared to resent its extension to themselves. On this subject there was angry debate and a resolute deputation to the King, who made a virtue of necessity and granted them all a free pardon. No progress was made towards the divorce. In vain books and pamphlets were circulated in favor of it, in vain Henry lectured the Commons in person, in vain the council practised, so Chapuys heard, every art of intimidation and bribery, and, as the weary session dragged on, were free with leaves to depart to all the tired members of the opposition while those members thought most friendly to the King were kept sternly in their places. The House refused to bring in any useful bill.[10]

Much of this obstinacy was blamed by the Boleyns and their friends on John Fisher. It was Fisher who had defended Catherine most ably at Blackfriars, and Fisher who had dared remind the enemies of the Church in the lower House of the fate which overtook the kingdom of Bohemia. Now it was Fisher who led the fight in Convocation, and threw all the weight of his learning, eloquence and spotless reputation into the battle of pamphlets, firing salvo after telling salvo for the Queen, and only wishing, so he told Chapuys, that he had the strength and time to answer every book Henry's mercenaries published. Among the Lords where he sat, and increasingly among the Commons who respected his integrity even when they resented his plain speaking, Fisher carried great weight. Before Parliament assembled Chapuys had heard threats against John Fisher's life, threats which grew louder with the exasperation of the radicals, and in March something very queer happened at Fisher's London dwelling. A dozen people who ate the broth at one of Fisher's modest dinners were made violently ill. Several died, and the Bishop himself was prostrated by convulsions, and so weakened that he could not walk or stand for nearly a month. The Bishop's cook, promptly arrested, confessed under torture that he had put a white powder someone had given him into the broth, just for a joke. He hadn't known it was poison.

Henry was horrified. Poison was as mysteriously dreadful as the plague, and like the plague might not spare even the person of a king. Parliament needed little urging to pass a statute ordering for poisoners the most excruciating death they could think of, and with sublime disregard for the rule of *ex post facto*, the Bishop's wretched cook was hung in a cradle of chains, and slowly dipped and redipped in a caldron of boiling oil. Only one point was left unclear: who had persuaded the unlucky cook to play his fatal joke? No disclosures on that subject which the rack and the thumbscrews extorted were thought fit for the ears of the public. In the absence of an official version, the gossip of court and city was left to draw its own conclusions, and Anne Boleyn and her brother George had added to their already unenviable reputation another and more sinister stain.

Henry's violent reaction cleared him in the popular mind of complicity in the poisoning, but he was not above taking advantage of its results. On March 30, while Fisher lay ill and Warham and

Tunstall were absent, Brian Tuke brought the Lords an unexpected and unwelcome message from the King.[11] He read them a long letter from Henry, exposing the troubled state of his conscience and recounting the opinions of the universities against his first marriage. The Bishop of Lincoln, Henry's confessor, thereupon delivered a prepared harangue in favor of the King's divorce, and was seconded by the Bishop of London with another. To the dismay of the government, two other bishops, Bath and St. Asaph's, offered instant hot rebuttal; More, appealed to, refused to support the divorce; the Earl of Shrewsbury bluntly showed his displeasure, and the hum of comment made clear the opposition of the peers. Hastily, the Duke of Norfolk rose to say that the King's message was only for the information of the Lords, not for their action, and at his signal Brian Tuke retreated, flanked by his supporting bishops, to try his luck in the Commons. Again Tuke read the King's long message, again the two bishops spoke in turn, taking it upon their consciences that the King's marriage was null. But the Commons, "little edified, returned no answer." Even the Speaker was silent, and Tuke and his bishops beat a second retreat. The next day Henry abruptly prorogued Parliament until October.

iv

Queen Catherine was less surprised than Chapuys that Henry's ingenious attacks had been defeated. When Henry's line had become clear, the imperial ambassador was convinced that nothing could stop him, that, in a few weeks at most, he would break with Rome, marry Anne, and – a consequence which Chapuys had come to regard as inevitable – be at war with the Emperor. All that Chapuys saw left to do was to ask for his passports as a final gesture of protest, but when he told Catherine as much she vetoed his decision at once. She needed her friend the ambassador, both to keep her links with Rome and to organize her defense in England, and she by no means despaired of victory. She was confident that the English were not ripe for schism, and she felt that resolute action could still avert that catastrophe. Parliament and Convocation proved her right, and opposition to Henry in another quarter exceeded her expectation.

Since Parliament declined to act, and Henry's victory over Convocation had been less complete than he had hoped, there was only one legal way in which his marriage could be dissolved independently of Rome – by action of the archiepiscopal court of Canterbury. After the incident of praemunire, Chapuys felt sure such action was unescapable, and though he gloomily obeyed Catherine's injunction to do everything he could to prevent it, – to try to get Del Borgho, the papal nuncio, to dissuade the Archbishop from taking up the case, and to serve a copy of Clement's latest brief on him, personally, if he could, – Warham's age, his notorious timidity, and his habitual subservience to the King made it seem certain to the ambassador that the Archbishop would yield to Henry's pressure. But when Chapuys, armed with papal briefs and every argument his legal ingenuity could supply, was received at Lambeth, he found all his precautions unnecessary. It was quite impossible, Warham told him with dignity, for the court of Canterbury to hear the King's case; the Pope had forbidden it. Del Borgho had already inquired and been assured that under no circumstances would Canterbury disobey the papal prohibition.[12] The King, himself, would get the same reply. And though the royal councilors battered him with arguments, though Norfolk stormed and fumed and wondered that a subject should disobey his King, though Henry himself was reported to be furious, the old Archbishop only repeated his refusal. No counselor had been more deeply attached to the crown and to the Tudor dynasty, none had been more emphatic about the duty of obedience to the King, but the law of Christ forbade his servants to pervert the justice of the Church at any earthly command, and to this point Warham clung. The stormy interviews at Lambeth made quite clear what the qualification Warham had carried in the silence of the chapter house at Westminster really meant.

Catherine was more afraid of weakness at Rome than in England. Whether she was wrong or not about the innate goodness of Henry's heart, she had watched his conduct of diplomacy for more than twenty years and she was convinced that he would take every effort at conciliation or compromise as an encouragement to further aggression, whereas he could be pulled up short by resolute resistance. After Blackfriars she told Chapuys that if she could get a prompt decision from Rome, all would be well, but more than a year had elapsed and Clement had not even opened the case. Meanwhile – although her own party in the kingdom was, if anything, stronger than it had been, and every few days she received cheering messages from noble friends who were sick of the Boleyns, secret assurances that more and more of the clergy were swinging to her side, and public tokens of the unflagging partisanship of the masses of the common people – the supporters of the papacy, confused and disheartened by Clement's inaction, were weaker than ever. Among the many blunt Englishmen who found their dislike of Italian priests confirmed by Clement's behavior, and who took the silence of Rome and the apparently friendly presence of the papal nuncio as conclusive proof that the Pope and the King were in a plot to ruin the good Queen, there were but few thoughtful enough to distinguish between the policies of Giulio de' Medici and the interests of the universal Church. Thanks to Wolsey, the prestige of the papacy was so low after Blackfriars that Chapuys thought that if the churchmen had no more than the Pope's authority to protect them, the King would make short work of their goods and privileges. Two years later he was obliged to record that that authority had fallen lower still, chiefly because of popular disgust at the Pope's failure to protect the Queen.[13]

Catherine herself put the case another way. While the Boleyns surrounded the King, Henry, who was fatally susceptible to the nearest influence, would favor heresy, and, though he meant his sallies against the Church only as threats to coerce the Pope, they might, if unchecked, gather a fatal impetus. "People here," she wrote to Dr. Ortiz, the Emperor's proctor at Rome in April, 1530, "expect its own Head to give the Church a great fall. The evils here increase daily, and will go on doing so unless the Pope applies a remedy. Learned men assure me that a stronger medicine than the last papal brief is needed. Nothing will suffice except a final decision about my marriage. Anything else will bring only a temporary relief at the cost of greater ills to come."

She did not confine herself to writing to Ortiz or sending messages to the Pope through Chapuys. At every opportunity Chapuys' pouch for Rome inclosed a weighty missive in Catherine's bold impetuous scrawl, addressed to His Holiness, in person. There was neither order nor elegance in these epistles, little humility and less concern to spare Clement's feelings. The Queen's thoughts boil out faster than her racing pen can set them down – a turbid flood, full of Latin hyperbole and frenzied repetition. Her own woes are greater than any mortal can bear; those of her unhappy country are still worse. The Pope's delays are responsible for both, and against them she can only appeal to the judgment of God. To these themes she recurs again and again with savage vehemence, as if she were shouting at a deaf man.

Catherine understood that the Roman Curia was bound to act with due deliberation; what exasperated her was the Pope's failure to act at all. She had known after Blackfriars that a year or more might elapse before a final decision at Rome, and in her first communications with Chapuys she had made a number of sensible suggestions for steps to be taken in the interim, chiefly a really firm ban on discussion of her case, and a brief ordering Henry to separate from Anne pending the trial. But in fifteen months her case had not even been opened. Just before the attack on the clergy she wrote to the Pope:

Miçer Mai [the Emperor's agent at Rome] wrote me that Your Holiness had promised to renew the brief issued at Bologna, and to issue another commanding the King, my lord, to dismiss and utterly to cast away this woman with whom he lives. Merely on hearing of it, the fine folk who have managed to maneuvre the King, my lord, into his present position, and to keep him in it, began to give way, thinking all was lost. . . . May God forgive him who was the cause of the briefs' not being delivered, for the mere news of them produced a marked improvement, besides which, had the potion, though bitter, been administered in time, later remedies might have seemed sweeter.

Your Holiness should mark that my complaint is not against the King, my lord, but against the instigators and abettors of this suit. I trust so much in my lord, the King's natural virtues and goodness that if I could only have him with me two months, as he used to be, I alone would be powerful enough to make him forget the past. But they know this is true, so they contrive to prevent his being with me. These are my real enemies; these wage constant war against me, some of them for fear that the evil counsel they gave the King – for which they have already been well paid – may become known, others so that they may rob and plunder at will, endangering my lord's estate, his honor, and his soul. From these people spring the threats against Your Holiness. Therefore, put a bit in their mouths! Proceed to sentence! Then their tongues will be silenced and their hopes of mischief vanish; then they will set my lord at liberty and he will become once more the dutiful son of Your Holiness, as he always was.[14]

She could write of Henry's returning to her and becoming again a dutiful son of the Church when Chapuys was ready to ask for his passports; when, two months later, many of her friends thought that Henry's failures with Warham and with Parliament had averted immediate danger, she was more anxious than ever. In April, 1531, she wrote the Emperor that the time in which the Pope could still act effectively was growing short. For an account of the proceedings in Parliament and the effect of the decision of the universities she referred him to Chapuys, for whose services she could never be grateful enough, and went herself to the heart of the matter. "If the Pope grants a further delay, as the King of France is said to have requested him to do, you may expect that before long these people will obtain all they are aiming at . . . I beg you not to consent to the delay but to insist on the pope's giving sentence before next October, when Parliament reconvenes. . . . I am sure that the delay is solicited only to work my ruin." Throughout the summer of 1531 Catherine's letters have all one burden: "Let the Pope proceed to sentence!" "His dallying keeps my lord, the King, bound hand and foot by his enemies." "These delays are the cause of all the attacks upon the Church, and all the things that are being planned against the honor and conscience of my lord, the King." "Let the Pope decide!"

Catherine could not have asked anything of Clement VII more difficult than decision. Since his painful experiences at the sack of Rome his hesitance and timidity had become almost pathological. He wept often, ate and slept little, and his agitated breathing and constant wringing of his hands whenever any action was called for were noted by most of the ambassadors at Rome.

Catholic writers have often been eager to excuse his inaction, and indeed there were many reasons for it. Legally Henry's case was a difficult one, one on which learned men might honestly differ. As long as there was the faintest chance of reconciling the parties to the suit, the Church was bound to try it, and it was bound too, by the custom of the Curia, and a regard for the opinion of Christendom, not to give the appearance of a hurried, predetermined verdict. On such grounds one might excuse a delay of months, though hardly a delay of years.

But Clement had others. Henry had repeatedly threatened schism if the case went against him; as long as the case remained undecided he might remain at least ostensibly a Catholic. Whether one estimated the loss from schism in thousands of ducats to the papal revenue or in thousands of souls to God, it was serious enough to give anyone pause, especially at a time when in Germany losses of both were increasing annually. Catherine believed that the loss could be avoided by decision; Clement hoped it might be avoided by delay. But Clement was not thinking of England alone. Though Charles had restored the Medici to Florence and withdrawn his troops from the papal states, the Pope still chafed under the Emperor's yoke, and like most Italian politicians of the period he could think of no way of reducing the influence of one foreigner in Italy without calling in another. The "liberties of Italy," the Pope's freedom of action, depended he thought on reviving the broken power of the French. But the French made a great point of their English alliance, and to refuse them the delays they asked in Henry's name might be to end forever the chance of reviving anything like the League of Cognac.

Finally, the Emperor, since his arrival in Germany, had become quite convinced that the only real hope of ending the Lutheran revolt was another General Council of the Church, like the great Councils of Constance and Basel, and was quite prepared to support any moderate reforms of church discipline and doctrine which would offer a basis for restoring Christian unity. Everyone knew that such reforms would be at the cost of Rome; and Clement was frantic to prevent the revival of that threat to papal absolutism and to the Italian domination of the universal Church which, in the fifteenth century, fifty years of skillful diplomacy on the part of his predecessors had only just managed to defeat, and which, for the last fifty years, the Curia had always been alert to scotch. Only the co-operation of the French, who were not sorry to increase Charles's difficulties in Germany and were willing to exchange their help for Clement's political aid in Italy, could save Clement from a General Council, and if he condemned Henry,

Henry and Francis might combine in revenge to make a Council inescapable.

No one can know, now, just which motives weighed the most with Clement. Had some of his great medieval predecessors been called to witness, they might have said that Clement confused the headship of the universal Church with temporal power in central Italy, and the spiritual leadership of a united Christendom with a religious absolute monarchy that fell not much short of despotism. But the confusion of freedom of religious action with the independence of the temporal power was common to all the popes of a very long period, and the confusion between monarchy and absolutism is always natural and easy to an absolute monarch.

Whatever the springs of his action, Clement's policy resembled the policy of weary, timid conservatives everywhere, defending privileges about which they are uneasy against a revolution arising from contradictions they do not understand. He hesitated, temporized, delayed, alternated unsatisfactory concessions and ineffectual threats, could neither bring himself to give in to Henry's demands nor summon the courage which might have crushed his enemies. He had promised the Emperor to open Catherine's case by September, 1530; in June, 1531, he still had not done so. When he saw that it could be delayed no longer, he offered, in response to a French suggestion, to open it not at Rome but in Cambrai.

Clement had some reason to believe that the compromise of a legatine court at Cambrai, though suggested by the French, would be acceptable to the Emperor. Not a few of Charles's counselors were frankly uneasy at the drift towards hostilities with England, and would be glad of any settlement that would remove the cause. The Emperor, himself, though feeling bound in honor to support his aunt as long as she demanded his support, had long ceased to regard Catherine as anything but a liability. If she accepted Cambrai, and the court, which would probably have at least two cardinals of the French party, invalidated her marriage, at least the chief obstacle to a renewal of his alliance with Henry would be removed. Clement was not sure how Henry would receive the suggestion of a court at Cambrai, even though his friends the French had first proposed it, and Del Borgho was instructed to introduce the subject by indirection. But Henry leaped at the chance.

He was not, Chapuys remarked maliciously, leading an easy life, this King of England. On the one side more and more of his nobility and clergy were aligning themselves, almost openly, behind his unbending Queen. Anne had succeeded in offending the two Duchesses of Suffolk and Norfolk, among others; forthright old George Talbot, Earl of Shrewsbury, made no secret where his sympathies lay; and not even Norfolk, Anne's uncle, could muster a convincing enthusiasm for the new marriage. On the other side, Anne was harder than ever to manage. Henry was still in love with her, but sometimes he stormed out of an interview with her, purple with anger, vowing that in all her life his first queen had never dared use such language to him. Anne would not or could not understand the difficulties in the way of moving the case an inch forward, either at Rome or in England, and at times she was scornful of a lover unwilling to defy pope and emperor and all the world for her sake. Sometimes her royal lover was driven to undignified shifts to appease her. On one occasion Chapuys was astonished to find himself assailed by an unexpected volley of arguments and reproaches about the divorce when he came to see Henry on quite another subject. The ambassador's efforts to shift the discussion were unavailing, and he was quite unable to understand why Henry talked so much more threateningly than usual, using terms of the Emperor that were almost abusive, and speaking almost at the top of his voice, until shifting his ground the ambassador noticed at a little window giving on the great gallery a listening head that could only be the Lady's. Chapuys was malicious enough to pretend to take offense and to begin a heated rebuttal, whereupon the King, seizing him by the arm, marched off with him down the gallery, dropping his voice as he did so and changing from threats to explanations and apologies, although his manner (Anne could still see if she could no longer hear) was as imperious as ever.[15] To be forced to play such comedies was not good for Henry's disposition.

As soon as Del Borgho had made his suggestion, adding that unless it was accepted His Holiness would have no recourse except to open the case at Rome, Henry assembled his council and prepared another assault on the Queen. On the Tuesday evening after Whitsunday, while the Queen was preparing to retire, she was waited upon by a solemn deputation of more than thirty councilors, headed by the two dukes, and including Talbot, Dorset, Northumberland, Wiltshire and other peers, half a dozen bishops, and an array of doctors. Norfolk led off for the council with a speech characteristically pompous and confused. He got lost in a maze of thirdlys, and in the course of reminding the Queen of what she owed her husband wandered off into an account of how the English had helped her father conquer the Kingdom of Navarre, but he managed to convey that Henry was pained and surprised that she should be pressing for the opening of her case at Rome, provoking the Pope to summon the King to appear there in person, a thing unheard of, and subjecting him to unparalleled humiliation; Henry expected her to be contented with a neutral place, Norfolk said, and impartial judges.

Catherine's answer was clear. Her mind was more orderly in speech than in writing, and she had had warning of this ordeal and prepared for it, not by consulting council or going over papers, but by confessing, communicating and spending several hours in prayer. No one living, she said, could regret any pain or shame this case might have caused the King more than she. But since nothing was asked of either party that was not asked of the other, she did not believe that her proctors could have sought or the Pope granted any terms especially disadvantageous or humiliating to the King.

(She meant, of course, that, although Norfolk chose to pretend that he was outraged by the Pope's insistence on Henry's coming to Rome in person, actually all that was expected was that the King should send a proctor there as Catherine had done.) She had, she said bitterly, no especial reason to expect favor at the hands of the Pope, who had helped her little and injured her much, but Henry had first laid this case before His Holiness, "who is, indeed, he who keeps the place and has the power of Our Lord Christ on this earth, and is, in consequence, the mirror image of eternal Truth," and now it was necessary for the repose and example of England and of all Christendom, that right and justice be declared, and the Pope show himself the true vicar and servant of the Truth which is God. She would persist, therefore, in her appeal to Rome. As for the King's new title of Supreme Head of the Church of England, which Norfolk had dwelt on, she acknowledged Henry lord and master of the whole kingdom in things temporal, and for these she owed him obedience more than anyone as both his subject and his wife, but for what concerned the sacraments and in all spiritual matters there was on this earth for all Christians only one true supreme head and judge, the Pope. This she must confess, and God forbid that her husband should think otherwise.

All round the circle of her persecutors (mostly reluctant persecutors) it could be seen her shots had told. They nodded and nudged each other, Chapuys heard, at every point, and on the face of Dr. Stephen Gardiner, royal secretary, and soon to be Bishop of Winchester for his part in the divorce, could be read approval and a kind of awe. Lee spoke next, then Dr. Sampson, and after him Longland, Bishop of Lincoln, and to each the Queen replied. She did not have to fence with them. They could take their legal subtleties and distinctions to Rome, she told them, where they would find men to deal with, instead of assailing with a display of pomp and wisdom enough to astound the world one helpless woman, unlearned and unadvised. But she nailed each lie offered. "I love and have loved my lord, the King," she told them steadily in conclusion, "as much as any woman can love a man, but I would not have borne him company as his wife one moment against the voice of my conscience. I came to him as a virgin, I am his true wife, and whatever proofs my lord of Lincoln or others may allege to the contrary, I, who know better than anyone else, tell you are lies and forgeries."

Wiltshire made some final, feeble observations, but the rest were silenced, ashamed, more than half won over. Sir Henry Guildford was heard to mutter as they filed, defeated, from the Queen's presence, that it might be as well if all those who had suggested this accursed case to the King were tied in a cart and sent to Rome to answer it, and in reporting the interview to the King, beef-witted Charles Brandon rose, for the only time on record, almost to epigram. "The Queen is ready to obey you in everything," he told Henry, "except for the obedience she owes two higher powers."

"What two," said Henry eagerly, smelling treason and praemunire, "the Emperor and the Pope?"

"No, sire, God and her conscience." Perhaps Suffolk really said that, for it was, in fact, an old saying and so not beyond his reach. But if he understood it, it must have made him sometimes very uncomfortable.[16]

Catherine's nocturnal debate with the council had been at Greenwich, on May 31, 1531. In the middle of the next month the whole court moved for a few days to Hampton Court and thence to Windsor, Catherine accompanying her husband as usual. Henry still dined with her on state occasions though he spent more and more time with Anne, and though the Queen was torn with anxiety at the Pope's delays, and missed her daughter Mary whom Anne's spite kept away from court, Catherine still wore a brave face before the world so that Chapuys heard praise of her courage and apparent cheerfulness even from her enemies. Her ambiguous situation had gone on so long, and her hours with Henry were now so formal and so infrequent, that she may not have guessed that he was nerving himself for the final break, working himself up into a state of resentment in which he could believe that his wife was responsible for his unpopularity, his foreign difficulties, his humiliating summons to Rome, that she was, in fact, persecuting him maliciously, and conspiring with others to make him an object of hatred and, what was worse, of ridicule. He had ceased to take her with him on the short hunting trips organized from Windsor, and when he rode off with a party that included Anne on July 11 he did not even say good-by. Perhaps he had meant to, for he knew, and Anne knew, that this was the definite parting; he would never see her again; but to face the wife he had once loved and had since respected, and feared a little, for more than twenty years, called for a moral courage Henry lacked. The hunting party was larger than usual, and burdened with unusual baggage, but it passed softly out of the courtyard of Windsor just at dawn in a manner almost surreptitious.

Catherine waited a few days; then, as more and more of the courtiers that remained rode off to join the King, she wrote her husband a letter. She was sorry she had not been roused before he left to bid him Godspeed. She would be happy to know that he was well. Back came a curt and querulous reply. Little she cared about his health or peace of mind. Her obstinacy was destroying both. He was better when he did not see her. Catherine wrote again, submissively, but with a dignified hint that if this was good-by, at least their long life together made it only decent that good-by should be spoken face to face. This time Henry chose to treat his wife's letter as a state document. He made it the subject of a council meeting which consumed several days in drafting a short, harsh answer, the gist of which was that the Queen's disobedience in refusing the neutral court at Cambrai had so displeased the King that he did not wish to see her again. Two weeks later there was another message from the council. The King was returning to Windsor, and insisted that the Queen remove to Wolsey's old house, the More, before he did so. Mary, who had taken advantage of Anne's absence to visit her mother, was ordered to separate from her. On top of this another message directed Catherine to choose a permanent place of retirement, a nunnery or one of the smaller royal manors. Her suite was to be summarily reduced; she was not to see her daughter.[17]

Chapuys, who was almost less an ambassador by now than he was Catherine's chief counselor, working with her over the long file of documents about her marriage, discussing with her all the implications of her position, admiring more and more her courage, constancy, and grasp of affairs, was permitted to see something of how much the King's blow had wounded and shaken her, but to her husband's council she replied with spirit. She would go wherever her husband ordered, but she would prefer to go to the Tower, since the people of England would then know what had become of her, and she would have their prayers in her affliction. It was a warning not to go too far.

In October another deputation from the council, Sussex and Fitzwilliam for the barons, Doctors Lee and Sampson for the clergy, came to try whether her spirit had been broken. Warned of their approach to Easthampstede Catherine received them this time in state, with all her household about her, parrying their arguments as she had at Greenwich, in a voice which she made sure reached to every corner of the hall. When they fell upon their knees in mock supplication to beg her not to disobey her husband, she fell upon hers and loudly exhorted them, as they were true and Christian councilors, to advise the King to return to his obedience to the Pope and his duty to his wife. When they threatened her with removal to a still more retired manor, she answered clearly that she would go anywhere her husband sent her, even to the stake. Unmoved she watched them retreating in confusion.[18]

She was not afraid of councilors, and her own unbending courage and the knowledge that news of her ill-treatment would arouse the

English prevented harsher measures. Perhaps Chapuys, who deliberately threw obstacles in the way of the impending commercial negotiations, and managed on very slight warrant from his master to convey the impression that the Emperor expected war, increased the caution of the council. Catherine was allowed to return to the More, and her suite was restored to respectable proportions. In November, 1531, two Venetian diplomats[19] saw her dine there, among thirty maids of honor, with fifty more young ladies to wait on the table, and about her a court of some two hundred persons (exclusive, of course, of the humbler servants), though her attendance was less than it had been, and fewer of the magnates visited her than of old. The diplomats had heard on every side that "all the people of this realm, and almost all the peers spiritual and temporal are opposed to the divorce" and the Queen, herself, "is beloved by these islanders more than any queen who ever reigned." They heard her praised as "virtuous, just, replete with goodness and religion" and that everyone admired her "prudence, constancy and resolution" in her trials. She was forty-five, they said, and had lived thirty years in England, "of low stature," "plump" ("*piutosto grassa*," says one, "*grassetta*," the other), "of a modest countenance" ("*di faccia honesta*"), "not handsome, but certainly not ugly," and very careful of her own appearance and of that of all about her. Her household they found cheerful and well ordered, and the Queen, herself, always with a smile upon her countenance. Indeed the More might have seemed to outsiders a gayer place than Greenwich, where Henry had returned with Anne, for even the loyal Hall was obliged to record that "all men said that there was no mirth in that Christmas [of 1531] because the queen and her ladies were absent."

What mirth there was at the More was only for the public. Chapuys was shocked at the change grief had made in Catherine. Her letters to her nephew take a sadder tone. She still urged Charles to try to get the Pope to act – if her case could be decided before

Parliament met again, it might still not be too late; she still wrote tenderly of Henry, of the pity that a prince so good and virtuous should be daily deceived and misled, goaded by those about him like a bull in the arena; she still hoped that once freed from the toils he would acknowledge that God had restored his reason. But she confessed that only her fears for the peril to England and to all Christendom if she should falter, and her trust in God's providence, sustained her in her present grief, and she signed herself pathetically, "from the More, separated from my husband without ever having offended him, *Katharina, the unhappy Queen*." [20]

𝔥

In January Parliament met, and though, as Chapuys learned from the Queen's friends among the members, the government had been busy with bribery and intimidation, and though the country had been flooded for a year with books and pamphlets in favor of the divorce, the news of Henry's separation from his wife was stirring a rising tide of indignation which not even intimidation could suppress, and even Parliament reflected. A priest who was inveighing against the divorce from the pulpit at St. Paul's was arrested in the midst of his harangue, but when Henry, relying on his new authority, commanded every priest in the kingdom to preach his side of the case, few dared to do so, and at Salisbury one who did was hissed and torn from the pulpit. At Easter the King himself had to listen to a sermon, preached by the provincial of the Observant Franciscans in the oratory at Greenwich where he had been married, full of unmistakable allusions to kings who listened to false counselors and persecuted the Church, and when Henry put up a preacher the following Sunday to answer the criticism, and his champion waxed warm under the beams of the King's approval, the warden of the Observants rose in his place and denounced the preacher as one of Ahab's lying prophets, adding the pointed observation that Ahab had refused to be warned, and the dogs had licked his blood. Prompt arrest of the offender scarcely salved the King's wounded feelings. In the Commons a member named Temse took the occasion of a money bill to say that if the King would take back his true wife, he would not have an enemy in Christendom and would not need to oppress his people with exactions, and all the London merchants who traded with Flanders and feared war with the Emperor applauded his opinion. After his staunch supporters, Dr. Edward Lee and Dr. Stephen Gardiner, had been rewarded respectively with the archbishopric of York and the wealthy bishopric of Winchester, Henry found them much cooler than formerly towards his "great matter" and Chapuys estimated that most of the bishops had swung over to the Queen. Among the lay peers Anne's insolence had alienated many of her earlier supporters, and though for a year she had fought back at them, slandering Suffolk, forcing Guildford's dismissal from the council, boasting always that a few months would see her married, she could not fight them all. Even the Duke of Norfolk, Chapuys thought, was so disgusted with his niece, and so frightened by the popular outcry, that he would have opposed the King's divorce except that he was "one of those men who will do anything to cling to power."

Actually, however, it was only the shadow of power Norfolk clung to. Moving as yet in shadows, hidden, behind the scenes, even from Chapuys, a tougher, subtler brain than Norfolk's was directing the royal operations. Thomas Cromwell had no traditions to make him reverence the past, no sensibilities to be outraged, and no scruples to give him pause; he had only contempt for an aimless opposition which hoped to triumph by dint of noise and argument. In the arrests of the Observant Friars, and of the preacher at St. Paul's, of Catherine's rash friend, Rhys ap Griffith, the son and heir of the great Welsh magnate, and of her chaplain Thomas Abell who had finished and published his book in her defense, Cromwell was experimenting cautiously with terror. He was perfecting a system of espionage, a sort of unofficial secret police, modeled on Wolsey's but improved to a perfection hitherto unknown outside of Italy, and he was learning how bribery, pressure, and expert manipulation might control Parliament. It was a slow process, but as long as the decision at Rome could be staved off, and all the pleas of Catherine and the diplomacy of the Emperor could extort from Clement no more than the "weak, inane, meager" brief exhorting Henry to return to his wife which the nuncio finally presented in April, 1532, Cromwell looked to win.

He was probably scornful of such clumsy efforts as those of the Boleyns, who, when they heard that John Fisher, Bishop of Rochester, meant to take his seat in the House of Lords even though he had not been summoned, sent him word to stay away lest he catch fatally, this time, such another fever as last year's. He probably did not count much on efforts to pack either House, though he must have approved, and may have suggested, such devices as the omission of Fisher and Tunstall from the list of bishops summoned, and of Dorset and Shrewsbury from the peers, and the granting of licenses to be absent to members of the Commons who were not safe for the government. He did not disdain propaganda, as his negotiations to lure the fiery protestant William Tyndale back into Henry's service indicate, though whatever direct bullying of Parliament in Wolsey's style was to be done, he had to leave to Henry himself. But the experience of the past year had shown him the line by which all Henry's objectives could be achieved. The Commons could not yet be used directly to hasten the divorce, but they could be pricked into attacking the clergy. As long as the interlocking issues – the power of the Pope, the power of the clergy, the King's marriage – were kept separate, the wedge that had been driven between the churchmen and laity could be pressed down until the old constitution was split in pieces, and the opposition destroyed in detail.

The first step in Cromwell's campaign was the famous "Supplication of the Commons against the Ordinaries," which a deputation of the lower House presented to the King not long after Parliament reconvened in January, 1532. In it the Commons complained of the excessive fees demanded in church courts, of their delays, corruption and unfairness, particularly in cases of heresy, and of other ecclesiastical abuses for which they begged a remedy, but they emphasized as the head and front of the clergy's offending that "they do daily make divers and many fashions of laws, constitutions and ordinances without your knowledge or most royal assent and without the assent and consent of any of your lay subjects" – in other words that the Church was independent of the lay power. It had always been so, and few Englishmen had been appalled by the fact in the past, but the specific grievances were some of them real enough, and many had been indignantly discussed, so that the Commons who voted for the Supplication probably fancied that they approved its whole content even if they might not have thought of its precise language. But the precise language was important Thomas Cromwell had meditated every phrase, going over four clean copies by his secretaries and filling three of them with corrections and interlineations in his own hand before he had got the wording to suit him.[21]

Henry did his best to preserve the appearance that the Supplication was spontaneous. He was bound to consider it, he told the deputation, but he would not act upon it until he had heard what the clergy might allege in their defense, and he even had the royal effrontery to lecture the members on their neglect of duty (they had thought, simple men, that the Supplication was all that was expected of them, and that now they would be allowed to go home), and to offer to accept it provided they would accept another obnoxious royal bill which was hanging on their agenda. Henry was learning politics under Cromwell's tuition faster than he had done under Wolsey's. The Supplication was turned over to Convocation, and the next item in Cromwell's program brought forward, an act to abolish the payment of annates, or the first fruits of bishoprics to Rome, with the curious rider that its application was to be at the King's pleasure, and was to be confirmed or repealed within two years. The purpose, of course, was to put Henry in direct control of one of the principal sources of papal revenue from England, and to give him thus another whip with which to threaten the Pope; but the exactions of Rome, from which England suffered only less than Germany, were generally unpopular with both clergy and laity, and it is therefore remarkable that the bill met with such stiff opposition in both Houses that it could only be jammed through by actual divisions, then a most unusual expedient, the divisions being conducted, an even rarer thing, under the King's own eye.

Meanwhile Convocation was drafting its answer to the "Supplication." The clergy could understand, whether the Commons did or not, the meaning of Cromwell's language, and while they admitted the possibility of abuses, and sought to conciliate the complainants, they refused to acknowledge as abuses the liberties which more than three hundred years of custom and public law had embedded in the constitution of the kingdom. Henry, that impartial judge, transmitted their reply to the Commons with the remark that he thought the house would be ill-pleased with so slender an answer, and royal councilors interviewed the more influential clergy, singly and in groups, applying skillful pressure. Convocation made a second answer, yielding some substantial points, but not enough to please the King. Then Henry went suddenly to Parliament, and announced that he had just discovered that his own clergy were scarce half his subjects, "for the prelates at their consecration make an oath to the Pope clean contrary to the oath they make to us, so that they seem his subjects and not ours." Parliament, Henry concluded, should take steps to secure to the crown the loyalty which was its due. The hint of wholesale clerical treason, the invitation to bring in a sweeping general act of attainder, was just below the surface; but the Commons were, for the moment, merely bewildered by the King's astounding discovery. Only the cynical could suggest a reason for his making it now, after reigning three-and-twenty years, when the fact of the oaths had been a commonplace, known to them and their ancestors time out of mind, alluded to – though this they may not have known – in Magna Charta. Few who read the copies of the oaths presented to the speaker would have found anything contradictory about them, and to fewer still would it have occurred that a man may not have two loyalties, or that, just because the state was not supreme in every department of life, the realm was a monster with two heads. Before they could indicate their bewilderment, Parliament was prorogued.

For the panicky benches of Convocation, the mere threat had been enough. They looked in vain to Rome or to the papal nuncio; for all they knew the King and His Holiness might have a complete understanding, in which case resistance would invite utter ruin. The weaker prelates broke in disorderly rout, and on May 15 they all gave in completely to the King. They would make no new laws without the King's license; all their existing ordinances should be revised at the King's pleasure, and none, even of the old ones, should be valid without royal approval. This was no formal concession like the qualified Act of Supreme Head, this was the abject surrender of the inner citadel of the Church. Hereafter, the Church of England was to be Henry's; he could do what he liked with it. With the historic "Submission of the Clergy" Cromwell's revolution really began.

The date was marked when the next day, May 16, 1532, Sir Thomas More laid down his seals of office. Ever since he had taken them up, after the fall of Wolsey, he had been in a position increasingly ambiguous and painful. He was one of the Queen's closest friends, and the divorce made him heartsick; he was a man of peace, and though too much an Englishman to favor any foreign prince, he was in the main, like almost all Londoners, inclined to be pro-imperialist, and he had seen his master becoming more and more dependent on the French, following that part of Wolsey's policy which he had hated most. More was deeply attached to the old religion and he had been dismayed by the noisy attacks of the Boleyns on the Pope and by Henry's covert encouragement of anticlericalism. He must have realized for some time that he was lending the prestige of his scholarship and his integrity to a course which he could not honestly approve. But he was vulnerable, as most men were, to the charm that Henry knew so well how to exert, and he had hoped, as Catherine hoped, that the King would recover from his infatuation and return to better ways. Also he had a high sense of his duty to the King. Could a philosopher who believed that philosophy should issue in action, a wise lover of the institutions of his Church and of his country who saw how much both wanted perfection, refuse the great office of Lord Chancellor, judge of the highest court of equity, Keeper of the King's Conscience, guardian and mediator of the constitution of the realm? To do so would be to betray the humanist hope of moderate, just, and philosophical reform. Men of good will, believers in orderly progress and rational improvement, have often been induced by such arguments to make their reputations the bridge over which revolutionaries have walked to power, but none ever did so from purer motives than those that animated Thomas More. He had held scrupulously aloof from the debate over the King's divorce, which his conscience forbade him either to attack or to defend. He had refused even to talk to Chapuys, lest his sympathies betray him. He had administered such speedy and even-handed justice as England had never seen, and was not soon to see again, and he was leaving an office which had enriched most of its holders as poor as he had entered it. But moderation, virtue and good will, honesty, learning, and genius were all unavailing against the dark tide of history. The last great medieval Chancellor laid down his seals a failure. The office passed to the undistinguished keeping of Thomas Audeley, a sycophantic mediocrity; but the power passed from the experts in equity to the experts in finance, from the rule of law to the rule of chicanery and force, and first into the hands of Thomas Cromwell. For all his high hopes of reform, More's short tenure of office had merely expedited that transition, and the short tenure of life left him would have to go, he saw clearly, to expiate his involuntary treason.

As the office of Lord Chancellor was the keystone of the medieval constitution of the realm, so the office of Archbishop of Canterbury, Primate of All England, *legatus natus* of the Holy See, was at once the keystone of the Church of England, and the stone which locked the structure of the island Church into the great vault of Christendom. Often and appropriately in the past, the two offices had been held by the same person, and in the coming revolution the fate of their two last medieval holders could not be much different. After the Submission of the Clergy, William Warham, like Thomas More, faced the inevitable. The Archbishop had yielded farther than the chancellor. He was made of more malleable stuff, and for a man of his years and lifelong habits of subservience to be forced into opposition to the King was especially terrible; but, whereas More had only his conscience to sustain him, Warham had the traditions of his office, and from that office, in the end, he drew the strength he needed. He had shuddered away from advising Catherine with the phrase, "the wrath of the prince is death"; he had recommended one damaging concession after another. But he had steadfastly refused to disobey the Pope, and on his last appearance in the House of Lords he had given notice that in the next session he would move the repeal of all the statutes passed against the Church since the beginning of this parliament.[22] It was a futile gesture. For Henry's purposes the full control of the archbishopric of Canterbury was the next essential step. If Warham could no longer be cajoled, he might be frightened. If he could not be frightened, he could be destroyed. Before Parliament had been prorogued a month, Warham was assailed with a writ of praemunire, in that he had consecrated the Bishop of St. Asaph's before the bulls for the see had been exhibited to the King, and royal confirmation of the temporalities procured. No disobedience had been intended, but behind the technical charge Warham could see a vital issue, as beyond the King's vague threat he saw, as he was meant to see, impeachment and the block. Warham was eighty-two. The nervous strain of the last session had broken his health, but as he lay propped by his window on the Thames, dictating in measured sentences the speech that he would make in his defense at the bar of the House of Lords, the spirit in his feeble body was stronger than the spirit of William Warham, creature of kings and obsequious royal servant, had ever been.

"I intend nothing against the King's highness," he would say in beginning, "but I intend to do only that I am bound to do by the laws of God and Holy Church and by mine order, and by mine oath that I made at the time of my profession. . . .

"It is thought that I should not consecrate any bishop until he had exhibited his bulls . . . and that I should not give any bishop his spiritualities until he had agreed with the King's highness for the temporalities . . . [but] if the Archbishop of Canterbury should not give the spiritualities to him by the pope provided as bishop until the King's own grace had granted and delivered unto him his temporalities, then the spiritual power of the archbishops should hang and depend on the temporal power of the prince and thus be of little or none effect. . . . It were, indeed, as good to have no spirituality as to have it at the prince's pleasure. . . . The Archbishops of Canterbury from time out of mind have been in possession of the right to consecrate at their liberty bishops of their province without any interruption or impediment, or any question made to the contrary heretofore. . . ."

He would remind his hearers that this royal claim had been one of the articles of the Constitution of Clarendon, over which Church and Crown had fought in the twelfth century, and continue: "This article was one of the causes of the death and martyrdom of St. Thomas. And now St. Thomas is canonized for a saint . . . all for speaking and laboring and taking his death to fordo and destroy this same article. . . . [And his martyrdom] is the example and comfort of others to do the same for the defense of the liberties of the Church. . . .

"And if in my case, my lords, you think to draw your swords and hew me in small pieces [as once St. Thomas suffered] . . . I think it more better for me to suffer the same, than against my conscience to confess this article to be a praemunire for which St. Thomas died." [23]

The main issue was joined at last; at last the right tone was struck, ringing, triumphant, a trumpet call to the disheartened legions of the Church. A timid man may find beyond the extremity of his fear a hardihood to awe the brave. But the effort of mind and heart had exhausted the frail body; the courage to seek martyrdom had come too late. In a few years the high altar of his cathedral would be stripped of the gifts with which the gratitude of the humble and the piety of princes, acknowledging their conqueror, had adorned it for three centuries. The bones of Thomas à Becket would be tossed by royal hatred on the common dust heap. But the bones of William Warham would be undisturbed. There was to be no Saint William of Canterbury. On August 23, 1532, death proved more swift than the wrath of princes.

Chapter Four

HOWEVER SALUTARY its effect on the morale of the rest of the higher clergy, the butchery of an Archbishop of Canterbury would have taken longer in the sixteenth century than by the summary methods of the twelfth, and might have landed Henry VIII in almost as many difficulties as it once had Henry II. Now Warham was dead without a scandal, clever handling might postpone the open breach with Rome until a new Archbishop could be found, pliant enough to give Henry his divorce at Canterbury and to marry him with all due ceremony to Anne Boleyn.

So, at least, Anne must have calculated, for she agreed at last to yield to her impatient lover. Passion gratified would surely hold Henry for these few remaining months, since passion denied had kept him dangling for upwards of six years. For six years this woman, neither very beautiful, nor very intelligent, nor very virtuous, brought up in the lax morality of the French and English courts, her brother a libertine, her sister the King's cast-off mistress, none of her nearest relatives, not even her mother, free from the impeachment of scandal, had managed to defend her technical honor against the King's assaults while living, during most of that time, unprotected in his household, constantly in his company, and publicly believed to be his mistress. For six years she had maintained her suitor's besotted infatuation, had kept him constantly keyed up to the point of daring for her sake the gravest political dangers, driven him along a course which was a continual defiance of the public opinion of his own kingdom and of Christendom, against outcries so bitter that sometimes even her own family and those who stood to profit most from her desperate game drew back, and yet always denied him her ultimate favors. No wonder observers found Anne strained and pale; no wonder she lashed out venomously at times, even at her friends, and at times gave way to a sort of hysterical frenzy. The wonder is that her nerve never broke altogether, that at every crisis she mustered somehow the coolness and judgment to put aside the earthly supplications which Henry cannot have confined wholly to his letters. Even if she cared for nothing about the man except his crown, it was a remarkable feat. All Europe was betting against her. When the Pope and the Emperor agreed that time might show a way out of the difficulties with England, they were thinking, first of all, of the fragility of Anne's virtue. The shrewdest foreign diplomats foresaw her failure, and Queen Catherine herself, piously hoping for the restoration of her husband's reason, was counting in large part on what she knew of Henry's habits with his lights of love. When Henry told the Queen, in the course of one of their last quarrels, at a time when all the world believed that Anne was his mistress, that all the world was wrong, and the Lady was living in perfect virtue, Catherine, who usually knew when to believe her husband, began for the first time to be really afraid of the outcome, sensing in her enemy a woman whose moral qualities were, in their way, as unusual as her own.

That Henry told the truth when he said Anne had not yielded to him we may believe, not simply because Catherine believed it, but because of the public terms Anne arranged for her surrender. On September 1, 1532, eight days after Warham's death, the Lady Anne Rocheford was created Marchioness of Pembroke, with a settlement of a thousand pounds in land, and remainder in lands and title to the heirs male of her body, the usual phrase "lawfully begotten" being significantly omitted from the patent. Anne felt almost sure of marrying the King, but if anything went wrong at the last moment she was determined not to prove as big a fool as her sister Mary.

The timing of her surrender was masterly. Had she waited longer after Warham's death, Henry, whose infatuation for her did not exclude resentment at the way she had treated him, might have had leisure to reflect that once he had his divorce he would be free to choose a more docile and respectable wife. Had she yielded sooner, she might have lost her one hold upon the King before she had secured another. For all his stubbornly inflamed imagination, Henry was easily sated by possession. As far as the eager spies of courtiers and diplomats had ever been able to learn, Henry had been faithful to his passion for Anne as long as it was unrequited, but within six months after her surrender his fancy was straying, and when Anne made his infidelities the occasion for a scene he told her callously that she must learn to close her eyes as her betters had done before her.

In September, however, the honeymoon was full. Henry paraded his conquest before the court and prepared to parade it beyond the Channel, for he would need close French co-operation in his next step, both to influence the Pope and to ward off the hostility of the Emperor. All summer he had been negotiating for an interview with Francis I, to be held at Calais and Boulogne, and he planned now to take Anne with him as a sort of official introduction into the circles in which she would move henceforward. The introduction proved difficult. Francis I exemplified Chesterton's definition of a gentleman: he could not keep the ten commandments but he kept with ease ten thousand; and, consequently, he had no intention of exposing his wife, the Emperor's sister and Catherine's niece, to a meeting with Anne Boleyn. He was sure the sight of a Spanish dress would be displeasing to the King of England, and felt it would be better if his sister received the Marchioness of Pembroke. Margot, however, had already given vigorous expression to her disgust at Henry's divorce, and now she said plainly she had little wish to meet the King of England and none to meet his mistress – except that instead of the euphemism, she used a shorter word. Francis was obliged to make his sister's excuses, and Anne found herself insulted by his next suggestion of the Duchess of Vendôme as hostess, less, perhaps, because the lady's rank was insufficient, than because the sort of parties at which the Duchess could be expected to preside might be thought improper for prospective brides.

In the end Anne did not go to Boulogne, though she did cross to Calais, for Henry would let nothing interfere with the meeting; he needed the French too badly. Anne was appeased by being decked out in Catherine's jewels, even though Henry finally had to write in his own hand an order to Catherine to surrender them, since Catherine told his messenger that nothing less would convince her that her husband had so far taken leave of his sense of what was fitting as to demand them of her. To charm the French Henry was all smiles and determined cordiality, taking care to lose great sums at play to the more important nobles, scattering gifts of jewels, gold chains, and money with a lavish hand, forcing pensions on the chief councilors, and presenting the French princes with the I O U's their father had given him when they were ransomed out of Spain. Times had changed since England had collected pensions and indemnities as a sort of annual blackmail from France. The two kings had changed, too, since their meeting twelve years before on the Field of Cloth of Gold. Time had battered both of them, and if it had made neither of them really wiser, it had made them more anxious and more wary. They still disliked and distrusted each other, but they were both, now, afraid of the Emperor, and, needing each other, they masked their dislike wonderfully well. Besides a mutual defensive alliance, good as long as it was to the interest of both parties to keep it, Henry got for his money Francis's promise to send two French cardinals to Rome to suggest again the possibility of a neutral court at Cambrai, and to present the King of England's case to His Holiness in the most favorable possible light. This move, by soothing the Pope's suspicions, would make it definitely easier to get the bulls for the new Archbishop of Canterbury.[1]

Choice of the new Archbishop was not hard. The ablest cleric in England, Stephen Gardiner, had made himself impossible by his recent intransigence, but Cromwell and Anne Boleyn had a candidate ready, a learned and respectable person – not very well known, certainly, but without an enemy in the world: Thomas Cranmer, ex-chaplain in the Boleyn family, the shy, mild-mannered, fusty little tutor who had suggested to Henry polling the universities about his divorce. Cranmer was the ideal ecclesiastical tool, without vice or ambition, but wax to the stamp of power, loving authority because it was authority, capable of evolving the most disinterested and elevated reasons for carrying out practically any sort of royal order. Dr. Cranmer had recently been sent to Germany to collect the opinions of the reformed divines on the question that troubled the King's conscience, and if he had succeeded in getting few Lutheran endorsements of Junker Harry's divorce, he had convinced everybody, up to and including the Emperor himself, that he was a thoroughly good-natured, inoffensive little man. If Cromwell knew that Dr. Cranmer had consoled himself for his failures in debate by winning a softer argument with the niece of a Lutheran parson, and had subsequently yielded so far to Lutheran views as to marry the young woman in secret, the knowledge would not have made Cranmer less useful in his eyes. If the new Archbishop were ever to develop unexpected scruples, a hint that Henry held strong views on clerical celibacy would work wonders in restoring his pliancy.

In October Cranmer was summoned home from Mantua, whither, as ambassador, he had followed the Emperor's court, and on his tardy arrival in London – he was by his own account a laggard and fearful traveler – he was promptly apprised of the honor destined for him, and hustled, still bewildered, through the form of application for his bulls. The application, with gratuities for the cardinals and threats and promises for the Pope, went posting on the road to Rome. Henry had no intention of risking the usual year's delay in installing his servant.

Queen Catherine and her indefatigable counselor, Chapuys, were not blind to the drift of events. In September Catherine, almost despairing of the Pope, but not despairing of the Church if Clement could be forced to act, wrote at length to her nephew.[2]

"Though I know that Your Majesty is engaged in grave and important Turkish affairs [she said, in part] I cannot cease to importune you about my own, in which almost equal offense is being offered to God. . . . I see no difference in what these people are attempting here and what the Enemy of our Faith aims at where you are [on the Hungarian frontier]. . . . Your Majesty knows that God gives the victory to those who do in his service works good and deserving of merit, and that among the most deserving is to try, as you have been doing, to end this case, which is no longer mine alone, but concerns all those who fear God, as may be seen from the evils it has already entailed, and those it will bring on the whole of Christendom if His Holiness does not look to it quickly. There are many signs of the wickedness being meditated here. New books are being printed daily full of lies, obscenities, and blasphemies against our Holy Faith. These people will stop at nothing, now, to determine this suit in England. . . . The prospective interview between the kings, the companion the King now takes everywhere with him, and the authority and place he allows her have caused the greatest scandal and the most widespread fear of impending calamity. Knowing the fears of my people, I am compelled by my conscience to resist, trusting in God and Your Majesty, and begging you to urge the pope to pronounce sentence at once." And she added the heartsick final sentence: "What goes on here is so ugly and against God, and touches so nearly the honor of my lord, the King, that I cannot bear to write it."

Chapuys told her of the impending mission of the French cardinals almost as soon as it was decided, and she wrote in her own hand to Dr. Ortiz, to the Emperor,[3] and apparently also to the Pope, emphasizing Chapuys' warning that the proposal they were reviving of a court at Cambrai was meant only to win time for the total destruction of the Church in England. She and the ambassador were both sure, after Warham's death, that Henry meant to try for his divorce through Canterbury. When Chapuys learned in January that the nominee to the see was Thomas Cranmer, he sent off a whole volley of warnings to Charles, himself, who was actually at the moment interviewing Clement at Bologna, and to imperialist councilors and agents. The haste to secure Cranmer's bulls, he wrote, was dictated by the desire to have him pronounce the divorce at once so that it could be confirmed by the Parliament now in session. More warnings followed by a second courier, who took only twelve days to spur along muddy roads and over snowy passes to Bologna. "If the Pope knew," Chapuys wrote, "the reputation Cranmer has here of being devoted heart and soul to the Lutheran sect, he would not be hasty in granting the bulls. . . . He is a servant of Anne's and at least should be required to take a special oath not to meddle with the divorce." In case the Emperor should fail to convey all this information to the Pope, Chapuys took the precaution of repeating it to Dr. Ortiz, who had means of communicating with His Holiness directly, and was zealous enough to be sure to do so. To the Emperor Chapuys added another urgent appeal from Catherine. "The Queen begs once more for the immediate decision of her case. . . . She takes upon herself full responsibility for all the consequences, and assures Your Majesty that there need not be the slightest danger that war will follow. She believes that if His Holiness were to decide in her favor the King would even now obey him, but even should he fail to do so, she will die comparatively happy, knowing that the justice of her cause has been declared, and that the Princess, her daughter, will not lose the right to the succession. . . . [The Queen wishes me to say, further, that] this king has already seized and converted to his own use much of the wealth of the Church, and he will be encouraged to follow in this path of usurpation because of greed and because of the kind of people who now surround him, like the Lady and her father, staunch Lutherans both. . . . Should sentence be pronounced at once, the majority of people here are still such good Catholics that they would compel the King to obey. But unless the Pope acts at once, he will be deprived little by little of his authority here, and finally his censures will go unheeded."[4]

Chapuys' facts were sound; his predictions were accurate; both were in the hands of the Emperor by February 22, and transmitted to the Pope not more than a day or two later. Chapuys' arguments against Cranmer were known to many of the cardinals, and it would be strange if the Curia had no independent confirmation of them from Del Borgho, the nuncio in England, or from its observers in Germany. Nevertheless, some three weeks later, Cranmer's bulls for Canterbury were issued in full consistory, and rushed at once to England.

There was need for haste. Shortly after he wrote his second warning Chapuys heard of a curious scene. In the midst of a court gathering Anne Boleyn had said loudly to Sir Thomas Wyatt: "Will you send me some apples, Sir Thomas? I have such a longing to eat apples! Do you know what the King says? He says it means I am with child! But I tell him no. No! It couldn't, no!" And she laughed suddenly, hysterically, and fled from the room still laughing, leaving the spectators thunderstruck with dismay and embarrassment.[5] Cranmer would have to work fast if the expected child were to be born in wedlock.

This need for haste was what Clement failed to understand. The Roman Curia had not become suddenly either more venal or more naïve than it had been for the past three years; it would be a mistake to assume either that the cardinals were bribed by payments not much larger than were customary when so fat a plum as Canterbury was awarded, or that anyone at Rome was much deceived either about Cranmer's orthodoxy or about his probable attitude towards the divorce. But Clement apparently took the overtures of the French about Cambrai seriously, as the French themselves undoubtedly did. He had obtained the Emperor's reluctant consent to a court at Cambrai, and probably imagined that the case might be prolonged there another year, and that only then would Cranmer act, if he had to act at all, and then only with the glacial deliberation usual in ecclesiastical courts. Possibly Del Borgho, the nuncio in England, had deliberately deceived the Pope about the tempo of events in England; perhaps Del Borgho was himself deceived by the rumor which momentarily encouraged Catherine to believe that the marquisate of Pembroke was not just a first payment, but the full price of Anne's surrender. Whatever information he acted on, Clement let himself be persuaded by the French, to whom he was drawing constantly closer, into granting the bulls for Henry's nominee. In so doing, he made another contribution – his greatest and almost his last – to the destruction of the papal power in England.

If Clement contributed to catastrophe in England through weakness and folly, what is to be said of his nuncio? When Parliament opened in February, members were astonished and confused to perceive the Pope's ambassador seated in his robes on a kind of throne at the King's right hand. Thereafter Del Borgho was so petted at court, and paraded so constantly in Henry's company, that everyone felt sure Henry had finally come to an accommodation with the Pope. Loyal Catholics hung their heads, and Catherine's partisans were both furious and dismayed. All this time there reposed in Del Borgho's custody the brief Catherine had been seeking, commanding Henry to separate from the woman with whom he was living and to return to his lawful wife. Dr. Ortiz, coached by Chapuys, had finally obtained it in November, but Clement had weakly qualified his concession with the proviso that Del Borgho should not present it until he saw an appropriate occasion, and as often as Chapuys demanded its presentation, Del Borgho replied that the occasion did not seem appropriate. When finally Chapuys reproached the nuncio with outright treachery, Del Borgho, with a shrug, replied that he was a poor man, but he had to live like others.[6] Just how he earned his living no one can say now.

Del Borgho's ambiguous behavior, and Cromwell's increased parliamentary skill, completed the rout of Catherine's friends in Parliament. A bill was introduced declaring that the Church of England was sufficient and meet of itself to determine ordinances, laws, statutes and provisions; and that, because of the great enormities, dangers, long delays and hurts involved in appeals to Rome, all spiritual cases should henceforth be finally determined within the King's jurisdiction. The pious generalities in which the statute was wrapped did not conceal from anyone that this Act of Appeals, which the government was pushing through with all its weight, was meant first of all to outlaw Catherine's appeal to Rome, even if it was necessary, in order to do so, to alter the ancient constitution of the realm and sever England completely from the jurisdiction which united Christendom. Chapuys had given much time since his arrival to a study of Parliament, and had built up on the basis of the Queen's popularity and his master's power something like the nucleus of a coherent party among the members, but though the Commons resisted for three weeks and the Lords were equally reluctant, in the end the lines crumbled. The Act of Appeals passed both Houses, by force of "the King's absolute power," and even before the King signed it, the great majority of the clergy in Convocation had been forced to sign two propositions declaring the marriage of Henry and Catherine null and invalid from the beginning. The stage was ready for Thomas Cranmer.

Cranmer had been carefully coached. As a dutiful royal servant he had (Henry saw that he had) all the proper scruples about the oath of allegiance to the Pope which he would have to take on his consecration, the same oath the discovery of which had so opportunely shocked the King just a year before. Therefore, on March 26, in the chapel of the palace at Westminster, Thomas Cranmer made a secret declaration, before a notary and the requisite witnesses, that he would not consider the oath to the Pope as binding him in anything contrary to the will of his sovereign lord, the King. Four days later, publicly swearing allegiance to the Pope before the high altar, in the time-hallowed words, amidst the pomp and glitter of the accustomed ceremony, the new Archbishop began his public career in deliberate perjury. Poor man, he had very little choice.

From the first Cranmer was taught his place. He had not been consecrated a fortnight before he wrote the King, begging permission to take up His Highness's great cause of matrimony lest, bruited about among rude and ignorant people, it prove a scandal and danger to the realm. The letter, in its first draft, was already a masterpiece of official absurdity, bare-faced falsehood, and servile adulation, but its crawling phrases were not abject enough for Henry. He sent it back with alterations in the royal hand, requiring his Archbishop to call upon Our Lord to witness his impartial zeal, and changing the words "beseeching Your Highness most humbly upon my knees," to "prostrate at the feet of Your Majesty, beseeching."[7] That phrase indicated exactly the position in which Henry wished to see the English Church.

ii

Even before Cranmer wrote his cringing letter, another deputation of the royal council, headed by the Dukes of Norfolk and Suffolk, called upon Catherine at Ampthill, a retired manor in Bedfordshire to which she had recently removed, to require her on her allegiance to renounce the title of Queen and to submit herself to the King's will in the matter of her marriage, with the promise that in return the King would provide for her "more generously than she could expect." Until she submitted she was to be nominally as well as actually a prisoner, in the custody of her former chamberlain, Lord Mountjoy. Catherine made her usual reply. She was, and would remain, Henry's wife and England's Queen. After the deputation withdrew, her chamberlain and warder, Lord Mountjoy, remained to discuss future arrangements. Since she could no longer use the title of Queen, her servants must call her Princess Dowager; in view of her disobedience, her allowance was to be reduced to less than a quarter of the sum she had received hitherto. Catherine was unco-operative. Those who waited on her, she said, however few, would have to address her as Queen. For her household she declined to take any responsibility; she was at her husband's mercy. She hoped he would allow her enough to keep herself, her confessor, her physician, and two maids to care for her chamber. If that seemed too much she would gladly go about the world begging alms for the love of God. She could not be interested in details. As the Dukes had withdrawn, Norfolk had confirmed her worst fears. Her resistance, he told her not unkindly, was futile. Henry was already married – had been married to Anne for two months.[8]

The news meant that her five years' fight had ended in defeat. Ever since she had determined on an appeal to Rome, she had hoped that the Pope's decision would bring her husband to his senses, hearten him to shake off the yoke of the Boleyns, and thus prevent the evils of schism and heresy, internal strife and the robbery of the Church which otherwise must follow. She had begun by thinking of her divorce as a family, or at most a dynastic, problem – an ambitious plot of Wolsey's to injure Spain, and to make a liar and adulterer of her husband in order to drag him at the heels of France. After she faced Henry at Blackfriars it had seemed more like a plot of the devil's to involve them all in ruin; the stakes had become not merely her honor and her daughter's right but the soul of her husband and the salvation from heresy of all the people of England. As she watched the course of events in Europe she had become convinced that the largest of all stakes was involved, the future unity of the Christian faith. But her tactics remained unchanged. Even at the eleventh hour the Pope might have saved her, and himself, and Christendom. Now it was too late. Though her own iron endurance had not failed, this was failure. She would have to think what to do next.

To her friend and adviser, Eustache Chapuys, the new course was obvious. He had foreseen it almost ever since his first arrival in England, forty-two months before, and as he became more and more the partisan of the Queen, subordinating all the functions of his ambassadorial office to the problem of her defense, he had taken pains to prepare the minds of the Emperor, and the Emperor's chief advisers, for this probable eventuality. He had done everything in his power to postpone it, loyally implementing Catherine's program and adding his own grave warnings to hers, but as the Pope still delayed, and as Chapuys sensed the hastening tempo of Henry's progress towards schism, at no small risk and inconvenience to himself the ambassador had taken every possible step in England to make sure that the new policy when it had to be applied should prove more successful than the old. The passage of the Act of Appeals and the definite news that Henry was married signaled the hour of decision. On April 10, 1533, he wrote to the Emperor: —

Considering the great injury done to Madame, your aunt, you can hardly avoid making war now upon this king and kingdom . . . an undertaking which would be, in the opinion of many people here, the easiest thing in the world at present, for this king has neither horsemen nor captains and the affections of the people are entirely on the side of the Queen and Your Majesty. . . . The Pope should invoke the secular arm . . . and Your Majesty should forbid all intercourse of commerce between your dominions and this kingdom, whereat the people would rise against this accursed marriage. . . . The Scots are eager to help . . . and the King of France, according to his ambassador here, would not stir.[9]

Chapuys knew something of the Emperor's multifold difficulties, the danger from the Turks in Hungary and in the Mediterranean, the unrest in Germany, the intrigues in Italy, the sulky, vengeful attitude of France, and he must have guessed that his insistence on war with England would grate on many of the Emperor's councilors, but he was prepared to risk his own career on the chance of pushing Charles into intervention. He had explained carefully how dependent English economy was on trade with the Netherlands, how much confusion an embargo would create. He had spent much more than he could afford on spies to confirm his own estimates of popular discontent, had conferred in secret with the Scottish ambassador, and gone much further in conspiracy with English nobles than he had any warrant for. He hoped for several simultaneous local risings while the King of Scots, a dashing youth who would make a first-rate leader, Chapuys thought, could take the lead in the north and be rewarded by the hand of the Princess Mary. The Emperor would be quit at the price of a demonstration on the east coast; though his captains, if they landed, could enroll as many men as they wanted in any part of the kingdom. Except for Norfolk and the Boleyns, he thought, hardly a gentleman would stir to support the government; the panic in London was already general, a rising in the City was expected, and the King and his ministers understood popular feeling so well that "should the least mishap occur" they would think only of flight. The chief point, Chapuys wrote, was to strike at once, before Henry had time to hire mercenaries in France or Switzerland, and while the whole country was boiling with anger and alarm. Chapuys stirred up Dr. Ortiz to write from Rome, exhorting the Emperor to draw the sword without delay, while he, himself, with a shrewd appreciation of the argument that would move Charles most, wrote as if he felt that every hour he remained in England reflected on the Emperor's honor. Meanwhile he advised his friends among the merchants how to secure their goods in Flanders until the storm was over, and held a kind of continuous reception at the embassy for the nobles who came to wish him Godspeed and to assure him of their devotion to the Emperor and the Queen. He bought horses for his suite, ostentatiously packed his furniture, and gave to his formal interview at court on Maundy Thursday, 1533, something of the tone of an ultimatum and farewell. He had, apparently, made plans for the removal of the Queen and the Princess Mary, either to the Netherlands or to a place of safety in the north, and he had cultivated friendly relations with the Germans of the Steelyard, who had an armed squadron of their Baltic merchantmen lying conveniently in the Thames. If the Emperor could have been prodded into war by his ambassador, there would have been war that spring.[10]

But, for the first time since he had come to England, Chapuys' course was not Catherine's. In the past three years there had come to be a close bond between the ambassador and the Queen. She did not see Chapuys very often, but she had found him loyal, devoted, and understanding beyond anything she would have expected of any ambassador, even one of her own countrymen; and she had come to trust him as she had trusted no one in her life, except, perhaps, in her youth, her confessor, Fray Diego. She took no step without consulting him; she never forgot, in her letters abroad, to mention her gratitude for his services; and it is significant of their relationship that she no longer wrote to him formally in French as *Mons. L'ambassadeur* but in Spanish, the language of her heart, as *especial amigo* – special friend – a salutation not to be found elsewhere in her correspondence. Yet, though in his eagerness to persuade the Emperor Chapuys did his best to minimize the fact, he could not conceal that he and the Queen were poles apart on one point. Catherine would give no countenance to war.

She had considered the possibility as thoroughly as Chapuys had done, and, coming as always to her hardest decisions alone, had set her face resolutely against it. "I shall not ask His Holiness for war," she had written to Chapuys, "that is a thing I would rather die than provoke." [11] And to Charles, "there can be no danger in what I ask, since as you know, the thunders of this land hold no lightenings for any head but mine." [12] By her own letters to Charles and to the Pope, and by her repeated messages to both through Chapuys, she had made her position quite clear. In February, 1533, she had solemnly taken it upon her conscience that no matter what the Pope's decision was, and no matter what Henry's subsequent action, no bloodshed would follow.[13] She felt strong enough to prevent, by herself, the civil war Chapuys was busy in fomenting. Chapuys, who had remarked with a mixture of irony and reluctant admiration her tenderness for her husband and his people, had been reluctant to disclose his plans to her. When he did, he found that at one crucial point she imposed an absolute veto. She would take no steps to escape from custody, or to place herself in safety, nor would she be a party to any such plan. Such an action, she said, "would be a sin against the law and against my lawful husband of which I shall never be guilty." [14]

"The Queen," Chapuys was obliged to write, interrupting his own clamors for his recall, "is so overscrupulous that she would consider herself damned eternally were she to consent to anything that might provoke a war." [15] And he was obliged to record that so far from wanting him recalled, Catherine hoped he would remain, so that she might continue to consult him, and no breach might appear to have occurred between her husband and her nephew on her account. In her youth Catherine had stood one lonely siege to an ultimate unexpected victory; in her middle age she was prepared to stand another, equally determined to yield no jot of her own rights, and not to involve any innocent person in her misfortunes. It was as if she thought the single barrier of her unbreakable will could turn aside all the forces of history.

Her resolution was soon to be tested. The sleepy little market town of Dunstable had the double advantage of being near enough to Ampthill so that the Queen could not allege lack of notice or convenience in her trial, and far enough away from London to make the interruption of the Archbishop's proceedings by a popular tumult unlikely. There, on May 8, 1533, Cranmer timidly opened his court and summoned the Queen to attend, fearing nothing so much as that she might accept his summons. His alarm was needless. After consulting Chapuys, and signing two formal protests which the ambassador prepared for her, Catherine ignored the court at Dunstable. On May 10 the Archbishop found her contumacious, and on May 23, the first day which the barest observation of the forms permitted, he declared her marriage to Henry null and void from the beginning, on the grounds that her former marriage to Arthur had been consummated, and no dispensation could remove the impediment thus imposed by the law of God.[16] He had to hurry, for on May 28 he was back at Lambeth, declaring that he had investigated fully the marriage between the King and the Lady Anne (though he did not say where or when it had taken place), and found it good and valid.

Quick as he was, he was only just in time. Four days later, on June 1, Anne Boleyn passed through the streets of London, surrounded by all the customary pomp, but greeted with far less than the customary enthusiasm, to be crowned Queen of England. Cornhill and Gracious Streets were hung with scarlet and crimson, and in the Cheap a conduit ran white wine and claret all that afternoon; Juno and Venus and Saint Anne were invoked in pageantry, and loyal verses in English and Latin went even higher for comparisons; but Anne, a foreigner reported, saw few bare heads in the staring crowds and heard few "God save you's." George Talbot, Earl of Shrewsbury, found himself too old to pay homage to a second queen, and all over England long after the coronation Cromwell's informers had regretfully to report that such a one had said "that the Queen's Grace was a goggyl yed hoore" and cried "God save Queen Katteryn, our own righteous Queen," and such another had declared that he was not such a fool nor such a sinner neither as ever to take "that whore Nan Bullen to be Queen."

If Anne saw black looks among the commons, and detected the smirk behind the masks of kneeling courtiers, she only held her head the higher. The people might grumble, the Pope, stirred to unusual wrath and expedition by Cranmer's haste, might declare her marriage null; but the leaderless nobility were like sheep before a lion, and the Emperor, everyone saw, was grateful for his aunt's forbearance and not inclined to stir. The unorganized opposition only hardened Anne in her vengeful determination to make her enemies feel the sting of her triumph.

Steps to humiliate Catherine, her chief enemy, were the easier to procure because Henry, as long as his former wife defied him, could not feel secure in his own kingdom, and even aside from the King's vague fears and Anne's vindictiveness the political advantages of some gesture of submission on Catherine's part were obvious. In July, therefore, another full strength deputation headed by Lord Mountjoy was sent to Ampthill to try whether the accomplished facts of Cranmer's decree and the Coronation would win the surrender they had failed to secure in April.[17] They found Catherine much troubled with a cough, lying on a pallet, because she had lately pricked her foot with a pin so that she could neither stand nor go. But her spirit was as erect as ever. She asked them to read their instructions publicly to as many of her servants as could crowd into her chamber. She took immediate exception to the title of "Princess Dowager." She was and would be called Queen. To a long harangue reciting the King's recent actions and the acquiescence of the Lords Spiritual and Temporal therein, she replied that "all the world knoweth by what authority it was done, much more by power than by justice . . . without a lawful separation or divorce, the case being pending at Rome. . . . The King may do in his realm by his royal power what he will, but those [the Lords Spiritual and Temporal] who decided against me, did so against their consciences. . . . My matter dependeth not on the universities nor on the realm, but in the court of Rome, before the Pope, whom I account God's vicar and judge on earth as I have answered heretofore."

To the charge that she had departed from obedience to the King and seduced her servants also into disobedience, she replied that she had obeyed and would obey her husband in all lawful things, but could not obey him against God and her conscience, and turning to her own servants she praised their faithfulness, regretted that she could not reward it as it deserved, but warned them that they must not expect her to put her soul in danger for their sakes.

She scorned to answer the bribe of a handsome estate in return for her submission, and to the charge that her attitude was assumed to arouse the sympathy of the people and stir them to rebellion she answered that she had never sought dissension in the realm and trusted there would be none, but neither for the favor of the people, nor for any trouble or adversity that could be devised for her would she lose the favor of God. To the meanest threat of all, that her stubbornness would be visited upon her servants and her daughter, she replied that they and she must trust to the King's mercy, remembering the injunction not to fear those who have power over the body, but only Him who hath power over the soul.

The next day the deputation brought her, as she had asked, a written version of their arguments and her replies, and she struck out with vigorous pen strokes the words "Princess Dowager" wherever they occurred, commenting further that Cranmer's court had been held at a time when the King's own excusator at Rome had been suing to have the case adjudged at Cambrai. Notwithstanding which "it was brought to be determined here, within the King's own realm, by a man of his own making, the Bishop of Canterbury, no indifferent person, and the place also partial and suspect, considering that the King now has over the Church in England, as much or more authority than if he were the Pope. Indifferent!" she cried. "The place would have been more indifferent had it been adjudged in hell, for I think the devils themselves do tremble to see the truth so oppressed!"

To the threat of prosecution for treason she replied firmly, "If it can be proved that I have given occasion to disturb my lord, the King, or his realm in any wise, then I desire that my punishment according to the laws should not be deferred . . . but should I agree to your persuasions, I should be a slanderer of myself and confess to have been the King's harlot these four and twenty years. . . . As long as the King, my lord, took me for his wife, as I was and am, I am also his subject, but if the King take me not as his wife, I came not into this realm as merchandise, nor yet to be married to any merchant. If it can be proved that either in writing to the Pope, or in any other [of] my writings (which my lord the King may see at all times if he pleases . . .) I have stirred or procured anything against His Grace, or been the means to any person to make any motion that might have been prejudicial to him or his realm I am content to suffer for it. For," she added sadly, "since I have brought England little good, I should be the loather to bring it any harm."

The deputies attempted no further answer. Their leader, Lord Mountjoy, was already making up his mind that this was the last occasion on which he could be used to persecute the Queen, and that if his office of her chamberlain in which he had served her with loyal affection ever since her coronation was to be changed to that of jailer and inquisitor, he would lay it down, whatever the King's displeasure. Even those loyal councilors who were not ashamed of their part were aware that every word Catherine spoke to them would be repeated by twenty tongues before nightfall, and spread in shocked whispers from end to end of England, faster and farther than the propaganda of the royal printing presses could ever reach. Henry could maltreat his wife, but he could not – as Anne had told him – either in person or by deputy win an argument against her.

iii

No one seemed to enjoy the discomfiture of Mountjoy's delegation more than Thomas Cromwell. "Nature wronged the Queen in not making her a man," he told Chapuys with relish. "But for her sex she would have surpassed all the heroes of history." [18] Chapuys was touched by the genuine warmth of the praise. It showed, he thought, that he might yet make a good imperialist of the King's new minister. Later, the ambassador was to understand that it showed nothing but Cromwell's impersonal detachment from the problems of his office. No one saw more clearly the menace to the new order implicit in Catherine's obstinacy; no one had greater reason to fear it; but Cromwell was perfectly capable of admiring the Queen, and even of wishing to make her as comfortable as possible, until he was ready to destroy her.

In the summer of 1533, Chapuys had not yet learned to gauge his new antagonist. As far back as the spring of 1531 Cromwell had begun to be one of the moving spirits in the royal council, but for the first two years he kept so adroitly in the background that his name never appears in the ambassador's despatches. In February, 1533, Chapuys first mentioned him as the councilor most concerned in the application for Cranmer's bulls; in March he noted that Cromwell, not Norfolk, was in charge of certain mysterious negotiations with a German captain of mercenaries; in April he spoke of him as "the man who has perhaps the most influence just now," and in May, without qualifications, as leading person on the council and enjoying the most credit with the King. That month Norfolk went to France on a mission, and thereafter Cromwell was the person with whom Chapuys dealt. Chapuys found the change refreshing, a great help in his own readjustment to remaining in England after he had expected to be recalled. Slowly he realized that he had exchanged a clumsy, irritating antagonist for an agile, deadly one, but even after he had come to write "Cromwell's words are fair, but his deeds are bad, and his intentions much worse," he still preferred fencing with Mr. Secretary to bouts with the Duke or with Henry.

Norfolk and Henry both set Chapuys' teeth on edge. For the ponderous, cold-hearted, chicken-brained Duke, moving sluggishly in the mists of the feudal past like some obsolete armored saurian, Chapuys came to have only a chilly contempt. Towards the complex, protean, temperamental King, the ambassador's emotions were more various: reluctant liking, helpless exasperation, awe, amusement, pity, distrust, admiring wonder, horrified and incredulous loathing. After a while Chapuys could predict, within limits, what Henry would do or say next, but the inwardness of that majestic childishness, that absurd mixture of naïveté and cunning, boldness and poltroonery, vindictive cruelty and wayward almost irresistible charm always eluded him. Interviews with Norfolk were pure boredom. Interviews with Henry, even successful ones, left Chapuys feeling somehow baffled and overcome. But Thomas Cromwell, though he might be an unmitigated scoundrel, was also a witty and a reasonable man, one who never told unnecessary lies, and did not feel obliged to begin a policy of deception by deceiving himself. Confronted with one of Chapuys' frequent and scarcely veiled threats of the Emperor's intervention, Norfolk would invariably try to talk like a hero out of Malory; Henry, according to his mood, might bluster, or wax tearful over his nephew's ingratitude, or grow suddenly compliant and ingratiating, swearing that black was white and making promises he never intended to fulfill; but Cromwell, on the first of such threats, was frank and almost casual. "Yes," he admitted at once, "the Emperor could ruin us all if he liked. But," with a sly, sidelong glance, "what good would that do the Emperor?"

The thrust went home, but at least one knew where the steel was; one did not merely beat the air. Chapuys knew that Cromwell knew that his Imperial Majesty, Charles V, did not want at present to add trouble in England to his other burdens. The bland Secretary might almost have read the dispatches in which the Emperor instructed his ambassador to stay at his post, speak softly, and not irritate the English unduly. Chapuys knew also, though perhaps Cromwell did not, that only Catherine's repeated praise of his services and his loyalty kept him from being replaced by an ambassador more peaceably inclined. Under the circumstances, with nothing left to do except "try to keep matters from growing worse," and "prevent, as far as I can, any fresh attempt to injure the Queen or the Princess," Chapuys could be grateful for Cromwell's realism. The secretary was, at least, too intelligent to wish to inflict pain or humiliation without a purpose, or to take unnecessary chances with the patience of an emperor who might be provoked too far.

Besides, the two men had more in common than a preference for realism. Both were of the middle class; both had been touched by the Italian Renaissance. They liked to ride hawking together, to dine together, to lend each other books, and sometimes to slip away together from the wrangles of the council table to a garden by the river and let the talk wander from world politics to scholarship, the goldsmith work of Antwerp, ancient intaglios, sculpture, painting, and reminiscences of the Italy they both had loved. Chapuys believed that Cromwell was a conscienceless scoundrel, without scruples or remorse; Cromwell judged Chapuys an inveterate intriguer, as resourceful and dangerous, bent on his ruin. But they enjoyed each other's company.

That autumn of 1533, Cromwell was elaborating a scheme to strike terror into the Queen's supporters, a scheme which, with luck, might bring down Catherine herself. Even though Chapuys had been obliged to hedge his half-promises of the Emperor's support, the murmurs against the government and particularly against the King's new marriage had not grown less. Cromwell's own power and all the wide plans he had for making the King rich and powerful, as absolute in his domains as the Grand Turk, depended on Henry's not being turned from the course he had taken when he married Anne, a course sure to meet a mounting opposition. Cromwell knew of no way to make Henry popular while he followed it, but the book he studied most told him that the surest foundation for power was not love but fear. He knew of ways to instill fear. In September a trick of fate made fear more necessary than ever.

Just before Anne's coronation, when Chapuys, in protest against the King's assertion that he had to marry Anne in order to have a male heir, had pointed out that he could not be sure of having one, Henry had exploded with wrath. "Am I not a man like another?" he shouted. Then grinned complacently, "You do not know all my secrets." Physicians, astrologers, wise women, beggars with second sight, all assured him that the child Anne was expecting would be a boy. How could it fail to be "since God who knows my righteous heart, always prospers my affairs?" And since a male child was most urgently needed to quiet popular murmurs, insure the safety of the dynasty, and, most of all, to justify what could not be undone? When Anne was brought to bed, three months after her coronation, Henry was already triumphing in expectation. They scarcely dared to tell him that the child, for whom he had hustled Cranmer into Canterbury, bullied his nobility, broken with the Pope, defied Christendom, was of the same sex as the child whom Cranmer at his bidding had so recently declared a bastard. Even so thick-skinned a man as Henry may have puzzled for a moment over whose affairs God really favored, and Anne, huddled in the great bed at Greenwich, may have begun to guess how her predecessor once had felt. To Cromwell, who never relied much on special interventions of divine providence, the birth of a princess instead of a prince merely confirmed the wisdom of a policy of terror. He could congratulate himself that, with the able assistance of Archbishop Cranmer, he had already begun to investigate the prophecies of the Holy Maid of Kent.

Before she was received as a nun into the Convent of Saint Sepulcher at Canterbury, Elizabeth Barton had been a servant girl who spoke with angels. After she took the veil the prophecies resulting from these conversations continued, sure sign that their origin was not diabolic but divine. Every fortnight more or less she fell into a trance, and the words she muttered in her ecstasy might warn of an impending calamity, or report the place in purgatory of a departed spirit, or even convey, when properly interpreted, some highly practical bit of advice about finding a missing brooch, or opening a new shop, or bringing an aberrant husband to his senses. Her miraculous powers made her convent a place of pilgrimage and consultation even for some of the greatest in the kingdom; her revelations, full of detailed information about the bright world beyond the grave, circulated and found credence among high and low; and as she became more accustomed to her function she was able to report quite coherently the content of her trances. A modern psychologist could, no doubt, find a term for Elizabeth Barton's condition, but in a world in which a distinguished professor of theology could be constantly annoyed at his studies by the horseplay of devils, and the founder of an extremely efficient society could receive its constitution and bylaws in a face-to-face interview with the Trinity, no one needed more than the simplest explanation. The Holy Maid of Kent talked to angels, and the proof that she did so was that those who heard angelic discourse from her lips went away comforted and uplifted, often to lead better lives.

In the excitement after the Queen's divorce was first talked of, it was natural that Elizabeth's angels should discuss it with her. What they told her was much what she might have heard from Dr. Bocking her confessor, or on a sunny bench before any inn on any road in Kent, but not, therefore, less convincing: The King had sinned in his heart, and God's favor was withdrawn from him. Terrible punishments were in store for a realm where such sins went unrepented and unchastised. People listened eagerly, and the Holy Maid and her advisers began to be obsessed with the importance of her mission. She communicated with the papal nuncio, offered to advise the Pope about his duty, sought and received an interview with the King himself. As her prophecies spread broadcast, she was moved to voice what she thought the divine will more and more plainly. Whatever else she was voicing, it was surely the overwhelming sentiment of the people of England. No one thought it odd that an illiterate nun should admonish a king. Saint Catherine of Siena had scolded popes, and a Lorraine peasant girl had led armies and re-established a monarchy. For a moment Elizabeth Barton was as bold as Joan of Arc. The King, she said, would no longer be king in the eyes of God should he make a second marriage, and if he disregarded God's warning he would not live a month. This was to invite the fate of Joan of Arc without her triumphs. To prophesy the death of the King, to seek, or even to listen to such prophecy, was treason – the treason for which the Duke of Buckingham had died.

Cromwell was not interested, however, in the death of a mad Kentish nun. In silencing the Nun, he meant to make her prophecies a net to ensnare persons who could command the legions of this world. Archbishop Cranmer proved an apt collaborator. In examining Elizabeth Barton on the authenticity of her revelations, as he was bound by his spiritual office to do, Cranmer was on familiar ground. Just so might professorial guile lead an unwary undergraduate to confound himself. One must be mild at first, benign, sympathetic; one must ask merely for information, wreathing elaborate convolutions about the unsuspecting prey, tightening the noose ever so gently, until the examinee, emptied of everything he knows, struggles helplessly in a mesh of contradictions and damaging admissions. So in the end Elizabeth Barton told Cranmer everything, and no longer knew herself whether her revelations were from God or from the devil, or which had come to her alone, and which had been suggested by others.

In November, 1533, two months after the birth of the Princess Elizabeth, the Nun and five others – two monks, a friar and two secular priests – stood on a scaffold outside St. Paul's while a preacher held forth on lying prophets, and their confession of imposture and treason was read aloud to the gaping public. Then they were taken back to the Tower to await sentence.

It was an intellectual triumph for Cranmer, but slightly disappointing, so far, for Thomas Cromwell. He could still use the Nun's treason, when the time came, to terrorize Catherine's partisans, but he had aimed at larger game than monks and friars. He aimed at the Marchioness of Exeter and the Countess of Salisbury, Catherine's two chief friends among the ladies of the higher nobility, at John Fisher, Bishop of Rochester, Catherine's chief champion among the clergy, at Sir Thomas More, the most distinguished lay adherent of the old faith, and, of course, at the Queen herself. But the Marchioness of Exeter had consulted the Nun on a purely family matter, and the Countess of Salisbury knew no more of her prophecies than thousands of others. It would be hard to strike at Sir Thomas More on the ground that he had once written the Nun a letter advising her to leave politics alone, or at Fisher because he had failed to report to the Government a possibly treasonable prophecy he had heard from her after she had made it to the King's face. Such trivia could be used to harry the persons aimed at, but hardly to destroy them. As for the Queen, Cromwell confessed frankly to Chapuys that he had used every trick he knew to make the Nun confess that she was in collusion with the "Princess Dowager," but that Catherine had been too sensible to involve herself in the least.[19]

iv

Having failed to entrap Catherine, Cromwell was delighted to leave the unprofitable task of bullying her to persons better fitted by their rank to undertake it. If it amused him to note that Henry did not dare to murder his wife and could not ignore her, he gave no sign. Shortly after her interview with Mountjoy in July, 1533, Catherine had removed her household, at her husband's order, from Ampthill to Buckden in Huntingdonshire. The farther away Catherine was from her partisans in London, the safer Henry felt, and Buckden, in a wild and sparsely populated country on the edge of the great fens, a spot beyond the limits of his most ambitious progresses, seemed very far away. The palace at Buckden of the Bishop of Lincoln would be large enough to accommodate her diminished suite, the place was unfrequented, and the scandal of her desertion and ill-treatment would be the sooner forgotten if its scene was remote.

At Buckden,[20] though Catherine was harried from time to time by visits from royal commissioners and found that even the meager income allotted her was doled out by the King's accountants, she was, at first, neither ill-treated nor ill-lodged. The fields and woods around Buckden are pleasant in late summer and early autumn, the red brick pile of the episcopal palace, half-residence, half-fortress, had been rebuilt in the 1480's in a fashion then almost modern, and the Queen still had enough furniture and hangings to make it fairly comfortable. Her old favorite, Maria de Salinas, the widowed Countess of Willoughby, did not follow her from Ampthill, but she retained some eight or ten ladies in waiting, several of them Spanish, her *maestrasala*, the faithful Francisco Felipez, her physician, Miguel De la Sá, her apothecary, the Licentiate De Soto, and two chaplains, Jorge de Ateca, Bishop of Llandaff, and the indomitable Thomas Abell, her unexpected champion, whom she had been glad to welcome back into her service on his release from the Tower. The house offered a pleasant garden, a dignified great hall, and, from the Queen's own apartments, a sweeping view over the fens. Only as winter approached did Catherine discover how dank and unhealthy, alternately beset with east winds and marsh mists, was the residence appointed for her.

In one expectation, however, Henry was disappointed. All the way northwards her party found the roads lined with friendly people who shouted blessings and encouragements as she passed, gentry, yeomen, humbler folk, all alike, so they called out to her, ready to live and die in her service. Every mile was a spontaneous demonstration of loyalty and devotion which moved the Queen to tears and her warders to profound uneasiness, and at Buckden itself she was welcomed as if she had been coming home to Greenwich. She could no longer distribute her customary alms. Anne Boleyn had suggested that Catherine had won the love of the poor commons by feeding them, and the strict control which the royal commissioners now kept over her accounts was designed to make sure that there was nothing over for charity. But the villagers of Buckden watched as eagerly for her infrequent appearances, and cheered as heartily under her windows as if they received at her porter's lodge her customary royal dole of food and drink and small silver coins, instead of bringing there, timidly, fruit and fresh cheeses and simple country gifts which they hoped their Queen might like. By the firesides for forty miles about, people told each other how the ill-used Queen spent most of her days shut in a small room, off her bed chamber, that had a latticed window looking into the chapel, weeping and praying until the window ledge was wet with her tears as with rain, and the stone beneath began to be worn in hollows by her knees.

At Buckden, shortly after her arrival, Catherine learned that Clement had mustered the courage to condemn Henry's remarriage in a bull that was tantamount to excommunication, and then had let himself be persuaded not to make his censure public. At Buckden, in September, she heard that Anne had given birth to a daughter, for whose christening as Elizabeth Henry callously demanded that Catherine surrender Mary's christening robes, getting a stinging rebuff for answer. And from Buckden, in November, just after she heard of the "confession" of the Nun of Kent, she wrote Chapuys to urge again that the Pope proceed to sentence. Should a just sentence be pronounced, she said, many souls now in danger of perdition would be saved, her daughter's rights would be established, and the end of her own troubles would be at hand. But she reiterated that she did not ask for war, and the end of her troubles which she foresaw was apparently not a worldly triumph. "I am told," she wrote, "that the next parliament is to decide whether I am to suffer martyrdom. If it is to be so, I hope it may be a meritorious act. . . . I do not fear . . . for there is no punishment from God except for neglected duty."

Had Chapuys shown that letter to Henry, the King might have been easier in his mind. But one of the ambassador's best cards was the repeated hint that harsher measures against Catherine and Mary might precipitate a rebellion, and he took care not to make the Queen's revulsion from such a course too unambiguous. And to Henry, who could not distinguish between obedience of the will, and submission of the spirit, Catherine's obstinacy could only mean that she was conspiring against him. Buckden had proved, after all, too open and unsafe. It had been visited by two recalcitrant Observant Friars whom Cromwell had since clapped in the Tower but from whom he could wring no confession of the Queen's treason, and by other persons, muffled in their cloaks, whom Cromwell had not caught. The country people were obviously ill affected, and the Queen was not a prisoner at all except by her own consent, a circumstance galling to Henry's pride. Henry seized, therefore, on Catherine's request to be allowed to move to a drier house, as an excuse to arrange for her closer imprisonment.

Earlier in December, the Duke of Suffolk, grumbling that he would rather break a leg than go on such an errand, was sent northwards with harsh instructions. He was to exact an oath from all Catherine's servants to call her nothing but "the old Princess Dowager" (a method of separating her from her most loyal followers), to dismiss those who refused, and to convey her and the rest either to Fotheringay, a decent residence but strongly fortified and notoriously malarial, or to Somersham, a lonely, decaying house in the midst of the Cambridge fens, surrounded by ponds and marshes and accessible only by a single road that was in part a causeway, easy to watch and defensible by a handful against an army. Either residence would make conspiracy difficult and rescue almost impossible. Somersham was reputed to be even more unhealthy than Fotheringay. Perhaps Henry hoped that, with a little help, Nature might relieve him of the embarrassment of his wife's continued existence. Or perhaps he only hoped that the dampness, acting on her rheumatism, would make her willing to agree to anything for the sake of drier lodging.

Suffolk reached Buckden about December 18[21] and opened his first interview with Catherine by repeating the bribes offered her if she would acquiesce in the Dunstable decree. When she merely looked scornful, he added that he was obliged to warn her that her refusal would incur the King's severest displeasure. She answered then, vehemently, that she would rather die a thousand deaths than blacken her honor and her husband's. Suffolk explained the rest of his charge. He might put his oath to her servants if he liked, Catherine told him, but she would not be served by any who did not call her Queen. At the mention of Fotheringay, she cried out; she had always hated the place; she would not go there. Somersham she refused also. The dampness there would be worse than at Buckden; she would take her death of it. They might drag her there by force, but for her to consent to go there unforced would be consenting to her own death, therefore a sin. Suffolk had no tact, and the unpleasantness of his task made him brutal, but the Queen was not to be bullied by Charles Brandon. When he went on shouting, she swept into her bed chamber and shut the door on him. Thereafter Suffolk addressed his threats, his arguments, and his appeals to two inches of iron-studded oak.

In exasperation he turned to the servants, but the disloyal or faint-hearted had fallen away before the Queen came to Buckden. One by one, English and Spaniards alike, they made him the same answer: They had sworn loyalty to Catherine as Queen; they could not address her by any other title. . . . Servants the Duke of Suffolk thought he could deal with. His own men had occupied the house, and he clapped all of the Queen's household into the porter's ward, threatening dire things, and hoping they would be as uncomfortable as he was. He went back to shout through the closed door to the north tower where Catherine and two or three maids stood siege, and got no answer. On second thought he released three Spaniards, Llandaff, the confessor, De la Sá, the physician, and De Soto, the apothecary, and saw them cautiously admitted past the great oak door, but his consideration for Catherine's comfort and his belated effort at diplomacy had no effect. That night Buckden had the air of a castle taken by storm with the last of the garrison holding out in one tower.

Suffolk and the Earl of Sussex and Dr. Sampson held a council on the morrow and got nowhere. The door was unconvinced. In the street of Buckden village there were more men than usual, standing about in puzzled knots, some of them handling choppers or bill hooks with unconvincing casualness, giving black looks to Suffolk's armed guard. Suffolk again tried arguing with the door. Then he sat down and wrote a disheartened letter to Henry, a desperate one to Cromwell, a gloomy one to Norfolk. There was no provision for an emergency like this in his instructions. What was he to do? He looked out in the street where the crowd seemed to be thickening, and decided to send off appeals to all the local magistrates he could think of. That crowd had an ugly look.

Five days passed, and no courier came from London, where by now the Christmas revels would be merry. More oddly still, no word came from any of the local magistrates; no justice of the peace whom these yokels knew and would listen to appeared to tell them to disperse. The crowd outside, silent, watchful, seemed to change but never to diminish. One saw now and then a steel cap, or a man on horseback, or faces which at a distance might be those of Gostwicks or Allingtons or Hyndes, Tanfields or Mordaunts or Malorys, or others of the local gentry, but no one offered the Duke of Suffolk Christmas courtesies, and from the tower room came no token of surrender. It was a siege within a siege.

Desperate to do something, Suffolk ordered the hangings in the great hall taken down, the beds dismantled, the table furniture packed, the sumpter mules loaded, a litter made ready in the courtyard. The crowd only watched with a subdued alertness. Suffolk went back to shout through the closed door. All the furniture was packed. Buckden was to be abandoned. Since the Princess Dowager would not yield to persuasion, she must yield to force. She was to be taken to Somersham, whether she consented or not, by order of the King.

Catherine's voice answered. Force was force. The Duke must break down the door and have her carried to the litter. She would not walk a step. The beef-witted hero of a thousand tourneys, and as many love affairs, the victorious invader of France, the King's former brother-in-law and always loyal echo, perspired in the December cold. Charles Brandon did not lack physical courage. But to break down that door and face the lady behind it, with every prospect afterwards of seeing his company torn to pieces by the crowd, and of being ingloriously knocked on the head, himself, by some bumpkin armed with a flail or a paddle – no, he would rather risk the wrath of Henry VIII. Abruptly Suffolk ordered his men to release the Queen's servants and rally in the courtyard, prepared to ride. To cover his chagrin he arrested, more or less at random, some of the Queen's English household and had them bound with ropes. Among them was Thomas Abell, who went back thus to the Tower, after brief liberty, to wait there five years for his death. Suffolk left a token guard in the gatehouse, had a last word with Sussex and Sampson and Paulet in the devastated great hall; then they all clattered off, councilors, pensioners, men-at-arms, towards the London road. The puzzled crowd of country folk watched their retreat in silence; then, sure the strangers were gone, dispersed in little groups to their homes. Buckden looked like a castle sacked by mercenaries, but Catherine and her faithful few were left in possession.

ii

Between the lines of Chapuys' second report on the affair at Buckden, written after Mr. Secretary had given him a semiofficial version of it, one catches the flicker of Cromwell's grin. Among the things Chapuys and Cromwell had in common was an appreciation of the heroic Duke of Suffolk as a faintly comic figure. Their enjoyment of the picture of Suffolk kicking his heels outside a locked door was unshadowed by the fact that in this December of 1533 Cromwell was maturing plans which included presenting Henry with a legal excuse for Queen Catherine's execution, and Chapuys, thoroughly aware of what Cromwell was doing, was frantically counterworking him in England and abroad.

To Cromwell, the attack on Catherine's life was hardly more than an incident in his larger plans. He had always seen Henry's divorce as an opportunity for the monarchy to seize all the powers held in England by the Pope, and thus make the King more absolute in his own domains than any other ruler in Europe – or at least more independent of outside interference. Whether it ever occurred to Cromwell that by making a system of what had begun as an accident – the reliance on Parliament to legalize every step of his revolution – he was actually producing a limited monarchy in an absolute state, we have no means of knowing. If Henry himself ever thought of the matter, he probably considered that when to his ordinary sources of revenue he could add absolute control of the enormous wealth of the English Church, he would be rich enough to dispense with Parliament forever. Cromwell's business sense may have told him that, impressive as he knew the wealth of the Church to be, it would be evanescent in royal hands; his political shrewdness certainly told him that Henry's subjects would never permit the King to steal so much unless he shared the plunder with them. Whether he foresaw at all that the dispersion of the Church lands among those rich enough to pay for, or influential enough to demand, part of the loot would create in England a new ruling class, more dangerous to the personal authority of the King than the old feudal aristocracy and the authority of Rome combined, seems doubtful. In the political thinking of the early sixteenth century the personal power of the prince and the authority of the crown were scarcely distinguished, and Cromwell seems to have had little taste for abstract speculation. If the King could defend himself from outside interference and enforce his views on Parliament while the revolution was being carried through, the remoter future could take care of itself.

In every step the English government took, at home or abroad, after Anne's coronation, one can see the practical business mind of Cromwell at work. Up to the time Cranmer's bulls were issued, the government needed the co-operation of the Pope to legalize Henry's second marriage, and had obtained what it wanted through French influence at Rome – therefore, from the English point of view, the closer Francis I and Clement VII drew together, the better. The policy Cromwell now had in mind, however, made the hostility of the Pope at no distant date inevitable, and consequently the more

French and papal policy converged, the farther France would eventually draw from England. This may explain the apparent ineptitude with which the English ambassadors behaved during the friendly conference between Francis and Clement in November, 1533. "As fast as I study to win the Pope, you study to lose him," Francis raged at them. He thought they were merely stupid. He realized only later that English policy was anticipating his choice between England's friendship and that of Rome.

France, however, was a Catholic monarchy, with serious interests in Italy. Francis' final choice was uncertain. Even before the Marseilles conference Cromwell had begun to look for allies capable of checking the Emperor and not susceptible to papal influence. With sardonic amusement Chapuys watched Cromwell's expensive and useless involvements with the Lutheran princes of Germany and the radical burghers of Lubeck. The idea of an alliance with the German protestants was so logical that Cromwell continued to worry at it whenever he felt a danger of the Emperor's intervention, but England's need never supplied material enough to lay the foundations of a stable foreign policy on the quicksand of German politics.

The most logical alliance of all for England, of course, was with the Emperor himself. It was the defect natural to Cromwell's qualities that he found it difficult to understand chivalric notions of duty and honor and the sanctity of tradition, and was impatient of the folly of preferring an ideal to a practical advantage. That the Emperor should refuse the profits he could draw from alliance with England simply because of concern over the treatment of his elderly aunt seemed to Cromwell an affront to human intelligence, and he was startled to find his sensible friend Chapuys failing to agree with him. Instead of nodding when Cromwell suggested that it would be an excellent thing if Queen Catherine were to die quietly, since only her troubles prevented an Anglo-Imperialist alliance, Chapuys sputtered with alarm and indignation. The ambassador found the suggestion outrageous, and he added stiffly that the Queen's sudden demise would provoke the gravest suspicions, which he, for one, would consider only too well founded. In fact, he was obliged to warn Cromwell that, as the Emperor's representative, he would hold King Henry and the English ministers directly responsible should anything untoward happen to the Queen or the Princess. Cromwell shrugged.[22]

Chapuys went back to the embassy to repeat to Catherine his warning never to eat any food not prepared in her presence by her own maids, and tasted by them in advance, and to take what additional precautions he could against Mary's being given "something too much to eat" by her guardians, as, he gloomily told the Emperor, seemed very likely to happen. But Cromwell was not thinking of poison. Whatever his own preference for direct methods might have been under other circumstances, he was the readier to respect Henry's old-fashioned prejudices because the parliamentary campaign he was planning offered, among other, greater advantages, a way of eliminating Catherine and Mary, or rendering them harmless.

In spite of Chapuys' threats Cromwell felt fairly confident that there would be no foreign intervention for the moment. This was the time, then, to complete the legal structure begun by the Act of Appeals, and place all the Pope's former authority firmly in the King's hands. There would be opposition from the Queen's friends, and from other conservatives, but the government was learning to deal with parliamentary opposition. When Parliament reassembled in January 1534, the chief proved friends of the Queen in the House of Lords were conspicuously absent. Their attendance had been countermanded by royal order which none of them except Fisher, who was already practically in custody, had the courage to ignore. Others in both houses were spared the dilemma of having to vote either against the King or against their consciences by royal licenses to be absent. The printing presses ground out propaganda attacking the Church and in favor of the King's new marriage, every preacher in the kingdom was ordered to preach on the same theme, and "against the authority of the bishop of Rome," and Henry and Anne exerted themselves to be affable to doubtful members, some of whom could be caught with smiles and flattery, some with more substantial favors. But again Cromwell's chief weapon was terror.

The Nun of Kent and her unfortunate associates were still in the Tower. That no adequate evidence had been secured to convict any highly placed person of complicity in her pitiful "treason" did not prevent the circulation of rumors, involving her with now this prominent conservative and his friends, now with that. When the government brought in against her a bill of attainder, most terrible legal weapon of the Tudor despotism, which included among those to be executed without trial the two greatest Englishmen of the age, John Fisher, Bishop of Rochester, and Sir Thomas More, and when the rumor spread that other names, many others, might be added, a general *sauve qui peut* began among the Queen's friends and the defenders of the old religion, most of whom could remember some incident connecting them with the Nun. The mysterious arrest on Cranmer's orders of Bishop Nixe, an arch-conservative, increased the panic. Chapuys heard that the guns of the Tower were pointed against the city, and that the houses of the Boleyn faction were full of armed men. It is to the credit of Parliament that, in spite of these alarms, there were still some spurts of opposition. Catholic members came to assure Chapuys that if only the Emperor, or the Pope, would make some sign, if only they had some point round which to rally, they could still muster enough strength to defeat the government's bills. And when More boldly asked the right to defend himself before the Lords, his name and Fisher's were taken out of the act of attainder. That gesture had already served its purpose. In the atmosphere of terror it created the divided and discouraged opposition resisted but weakly. By March 30, 1534, every point in Cromwell's program had become a law.

The steps were simple, meant in the main to transfer to the King all that was left of the power of the Pope. An act suppressing annates completed the statute of 1532, and reduced the bishops in law to what most of them had long been in fact, mere royal appointees. An act confirming the submission of the clergy terminated what was left of the independent powers of Convocation, and made the King's court of Chancery the supreme court of ecclesiastical appeal. These two acts riveted the royal supremacy on the secular clergy. An act suppressing Peter's Pence ended the last payments left to Rome, asserted the complete independence of the English Church, and carried an inconspicuous rider affirming to the King the right to visit and reform all religious houses in the realm. This completed the constitutional breach with Rome, subjected the regular clergy to the King, and left them helpless against the spoliation that was soon to come. The capstone of the program was the Act of Succession. An argumentative preamble declared the King's first marriage null, his second valid; the body of the act entailed the succession to the throne on the children of the King by Anne Boleyn, and made it high treason to slander the King's marriage or question the succession by "writing, print, deed or act," and misprision of treason to impugn it in words; the sting in the tail of the act required every subject to take an oath to observe its contents upon pain of misprision of treason.

Every revolution invents new treasons. Cromwell's now had its test of loyalty, and the commissions to collect the oaths provided its revolutionary tribunals. It was almost incidental that Catherine and her daughter could not escape the operation of the act, if the government chose to use it against them, without renouncing, the one her claims as a married woman, the other her right to the throne. No other honest Catholic could escape it either. Henry and Cromwell had the means now to silence any opposition short of rebellion. The ax, as Henry had learned from Wolsey, is a sharp argument. Having served their purpose, the Nun and her companions, the first excuse for launching the terror, were taken from the Tower on April 20, 1534, and executed at Tyburn with the full barbarities of the penalty for treason.

All this while Catherine remained in the gutted castle of Buckden. Some of her staff had been arbitrarily carried off by Suffolk, some of the tapestries were never rehung, some of the bed-stuffs and the plate were missing. With strange men-at-arms in the courtyard and the great hall, the Queen kept to her own apartments, hearing many masses through the window into the chapel, sewing a little, shivering in the great bed while her maids cooked her dinner before the bedroom fire. In February she wrote at length to her nephew her opinion of the negotiations that still dragged on at Rome, sparing Charles nothing of her indignant scorn at the Roman dallying which had caused her misfortunes, and letting him see that she held him, too, in part responsible. She had heard from Chapuys of the threat to Mary and herself in the pending Act of Succession, but her anxiety was still for the shattered prestige of the papal see. "I would not for anything in the world fail to inform . . . all persons capable of giving them remedy, of the evils before my eyes. . . . Beg his Holiness to act as he ought for God's service and the tranquility of Christendom. All the other considerations, even the lives of myself and my daughter ought to be put aside. . . . There is no need to tell you of our sufferings. . . . I could not endure so much, did I not think these things suffered for God's sake. . . . As long as I live I shall not fail to defend our rights." And in a desperate postscript: "I beg you to show more affection for me, and for my daughter." [23]

At last, in March of 1534, the very month in which Henry's submissive Parliament was passing the acts which confirmed his triumph over the Church, the long hesitation at Rome was ended. On

March 24, Clement VII in full consistory gave his final sentence on the marriage of Henry and Catherine, pronouncing it good and valid in the eyes of God and the Church. Rome blazed with torches and rang with cries of "Empire and Spain!" and Dr. Ortiz wrote that this was a victory over enemies let loose from hell, but the deputation which came to Catherine at Buckden six weeks later did not invite her to return to her husband. Instead the royal commissioners were directed to exact from "the old Princess Dowager" and the servants remaining in her household the oath recently required by Parliament to maintain and defend the unlawfulness of the King's first marriage and the legitimacy of Anne Boleyn's child, under pain of treason for refusal. Clement's decision had come too late.

Chapter Five

CATHERINE MADE her formal appeal to Rome on the eighteenth of June, 1529. Rome finally decided in her favor on the twenty-fourth of March, 1534. There was, actually, no fresh trial at all. The evidence given at Blackfriars was reviewed in so far as it was held pertinent; Dr. Ortiz submitted a brief and affidavits, but no point in the Roman ruling turned upon them because the question of the consummation of Catherine's first marriage was held to be irrelevant; Rome ruled simply that the dispensation of Julius II was adequate, basing its judgment on the bull known in England from the first, without finding the support of the brief, subsequently produced, in any way necessary to the case. The power to dispense was asserted, and the marriage declared valid by reason of the dispensation. Even in its strictly legal aspect, the decision was less comforting to Catherine than it might have been, but had it been given four years earlier, it might have served.

During that four years of delay, however, while Clement's hesitations and ill-timed concessions surrendered one citadel after another into Henry's hands, a legal revolution had taken place in England. The English Church had seceded from the papal jurisdiction, and unless the whole work of the revolution could be undone, no papal decision would have any force in England. For four years Catherine had kept demanding the final sentence, kept pointing out that the longer the delay, the stronger the measures that would be needed, kept hoping, long after others despaired, that the Pope might act in time. Now it was clear that no action, short of the application of physical force, could have any effect. The parliamentary session of 1534 had flung down the challenge to Christendom.

Had those four years and more since she faced Henry at Blackfriars not held so many disappointments for Catherine, she might have found the final realization harder to bear. As it was, she had had a long time to make up her mind, and many warnings from Chapuys of the hard dilemma she would have to face; and she felt she knew her course. As she told Mountjoy's delegation, the preceding July, she would obey the King in all things not contrary to God's laws, but she would not deny her marriage. If martyrdom was required of her, she was ready.

That was not an idle phrase. The first commission which came to Buckden to ask her to take the oath laid down by the Act of Succession had made no threats, and retired after she told them that she stood on the Pope's final sentence, recently given at Rome. But the second, a fortnight later, headed by Lee, Archbishop of York, and her former councilor, Cuthbert Tunstall, Bishop of Durham, had sterner instructions.[1] They obliged Catherine and her household to listen to a reading of the Act, the rambling argument of its preamble punctuated by scathing comments from the Queen, and then Lee, turning to her, warned her solemnly that she was not exempt from the penalties set down.

"If one of you has a commission to execute this penalty upon me," she replied instantly, "I am ready. I ask only that I be allowed to die in the sight of the people."

Such was, of course, the melancholy legal right of any person convicted of treason. Possibly Catherine was thinking only of the example of firmness which her death might set to all those whose faith the policy of the government was sure to try. She never expressed, one is tempted to think she never felt, the slightest doubts of her own courage, even on the scaffold, and she seems to have thought a great deal of the encouragement her constancy might bring to weaker souls. Now and then it seems to have crossed her mind that such a martyrdom would expiate the harm she had unwittingly brought her adopted country. But public martyrdom was the satisfaction Henry's government could least afford to give the Queen. No one, so far as we know, in the royal council dared to advise such a course. No jury of the Lords, however packed, could be relied on to convict her. No prison in the realm could hold her, once the people knew she was a prisoner. And even if the people were unable to set her free before she reached the scaffold, they would surely have had the lives of every one of her executioners.

Lee and Tunstall dropped their idle threat. They could not bully the Queen; they found it hard enough to bully even the poorest of her servants. All her household made the same answer they had made to Suffolk; they could not swear that their queen was not Queen. In the end, the bishops arrested some of Catherine's people, accepted from others a modified oath or none at all, and went back to Huntingdon to write their unsatisfactory report.

Not daring to kill Catherine, not even daring to commit her to the Tower, yet knowing that while she lived she was the potential leader round whom all the growing forces of discontent would rally at a word, the government was in a quandary. The best interim solution anyone had been able to think of was to take advantage of her application for a drier residence to remove her, and the handful of her followers, to Kimbolton, half a day's ride from Buckden, a gloomy fortified manor house whose thick walls and wide moat, recalling the lawless days of the Wars of the Roses, made it a somewhat stronger prison than the episcopal palace at Buckden. At Kimbolton Sir Edmund Bedingfield and Sir Edward Chamberlayn, two gentlemen on whose loyalty Henry thought he could rely, were appointed respectively steward and chamberlain of her household. Bedingfield's servants replaced those she had lost, and the steward was given strict orders to permit no one to visit her without special license from the King.

Catherine's removal to Kimbolton took place in the middle of

May, 1534, apparently while Lee and Tunstall were at Huntingdon. After the change of residence her mode of life was curious. The new officers of her household were sworn to address her only as "Princess Dowager." She would recognize no one who did not approach her as if she were still Queen. In consequence, she remained shut up in her own apartments, seeing no one except her few remaining personal attendants, more strictly imprisoned by her own pride than by her husband's orders. Her attendants included four faithful Spaniards, her confessor, her physician, her *maestrasala* and her apothecary, two grooms of the chamber, three maids of honor, and some six or eight other women including inferior servants. Her apartments were drier and more comfortable than those at Buckden; some of her windows looked out across the moat and over the village roofs to the gently rolling country beyond; behind her chapel was a narrow walled garden where on fine days she could walk undisturbed, warming herself in the sunshine. But for nearly a year after she entered Kimbolton she never penetrated the rest of the house or held any direct communication with her jailers, and when the drawbridge was raised after her entrance it was lowered for her only once again.

The Queen's seclusion in Kimbolton worried Chapuys the more because in the first month after her removal there he had little information about her circumstances, and heard nothing from her directly beyond the contents of two enigmatic little notes, each suggesting that he visit her. The fear of foul play was never far from the ambassador's mind. He imagined the Queen's imprisonment as even more strict than it was, and his anxiety was not allayed when his repeated applications to Cromwell, and finally to Henry himself, for license to visit her were put off with lame excuses. When he had waited in vain for a month, constantly promised a license to visit Kimbolton and constantly put off, he could bear it no longer; he announced that he was going on a pilgrimage to Our Lady of Walsingham and expected to see the Queen on the way.[2]

He took care to give this act of defiance the widest publicity. He spread the news of his journey through the City, invited the leading Spanish merchants to accompany him, mounted all his own suite, even to the lackeys, and dressed them all in fresh liveries — and thus assembled for his start more than sixty horsemen, caparisoned as if they were a king's escort. Before them went all the drums and trumpets to be hired in London. To this defiant music the cavalcade paraded up one London street and down another, and when the City gates were behind them and the cortege was raising the July dust along the Old North Road, Chapuys kept his musicians in the van, with orders to blow their loudest at the entrance to every village, that all the world might note the Black Eagle and the Castles and Lions, and know that the ambassador of Spain and the Empire was en route to Kimbolton.

Halfway on their journey the procession was overtaken by a gentleman of the court with a message from Henry: The ambassador was by no means to visit the Princess Dowager. Chapuys thanked the messenger noncommittally, without showing signs of turning back, and the gentleman, after eying him dubiously, spurred on ahead of him to Kimbolton. Not till they had passed St. Neot's did the troop finally halt. Less than five miles from Kimbolton, Francisco Felipez brought Chapuys a message from the Queen. The King, her husband, had forbidden her to receive him, therefore it would be as well if he came no farther. In recognition of his courtesy there would be a present of wine and game for all his escort. In deference to the Queen's wish, Chapuys halted where he was, but he saw no reason why his gentlemen and some of the young Spaniards who had ridden with them should not go forward to within sight of the castle. They rode on, in fact, to the very edge of the moat, a gaily dressed band, singing the songs of Spain, making their horses leap and curvet under the Queen's windows. With them was a servant of the ambassador's, one of those Spanish fools in whose antics Catherine had once delighted. His acrobatic buffoonery drew more eyes than the prancing cavaliers; he tossed a locked casket over the wall; he capered on the edge of the moat with extravagant supplications for admittance until, tumbling into the slimy waters, he was hauled out amid crows of delight from Bedingfield's servants and the Queen's maids at the windows. It may be that the fool's behavior was as calculated as the band of musicians and every other move of the ambassador's journey. At any rate, it led to the exchange of volleys of Spanish banter between the household and the cavaliers, under cover of which any information desired could have been conveyed without the English being the wiser, and to the appearance of the Queen herself, smiling at an upper window. It had given the whole affair an air of innocent festivity, relaxing both Catherine's rigidity and Bedingfield's suspicions, and in the end the visiting Spaniards were entertained at supper in the great hall. When Chapuys turned back towards London, going another way so that as many people as possible should see that he had been to visit the Queen and been refused admittance, he professed not to have learned why Catherine had wanted him to come; but he had a clearer notion of the state of affairs within Kimbolton, and (though he took care not to boast of it in his letters) he seems to have established the channels which did not fail thereafter to keep him in close touch with the Queen.

ii

Besides his personal anxiety about Catherine's welfare and his wish to underline for English eyes the continued interest of the powerful Emperor in the discarded queen, Chapuys had other motives for his journey to Kimbolton which he did not care to make too explicit in official dispatches. He needed first-hand knowledge of the place of Catherine's detention, and surer and more private means of communicating with her household, because he had not yet given up the hope that the Queen might yet be persuaded to place herself at the head of a movement to overturn the throne. By the spring of 1534, Chapuys was already at the center of a widespread network of conspiracy for counterrevolution. In spite of every discouragement, he was busily digging underground galleries to connect one powder magazine of discontent with another, twisting every filament of treason that came to his hand into a single fuse, blowing on the tinder of rebellion, ready to spring his complicated mine as soon as he could get the signal.

His predecessor Mendoza's dispatches had presented Chapuys with the first sketch of a possible insurrection, but Mendoza's contacts had been mostly with Spanish merchants in London and with a few rash enthusiasts whose names he could have learned from de Praet, and though he thought the idea a sound one, during his brief embassy he had not given the malcontents much encouragement. Without serious leaders, Mendoza had written, the popular unrest, widespread as it was, would pass off in smoke. Chapuys was as contemptuous as Mendoza of the utility of a mere leaderless mob, but the longer he stayed in England the better he understood how much of Henry's rule depended on popular support, and the more pains and money he spent in trying to gauge the pressure of public opinion. All his reports confirmed that the King and his government were increasingly unpopular.

The country folk were ripe for revolt. There had been no serious popular insurrection in England for a generation, not since the rising of the Cornishmen in '97; but the English peasantry, better fed, better armed, and reputed more turbulent than any of the Continent, were apt to such occasions, and the riots of 1524, and widespread tax resistance in 1525, had shown that the old temper was not dead. In the decade since 1525 the causes of discontent had deepened. Taxation was not heavy by Continental standards but, even though Wolsey, the master extortioner, was ruined and dead, it had grown heavier, year by year. Crops were poor in 1533 and

1534. Inclosures had gone on, on the whole, more rapidly since Wolsey's fall; the old complaints that plows were stopped in the furrow and the sheep were eating up the men had not diminished; there were more homeless than ever on the roads, and for every yeoman or cottager turned from his land fear flickered at a hundred neighboring hearthsides. To all this vague unrest, the King's policy gave a focus. The word going about at country taverns that the crops had never done well since the old queen was put away could be more dangerous than a new tax. Religious innovations, also, always unsettle the minds of peasantry. And not only peasantry. There would be fewer squires to rally to the King, and fewer parish priests to preach submission and contentment. The regular clergy, very influential in some sections, were taking alarm at the King's policies, and some of the old queen's favorite order of Observant Friars were thought to be spreading active sedition.

If the towns stayed loyal, however, the King could ride out a serious revolt in the country. But Chapuys felt he knew how to create dissension in the towns as serious as any peasant rising. Study of the question had convinced him that a stoppage of trade with Flanders would produce panic and revolt in England before the Netherlands could be seriously affected. If the towns were not so hostile to religious change as the countryside, it was the townsmen who most feared the consequences of a papal interdict and the Emperor's hostility. If Henry had his greatest personal popularity in and around London, so had Catherine. Chapuys had cultivated immediate contacts, chiefly with Londoners. A man of the middle class himself, he had no contempt for tradesmen, and he took as much pains with the merchants – not even confining himself to the great ones – as most conscientious ambassadors took with Dukes and royal counselors. He entertained English merchants at the embassy, was always ready with helpful information and free legal advice about the pitfalls of trade in all corners of the Emperor's far-flung dominions, and quick to show his sympathy and exert his influence when called upon. In return he patiently probed their attitudes and their knowledge of their countrymen, and it was chiefly what he knew of Londoners that led Chapuys to be confident that his mine would not fail to explode.

Neither merchants nor peasants, however, could lead a successful revolt in England in the 1530's. The peasants were incapable of planned action; the merchants would act only to protect their profits. The prestige and the political experience necessary for a real counterrevolution were still the monopoly of the old feudal ruling class. The nobles were no longer that formidable strength which had tossed the crown from hand to hand fifty, sixty, seventy years before. No one or two or three of them, in these days, could raise anything like an army among his own tenantry and vassals, and if the activity of royal courts and royal officials had clipped the barons' local power, the events of the Tudor reigns had gravely impaired, also, their solidarity as a class. But, under the crown, they were still the ruling class, still the only possible captains and high functionaries, and the loyalty of a preponderant majority of them was still necessary for a stable government. And it was still psychologically possible for the preponderant majority to refuse their loyalty. Fifty years had failed to produce among most of them any rooted attachment to the Tudors, and the sturdy traditions of their warrior caste had not been much infected as yet by the middle class sentiment of national patriotism. Their strongest feeling about the Crown was that only men of their own station should be the executors of its authority and the beneficiaries of its favors, and they were not yet far enough removed from feudal independence not to feel cramped and crushed between the descending millstone of royal absolutism and the thrust of the rising moneyed class. The appearance from among this class of a royal favorite lording it over them could still make them think of rebellion.

When Chapuys first came to England all the nobility were pleased by Wolsey's fall. They saw, in the ostensible leadership on the council of the Dukes of Norfolk and Suffolk, and the return to an active place on it of other men of old names, a promise of the kind of government they liked best, completely dominated by the aristocracy and guaranteed by the appointment of More as Lord Chancellor both against the excessive influence of the Church and against too wide a divergence from doctrinal orthodoxy. In the first two years of his embassy, Chapuys received from highly placed persons many vague messages of sympathy and encouragement, many more or less open expressions of regard for the Queen and the Emperor, and of hopes for Henry's reconciliation with both, but few signs that any persons of consequence were ready to consider open rebellion. At the time, that attitude accorded with Chapuys' conciliatory instructions from the Emperor, and suited his own unfixed views.

The same events, however, which convinced Chapuys that Henry's government could and must be overthrown had crystallized the feudal opposition. The nobility were shocked by the treatment of the Queen. They were disturbed by the attacks on the Church. They were alienated by the emergence into power of Thomas Cromwell. And they were tempted to rebellion by the very fact that the widespread popular discontent offered the opportunity for a successful rising, and the profits of palace revolutions had always been among the perquisites of their class. Many of the oldest and most influential families among the higher nobility had been attached to Catherine by particular ties of gratitude and affection. Most of the heads of those families would have acquiesced, however, in the divorcc proceedings, even though acquiescing sadly and reluctantly, had the divorce been decently carried out and followed by a remarriage they could approve; but Anne's arrogance, their dislike of the Boleyns, and the irregularity and brutality of Henry's behavior inclined a number of the greater nobles to listen to the indignation of their wives. As a whole, the barons had little regard for the Pope, and were incapable of being interested in a dispute over the constitution of the Church; Clement VII must have seemed to many of them merely an interfering Italian priest, and the Submission of the Clergy no more than the assertion of royal prerogative as against privileged royal officials; but by instinct they were conservatives in religion, suspicious of Lutheranism and other new-fangled innovations, and the very lines of class tradition and interest which weakened their national patriotism made them more conscious of the ancient unity of Christendom, of the interests and loyalties they shared with their fellow nobles on the Continent. Moreover, the growing threat to the religious houses touched most of them on a sensitive spot. Hardly one great family but felt a vested interest in at least one monastery or convent: their ancestors had founded these asylums, and now slept in tombs lining their aisles and choirs; they, themselves, expected so to sleep in their turn, profiting by the prayers contracted for centuries ago; meanwhile the monastery was a kind of annex to the family property, its abbot often a kinsman, its bailiffs and stewards clients, and its revenues frequently subject to a charge for the benefit of some relative whom otherwise primogeniture might have disinherited. A threat to the monasteries was a threat to themselves. Most of all, perhaps, they were outraged by the source of that threat: the plebeian, Thomas Cromwell. They had resented the pre-eminence of Wolsey, because, even though a Cardinal Archbishop, he was unmistakably a vulgarian; but the unsanctified Cromwell was no better than Wolsey's lackey — Edward II and Richard II had lost their crowns for cosseting favorites less unsuitable. Among the descendants of barons who had often rearranged the succession to the English throne, and usually profited by doing so, ancient memories stirred.

One by one, from different motives and with different degrees of sincerity, one peer after another got in touch with Chapuys, and the ambassador, who had studied them all more diligently than they supposed, had for each an appropriate word and, for each whom he thought he could trust, an appointed place in the puzzle he was fitting together. Not even to the secrecy of cipher, not even to those special couriers who slipped away from London on merchant vessels bound for Antwerp or crossed inconspicuously from Orewell amid bolts of Norfolk cloth, – thus escaping, Chapuys hoped, the constant vigilance of Cromwell's agents, – did the ambassador ever commit a full outline of his plan. Sometimes a hint in a private note to Granvelle reveals the name of "the good old lord" cautiously referred to in the next official dispatch, sometimes clues in a whole series of letters have to be fitted together to make even one part of the scheme coherent. And some parts Chapuys kept entirely to himself, being anxious to tell the Emperor only enough to convince him that the rising would be easy, widespread, and certain to succeed. Parts of what Chapuys suppressed came out later, some in 1536 at the time of the Pilgrimage of Grace, some in 1538 after "the Exeter conspiracy," some later still in bits of the ambassador's own correspondence or scraps picked up by the pertinacious Monsieur Castillon, ambassador of France. An enigmatic ciphered list of names with figures that may mean "horse" and "foot," in the Brussels archives, has a place in the picture, and a document headed "What the ambassador's nephew told the Council about England." Some of the plot must remain obscure forever. But some parts are perfectly clear, and we can identify several main groups of conspirators by 1535.[3]

The boldest and most outspoken were the northern lords, chiefly John Hussey and Thomas Darcy, both great barons on the northern marches, and both, later, taken and executed for treason. Lord Hussey, whom Henry had trusted with the guardianship of the Princess Mary, sought out Chapuys secretly to tell him that the lords and gentlemen of the northern counties were determined to remedy the evils of the kingdom and appealed to the Emperor for aid, referring Chapuys for further information to his "brother" Lord Darcy of Templehurst. Chapuys had already been in touch with Darcy, who had sent him, the Christmas before, a little medal with the significant arms of the Poles; he found Darcy ready to talk frankly. The King's conduct, Darcy said, was such an offense against God and reason that, although he had always counted himself the most loyal of subjects, he could countenance it no longer. He was going north, where every parish priest could be relied on to preach against a heretic king, and where sixteen hundred lords and gentlemen of his opinion would rally to the banner of the crucifix and the imperial standard. He and Hussey, he said, Sir Thomas Dacre ("lord Dacre of the North"), and the Earl of Derby were the leaders, and they were sure of every great man north of Humber, save only the Earl of Northumberland, with whom they were ready to deal. Of the Emperor they asked help in reaching an understanding with the Scots, arms to equip the poorer gentry, a small force of gunners from Flanders, and some sort of naval demonstration at Thames' mouth to hold Henry's attention until their host could gather. Chapuys counseled patience for the moment, held out hopes about the arms and the Scots, and was pleased to hear that, with or without the Emperor, the North would not wait much longer. When he went north, after Christmas, Darcy sent Chapuys a New Year's gift of a handsome dagger, "as a sign it was time for sword play."

Darcy was a tower of strength, an experienced soldier in foreign and border wars, Knight of the Garter, and one of the greater magnates of the North, boasting that he could raise eight thousand men among his own tenants and friends. Thomas Dacre of Greystock was even more formidable, warden of the Western Marches, tough fighter, slippery negotiator, chief prop of Henry's rule in the border counties. Made uneasy by the royal flirtation with heresy, Dacre had been talking with his friends across the border, and had gone so far that Henry and Cromwell had brought him before his peers on a charge of treason. The outcome showed how much loyalty Henry had lost in recent years. Dacre was less highly connected than Buckingham had been, had made more enemies, and was accused on more substantial grounds, but the peers acquitted him, a result almost unheard of in Tudor trials for treason. Now he had gone northwards, thoroughly disgruntled and determined on revenge.

Once satisfied of Darcy's good faith, Chapuys put him in touch with two important recruits: Harry Percy, Earl of Northumberland, the one great noble they had not counted on, and William, Lord Sandys, Grand Chamberlain and Governor of Guisnes, "the first soldier in England," Darcy said, and worth an army in himself.

In the west, a second group of conspirators sought Chapuys' aid, their most formidable member the head of the Neville family, George, Lord Abergavenny, one of the last of the great barons of the Welsh marches, a tough old specimen of a breed nearly extinct. Abergavenny had fought at Bosworth and Stoke for the Tudors, been Warden of the Cinque Ports, and led a wing of the English host in France, but as a boy he had seen men with armor still spattered from the bloody fields of Barnet and Tewksbury, at a time when his family had boasted that the crown of England was in their gift. His loyalty to Henry VIII had been weakened first when his father-in-law, the Duke of Buckingham, had gone to the block and he, himself, briefly to the Tower, in 1521; he was a strong friend of the Queen's, and had been one of the first of the greater barons to show displeasure with Henry's policies and take himself off to his estates. His contemporary and chief rival in the marches, George Talbot, Earl of Shrewsbury, had been equally outspoken in his opposition to the King, and Chapuys counted on him to hold off, ... if he did not join the rebellion.

... ntented marcher lords and allied with them, ... ed about Henry Courtenay, Marquis of ... re, the most powerful nobleman in ... s thought, and since he was the ... rd IV, one of the nearest to ... hapuys was in touch chiefly through the Marchioness of Exeter, the daughter of Catherine's old chamberlain, Lord Mountjoy, an energetic, high-spirited woman who had been one of the first to talk openly to Chapuys of treason, and after her father's death, promised the adherence of the Blount connection to any revolt. Sir Thomas Arundel, Sir Henry Parker and Sir George Carewe were among those knit to the interlocked western groups, and so were the Poles, Henry, Lord Montague and his brother Sir Geoffrey, the sons of Catherine's friend, the Countess of Salisbury.

Support for the western rising could be counted on from Wales, where Henry's policy of assimilation, and the English officials he had sent to rule the Welsh, had alienated the sentimental affection of the mountaineers for their kinsman on the throne without as yet establishing his authority. Rhys ap Griffith, grandson of the great Welsh magnate who had helped crown Henry VII and the son of Catherine's former page, a bookish, dreamy young man, had quarreled with the government, transferred his loyalty to the Queen, been taken in a muddle-headed conspiracy from which Chapuys had held aloof, and hanged in 1531, the first of Catherine's partisans to die for her. Instead of breaking the power of the clan, the execution had transferred its leadership to a tougher and more formidable intriguer, the young man's maternal uncle, Sir James Griffith ap Howell of Castle Maelgwyn in Pembrokeshire. Sir James had been arrested in Wales, had talked his way out of prison, and since had been appearing in '33 in Scotland, in '34 in Ireland (whence he sent Chapuys information about the rebellion of the Fitzgeralds), in 1535 on the Continent. Wherever Sir James went, an atmosphere of conspiracy followed, alarm among English agents, activity among imperialist ones. Whenever the marche lords revolted, Sir James was ready to raise half Wales for t Queen. Altogether, the chances of a western rising looked so h ful to Chapuys that he was inclined to favor Wales or C over Yorkshire as the place to land the Emperor's merce

Of all these conspiracies, however, the one which drew its strength from the southeast and the home counties seemed the most ominous for Henry, and consequently the most encouraging to Chapuys. The very lords on whom Henry would have to rely, to protect the center of government and suppress the riots which Chapuys hoped to be able to produce in London, were seriously disaffected. Lord Edmund Bray assured Chapuys that at least twenty peers and great gentlemen, and more than a hundred knights, all eager to take up arms in defense of the Queen and the old religion, could be rallied on short notice in the heart of the kingdom. Sir Thomas Burgoyne, another son-in-law of Buckingham's and an able soldier, would be among them, and Sir Thomas Elyot, lately Henry's ambassador to the Emperor. The most distinguished of this group was probably Thomas Manners, Earl of Rutland, but their most surprising recruit was none other than Sir William Kingston, Constable of the Tower of London, on whose loyalty Henry relied completely. Nevertheless Chapuys felt sure of him, and sure with his help and Bray's of controlling the situation around London if need arose.

These three groups were merely the most active conspirators, those actually committed to armed rebellion. From many other magnates whom he thought less trustworthy, Chapuys had received assurances more or less treasonable in some fashion more or less direct, and beyond them again, he estimated that most of the remainder would be lukewarm in loyalty, and would wait to see which way the cat jumped. Suffolk, for instance, had just married again, this time the young daughter of the Countess of Willoughby, Maria de Salinas, who reported with pride that her new son-in-law would certainly not draw his sword against the Queen, might even be induced to strike in her favor. Norfolk, himself, was said to be wavering, offended at Anne, enraged by Cromwell's rise, alarmed for the old religion, and unlikely to risk his neck in defense of the King. Except for the Boleyns and their immediate party, the nobles on whom Henry could count with confidence were very few.

All this web of conspiracy, as Chapuys saw clearly, had one grave weakness. It had no center except the ambassador himself. Each group of feudal lords appealed to Chapuys for aid from the Emperor, avoiding contacts with the other groups. Only Chapuys had all the threads in his hands, and while the combined domestic strength of the malcontents seemed great enough to overthrow the government without foreign aid, there was no way to exert that strength without impetus and leadership, which none of them could supply of themselves. Unless they united, Henry could divide them by concessions and destroy them in detail. If any group rose before the others, and without a chief who could appeal to them all, the rest would hold off, and if the first revolt seemed to be going badly, common prudence would urge these wary, self-regarding nobles to join the King in stamping it out. Chapuys stirred and stirred the bits of his puzzle without much hope that they would click together unless he could supply the missing piece.

Obviously the missing center of the picture was Catherine herself. Not even a papal interdict and the Emperor's intervention would so surely bring all the latent feudal opposition out into the open as Catherine's declaration against her husband in her own and her daughter's name. It would be a secondary advantage that, once Catherine took the field, the Pope could hardly refuse to publish the brief deposing Henry which his chancery had already drawn up, and the Emperor could not deny his aunt's appeal for aid without intolerable loss of honor and prestige, and the risk of grave political disaster. If Catherine raised her standard, the rebels would probably never need more than the moral aid of papal and imperial support. She alone could give the signal to precipitate a general rising; her cause had become the center and symbol of all the forces of discontent in the kingdom. All the nobles would rally to her, because of personal friendship, because they recognized in her their idea of a leader, the one person whom the greatest of them could follow without loss of dignity, because her regency would offer the best chance of replacing Henry's rule by a stable, constitutional government under which they could consolidate their gains, and because they knew that her conservative views were close to their own, and that she would prefer to rule the kingdom through them. No one who knew her, who remembered the year of Flodden, or had seen her prompt decision and unbreakable courage in her recent trials, could think her incapable of leadership. And her personal popularity would be the best link between the nobles and the masses, would turn what might otherwise prove a mere feudal uprising into something like a national movement. Catherine's leadership would give Chapuys the counterrevolution he was hoping for, if anything could.

Henry VIII was only recognizing a naked political fact when, in 1535, he told his council: "The lady Catherine is a proud, stubborn woman of very high courage. If she took it into her head to take her daughter's part, she could quite easily take the field, muster a great array, and wage against me a war as fierce as any her mother Isabella ever waged in Spain."[4] The war Isabella waged in Spain had overturned the throne of Castile.

iii

It must have exasperated Chapuys sometimes to have the missing piece under his hand and be unable to fit it in. Not that he had any doubt, after he had reconnoitered Kimbolton for himself, of freeing Catherine whenever necessary. Even Henry knew, after Suffolk's fiasco at Buckden, that he could make no more than a pretence of holding Catherine a prisoner against her will. But it was her will to remain a prisoner. She agreed with Chapuys that stronger measures would have to be taken to restore England to the Catholic Church. What measures she would not say. Her horror of war, and particularly of civil war, her extreme reluctance to advance her own interests or even secure her own safety at the cost of bloodshed, her sense of the sacred duty of obedience to the King, and of her own further duty of obedience to her husband — strengthened, perhaps, by who can say what lingering fondness for the man — exactly balanced her outraged orthodoxy, kept her immobile at the fixed point where duty seemed to place her. In half-humorous despair Chapuys noted that the Queen had no further recommendations to make to the Emperor, and that all that had happened could not induce her to rebel against her husband, or even to speak harshly of him. The ambassador had never dared tell the Queen how far he had gone with the feudal conspirators; he dared do so now less than ever. To offer Catherine power and the opportunity for revenge would be the worst possible way to try to move her.

Chapuys had already attempted, and in vain, to play on a motive which he knew would be much more powerful with Catherine than any selfish one: her love of her daughter and her fears for Mary's safety. As soon as the Act of Succession was passed, Chapuys warned the Queen that Anne, whose fear and hatred of Mary had increased since she, herself, had failed to bear a son, would insist that Henry's daughter take the oath, swear that her mother was not married and that her own birth was illegitimate, or suffer the consequences. Chapuys may have intimated the two alternatives which he was considering for the Princess, the taking of the oath with private reservations which, under the canon law, would render it null, or instant flight beyond the King's reach. But for Catherine there were no alternatives. She could not recommend for her daughter any course she would not take herself. Before she left Buckden she wrote to Mary:

Daughter: I heard such tidings today that I do perceive if it be true, the time is come that Almighty God will prove you; and I am very glad of it, for I trust He doth handle you with a good love. I beseech you agree to His pleasure with a merry heart; and be you sure that, without fail, He will not suffer you to perish if you beware to offend Him. I pray you, good daughter, to offer yourself to Him. If any pangs come to you, shrive yourself; first make you clean; take heed of His commandments, and keep them as near as He will give you grace to do, for then you are sure armed. And if this lady [Lady Shelton, Anne Boleyn's aunt, who had just been placed over Mary by Anne's maneuvering] do come to you as it is spoken, if she do bring you a letter from the king, I am sure in the self-same letter you shall be commanded what you shall do. [The letter, of course, would contain the King's order to take the oath.] Answer with few words, obeying the King, your father, in everything save only that you will not offend God and lose your own soul [as Mary knew Catherine thought she would do if she admitted the legality of the divorce]; and go no further with learning and disputation in the matter. And wheresoever, and in whatsoever company you shall come, observe the King's commandments. Speak you few words and meddle nothing. I will send you two books in Latin; one shall be *De Vita Christi* with a declaration of the Gospels, and the other the Epistles of St. Jerome that he did write to Paula and Eustochium, and in them I trust you shall see good things. And sometimes for your recreation use your virginals or lute if you have any.

But one thing especially I desire you, for the love that you do owe unto God and unto me, to keep your heart with a chaste mind, and your body from all ill and wanton company, [not] thinking or desiring any husband for Christ's passion [Mary was to be told that if she consented to the oath, there would be no obstacle to her marriage either to the King of Scots or to a French prince]; neither determine yourself to any manner of living till this troublesome time be past. For I dare make sure that you shall see a very good end, and better than you can desire. I would God, good daughter, that you did know with how good a heart I do write this letter unto you. I never did one with a better, for I perceive very well that God loveth you. I beseech Him of His goodness to continue it; and if it fortune that you shall have nobody with you of your acquaintance, I think it best you keep your keys yourself, for howsoever it is, so shall be done as shall please them.

And now you shall begin, and by likelihood I shall follow. I set not a rush by it; for when they have done the uttermost they can, then I am sure of the amendment. I pray you, recommend me unto my good lady of Salisbury, and pray her to have a good heart, for we never come to the kingdom of Heaven but by troubles.

Daughter, wheresoever you come, take no pain to send to me, for if I may, I will send to you.

Your loving mother,
KATHERINE, THE QUEEN [5]

Without knowing the circumstances one might think that some news of impending victory was the occasion of this letter. The tone would not be calmer if Mary seemed likely to be going to court instead of to the scaffold. Catherine knew her daughter well enough to choose, not exhortations or heroics, but the quiet matter-of-factness which steadies the taut nerves. "And now you shall begin, and by likelihood I shall follow. I set not a rush by it." Death at the hands of the headsman could seem as simple and unimportant as that.

Not to Mary, however. Chapuys was not displeased to note that though the Princess Mary showed a stubborn courage worthy of her mother, she seemed to feel far less resignation. When, after Anne's child Elizabeth was born, Mary was summoned to attend as lady in waiting on the infant whom Chapuys always called baldly "the little bastard," the ambassador had not known whether to be more delighted at the spirit with which Mary repelled and retorted upon every snub and humiliation or more alarmed at the boldness which thus invited serious reprisal. Mary was stripped of most of her household, bullied by successive deputations of councilors, and prevented from having her meals prepared separately and served in her own chamber, so that Chapuys was frantic for fear of poison. She was threatened with physical violence, and on at least one occasion subjected to it. Surrounded by Anne's creatures and by spies of Cromwell's she lived in an atmosphere choking with petty malice and secret danger. But her spirit was unbroken. The commission which came to exact the oath to the Act of Succession locked up the last of the maids still loyal to her and finally terrified the girl into submission, but though the councilors hounded Mary with repeated demands, though she was deprived of her last friends, – her maid; then her tutor, Dr. Richard Fetherstone, who was sent to the Tower; finally, the good Countess of Salisbury, her mother's friend, who was harshly ordered away from court because she comforted the Princess, – though Lady Shelton told Mary exultantly that if she refused the oath again her father would have her head, the Princess was still defiant.

Fondness for his daughter or perhaps merely political caution prevented Henry from carrying out Lady Shelton's threat, and when he saw that Mary could not be bullied, he even took some steps to make her more comfortable; but Mary was not grateful. She was only nineteen, but her treatment, after years of love and pampering, was making her hard, reserved, secretive. She did not know when this calm might disclose a new danger. For fear of poison she continued to cut her meat only where others cut, and to drink only where others drank before her. She had lost any affection for her father, any desire to obey him. She would not take the oath, but she had no wish either to be a martyr. She wished only to escape from this stifling atmosphere of hate and dread. She was young. She wanted to live and be Queen.

Mary's longing for escape fell in exactly with Chapuys' plans. He was genuinely afraid she would be poisoned if she stayed at court. Moreover, despairing of Catherine's co-operation, he could see ways of using Mary instead of her mother. One way was to marry her to Reginald Pole, the Countess of Salisbury's second son, a young man of great charm, everyone said, and great promise, who was studying philosophy at Venice. In the unclouded years before the divorce the match had been spoken of more than once. The Countess of Salisbury's maiden name was Margaret Plantagenet. Her father was George, Duke of Clarence, brother of Edward IV. Her brother was the ill-fated Earl of Warwick, White Rose pretender to the throne, whom Henry VII kept so long imprisoned in the Tower only to have him executed there, at the instigation, some said, of Dr. De Puebla, just before Catherine sailed to England. If it was true, as people said, that Dr. De Puebla had insisted that it would be unsafe for Catherine to come to England while the White Rose was alive, if it was true that Warwick had been sacrificed to the Spanish alliance, then Catherine was indirectly responsible for what was little better than the judicial murder of the Countess of Salisbury's brother. Legend has it that Catherine felt the responsibility deeply, that she sometimes said that her first marriage was bound to prove unlucky – it was made in blood. Certain it is that even at Ludlow she was drawn to Margaret Pole, made her, after the coronation, the first of her friends among the older nobility, encouraged the education of her son Reginald at court, almost as if he were a royal prince, and was reported to have said that she might yet repair the wrong she had innocently done to the house of Plantagenet and restore their blood to the throne by marrying her daughter to Lady Salisbury's son. On the medal which Darcy sent Chapuys at New Year's of 1534 the arms of the Poles quartered with the leopards and lilies of England was meant to remind the ambassador that the feudal aristocracy thought Lady Salisbury's offspring acceptable claimants to the throne. If Reginald could be married to Mary, Chapuys hoped that the union might "remove some of the queen's exaggerated scruples" against countenancing rebellion, and even if it did not, Mary and Reginald Pole together might prove a workable substitute for Catherine at the center of Chapuys' puzzle. The solution appealed to the ambassador the more strongly since it promised to involve the Emperor almost as inevitably as the raising of Catherine's own standard would involve him. Nothing could be done until Mary was free. And if Mary escaped to the Emperor's domains, whether or not she married Reginald Pole, Charles would have to give her his protection and consequently would almost certainly find himself at war with

Henry and obliged, by the logic of the situation, to support the feudal counterrevolution in England.

Chapuys managed to arrange that the first suggestion for Mary's escape from England should reach the Emperor from Catherine's proctor at Rome, Dr. Ortiz, and then, when it was transmitted to him, backed it heartily on the grounds that it was the only way to preserve Mary's life. "The Concubine [Anne]," he wrote, "plots day and night against the princess. . . ." "These people believe that the lives of the Queen and Princess are all that stand between them and safety . . ." "Cromwell's words are fair . . . , but he really desires the Princess's death." "The king said recently that the Queen had a dropsy (which I know not to be the truth) and that she would not live very much longer. . . . I think he would be glad if the Princess were also to die." "Neither the Queen nor the Princess will be safe for a moment while the Concubine still has power . . . she is desperate to get rid of them."

The best way to save their lives, as Charles, his ambassador implied, was in duty bound to do, would be to authorize the English nobility to rise. The lords would do so on the mere promise of the Emperor's support, and their first act would be to secure the persons of both royal ladies.[6]

If, however, the Emperor was not ready to go so far (as the Emperor obviously was not), Chapuys could arrange at least for Mary's escape. A fast galley to come up the river to Greenwich, and armed ships to hover at the mouth of the Thames and beat off pursuit, would be all that would be needed. Chapuys would guarantee to get Mary aboard the galley at any time on a few hours' notice. Even when Mary was removed from Greenwich to a house some fifteen miles from the river, the ambassador was still sanguine. The Princess rode well. It would be easy to surprise her in the fields, overpower her guards, and gallop off with her to Gravesend. Resistance would be slight, the whole countryside would favor her escape, and even those sent in pursuit would make no haste, but bless her rescuers. The ambassador would undertake without fail to raise in less than twenty-four hours a force adequate to carry the Princess off and guard her to the ships.

Actually, of course, Mary's escape would have been the signal for the rising. Kingston and Burgoyne and Edmund Bray would furnish the initial force, the armed ships from Flanders would be drawn into making a demonstration in the Thames, Chapuys had fast horses in his stables and trustworthy English couriers in his suite, ready to notify the north and west, and if all went well, Mary might never have to leave the kingdom at all. At the worst, Mary and her partisans in the home counties could retreat to the Emperor's ships and land again in the north or west with the army which, once he was openly involved, the Emperor would have to furnish. Charles and his council saw the trap just in time.

Chapuys' letters to the Emperor might lead us to believe that Catherine approved his plans for her daughter's escape, had we not two letters of her own from the spring of 1535. While Chapuys was in the midst of his schemes, the Princess fell ill. Fear, excitement, and constant nervous tension might produce in a high-strung girl of nineteen all the symptoms of nausea and weakness Mary showed, but the thought of poison was never far from Chapuys' mind, and apparently not far from other minds either. Henry, for once, showed himself seriously disturbed and sent his own physician Dr. Butts to see to his daughter. Dr. Butts called in Catherine's own physician, Miguel de la Sá, who came as fast as he could from Kimbolton, and the two of them, besides taking what medical measures they knew, frightened Mary's waiting woman into hysterics by reminding her of the penalties for poisoning. De la Sá went back to Kimbolton, and reported to Catherine that Mary was making a slow recovery, hinting, apparently, that he and Butts suspected an unnatural cause for her malady.

On February 12, 1535, Catherine wrote Chapuys: —

My especial friend, My physician has told me something of my daughter's illness. He gives me hope that her health is improving, but her illness is so prolonged, and [my physician] is so hesitant about visiting her again (for some days, indeed, he could not because I was ill, myself) that I have a grave suspicion about the cause. Therefore it appears to me that what I ask is just and in the service of God. I beg you to speak to the King, and desire him from me to be so charitable as to send his daughter and mine where I am, because if I care for her with my own hands and by the advice of my own and other physicians, and God still pleases to take her from this world, my heart will be at peace, otherwise in great pain. Say to His Highness that there is no need for anyone to nurse her but myself, that I will put her in my own bed in my own chamber and watch with her when needful.

I have recourse to you, knowing that there is no one else in this kingdom who will dare to say to the King, my lord, that which I am asking you to say. I pray God to reward your diligence. *From Kimbolton, the first Friday in Lent. Catherine, the Queen.*[7]

It was a delicate message to ask anyone to convey. Catherine was asking her husband to give her the only assurance which she could believe that he was not deliberately having their daughter poisoned. De la Sá would not have been so reluctant to return to Greenwich had he not thought that Henry himself might be behind the business, and that consequently it would be unsafe for a foreigner to learn too much about it. At the same time Catherine was offering her husband her own assurance that while Mary was with her no other person would be able to contrive to poison her. She did not need to name the other person. Anne did not conceal her hatred of Mary, and long before this Henry must have heard what half the court was saying, that Anne was a witch and a poisoner. All the court saw, now, that Henry chafed at the chains which bound him to Anne, and some said that Henry was more afraid of his second wife than he had been of his first, and with better reason. Catherine guessed that fear and suspicion of Anne had made him send Dr. Butts so quickly to Mary's side, and wanted to point out that while Mary was under her care, Anne would be powerless to harm her.

Chapuys read the Queen's letter to Henry and got, at first, a blunt refusal. Nothing would more increase Mary's present willful stubbornness, he said, with some reason, than to be constantly in her mother's company. Moreover, and the flat hawk's eye gleamed a moment with malice as the King planted his dart, ill-intentioned persons were said to be plotting to steal his daughter out of the kingdom, and he did not mean to make it easy for them by sending her to such a lonely place. Perhaps Chapuys' blank look convinced Henry that a shot in the dark had gone wild, for in the end his persistence won a sort of compromise. Mary was to be permitted to go to a house near Kimbolton, where De la Sá could visit her, provided Catherine did not try to see her. In reply to Chapuys' report, Catherine wrote:

My especial friend, You have greatly bound me by the pains you took in speaking to the King, my lord, about my daughter's coming to me here. You must trust God for your reward, for (as you know) I have no power to thank you with aught but my good will.

Touching the answer made you that the King consents to send her to some place near me, provided I do not see her, thank him for the goodness he shows to his daughter and me, and for the comfort I have received thereby. As to my seeing her, assure him that if she were within a mile of me I would not see her, for the times do not permit me to go about in public, and if I would, I have not the means.

Say to His Highness, however, that what I wished for most was for him to send her where I am, for the comfort and mirth we should have together would be half her cure, as I have proved by experience, having been ill of the same disease. What I wished was so just and reasonable, and touched so nearly the honor and conscience of the King, my lord, that I did not think it would be denied me. Do not cease, I beg you, to do everything you can that this may be done.

I have heard that he has some suspicion of her surety, but I cannot believe that anything so far from reasonable could come from the King's heart, nor can I think he has so little confidence in me. If any such matter chance to be spoken of, I pray you say to the King, my lord, that I am determined (without doubt) to die in this kingdom, and I now offer my own person as surety for my daughter, to the end that if any such thing be attempted, the King, my lord, may do justice upon me as upon the most traitorous woman that ever was born. The rest I commit to your good wisdom and judgment as to my trusty friend, to whom I pray God to give good health.

Catherine's pathetic plea to be allowed to see the daughter she loved above everything in the world, and had not seen for nearly four years, was in vain. Mary was not permitted to come within thirty miles of Kimbolton. But, for Catherine's story, the important thing is the ring of absolute, indignant sincerity in her denial of any knowledge of a plan for Mary's escape. Chapuys had not dared to tell her about it, and her own mind was made up. Not only would she never raise a rebellion against Henry, she would never attempt in any way to evade his authority, not for the sake of her own life, not for the sake of her daughter's.

iv

Even as she wrote this letter to Chapuys, however, a consideration more compelling than her daughter's safety was struggling with Catherine's resolution. All that she had foreseen and feared for six years was now coming true. The bonds that bound England to the rest of Christendom and to the faith of a thousand years were snapping one by one. By the Act of Succession men were called on to swear, not only to maintain the validity of the King's new marriage, but to renounce the authority of the Pope as well, and no sooner had the Nun of Kent and her companions died on Tyburn than Cromwell's agents began going up and down the land, exacting the oath from all they suspected of holding to the old religion. Most men swore; those who did not were speedily on their way to the Tower. In the summer of 1534 preachers were ordered to expound from every pulpit the "falseness and imposture of the presumed authority of the bishop of Rome" and in November of that year Parliament passed an act declaring that the King's Majesty "justly and rightfully is and ought to be Supreme Head of the Church of England" (no equivocation about the "law of Christ" this time); in January the council baldly inserted the title among the King's dignities (along with the other title of "Defender of the Faith" given him by Leo X), and the crown thereupon assuming all the remaining prerogatives and perquisites of the Pope, the breach with Rome was complete.

Meanwhile the attack on the religious orders gathered momentum. The oath to the Act of Succession had sufficed to strike down the boldest Catholics among the regulars, and in the summer of '34 the first houses were dissolved, the monks of the Charterhouse in London, and the monks of Sion where Catherine had loved to visit, and most of the convents of the Observant Friars, including Catherine's favorites at Greenwich. From Sion Catherine's friend, the learned Richard Whitford, an "obstinate papist," was sent to the custody of more submissive brethren, and from Greenwich her friend Father Forrest joined Thomas Abell and the other Catholics in the Tower, while the humbler friars, transferred to Conventual houses, were "loaded with chains and treated worse than dogs." But more monks and friars took the obnoxious oath than Cromwell would have liked, and in the summer of 1535 his agents were merrily riding from monastery to monastery collecting the statistics of land and rent and treasure which were to seal the doom of all the religious houses, and the gossip about sin, superstition and corruption to be used to justify their rape. The time was close at hand when the holiest shrines in England, Canterbury and Walsingham and the rest, were to be desecrated and plundered, when the monks were to be driven from their ancient homes, their libraries scattered and the very leads torn from the roofs which had protected, not merely the most beautiful buildings in northern Europe, but learning and hospitality and innocent piety as well. Before long the wood of a crucifix before which generations of simple people had prayed was to be broken up for firewood to burn a victim whose crime was that he still held the faith of those simple generations; before long the toll of the Catholic martyrs would shock and sicken Christendom. Thomas Cromwell meant to be thorough, and no holocaust of bewildered Dutch Anabaptists and argumentative London artisans with queer views about the sacraments could blaze high enough to hide what he meant.

Through the spring and summer of 1535, the news of Cromwell's thoroughness and the prevision of what it meant tortured Catherine. In '34 she had written tenderly and cheerfully to Father Forrest, not doubting, she told him, his willingness to die for Christ.[8] Nor did she doubt that he and others would be called upon to do so. She had heard that her friend and Henry's, Thomas More, was in the Tower for refusal to take the oath to the succession, and that her councilor and champion John Fisher was there also; she had heard of the arrest of the London Carthusians and she was not unprepared for what followed.

On April 28, 1535, five men were brought up for trial under the new law: John Houghton, prior of the London Charterhouse, Augustine Webster, prior of the Carthusians of Axholme in Lincolnshire, Robert Lawrence, prior of the Carthusians of Beawale in Nottinghamshire, Richard Reynolds of the Bridgettine monastery of Sion, and John Hale, a secular priest, the vicar of Isleworth. The next day, a jury, terrorized by Cromwell, condemned them to die as traitors, and when the condemned were asked why they persisted in an opinion forbidden by the lords and bishops in Parliament, Richard Reynolds replied for all of them. All the rest of Christendom held opinion with him and his fellows, he told the judges, "and even in this realm of England, though the smaller part holds with you, I am sure the larger part is at heart of our opinion, although outwardly, partly from fear, partly from hope, they profess to be of yours." Pressed to reveal the names of those who secretly agreed with him he answered, "All good men." On May 4 the monks were drawn on hurdles to Tyburn, there hanged, cut down while still alive, their bowels and hearts ripped out, and their bodies hacked to pieces and impaled on spears, all this carried out with a singular brutality upon one victim at a time, while the others looked on, witnesses reported, without changing color or altering the tone in which those awaiting their turn exhorted the bystanders to do well and obey the King in everything not against the honor of God and the Church.

On June 19, three more monks of the London Charterhouse suffered at Tyburn. On June 22, John Fisher, Bishop of Rochester, a man of seventy-four years, "a long lean slender body, nothing in a manner but skin and bare bones, so that the most part that there saw him marvelled to see any man so far consumed" mounted the scaffold unaided, and lifted that high silvery voice for the last time to refuse the pardon offered him. The greater barbarities of the penalty were omitted for fear the compassion of the people might be too far aroused, but the naked corpse was left all day to view, before it was huddled in a shallow ditch beside the wall of All Hallows, Barking, and the noble head, so skull-like in life that death could hardly change it, was impaled on a pike on London Bridge whence it looked "sadly and constantly upon the people coming into London," until men began to talk of a miracle, and it seemed wiser to throw it into the river.

A head even better known replaced Fisher's on London Bridge. Sir Thomas More had been in the Tower for fifteen months, constantly examined and re-examined by agents of a government not less eager to trip him into treason than to publish his submission to the world. Henry had loved the man; Europe reverenced his genius.

For both reasons Henry had to have either his explicit approval or his death. "I know well," More told Norfolk when sentence was pronounced, "that the reason why you have condemned me is because I have never been willing to consent to the king's second marriage." But if More had never been willing to consent, he had been reluctant to condemn, and if the King's marriage had caused his death, it was because More's trained legal mind appreciated the issue at stake better, perhaps, than any other mind in England. Wittily, patiently, ironically he had explained to Rich, to Audeley, to Norfolk, over and over again. He did not set himself up against the statutes of the King in Parliament; he knew as well as any man that often the edicts of the state must override the subject's right of private judgment. But the moral authority of the state was delegated to it by the community of all Christian souls, and was limited by the great unwritten constitution of the whole community of Christendom – of which no state was more than a part. A state which put itself beyond the pale of the community, which recognized no authority above its own, and based its power on fear and naked force, was no better than the rule of a tyrant or a gang of robbers. There were laws which no Parliament could pass; and for that point of constitutional law, Henry's loyal subject and England's greatest Chancellor was willing to die. He put the same point more simply to the crowd around his scaffold. He had been told not to use many words. He did not need many. "I die," he told them, "the King's good servant, but God's first." [9]

Catherine could not have phrased it so well, but the point was perfectly clear to her. It was her duty, everyone's duty, she had repeated again and again almost in the very words of the monks of the Charterhouse, to obey the King in everything not against God's law. To feudal anachronisms like Dacre and Abergavenny and to pragmatists like Thomas Cromwell her position was incomprehensible, but everything from her girlhood training to her mature study of the humanists reinforced it, and it was shared by enough Englishmen, high and low, to go far towards explaining the history of her century. She did not flinch from the path that Richard Reynolds and Thomas More had traveled. She had seen for a long time that the logical end of refusing to obey a king like Henry VIII, while one also refused to resist him, was death.

What troubled her that summer of 1535 was a more perplexing thought. Houghton and Reynolds, Fisher and More, were quit for martyrdom, but would she be? They had done their whole duty by God and man, and Catherine had no doubt of their reward; but had she not a harder duty? In a sense their deaths lay upon her, and not merely their deaths, which so deeply religious a woman as Catherine could hardly consider unmitigated tragedy, but what seemed to her the worse fate of all the weak ones who had submitted to the King and were being led, they and their children, towards heresy. There is no evidence that she ever thought for a moment that she could have served God by denying His laws, but should she risk the sin of rebellion against the King for the sake of the souls who might be saved? In one form or another that question, posed wherever consciences found themselves in conflict with the religion supported by the state, was to be the gravest men would consider throughout Europe during the next century, without reaching, in the end, better than partial and controversial conclusions. It is not surprising, then, that the conclusion Catherine reached was a compromise, applicable only to her particular case.

She would not lead an army against her husband. Not because she lacked the means. If God meant her to take the field, he could get her out of Kimbolton, and age and ill health could no more stop her than they could have stopped her mother, Isabella. But she could not convince her conscience that it was laid upon her to go so far. To rebel herself, and lead others into what might be the sin of rebellion, to be, perhaps, the cause of her husband's death, and perhaps to profit by it, was more than God seemed to require. But short of that she must do what she could to save England from heresy. So far she had avoided anything that might lead to war. In the fall of 1533 she had cheerfully approved the Emperor's instructions for Count Cifuentes at Rome, which Chapuys had found so exasperatingly inadequate. Even in April, 1535, though she was obliged to admit to the Emperor that sentence on her divorce had come too late, she had refused to suggest any further steps. But there were further steps, for which she could ask.

Chapuys had been clamoring for them for over two years. The Pope must implement his bull, excommunicating Henry and depriving him of his throne, and call upon the secular arm. England must be laid under an interdict, and the Emperor must carry out the sentence of deprivation at the head of an army. Politically, conditions could not have been more favorable than they seemed in the autumn of 1535. The feudal conspiracy in England was ripe and could not be kept so for long. The Emperor had just returned victorious from Africa, having defeated Barbarossa, taken Tunis, and dealt the Moslem power in the western Mediterranean a heavy blow. His prestige had never stood higher, and for the moment his hands were free. After the shudder of horror that had run through Europe at the deaths of Fisher and More, even the cynical Francis I would hesitate to support the heretic king. Clement VII had died in September, 1534, and his successor, Alessandro Farnese, Pope Paul III, was said to be of firmer principles, and was certainly of firmer courage. But neither Pope nor Emperor would move against Henry without Catherine's direct appeal.

Before she took her decisive step Catherine must have struggled with herself a long time. At last, on October 15, she wrote to the new Pope: —

Most Holy and Blessed Father,

. . . I have for some time ceased from writing to Your Holiness, though my conscience has reproached me for my silence . . . [Now] once more . . . I do entreat you to bear this realm especially in mind, to remember the King, my lord and husband, and my daughter. Your

Holiness knows, and all Christendom knows, what things are done here, what great offence is given to God, what scandal to the world, what reproach is thrown upon your Holiness. If a remedy be not applied shortly, there will be no end to ruined souls and martyred saints. The good will be firm and suffer. The lukewarm will fail if they find none to help them, and the greater part will stray away like sheep without a shepherd. I write frankly to your Holiness, as one who can feel with me and my daughter for the martyrdom of these good men, whom, it comforts me to hope, we may follow in their sufferings though we cannot imitate their lives. . . . We await a remedy from God and from Your Holiness. It must come speedily or the time will be past! [10]

At the same time Catherine wrote in the same vein to her nephew, the Emperor, and directly in her own hand to Dr. Ortiz, making an unmistakable appeal for intervention. Chapuys had told her that long ago the Pope would have issued his executory brief declaring Henry excommunicated and deposed, laying England under the greater interdict and invoking the secular arm, except that Catherine, who was the injured party, had never applied for it. So far, she had always refused to do so. Now she authorized Chapuys to make formal application in her name, and, that nothing might be lacking, sent word to Mary that she must also appeal.

Chapuys lost no time. He had already heard a rumor that when Parliament reassembled bills of attainder would be brought in against Catherine and Mary, and though the Queen, if she had to give the signal for rebellion against her husband, might have preferred to do so by her death, the ambassador hoped to be quick enough to save her life and her daughter's. When the letters from Kimbolton reached him he began at once to draft the necessary documents, adding an urgent message of his own, and before morning his most trusted secretary was galloping for Dover with orders to ride post and by the shortest route until he reached the Emperor at Naples. But he was to do more than that. Chapuys had a shrewd and justified suspicion that the person who had been blocking the publication of the Pope's executory brief was Count Cifuentes, the Emperor's own ambassador at Rome, who felt, with many of his countrymen, that clearing pirates from the Mediterranean was more important than clearing heretics from England. Chapuys ordered his secretary to stop in Rome and deliver Catherine's letter and formal application to the Pope before he even saw the Emperor. As Chapuys knew from Ortiz, most of the cardinals had been clamoring for months for publication of the executory brief. Once it was published, Charles could not ignore it. The ambassador flattered himself that at last he had found a way to force his master's hand.[11]

The sequel was ironic. As Chapuys' secretary clattered through the streets of Milan, Francesco II Sforza lay dying in its gloomy citadel. The courier with the news of the Duke's death passed Chapuys' man almost at the gates of Rome, and when the secretary went to the palace of the Spanish ambassador to change his clothes before presenting himself at the Vatican he found Cifuentes considering the new crisis. Sforza's death reopened the whole question of Milan, and war with France would be a matter, probably, of weeks. Chapuys' secretary had no message for Cifuentes, but Cifuentes had no time for tact. He turned the unfortunate secretary inside out, and when he discovered what a bomb he was carrying, kept him locked in a room in the embassy, so close that even Dr. Ortiz did not suspect his presence there, until he could be conveyed under guard to the southern gate and ordered harshly to keep riding towards Naples and not to come back until the Emperor had seen all his papers. Six weeks later Charles sent the secretary straight back to Chapuys with a brief acknowledgment and a verbal message recommending caution. But long before that Chapuys, having heard the news from Milan, knew that his bid for intervention had failed.

v

Her decision taken, Catherine waited through two months at Kimbolton before she wrote again to her nephew and to Dr. Ortiz, brief appeals, reporting the contemplated attainders, urging haste, referring them to Chapuys.[12] She had been ill in November, confined to her bed with pain and nausea by a kind of attack from which she had suffered from time to time for more than a year, but early in December Chapuys was relieved to get a letter in her own hand, written with something like her old spirit: she wanted money for presents to her suite at the Christmas season, she hoped Henry would permit her to move after the New Year to a drier and healthier house, she hoped to repay the ambassador for all he had done for her and would again commend him, as she never failed to do, to the Emperor. In an oblique phrase she thanked him for his diligence in her affairs. About the results of that diligence the ambassador had by this time his own rueful doubts. Henry, having heard of Sforza's death, was in high good spirits. Francis was greensick for Milan, he assured Chapuys. There would be war – war, for certain. Would the Emperor let solicitude for his relatives stand in the way of a profitable alliance with England? With the Emperor's letter from Naples in his pocket, – reproving him for excessive zeal, refusing to believe that Henry would seek the death of his wife and daughter, saying that if worst came to worst Catherine and Mary must submit and take any oath required of them, – Chapuys was sure the Emperor would not, though he took a perverse satisfaction in letting Henry believe that Charles would prefer his aunt's welfare to the safety of Milan. Even though Catherine said she was better, he repeated his request to be allowed to visit her.

Then, on December 29, Chapuys had an alarming note from Dr. De la Sá. The Queen was much worse; if the ambassador expected to see her alive he must come at once. She was asking for him, also for her daughter. Chapuys rode back to Greenwich and, after hours of fidgeting, again saw the King.[13] Henry was positively beaming. Chapuys glowered his impatience to be off, but Henry, his arm thrown securely round the fretful ambassador's neck, dragged Chapuys through a long political discussion. This business of Milan would surely mean war.

Chapuys did not think so. Could he have permission to go to Kimbolton?

Oh yes, it would! And the French would give anything in the world to secure his alliance. Francis knew he could not win without England's help.

Chapuys was not interested. How about the Queen's request for money and a change of residence?

Such things were of no importance. They could be arranged. Better see Cromwell. Now about this French alliance. It would have many advantages for England, but still—

And how about the Queen's request to see her daughter? Chapuys interjected.

Ah, that was more serious. Henry would have to consult his council about that. This French alliance, now, England might be forced into it as long as the Emperor was so stubborn about his aunt. If the Emperor could be made to see that it was to his own interest not to meddle in what did not concern him—

"His Imperial Majesty will never abandon Queen Catherine while she lives," Chapuys flared.

"It doesn't matter." Henry released his clutch on Chapuys' neck and swung away. "She won't live long. Go to her when you like."

At the gate the Duke of Suffolk intercepted Chapuys to give him the necessary letter for Bedingfield, to remark negligently that he had better hurry if he wanted to see the old queen alive, and to add in a burst of what Suffolk must have thought exquisite diplomatic tact: "When she's dead there will be no barrier between my King and the Emperor, your master."

Through the rain of a January morning, – the second of the new year, 1536, – the ambassador at last saw Kimbolton.[14] The mud was appalling, but Chapuys had given his small escort, and Stephen Vaughan who rode with him as a guide and Cromwell's spy, little rest. Bedingfield admitted them at once, and the Queen chose to make a little ceremony of his reception, lining all her slender suite about her chamber and commanding the presence even of Bedingfield and Chamberlayn, who, although they were the principal officers of her household, had not seen her for more than a year. Between rows of sober faces the ambassador advanced to kiss the hand extended from the bed, sinking on gouty knees to the foul rushes as if this were the great audience chamber at Westminster and all the barons of the kingdom were looking on.

In a voice still loud and clear the Queen thanked him for his visit as the ritual of a diplomatic reception required, and then, in a lower tone, as she motioned him to rise, "I can die now in your arms, not abandoned – like one of the beasts."

Vaughan's head seemed to sway forward, and there were other heads listening. Chapuys judged it best to speak slowly and clearly for the benefit of those not too skilled in foreign tongues. Her husband, the King, he said, and the whole kingdom, were anxious for news of her recovery. The King promised prompt payment of all the arrears of her pensions, and when she was better (this was rank improvisation) she might choose any manor she preferred as a place of retirement. The King was sorry – as the Emperor would be when he heard of it, as they all were – for her illness, and hoped, as they all hoped, that she would soon be better. She must give herself every chance. The peace, the welfare, the unity of all Christendom (the ambassador's slow spacing stressed the words) depended on her life.

It was a short interview. Catherine thanked him again, gave him her leave to retire. "You will be weary from your journey," she said. "We will speak further another time. I, myself, shall be glad of sleep. I have not slept two hours these past six days. Perhaps I shall sleep now."

Chapuys was tired, but he had hardly pulled off his muddy boots in the chamber in the Queen's wing assigned to him when Dr. De la Sá came to say that the Queen was asking for him, and, this time, the ambassador sitting on the foot of the bed, the waiting women crouched out of earshot at the other end of the room, they talked in low tones for more than two hours. Catherine wanted to know all about her nephew, his victory at Tunis, his plans for Italy, the unfortunate crisis over Milan; she wanted to know about Mary, whom Chapuys had seen as often as he could. She asked nothing more about Henry. When the news was exhausted she would not let the ambassador go, though he feared he was tiring her. There were things she had to tell him. By the English law a married woman could not make a will while her husband lived, but there were certain dispositions. There had been, she did not need to tell the ambassador, very little money since she had come to Kimbolton. She owed for drugs, and for the washing, and for the turning of some of her dresses. And she owed all her people for wages – a considerable amount. She had very few jewels left, but surely the King would not mind if the gold collar she brought out of Spain went to her daughter. And she would like the child to have her furs, though they were old. She wanted to be buried in some convent of the Observant Friars, she said, forgetting for the moment that there were no more Observant convents in England, and she wanted, she added firmly, five hundred masses for her soul. The ambassador begged her not to distress herself with such matters. There was plenty of time. Still she would not let him go.

When she spoke again it was of the past, her own tribulations and her daughter's, of the Pope's long delay, and so finally to what troubled her most: the woes of this unhappy country which she had wished so well and brought so little good. So many honest and worthy men had suffered already, so many souls had been endangered, and some, perhaps, gone to eternal perdition, and all on her account, yet she did not see how she could have done otherwise than she did. She was Henry's wife; it would have been a sin to deny it. Would it not also have been a sin to rebel against her husband? Just the same, because she had chosen as she had, all the kingdom was now full of heresy and sedition; and the spread of false doctrines, the breaking of the ancient bonds that bound England to Christendom, the blood, the violence, the lies – all these lay upon her conscience. The choice had been hers, must not the guilt be hers also?

Chapuys said what he could. No evil was irremediable. Her course of action had been throughout just what the laws of God and the Church prescribed, and by it she had secured in the eyes of all just men the validity of her marriage and her daughter's right to the throne. The Emperor would watch over her daughter always, and in time it might be hers to undo all the harm her father had done and restore England to the Church. But no need to talk of that yet. She, Catherine herself, might yet be the instrument. The Emperor, one day, would have time for England; the English people themselves remained loyal to her and to the Church, and perhaps – here the ambassador shamelessly stole a leaf from Catherine's book – when the Pope issued the brief she had applied for, God would restore her husband's reason, and Henry himself would confess his error and make reparation. While the candle guttered at the bedside and the waiting women yawned before the dying fire, the ambassador, thanking God that ten years in politics and ten in diplomacy had filed his tongue, talked as he had never talked before. At last it seemed to him the Queen was easier in her mind. She thanked him. She said she thought that she would sleep.

Chapuys stayed three days at Kimbolton. Catherine did sleep that night, and the next day she ate and retained her food. Each day she had a long conversation with the ambassador and each day she seemed better. "In our last conversation," said Chapuys, "I saw her smile two or three times, and after I left she was willing to be amused by one of my people whom I left to entertain her" – probably the Spanish fool who had convulsed Kimbolton on the earlier visit. De la Sá felt sure the Queen was out of danger. She, herself, did not wish to detain the ambassador longer.

Besides Chapuys' Spanish fool, she now had with her a dearer reminder of her youth. Late on the night before the ambassador's departure, the Dowager Countess of Willoughby demanded entrance at Kimbolton. Across the moat Bedingfield told her he could not admit her, and heard, sharply, that he would have to. It was a foul black night, the roads were filthy, she had fallen from her horse, she did not care what his orders were, she was not going another mile. Once within Kimbolton, the Dowager Countess went straight to the Queen's apartments, and Bedingfield saw no more of her. Maria de Salinas had come back to her first mistress.[15] It was in her arms, not the ambassador's, that Catherine was to die.

The day Chapuys left Kimbolton, the day of the Epiphany, the Queen seemed much stronger. She combed and arranged her hair without anyone's help that afternoon, and talked a long time to Maria, but the next day pain and nausea returned, and at midnight she woke her maids and asked if it were not near dawn. In alarm they sent for her confessor, and Llandaff, seeing her so pale and weak, offered to hasten the canonical hour and say mass at once; but Catherine forbade him, and when he would have insisted, overwhelmed him with citations from the relevant authorities. She had always been strong enough to wait. At dawn then she received the sacrament, and then dictated two letters, one to the Emperor, one to Henry. To Henry she wrote: –

My most dear lord, king, and husband, The hour of my death now drawing on, the tender love I owe you forceth me, my case being such, to commend myself to you, and to put you in remembrance with a few words of the health and safeguard of your soul which you ought to prefer before all worldly matters, and before the care and pampering of your body, for the which you have cast me into many calamities and yourself into many troubles. For my part, I pardon you everything, and I wish and devoutly pray God that He will pardon you also. For the rest, I commend unto you our daughter Mary, beseeching you to be a good father unto her, as I have heretofore desired. I entreat you also, on behalf of my maids, to give them marriage portions, which is not much, they being but three. For all my other servants I solicit the wages due them, and a year more, lest they be unprovided for. Lastly, I make this vow, that mine eyes desire you above all things.[16]

At ten that morning she received extreme unction, and then prayed, aloud, for more than two hours for her daughter, for the souls of all the people of England, and especially for her husband. At two in the afternoon of January 7, 1536, she died.

She was buried, by royal command, in the choir aisle of Peterborough Abbey, with no more than the honors due a princess dowager. Few of the dispositions in her will were ever carried out. Few of the hopes with which she died were ever realized.

vi

Eustache Chapuys heard the news of her death in London, on January 9. He was to remain at his post for nearly a decade longer, but his chief preoccupation, ever since he had first come to England, was now gone, and his letters changed after Catherine died. He remained a shrewd observer, a brilliant commentator, and, once he had no interests to serve except the Emperor's, a much more satisfactory negotiator; but his bursts of honest enthusiasm and indignation were less and less frequent, his phrases colder, warier, slyer, his indirections were more concerned with saving his own skin whole amid the wreck of the conspiracies he had fostered, and with building up at Antwerp the modest little fortune on which he looked forward to retiring. He had made his last crusade, and he could guide the Princess Mary through the difficult reconciliation with her father with a legal and diplomatic finesse undisturbed by any nicety about moral values.

For a time he took a savage pleasure in abusing Henry in his letters, a gloomy pleasure in impressing upon the Emperor the conviction that his aunt had been poisoned. When Henry heard of his wife's death, Chapuys wrote, the King dressed from top to toe in yellow with a white feather in his cap, gave a ball at Greenwich, and went about among the revelers with the Princess Elizabeth in his arms, showing her off to everyone and saying, "God be praised, the old harridan is dead, now there is no fear of war." At Kimbolton there had been no proper autopsy or inspection of the body, he told the Emperor, and when the chandler of the house opened it for embalming, being then alone except for another servant, he found all the organs healthy save the heart which was all black and hideous to see, with a black growth adhering to it. Dr. De la Sá, when informed, said that this was proof positive of poison. We do not know enough, even now, to make from the unverified report of a candlemaker any confident diagnosis, but we are less credulous today about the slow and secret poisons in which Chapuys and Dr. De la Sá and all their contemporaries believed. If Catherine was poisoned, it is hard to say what the poison was, or how it could have been administered except in the drugs of Dr. De la Sá, in which case Dr. De la Sá would hardly have been so forthright in confirming the suspicion. Catherine had long been careful to eat only food prepared in her own chamber and shared with her own maids. No one else is reported to have been ill, and Catherine had had repeated attacks of the same malady for over a year. Perhaps she died of some form of cancer.[17] But Chapuys was not alone in his suspicions. According to his reports one of the charges brought against Anne Boleyn shortly afterwards was of poisoning the old Queen, and seeking to compass the death of the Princess and the King by the same means.

Chapuys had, at least, the satisfaction of recording, in malicious detail, the ruin of the Concubine. "I am her death, as she is mine," Anne is reported to have said of Catherine, and so it proved, though in a strange manner. Henry had been tired of Anne for a long time. There is little doubt he was afraid of her also. It was unlikely, after her repeated miscarriages since Elizabeth's birth, that she would ever bear him a son. But while Catherine lived, to get rid of Anne would only have entailed useless complications. Catherine's death sealed the fate of her rival. Anne's protégé, Thomas Cromwell, stage-managed the affair; her former chaplain, Thomas Cranmer, gave it his reluctant blessing; her father, Lord Wiltshire, who kept his honors and his offices, sat unprotesting among the judges; and her uncle, Norfolk, pronounced the sentence: for treason, incest, and adultery the Lady Anne was to die by burning or beheading at the King's pleasure. Thomas Cranmer hastened to declare her marriage null and invalid from the beginning. By implication her daughter Elizabeth was a bastard. Four brave gentlemen of her party, involved in her ruin, among them her brother, Lord Rochford, and one poor weakling of a lute-player died before she died. But her death was not long delayed. On May 19, 1536, less than four months after Catherine's funeral, Anne knelt before the imported headsman in the courtyard of the Tower, and the sorry comedy was over.

When Chapuys wrote the Emperor the news he let none of the pity for Anne's death felt even by the English who had hated her creep into his letter, but he could add a fact which few of them knew so soon. Just twenty-four hours after Anne's execution, Henry had married his third wife, the Lady Jane Seymour.

In the intervals of negotiation Chapuys always found time to keep the Emperor posted on the intricacies of the King of England's connubial affairs. He was absent on business when Henry divorced his fourth wife, Anne of Cleves, and when Thomas Cromwell paid for that mistake and for his power with his head; but

Chapuys was back again in England to see the King, gray now and obese, eaten with disease and prematurely senile, struck suddenly helpless and blind with tears when, in the midst of a court ball, the cannon from the Tower told him that his fifth wife had suffered the same fate as Anne Boleyn. By that time Chapuys was too old himself to hate Henry any more. In their last interview, when the King's swollen body with the marks of death already upon it was lowered into the chair from which four men could hardly heave it, and His Majesty bade the gouty old ambassador seat himself also, there was a kind of reluctant friendliness about their conversation, and Chapuys could reflect, when his automatic riposte struck from the slobbering hulk a spark of the old boastfulness, that here was the wreck of a very great king, almost a very great man.

From that last interview, Chapuys went to say good-by to Mary in a garden beside the Thames. The Emperor had promised him that in a few months more he would be free from diplomacy, free to enroll as a student at the University of Louvain. After all, he was only fifty-five, and he had always felt that study meant more to him than kingdoms. He would be glad to forget most of what he had seen in England. But he did not quite forget Catherine's daughter. He wrote to her, once, from the quiet cloister of the college he had founded at Louvain. That was in the days when, Queen at last, she was vainly trying to win England back to her mother's faith. He thanked Mary for her recollection of him; he would keep her gift to pay the way of English students at Louvain, but he begged her to be more chary in her giving. Since the chief beneficiary of Mary's lavishness was the son of Chapuys' old master, the Emperor, the warning shows the persistence of Chapuys' first loyalty. In another letter, written the year before his death, he remembered Catherine, "the most virtuous woman I have ever known, and the highest hearted, but too quick to trust that others were like herself, and too slow to do a little ill that much good might come of it."[18]

Some modern historians have been tempted to concur in Chapuys' judgment. It is difficult to doubt that, had Catherine acted differently, the Reformation in England would have been delayed, might never have come at all. And had England remained in the Church, no one can say for certain that the unity of Christendom might not have been saved, perhaps by a victory for the moderate reformers and the consequent democratization of Church government in some General Council in the sixteenth century; perhaps, though more doubtfully, by the triumph of renascent Catholicism in the seventeenth.

Catherine, herself, would have accepted the responsibility. Had she behaved differently, the history of England would have been different. But she might have pleaded that the course she took promised as much chance of Christian unity as any other. By defending the validity of her marriage, by keeping her daughter true to the old Church and in line for the throne, she had at least preserved the possibility of a Catholic restoration when Mary became Queen. And Mary did become Queen, before Anne Boleyn's daughter. Catherine could not be expected to foresee that Henry's third marriage would produce a son who would live just long enough to root the Reformation in England, just long enough so that Mary would come to the throne too late to undo what had been done, too late to bear a child who might undo it. Catherine's dynastic hopes proved as vain as Isabella's. That, the Queen would have said, repeating her mother, was in the hands of God.

The only choice really open to Catherine was the one offered her once she saw that papal action had come too late to restore her marriage or prevent the breach with Rome. She might, as Henry said, have taken the field and waged war fiercely. Had she done so, no one can be sure that Chapuys' prediction of an easy victory would have proved correct. The forces of counterrevolution were strong in England, but the tide was setting towards the new times, and only the Queen's personality could have held the reactionaries together. It may be that she would have succeeded only in plunging England into such a bloody series of religious wars as thirty years later broke out in France, wars that would have embittered both parties, and distorted the development of her adopted country in ways beyond our guessing. She could not bring herself to do it; and, if she could have looked into the future, little as she would have liked England under Anne Boleyn's daughter she might have preferred the Elizabethan compromise to St. Bartholomew's and the Barricades. If she had brought England little good, she said once, she would be the loather to bring it any harm. There have been worse decisions than that.

NOTES

Abbreviations

A.R.B.	*Archives Générales du Royaume*, *Brussels. Papiers de l'Etat et de l'Audience.*
B.M.	British Museum.
Bib. Nat.	*Bibliothèque Nationale*, Paris.
R.O.	Public Record Office, London.
V.A.	*Haus-hof und Stadt Archiv*, Vienna.
Vat.	Archives of the Vatican.
Allen	Erasmus, *Opus Epistolarum* (R. 1429).
Cal. Ven.	*Calendar of State Papers*, Venetian (R. 712).
Cal. Span.	*Calendar of State Papers*, Spanish (R. 620).
D.I.E.	*Colección de documentos inéditos* (R. 623).
L. & P.	Letters and papers of Henry VIII (R. 70).

Notes

A NOTE ABOUT SOURCES

The publication of the *Bibliography of British History, Tudor Period, 1485–1603*, edited by Conyers Read, Oxford, 1933, should relieve most writers about Tudor history of any obligation to append long lists of printed works to their own books. Books and articles listed by Read will be cited hereafter in brief form, followed on the first occasion by the letter *R* and the number given them in Read's *Bibliography*, to which the reader may turn for more complete description. No attempt will be made to offer a complete list of books and articles cited or consulted.

Something will be said immediately below of the chief sources for the whole biography of Catherine of Aragon, and at the beginning of the notes to each chapter, the principal additional works used for that chapter will be noted.

ARCHIVAL SOURCES: Most of the public documents useful for a biography of Catherine of Aragon have been described in one of the series of calendars issued under the auspices of the British Public Record Office. It cannot be too frequently emphasized, however, that calendars merely describe the contents of the documents with which they are concerned; they cannot be expected to offer verbatim translations. Even from the most careful of them one must go to the documents themselves to find the turn and color of the original phrase, for although most of the documents for this period have been calendared, relatively few have been printed in full, and even printed documents are not always free from error. I have tried, therefore, to check all available originals of documents used in this book, although political conditions in Spain after 1936 obliged me to rely for Spanish MSS. largely on transcripts, chiefly those in the Public Record Office. In the footnotes which follow, however, I have cited documents by the volume and page number of the calendar in which they are most fully described, since few persons are likely to wish to verify the originals, and if they do, they can identify them most conveniently from the calendar's description. The addition in parentheses of a reference to the archives in which the original may be found means that the document in question is incompletely or inaccurately described in the calendar.

The *Haus-hof und Stadt Archiv* in Vienna contains a considerable mass of the correspondence of the Emperor Charles V, chiefly for the years 1521–1525, which was omitted from the *Calendar of State Papers, Spanish* (R. 620). I have prepared a supplement describing this material and hoped to see it published before this, but although the volume was ready last year, the war has delayed publication. In general the Vienna archives proved the richest single source for unpublished material about Catherine. The *Archives du Royaume de Belgique* at Brussels are supposed, as far as sixteenth-century Habsburg documents are concerned, to be composed of copies of originals preserved at Vienna, but this is not quite the case. Some of the documents in Brussels from this period appear not to be represented at Vienna. A few unpublished papers relevant to Catherine of Aragon are still to be found in the *Bibliothèque Nationale* at Paris, and the *Archives de la Ville* of Annecy yielded the family papers of Eustache Chapuys and some fragmentary private correspondence of that interesting ambassador. The archives of the Vatican revealed chiefly how thorough was the gleaning of Stefan Ehses for *Romische Dokumente zur Geschichte der Ehescheidung Heinrichs VIII* (R. 379), and the collections at Venice how admirable, on the whole, was the work of the editors of the *Calendar of State Papers, Venetian* (R. 712). British public archives still contain some uncalendared material for the reign of Henry VII, but the monumental *Letters and Papers of Henry VIII* (R. 70) adequately represents the major British collections for that reign, particularly since the supplements added in 1929 and 1932.

A further word should be said about the *Calendar of State Papers, Spanish*, which, containing as it does the reports of the Spanish ambassadors in England, describes the documents which constitute the chief source of this book. Volumes I and II, edited by G. A. Bergenroth, can be used only with extreme caution, Vols. III–VII, edited by Pascual de Gayangos, with hardly less, though Gayangos' errors, more numerous in dating and transcription of proper names than in translation, are less misleading. The whole series is disappointingly fragmentary. The contemplated supplement from Vienna and elsewhere should help to fill one of the largest gaps; another is filled by *Correspondencia de Gutierre Gomez de Fuensalida*, edited by El Duque de Berwick y de Alba, Madrid, 1907, which is invaluable for the last years of Henry VII and has been too little used. Other gaps may yet be filled by a more careful sifting of Spanish repositories.

Printed Books: The only thing approaching a contemporary biography of Catherine of Aragon is Father William Forrest's *History of Grisild the Second* (R. 362), a rhetorical narrative in verse, embellished with invented speeches and moral reflections, written in the reign of Mary I, and aiming more at edification than at factual accuracy. It does, however, preserve some recollections of Catherine by those who knew her, as does Nicholas Harpsfield's *Treatise on the pretended divorce* (R. 365), a more reliable book. Of the contemporary writers, the most colorful and in many ways the most valuable, Hall (R. 287), is disappointingly meager about Catherine, probably because of Hall's uncritical loyalty to her husband.

The few modern biographies of Catherine add little to Agnes

Strickland's brief account in the *Lives of the Queens of England* (R. 322). The most pretentious, W. H. Dixon's *History of two queens* (R. 396), is fantastically inaccurate and absurdly prejudiced. The most recent, and on the whole the best, *Catherine of Aragon* by Francesca Claremont, London (Robert Hale) 1939, contains useful genealogical information about members of Catherine's suite, and most of the legends and traditions about Catherine, but is frequently uncritical.

H. A. L. Fisher's *History of England*, 1485–1547 (R. 303), and A. F. Pollard's *Henry VIII* (R. 417), *Wolsey* (R. 418), and *Thomas Cranmer* (R. 1338), and R. B. Merriman's *Thomas Cromwell* (R. 412) have never been far from my hand as I wrote. Absence of more frequent reference to these books in the following notes implies not so much independence of them as a general indebtedness extending back over many years which I could not now disentangle if I would. I have deliberately excluded from the notes documentation of facts supplied as background and easily verifiable in standard books of reference like the above.

NOTE ON ILLUSTRATIONS

The Portraits of Catherine of Aragon

A number of portraits by Holbein and others have been described at various times as being of Catherine of Aragon, portraits of persons as different in appearance and station in life as Margaret Roper and Queen Louise of Savoy. Actually the number of likenesses which one can be moderately sure were meant to represent the Queen are very few.

1. *Frontispiece*. About the best of these, the portrait in the Vienna gallery used as a frontispiece, unnecessary doubts have been expressed. Even if the person represented did not strongly resemble

Isabella of Castile and the royal child at the Prado, and even if it were not possible to say with considerable certainty when the portrait was painted and by whom, the presence among the Habsburgs' portrait collection of a young woman in Spanish dress and hair arrangement of the early 1500's with a C embroidered on her dress, and the scallop shells of Santiago, and wearing an English necklace of red and white Tudor roses suspending a K, would leave no doubt as to the identity of the sitter. It could not possibly be anyone but Catherine of Aragon; and if the sitter's appearance did not agree with contemporary descriptions of Catherine as a girl, we should have to question the descriptions. Actually, the agreement is striking.

2. Opposite page 198. Of the few undoubted portraits of Catherine as Queen, the best I have seen is that at Chatsworth. It came to the Duke's family from Elizabeth Countess of Shrewsbury, the famous Bess of Hardwick, and is mentioned in her will in 1601 as a portrait of "Quene Katherine" hanging in the gallery at Hardwick. The very similar, but somewhat inferior, portrait belonging to Merton College appears to be a copy of the Chatsworth portrait, though both, of course, may be derived from a lost original.

The relation to this family of portraits of the one in the National Gallery, the only portrait with any pretensions to genuineness which has been widely reproduced, is curious. The pose, and the outlines of the English hood, are so similar as to suggest a close relationship. The face seems to be that of a different person. The grounds for believing that this portrait is of Catherine at all seem to be slight. It was not acquired by the National Portrait Gallery until the middle of the nineteenth century and its earlier history is obscure. The first catalogue of the gallery after its purchase authenticates it by reference to a reproduction of the same or a strikingly similar portrait in Agnes Strickland's *Lives of the Queens of England*. Miss Strickland believed that her portrait was of Catherine: (1) because it resembled a portrait said to be of Catherine at Versailles, (2) because the hand held a sprig of lavender, and (3) because the fullness of the lower lip and the shape of the jaw showed a strong resemblance to the Queen's nephew, Charles V. But (1) the Versailles portrait, now undiscoverable, seems to have been later catalogued as "Margaret of Austria," (2) the lavender is of absolutely no significance, (3) Catherine had no drop of Habsburg blood, and certainly did not have the Habsburg jaw. Yet the vague similarity to the Chatsworth and Merton portraits remains, and it does not take much imagination to see a pomegranate or two embroidered on the sleeves of this majestic but forbidding lady. Perhaps this is a rather bad copy of some portrait of Catherine as an older woman, in a headdress and pose that had become conventional. Or perhaps it is somebody else, and the apparent connection is quite accidental.

There is a figure meant to be the Queen in the Westminster Tournament Roll, and there are handsome full-length figures in stained glass in the Chapel of the Vyne in Hampshire, and in the east window of St. Margaret's, Westminster. Both the stained-glass representations may have been made from cartoons taken from life or from portraits, but they are not sufficiently individualized to be very helpful as to Catherine's appearance. All that can be said is that the likeness is not inconsistent with the Vienna and Chatsworth portraits.

PART I

Chapter One

Contemporary Authorities: Hernando de Pulgar, "Crónica de los Señores Reyes Católicos" to 1492, in *Biblioteca de Autores Españoles*, Vol. LXX, pp. 215–511, Madrid, 1878; Diego de Valera, *Crónica de los Reyes Católicos*, Madrid, 1927, to 1488; Andres Bernaldes, *Historia de los reyes católicos*, Seville, 1870; and Lorenzo Galindez de Carvajal, "Anales breves . . . de los reyes católicos" in *Colección de documentos inéditos para la historia de España,* Vol. XVIII are the chief chronicle sources for the reign of Ferdinand and Isabella. Further light on the movements of the court and the interests of the humanists in *Opus epistolarum Petri Martyris Anglerii,* Alcala de Henares 1530, and L. Marineo Sículo, *Epistolarum familiarum,* Valladolid, 1514, and *De rebus Hispaniae Memorabilibus,* Alcala de Henares, 1533. For Catherine's tutor, *Itinerarium ad regiones sub aequinoctiali plagas constitutas, Alexandri Geraldini a Merini episcopi civitatis S. Dominici apud Indos Occidentales,* ed. O. Geraldini, Rome, 1631, contains besides Geraldini's amusing account of his voyage to Santo Domingo in 1520, selections from his verse and letters, and a biographical notice of small value by his grandnephew. Gonçalo Fernandez de Oviedo, *Libro de la camera real,* Madrid, 1870, for Prince Juan's household, and [F. Eximeniç] *Carro de las donas,* Valladolid, 1542 (lib. II) for Catherine's education and Isabella's interest in the classics.

Later Works: Diego Clemencin, *Elógio de la reína católica Doña Isabel,* in *Memorias de la real academia de historia,* Vol. VI, Madrid, 1821, contains the pioneer account of the intellectual history of the reign of the Catholic Kings. W. H. Prescott, *Ferdinand and Isabella,* is still valuable. For diplomatic relations of the Catholic Kings, R. B. Merriman, *The Spanish Empire,* Vol. II (New York, 1918) Chs. XII, XIII, XIX and XX, with critical bibliographies. For Peter Martyr, J. H. Mariejol, *Pierre Martyr d'Anghera,* Paris, 1887. A. F. Bell, *Luis de Leon,* Oxford, 1925, has good first chapter on humanists under Ferdinand and Isabella; see also A. Bonilla y San Martín, "El Renascimiento . . . en España" in *La España Moderna* (Feb., 1902) pp. 90 ff., and *Luis Vives e la filosofia del Renacimiento,* Madrid, 1903. Caro Lynn, *A college professor of the Renaissance,* Chicago, 1937, gives a valuable account of L. Marineo Sículo.

[1] Pulgar, *Cronica,* pp. 266–267; Carvajal, *Anales breves,* p. 272; Bernaldez, *Historia,* I, 213.

[2] Carvajal, *Anales breves,* pp. 237 ff.; Peter Martyr d'Anghiera, *Opus epistolarum,* ep. 140–224 *passim;* L. Marineo Sículo, *De rebus hisp.,* ff. 116–117 *passim;* Marino Sanuto, *Diarii,* I, 55 ff. *passim.*

Before leaving for England, Catherine adopted as her badge the pomegranate. The punning reference to Granada (the pomegranate is *granata* in Spanish) is obvious. If Catherine was not enough of a classicist to intend a reference to Proserpina, Geraldini could have enlightened her. She was probably also thinking of the ordinary meaning of the pomegranate in Catholic symbolism. The Arabs (and I suppose the Spanish Moors) regarded the pomegranate as the special symbol of fecundity. If Catherine had that further meaning in mind, the choice was an ironic one. But a badge is the cleverer, the more things it can be taken to mean. The pomegranate certainly was not meant merely to say that Catherine was in any special way "from Granada."

[3] D. Clemencin, *Elógio*, p. 383 ff. and references there cited.

[4] "Journal of Roger Machado" in *Memorials of King Henry VII*, ed. James Gairdner (R. 335) p. 181; Jeronimo Zurita, *Anales de la Corona de Aragon*, Saragossa, 1610, IV, 358–359; *Cal. Span.* I, *passim.*

[5] P. Martyr, *op. cit.*, ep. 172, 174, 176, 182, ff. lxii–lxiv; Bernaldez, II, 133–134; Carvajal, 289–292.

[6] *Cal. Span.* I, 209–215; Rymer, *Foedera* (R. 67) XII, 741–747; Alba, *Corresp. de . . . Fuensalida*, pp. 117–137.

[7] P. Martyr, *ep.* 220, 221.

[8] *Cal. Span.* I, 220–253 *passim;* Wood, *Letters of Royal Ladies* (R. 266), I, 120 ff.; *Letters and Papers of Henry VII*, ed. James Gairdner (R. 333) I, 113 ff.; *Bib. Nat. Fonds Esp.* 318.

[9] Carvajal, pp. 300–301; Bernaldez, I, 154; *Cal. Span.* I, 246, 258, 261–262.

Chapter Two

The best chronicle source for the reign of Henry VII is Polydore Vergil's *Historia Anglica*, Basel, 1546 (R. 295), which now and then differs interestingly from Hall noted above. Leland, *Collectanea* (R. 2842), contains contemporary accounts of the arrival of Catherine in England, of the festivities following her marriage, and of the burial of Prince Arthur. *Memorials of King Henry VII*, ed. James Gairdner (R. 335) contains Bernard André's Chronicle, etc.; *Letters & Papers*

. . . *of Henry VII* (R. 333) and Pollard, *Contemporary Sources for the reign of Henry VII*, 3 vols., London, print useful documents.

Bacon's famous *History of King Henry VII* (R. 339a) is not, of course, a firsthand authority. Besides the points made by Busch, *England unter den Tudors* (R. 341), p. 416 ff., it should be noted that Bacon's didacticism, characteristic of Renaissance literary historiography, led him to rationalize excessively Henry VII's behavior, perhaps for the sake of admonishing James I. Modern biographies of Henry VII by James Gairdner (R. 345) and Gladys Temperley (R. 357) should be supplemented by C. H. Williams, *The making of the Tudor despotism* (rev. ed.), London, 1935, a brief and simple, but sensitive and scholarly study, also useful for the reign of Henry VIII.

[1] G. Mattingly, "The reputation of Dr. De Puebla" in *Eng. Hist. Rev.* (Jan., 1940), LV, 27–46, and references there cited, for an account of De Puebla's career.

[2] See E. H. Harbison, *Rival ambassadors at the court of Queen Mary*, Princeton, 1940, pp. 55–56, 64, 229, 307, for emphatic opinions by French and Spanish diplomats on the instability of the English in politics.

[3] Schanz, *Englishe Handelspolitik* (R. 2146) I, 269–272; C. L. Scofield, *Edward IV*, 2 vols., London, 1923, II, 108–109; E. Power and M. M. Postan, *Studies in English trade in the fifteenth century*, London, 1933, pp. 314–318.

[4] For Catherine's welcome in England, Leland, *Collectanea*, V, 352 ff.; *Cal. Span.* I, 262 (R.O.); Gairdner's *Letters & Papers of Henry VII*, I, 404 ff., II, 103 ff.

[5] For Ayala and De Puebla, *Cal. Span.* I, 168 ff., *passim; Cal. Ven.* I, 226, 269, 271, 276, 280, 282; Busch, *op. cit.*, 113–116; Mattingly, *Eng. Hist. Rev.*, LV, 30–39.

[6] Polydore Vergil, I, 1546; *Greyfriars Chronicle* (R. 286), p. 27.

[7] Leland, *Collectanea*, V, 356 ff.

[8] Supplement to *Cal. Span., Vols. I and II*, pp. 2–11.

[9] For Wales under Henry VII see "A life of . . . Rice ap Thomas" in *Cambrian Register*, 1795; D. Jones, *Sir Rhys ap Thomas* (R. 4248); J. B. Nevins, *Wales during the Tudor period* (R. 4261) and the valu-

able studies of C. A. J. Skeel (R. 4270–4273) and W. Ll. Williams (R. 4284–4287). For Ludlow, Thos. Wright, *A History of Ludlow*, London, 1841.

[10] For Arthur's death and burial, P. Vergil, *Hist. Ang.*, I, 1550; Leland, *Collectanea*, V, 368 ff.

Chapter Three

For diplomatic negotiations of the last years of Henry VII, besides collections already cited, see Le Glay, *Négociations diplomatiques* (R. 581); J. Chmel, *Briefe und Acktenstücke zur Geschichte Maximilians I*, Stuttgart, 1845; and *Lettres de Louis XII* (R. 576).

For Joanna I of Castile, A. Rodríguez Villa, *La reína Juana la Loca*, Madrid, 1892, based in part on the studies of L. P. Gachard, is still standard. Of the two most recent books about Joanna, Ludwig Pfandl, *Johanna die Wahnsinnige*, Freiburg, 1930, is largely speculation, on insufficient evidence, about the nature of Joanna's madness and its transmission to her descendants; Michael Prawdin, *The Mad Queen of Spain*, Boston, 1939, adds some fresh material for Joanna's life after 1522, but is vitiated by the contention, not substantiated by the evidence, that Joanna was attempting to pursue an independent pro-Castilian policy, and was not out of her mind.

[1] Misled by his name, English historians have informally elevated this gentleman to the Spanish peerage under the title of "Duke of Estrada." G. Bergenroth, first editor of the *Spanish Calendar*, is responsible for this error, though it is quite clear from the form of address employed in Hernan Duque's instructions (R.O. Transcripts) that he was not a grandee.

[2] *Cal. Span.* I, 267 (R.O.).

[3] See *L. & P.* II, 1019, 1184, 1301. The editor has quaintly disguised Catherine's tutor as "Alexander Fitzgerald."

[4] *Cal. Span.* I, 290, 294.

[5] *Cal. Span.* I, 295 (R.O.).

[6] *Memorials of Henry VII,* 223 ff.

[7] Rymer, XIII, 76–86.

[8] Alba, p. 458, and see below for negotiations to marry Prince Henry elsewhere.

[9] For Henry's negotiations with Flanders see Busch, pp. 171–186; Schanz, pp. 15–37; *Letters & Papers of Henry VII*, I, 134–177, 189–219; II, 106–112, 146–149, Alba, p. 129, and *Cal. Span.* I, 354–376 *passim.*

[10] Kervyn de Volkarsbeke, *Missions diplomatiques de Pierre Anchemant*, Ghent, 1873, p. 104; *Memorials of Henry VII*, 102, 168; Alba, 300–339 *passim.*

[11] *Cal. Span.* I, 371–373; R.O. *Transcripts*, 425–426.

[12] These include the Venetian ambassador to Philip I, Quirini, *Cal. Ven.* I, 308–324 *passim;* Philip's principal chamberlain, the Count of Fürstenberg, "Briefe des Grafen Wolfgang zu Fürstenberg," ed. R. Von Schreckenstein, in *Zeitschrift der Gesellschaft fur Beförderung der Geschichts-Alterthums-und Volkskunde von Freiburg*, I (1867), 125–163; an anonymous Fleming in L. P. Gachard, *Collection des voyages des souverains des Pays-Bas*, I, 389–480, apparently a member of Philip's suite; an anonymous Englishman, a herald, in *Mem. of Hen. VII*, and Don Pedro de Ayala and G. G. de Fuensalida, in Alba, *op. cit.* See also Chmel, pp. 223–235, 262–270 *passim*, Gachard, I, 481–509, *L. & P. of Hen. VII*, I, 294–300, for comment by diplomats and principals, and Polydore Vergil, II, 1553–1556, and Padilla, *Crónica de Felipe* I, in *D.I.E.* VIII, 136–140, for early narratives. It seems likely that the story of detention was invented by Flemings who disliked the commercial treaty.

[13] Rymer, XIII, 123–126.

Chapter Four

[1]*Cal. Span.* I, 375–440 *passim.* Even the summaries in the *Calendar* show that Catherine was mistaken about De Puebla; transcripts (R.O.) and photostats (Sim.) confirm this. *Cf.* letters of Catherine and De Puebla of the same dates, 7 Sept. and 4 Oct., 1507. For De Puebla's personal affairs, see also Bernard André in *Mem. of Hen. VII*, pp. 104–105, 108–111.

[2] *Cal. Span.* I, 417, 435, 439–440, 453. *Sup. to I & II*, 103, 126.

[3] See *Lettres de Louis XII*, I, 78; *L. & P. of Hen. VII*, I, 289–300; Chmel, pp. 238–266 *passim*, for the background of these negotiations. For Frauenberg's mission, Chmel, pp. 276–280. Treaties in Rymer, XIII, 181–200. Subsequent relations, *L. & P. of Hen. VII*, I, 323 ff.

[4] See the Duke of Alba's introduction to *Corresp. de . . . Fuensalida*, pp. ii–lx for Fuensalida's career up to 1508.

[5] "*No son estos humilldes sino quando maltratados*," Alba, p. 194.

[6] Alba, pp. 460–461.

[7] Alba, p. 464.

[8] *L. & P. of Hen. VII*, I, 342, 350–354.

[9] Alba, pp. 469–472.

[10] Alba, pp. 479–484.

[11] For this quarrel Alba, pp. 490–540 *passim*. Fuensalida's letters for the spring of 1509 are not all in the proper order, but may easily be rearranged from internal evidence.

[12] Alba, pp. 449, 484.

[13] Alba, pp. 515–517.

[14] Alba, p. 518 ff.

[15] *L. & P.* I. 45, (B.M., French Addit. MSS. 21404 f. 10.)

PART II

Chapter One

[1] *L. & P.* I (rev. ed.), 45.

[2] Wood, *Letters of royal ladies*, I, 158.

[3] Allen, I, 450.

[4] Sanuto, VIII, 58; *Cal. Span.* II, 23–32; *L. & P.* I, 145–146, 149; *Cal. Ven.* II, 2–47 *passim*.

[5] *Cal. Ven.* II, 26.

[6] Hall, pp. 516–519; *Cal. Ven.* II, 43; *L. & P.* I, 370–383 *passim*. This tournament is the one so magnificently illustrated by the "Westminster Tournament Roll."

[7] *Cal. Span. Sup.*, pp. 36–41.

Chapter Two

[1] P. Vergil, *Hist. Angl.* II, 1589–1593. *Cf.* Hall, pp. 528–532. Besides references cited in Fisher and Pollard, see Prosper Boissounade, *Histoire de la réunion de la Navarre à la Castile*, Paris, 1893, pp. 321–341; John S. C. Bridge, *A history of France from the death of Louis XI*, Oxford, 1921, IV, 180 ff.

[2] *Cal. Span.* II, 64–79.

[3] *Cal. Ven.* II, 87.

[4] The treaties, Rymer XIII, 358–363; *Cal. Span.* II, 104–105. For the double negotiations see *Cal. Span.* II, 83–98; *L. & P.* I, 759–766, 772–774; Guicciardini, *Opere inedite*, Florence, n.d., VI, 172–174, 176–180. Modern comment, Bridge, *op. cit.*, IV, 194 ff.

[5] *L. & P.* I, 1349.

[6] For Catherine's letters to Henry and Wolsey see Ellis, *Original letters*, first series (R. 270), I, 78, 82, 84, 88, 89; also *L. & P.* I, 968.

[7] Ellis, *Original letters*, I, 88.

[8] *L. & P.* I, 1065, 1078.

[9] Hall, p. 567.

[10] *Cal. Span.* II, 162–218 *passim.*

[11] *Cal. Span.* II, 248–249.

[12] Whether or not Henry VIII took steps looking to the annulment of his marriage to Catherine in 1514 was the subject of a short, sharp controversy between Professor A. F. Pollard and Mr. Hilaire Belloc several years ago in which Professor Pollard certainly made most of the points. Since one disagrees with reluctance with so eminent a Tudor authority, the argument had better be recapitulated:

Three pieces of evidence can be cited for Professor Pollard's view.

1. Peter Martyr writing on December 31, 1514, says that Catherine had recently had a miscarriage as the result of a quarrel with Henry who upbraided her with her father's desertion of him. (*Ep.*, p. 545.) There is no mention of a project for divorce but the letter is taken to prove that Henry's rage at Ferdinand extended to Catherine. The miscarriage referred to would be the stillborn (?) child of late November. Peter Martyr is writing from Spain, of course. In Spain it was only beginning to be clear how deep Henry's resentment against Ferdinand

was. But Henry had known of Ferdinand's desertion by April and was deep in negotiations with France by June. He would not have waited until the following November to assail Catherine for her father's treachery. Peter Martyr is obviously misinformed, as he often was about affairs in England. Caroz' letters not only contain no reference to such a quarrel but distinctly imply that none occurred, and that Catherine fully shared Henry's feelings about Ferdinand's conduct.

2. An anonymous Venetian wrote from Paris to Rome on August 15, 1514, that "the king of England wishes to leave his wife because he cannot have any issue (*sic*) and will marry a daughter of the duke of Bourbon." This rumor rates two entries in *Cal. Ven.* II, 464, 479 but it is one source. It is just the sort of rumor that the Venetians, allies of the French and very anti-Spanish, might be expected to embrace – but Sanuto notes it with caution. Badoer, the able and experienced Venetian resident in London, knew nothing of it. On the contrary, he knew that, so far from being unable to bear a child, Catherine was expecting one in November, and he writes of her in terms which show he still feared her pro-Spanish influence. Argument merely from silence is difficult in this period, but neither Gerard de Pleine, Maximilian's ambassador, nor any of the French diplomats in London show any more signs than Badoer or Caroz of suspecting any breach between Catherine and Henry. It was very different in 1527.

3. Probably the two bits above would have been dismissed as worthless gossip except for an entry in Garampi's eighteenth-century Index to the secret archives of the Vatican (Miscellanea, I, f. 173b) under the heading "England" and the date "1514," which runs "*Archetypus epistolae scribendae a Pontifice ad Henricum Angliae regem super pretensa nullitate matrimonia eis*" – that is, "Original of a letter to be written by the Pope to Henry, king of England, about the pretended nullity of his marriage." This seems very serious, but it proves almost too much. The phrasing indicates a brief taking formal cognizance of a question about Henry's marriage. If the entry is correct, we must assume not only that no one in England during all the subsequent pother over Henry's divorce ever thought it worth while to mention that the King's conscientious scruples dated back to 1514, but that a deci-

sion, so momentous that in spite of the pressure of a triumphant emperor in Catherine's favor it took Clement VII nearly five years to reach it, was taken by Leo X in something like that many weeks, although Leo at that moment was anxious to oblige England and spite the Spanish; and we must further assume that Leo got to the point of drafting an official and apparently decisive brief on the subject without that step becoming known to anyone in the Curia, not even to his nephew and secretary, Giulio de' Medici; for had such a brief of Leo's existed, Clement VII, in the years of his dreadful uncertainty, would have been the first to take refuge in it.

It seems easier to believe that, by a curious coincidence, the Venetian rumor is reinforced by an indexer's error. Such errors are always possible when an index is made up by pasting loose slips into a ledger, particularly when, as in this case, the slip itself bears no date; and such errors do occur in Garampi, though they are not frequent. One would conjecture that the entry really describes Clement VII's brief of 1534.

What makes any other explanation almost incredible is the overwhelming evidence that Catherine was pregnant during the months in question, that Henry VIII was optimistically counting on a son, this time, and treating his wife with all his customary kindness and solicitude, and that Catherine herself enjoyed her usual influence and was unalarmed. (See *L. & P.* I, 1317.)

Chapter Three

Such papers as survive for the administration of Catherine's estates are mostly in the P.R.O. and calendared (often very briefly) in *L. & P.*

R. W. Chambers, *Thomas More*, London, 1935; E. M. G. Routh, *Sir Thomas More and his friends*, London, 1934; Jervis Wegg, *Richard Pace*, London, 1932; Foster Watson, *Luis Vives and the Renaissance Education of Women*, London, 1913 and *Luis Vives, el gran Valenciano*, Oxford, 1922; and F. A. Gasquet, *Cardinal Pole and his early friends*, are useful additions to the exiguous list for English humanism in Read. Henry de Vocht, *Monumenta Humanistica Lovaniensis; texts and studies about Louvain humanists*, Oxford, 1934, has the best account of

Vives' relations with England. See also A. Bonilla, *op. cit.*, and Juan de M. Carriazo, "*Las ideas sociales en Juan Luis Vives*" in *Sociedad Española de Antropología, Etnografia, y Prehistoria: Actas y Memorias*, VI (Madrid, 1927), 49–134. Ines Thurleman, *Erasmus von Rotterdam und Joannes Ludovicus Vives als Pacifisten*, Fribourg, 1932, is a conscientious summary of humanist attitudes towards war. Vives is cited from *Opera Omnia*, Valencia, 1783.

[1] *Cal. Span.* III intro. iii, 206, 256 ff. *passim;* Lanz, *Correspondenz des Kaisers Karl V*, 3 vols., Leipzig, 1844–1846, *passim; Lettres de Louis XII*, vol. IV *passim;* and unpublished letters in Vienna archives.

[2] *Cal. Ven.* II, 242; *Cal. Span.* II, 270–272.

[3] *Cal. Span.* II, 273. Catherine often repeated this generalization in letters and in conversation with subsequent ambassadors.

[4] *Cal. Span.* II, 268–270, 273.

[5] *Cal. Ven.* II, 529.

[6] *Cal. Ven.* II, 248.

[7] More, *Utopia*, London, 1910, p. 356.

[8] Forrest, *History of Grisild the Second*, p. 46.

[9] Claremont, *Catherine of Aragon*, p. 99.

[10] It is noteworthy that Hall does not mention Catherine in his account of the pardoning of the 'prentices, but, much as he dislikes Wolsey, gives him a leading part. Hall, pp. 588–591. This is characteristic of Hall's exclusion of references to Catherine wherever possible. But Chieragato, an eyewitness who gives a detailed account of the Ill May Day, specifically attributes Henry's mercy to Catherine's intercession, and even confirms details in Churchyard's ballad. *Cal. Ven.* II, 385. *Cf.* Strickland p. 37.

[11] Allen, III, 602, IX, 401.

[12] H. E. Salter, *Registrum Annalium Collegii Mertonensis*, Oxford, 1923, II, 477 ff.; also Bodleian MSS., *Twine*, 17 ff., 149–151; Fiddes (R. 401), C. I, 34; Anthony à Wood, *History and antiquities of Oxford*, Oxford, 1796, II, 14 ff.

[13] *De Inst. Christ. Fem.* (1524) *Opera Omnia* IV, 65–301. (Later translated by Richard Hyrde with an independent dedicatory epistle to Catherine.)

Chapter Four

For the diplomatic negotiations of this period, unpublished correspondence at Vienna is a valuable supplement to the standard calendars.

To Brewer (R. 387), Busch (R. 693), Jacqueton (R. 607) and Mignet (R. 609), for modern analyses, should be added F. Nitti, *Leone X e la sua politica*, Florence, 1892, and Karl Brandi's brilliant and scholarly *Kaiser Karl V*, Munich, 1937 (Eng. trans. N. Y., 1939), on the whole the best biography of the Emperor.

[1] A. F. Pollard, *Wolsey*, for an acute analysis of the Cardinal's policies. *Cf.* J. S. Brewer, *Reign of Henry VIII* (R. 387) and W. Busch, *Drei Jahre englischer Vermittlungspolitik* (R. 693).

[2] F. Nitti, *Leone X e la sua politica* (Florence, 1892); *cf.* L. Pastor, *History of the Popes*, St. Louis, 1923, VII, 213 ff. *passim*, especially 223–232, 242–243; E. Charrière, *Négociations de la France dans le Levant*, Paris, 1848, I, 25, 31–68.

[3] Rymer, XIII, 624–649.

[4] *Cal. Ven.* II, 448, 450–451, 462, 468, 472; *L. & P.* II, 1370, 1375, 1385, 1394, 1424, III, 43, 70, 111, 435. Nitti, *op. cit.*, pp. 112, 120–121.

[5] Hall, p. 599; *L. & P.* III, 129–130, 144–145, 148; *Cal. Ven.* II, 540–543.

[6] For the following negotiations, *L. & P.* III, 158–159, 163, 187, 188–190, 214, 223, 232; *Cal. Span.* II, 322 ff.; supplemented by *V.A. Belgien* DD Abt. B fasc. i and 3.

[7] *L. & P.* III, 230, 255–256.

[8] For this interview, Hall, pp. 604–605; *Cal. Ven.* III, 46; *V.A. England* f. 2. esp. Charles to De Mesa 21 and 24 Jan., 1522, to Henry VIII, same date, to Catherine, same date, De Mesa to Charles V, 18 Feb., 1522, and correspondence between Charles and Gattinara 1521–1522 in *Belgien* DD, fasc. 1–3, only partially published by Lanz, *Mon. Habs.* See also Brandi, *Karl V*, pp. 99–102.

[9] Busch, *Drei Jahre*, pp. 88 ff., seems nearer right about these negotiations than either Brewer or Mignet.

[10] *Cal. Span.* II, 433, 438 and *V.A. England* fasc. 1, 2 and 5 *passim.*

[11] The letters of Louis de Praet, *V.A. England*, f. 1, 2, 5 give a vivid

account of Wolsey's predicament during these negotiations. Jacqueton, *La politique extérieure de Louise de Savoy*, prints the French correspondence.

[12] *Cal. Span.* III, 50–56, 62–65, 74–75; *L. & P.* IV, 508, 542.

[13] *Cal. Span.* III, 129.

[14] 2 April, 1523, and 21 July, 1523. De Praet to Charles V, *V.A. England*, fasc. i; *Cal. Span.* III, 108.

[15] For these negotiations *Cal. Ven.*, III, 443; *Cal. Span.* III, 168, 171, 174–179, 183, 185–186, 190–196, 201. *V.A.* "Memoir of the emperor's reply to the English ambassadors" (1525), *England*, fasc. 2.

[16] Ellis, *Original letters*, II, 19.

[17] Vives, IV, 40; *cf.* VII, 208.

PART III

Chapter One

Documents concerning the divorce printed in older books such as Strype (R. 1342), Wilkins (R. 1260), Burnet (R. 1295), Pococke (R. 377), Le Grand (R. 411), Theiner, *Vetera Monumenta*, and Laemmer, *Monumenta Vaticana*, are calendared in *L. & P. Jean du Bellay: Ambassades en Angleterre* (R. 568) adds full texts of Du Bellay's dispatches excerpted by Le Grand; and Ehses, *Romische Dokumente* (R. 379) is invaluable for Cardinal Campeggio's correspondence, previously uncalendared.

Friedmann's *Anne Boleyn* (R. 402) deserves most of the fine things that have been said about it, and is, perhaps, the best detailed history of the period 1527–1536 as it is reflected in diplomatic correspondence. It makes a very full, though not always precise or discriminating, use of Chapuys' dispatches. Gairdner, "New light on the divorce of Henry VIII" in *E.H.R.*, XI and XII (R. 405), based on Ehses, should be checked by Thurston, "The canon law of the divorce," in *E.H.R.* xix (R. 1465).

[1] 26 Nov. 1526, *Cal. Span.* III, 1018 (*V.A.*).

[2] *L. & P.* IV, 667.

[3] De Praet to Charles V, 17 Nov. 1523, *V.A. Belgien* DD Abt. B, fasc. 8; *Cal. Span.* III, ii, 16 ff.; *cf.* Wm. Tyndale, *The Practice of Prelates* in *Works* (R. 1439) I, 454, and Busch, *Ursprung des Ehescheidungs* (R. 391), pp. 270–274.

[4] *L. & P.* IV, 1066.

[5] *Cal. Span.* III, 677–681, 763–764, 1015–1017, ii, 16–84 *passim; L. & P.* IV, 1163, 1188.

[6] *Cal. Span.* III, ii, 187–191.

[7] *Cal. Span.* III, ii, 193–194; hearings began before Warham 17 May, 1527, calendared in *L. & P.* under May 31.

[8] See G. Constant, *La reforme en Angleterre*, pp. 349–350 for a good summary of the arguments. *Cf.* Chambers, *Thomas More*, pp. 162–163.

[9] See S. B. Chrymes, *English Constitutional Ideas in the Fifteenth Century*, Cambridge, 1936, pp. 11–62, for female succession.

[10] De Praet observed the Scottish negotiations of 1524 and repeats emphatically that no other marriage alliance could be half so popular in England.

[11] *Henry VIII's Love Letters* (R. 366).

[12] *Cal. Span.* III, ii, 194, 209, 276–277.

[13] *Cal. Span.* III, ii, 277, 300–303. For Felipez' mission see also *L. & P.* IV, 1480–1481.

[14] With Wolsey's journey to France, Cavendish (R. 360) begins to be of first-rate importance. The best modern account is, of course, in Pollard's *Wolsey*.

[15] Good analysis of these maneuvers by Gairdner, *E.H.R.*, XI, 681 ff.

[16] *Cal. Span.* III, ii, 443.

[17] "*Jeu de terribles mesteres*," *Du Bellay: Premieres Ambassades*, p. 158.

[18] Pollard, *Wolsey*, pp. 209–210.

[19] *L. & P.* IV, ii, 1753, 2146.

[20] *Cal. Span.* III, ii, 377 (*V.A.*). By reading "Winchester" instead of "Rochester," and then interpolating "Stephen Gardiner," Gayangos quite confuses this point. The Bishop of Winchester at this time was, of course, not Gardiner but Wolsey himself.

Chapter Two

The most recent book on Clement VII's conduct of the divorce case is a spirited defense, *Clement VII and Henry VIII*, by Pierre Crabites, London, 1936, good as to procedure under the canon law, but weak as to general history. The soundest judgment, severe but well-balanced, is that in Ludwig von Pastor's *History of the Popes*. Campeggio's dispatches are printed in full in Laemmer and Ehses.

[1] Ehses, p. 54.

[2] *Cal. Span.* III, ii, 855 (*V.A.*).

[3] The bull and the brief bulk very large in the documents about the divorce for several years. The best short discussion seems to be that of Herbert Thurston in *E.H.R.*, xix, 632–648.

[4] *L. & P.* IV, 1090, 2265–2266 (R.O.)

[5] *Cal. Span.* III, ii, 854.

[6] *Cal. Span.* III, ii, 877, 884–885, 890.

[7] *L. & P.* IV, 2265, 2267 (R.O.), 2277; *Cal. Span.* III, ii. 890–950 *passim* (*V.A.*); *L. & P.* IV, 2265 misreads "Chas" for "Thos" and calls the messenger "Charles" Abell. The royal councilors themselves confused Montoya with Felipez. Abell's own memorandum, 9 Jan. 1529, attached to Catherine's letter in *V.A.* (*cf. Cal. Span.* IV, i, 43). *Cal. Span.* calendars this letter from a contemporary copy at Simancas, and a modern transcript is in the B.M. (Addit. MSS.)

[8] *Ultīa*, misread "*altra*" by Ehses. (Vat.)

[9] Hall, pp. 754–755; Le Grand, III, 209.

[10] Hall, p. 735.

[11] The undated memorandum of what the counselors were to say is printed in Pocock I, 212. Not used, the editor of *L. & P.* thinks; but Mendoza's dispatch of Jan. 16, 1529 (*Cal. Span.* III, ii, 877), shows that it was, and supplies the appropriate date.

[12] For the Blackfriars trial we have at least three eyewitness accounts: Campeggio's, M. du Bellay's, and Cavendish's, and possibly a fourth in Hall, although Hall's details are so relatively meager and inexact that he may not have been present. In addition, several bundles of notes and depositions are preserved in B.M. and calendared, rather inadequately, in

L. & P. under more or less appropriate dates. Unfortunately neither Campeggio's letters nor M. du Bellay's give a full account, and Cavendish wrote some time after the event. In the main the three confirm each other and are confirmed by the documents calendared in *L. & P.*, but there are some inconsistencies which I have had to resolve rather arbitrarily. Direct quotations are from Cavendish, not because I am sure he got the speeches verbatim, but because the temptation to steal Cavendish's language when one can is irresistible.

Chapter Three

The chief source for this and the next two chapters is the correspondence of Eustache Chapuys, which has been the mainstay of every historian of this period since excerpts were first made from it for J. A. Froude. Chapuys' dispatches are calendared in *L. & P.* and *Cal. Span.*, and Froude's *Divorce of Catherine of Aragon* (R. 403) and Friedmann's *Anne Boleyn* quote extensively, but although search of the archives has turned up only some half-dozen uncalendared letters, none very startling, and a few odd related papers, re-examination of the originals has not been altogether unprofitable. Chapuys wrote a rich, but rather involved and provincial French, and his own handwriting, always somewhat eccentric, deteriorated rapidly because of gouty fingers after 1531. Incorrect and varying readings by earlier editors are thus, naturally, not infrequent and some of these it has been possible to correct.

The *Archives de la Ville* of Annecy preserve a number of bundles of papers relating to the Chapuys family, including records of the ambassador's education, business transactions and estate, and of the foundation of his colleges at Louvain and Annecy, and some of his letters to his family and personal friends, of little political interest. There is a short account of these papers, and of other materials for Chapuys' biography, in my article "A humanist ambassador" in *Journal of Modern History*, IV (1932), 175–185.

In general, as far as he can be checked, Chapuys appears to be a reliable witness – subject, of course, to discount for his partisanship for Catherine, and his ignorance of English affairs on his arrival. He was an industrious and cautious collector of information, and too good a humanist to have violent religious or national prejudices. He was also a brisk and colorful reporter, and his letters are the more welcome because Cavendish fails after 1530, Hall soon becomes thinner, and the Venetian sources are inadequate for the early '30's.

[1] Chapuys to Granvelle, 20 Aug., 1529, *V.A. England*, fasc. 9. For his instructions, etc., *Cal. Span.* IV, i, 45–46, 116, 174–175, 177.

[2] *Cal. Span.* IV, i, 220–238. (*V.A.*)

[3] *Cal. Span.* IV, i, 234–237, 305, 327, 342, 350, 361, 385–386, 392–393, 419, 433, 437, 533, 586, for Chapuys' summaries of Catherine's views.

[4] Chapuys' account, from several informants. *Cal. Span.* IV, i, 349–352 (*V.A.*)

[5] H. A. L. Fisher, *England*, p. 303.

[6] *Cal. Span.* IV, i, 368 ff. *passim;* Pollard, *Wolsey*, pp. 280 ff.; and, of course, Cavendish for Wolsey's last days.

[7] Merriman, *Thomas Cromwell*, I, 89 ff.

[8] *Cal. Span.* IV, ii, 61.

[9] *Cal. Span.* IV, i, 800.

[10] *Cal. Span.* IV, ii, 16, 39–40, 78–80.

[11] *Cal. Span.* IV, ii, 84–85.

[12] *Cal. Span.* IV, ii, 27 (*V.A.*)

[13] *Cal. Span.* IV, i, 366–367; IV, ii, 70–71.

[14] Catherine to Clement VII, Jan. 6 (?) 1531, *V.A.* (Cf. *Cal. Span.* IV, i, 808.)

[15] *Cal. Span.* IV, i, 802–803 (*V.A.*)

[16] *Cal. Span.* IV, ii, 169–177 (*V.A.*)

[17] *L. & P.* V, 361.

[18] *Cal. Span.* IV, ii, 264–266.

[19] Ludovico Fallier and Mario Savorgnano. Sanuto XLIV, 668 ff. (Venice-Correr).

[20] "*Katarina sin ventura* (sĩ vẽtə) *regina*," – the signature of another unhappy Catherine. 15 Dec. 1531. *Cal. Span.* IV, ii, 332. (Simancas, holograph.)

[21] Merriman, *Cromwell*, I, 96–97, 104–111.

[22] *L. & P.* V, 380–381, 386.

[23] *L. & P.* V, 541 (R.O.)

Chapter Four

For this and the next chapter the anonymous *Crónica del rey Enrico Otavo de Ingalaterra*, ed. the Marqués de Molins, Madrid, 1874, is of some use, the Spanish edition, careful as to MS. and with a scholarly introduction being much preferable to M. A. S. Hume's translation, London, 1889 (R. 360a). The author of this chronicle is careless as to chronology and proper names, and utterly uncritical; he was probably not himself in England as early as 1536; but he seems to have gathered information from Spanish merchants in London, from a Spanish member of Chapuys' suite, and from at least one of Catherine's former servants, so that several of his anecdotes and descriptions have every appearance of authenticity.

James Gairdner, *The English Church* (R. 1309) for religious changes.

[1] *Cal. Span.* IV, ii, 524 ff. *passim,* and Pollard, *Henry VIII*, pp. 294–295; A. Hamy, *Entrevue de François I*er, (R. 605).

[2] *Cal. Span.* IV, ii, 510 (*V.A.*)

[3] 11 Nov., 1532, *Cal. Span.* IV, ii, 553–554.

[4] *Cal. Span.* IV, ii, 585, 592, 597–599, 606. *L. & P.* V, 100.

[5] *Cal. Span.* IV, ii, 608 ff. (*V.A.*)

[6] *Cal. Span.* IV, ii, 592 ff.

[7] *State Papers* I, 390–391.

[8] *Cal. Span.* IV, ii, 628–629 (*V.A.*)

[9] *Cal. Span.* IV, ii, 630–632 (*V.A.*)

[10] *Cal. Span.* IV, ii, 636–642, 644–645, 650, 675, 681; *Cal. Ven.* IV, 404, 426.

[11] *Cal. Span.* IV, ii, 291 (misdated 22 Nov., 1531). (*V.A.*)

[12] *Cal. Span.* IV, ii, 554.

[13] *Cal. Span.* IV, ii, 596.

[14] *Cal. Span.* IV, ii, 688. (*V.A.*)

[15] *Cal. Span.* IV, ii, 649.

[16] *Cal. Span.* IV, ii, 647, 666–667; *L. & P.* VI, 219, 230–231.

[17] "Report of Lord Mountjoy etc.," *State Papers* I, 397 ff.

[18] *Cal. Span.* IV, ii, 737.

[19] *Cal. Span.* IV, ii, 864.

[20] For Catherine's life at Buckden, besides Chapuys' dispatches, see Clifford, *Life of Jane Dormer* (R. 622), Forrest, *Grisild the Second*, pp. 95–101; Strickland, *Queens of England*, IV, 140–147, *Tresham papers*, H. M. C. *Var. Col.* III; *Crónica del rey Enrico*, pp. 14–60 *passim*, and R. Langley, *Buckden Palace*, Peterborough, 1932.

[21] For Suffolk at Buckden, Chapuys' account, *Cal. Span.* IV, ii, 892–893, 895–899 (*V.A.*); Suffolk's letters, *State Papers*, I, 415–419; *L. & P.* VI, 622 (R.O.).

[22] For Chapuys' fears for Catherine's life etc., *Cal. Span.* IV, ii, 679, 883, V, 2, 13, 17, 63, 82, 130, 219–226, 250; *L. & P.* VI, 49.

[23] *L. & P.* VI, 603–605. (*V.A.*)

Chapter Five

Two recent lives of Mary I, Beatrice White, *Mary Tudor*, New York, 1935, and H. M. F. Prescott, *A Spanish Tudor*, New York, 1940, are both more useful accounts of Mary's girlhood than are to be found in Stone (R. 457). *A Spanish Tudor* makes excellent use of the calendared versions of Chapuys' dispatches.

[1] *State Papers*, I, 419–422; *Cal. Span.* V, 154–156.

[2] For Chapuys' ride to Kimbolton, *Cal. Span.* V, 197, 219–223; *L. & P.* VII, 415; *Crónica del rey Enrico*, pp. 61–65.

[3] M. H. and Ruth Dodd, *The pilgrimage of grace* (R. 397) is the best study of the Catholic reaction in the late '30's, but seriously underestimates the feudal conspiracy.

Analysis of all the evidence for this conspiracy would exceed the decent limits of a footnote, but for the northern group see: *L. & P.* VII, 369–370, XI, 714, 1143; *Cal. Span.* V, 354 (*V.A.*); also *A.R.B.* 371, ff. 32–38 and references cited by Prescott, *Spanish Tudor*, pp. 58–60. For western group: *Cal. Span.* IV, ii, 411, 459, 471, V, 104, 233–237 (*V.A.*), 301, 335, 813–814 (& Dodd *ut sup.*). For central group: *Cal. Span.* V, 354, 375 (*V.A.*), 413, 441–442 (*V.A.*); *L. & P.* VII, 38. Also Chapuys to Anthoine Perrenot, 22 July, 1536, *V.A. England*, fasc. 7, quite incorrectly calendared *L. & P.* IX, 65 and *A.R.B.* 371, ff. 18–19. Also *cf.* Kauleck, *Correspondance Politique* (R. 566), pp. 29–217 *passim.*

[4] *Cal. Span.* V, 430.

[5] *L. & P.* VI, No. 1126 (Arundel MS) undated and somewhat out of its proper order. *Cf. Cal. Span.* V, 96, 104 (*V.A.*), 153–154. Date is obviously April 1534.

[6] *Cal. Span.* V, 41, 374, 410–11, 432–3, 457; *L. & P.* VIII, 100, 105, 194. *Cf.* Prescott, *Spanish Tudor*, pp. 63–67.

[7] This letter and the next are calendared in *L. & P.* VII, No. 1126 and VIII, 328 from modern transcripts in R.O. as "Catherine to Cromwell" on the strength of the transcriber's indorsement. *Cal. Span.* calendars them from the contemporary copies at Vienna, but misdates them "1534." The originals seem to have been among a small collection of Chapuys' private papers – mostly royal autographs – which was destroyed in the conflagration of the Louvain library in 1914. (Private information from the late Joseph Orsier, who made some notes of the contents of the collection with a view to publication, but unfortunately failed to take copies.)

[8] N. Sanders, *De origine* (R. 1286) 2nd ed. Ingolstadt, 1587, p. 114.

[9] Chambers, *More*, p. 349.

[10] *V.A. England* fasc. 9 inaccurately calendared in *Cal. Span.* V, and inaccurately transcribed for *L. & P.*

[11] *Cal. Span.* V, 538, 550, 559–560, 565, 586, 588. (*V.A.*)

[12] Catherine to Ortiz, 13 Dec. (?) 1535. *V.A. England* fasc. 9, inaccurate in *Cal. Span.* This is Chapuys' copy. The simultaneous letters to the Pope and to the Emperor are lost.

[13] *Cal. Span.* V, 595–600.

[14] *Cal. Span.* V, ii, 3 ff. (*V.A.*). Friedmann gives an accurate account of these letters of January 1536.

[16] No original text of this letter survives. That it was written, and its general contents, we know from Chapuys. The differences and similarities of the two texts given, in Polydore Vergil (1556) II, 1742, and Sanders (1587), p. 119, point to the existence of English copies in the sixteenth century.

[15] Claremont, p. 246 ff.

[17] *Cf.* Friedmann II, 168–178; N. Moore, "The death of Catherine of Aragon"; *Athanaeum*, Jan. 31 and Feb. 28, 1885.

[18] *Archives de la Ville d'Annecy*, Liasse G G 198, No. 11, Eustache Chapuys to Guignone Dupuys, Louvain, 6 Aug., 1555.

[illegible] Cal. Span. V, 116.

[illegible] N. Sanders, De origine (R. 1585) and tr. Lewis (London, 1877), p. 114.

[illegible] Chambers, [illegible], p. [illegible].

[illegible] Cal. Span. V, 316, 570, 559–560, 595, 588, 588. (L. & P.)

[illegible] Cal. Span. V, 597–600.

[illegible] Claremont, p. 246 ff.

[illegible] Archives de la Ville d'Anvers, Cartas C C 108, No. 10, Eustache Chapuys to [illegible], Louvain, 6 Aug., 1535.

Index

M